On Whom to Lean:

The Life Stories of
the War-Torn Generation
of Chinese Americans at Rossmoor

By
Zong-Yi Li

Translated by Christine Yunn-Yu Sun

On Whom to Lean:

The Life Stories of the War-Torn Generation

of Chinese Americans at Rossmoor

Copyright © 2015 Zong-Yi Li

All rights reserved. No part of the book's content should be duplicated and/or distributed in any way or form without permission of the copyright holder.

ISBN-10: 0996743219

ISBN-13: 978-0-9967432-1-1

Author: Zong-Yi Li

Translator: Christine Yunn-Yu Sun

Editor for Chinese edition: Tianchi Zhao

Editor for English edition: Theresa Kuo, John Moe, Zong-Yi Li

Sub-Editor for English edition: Steve Goschnic

Cover Design: Tianchi Zhao, Peter Li

Publisher: Huaxia Renwen Publishing

First Chinese Edition: September 2015

First English Edition: July 2017

Printed in the United States of America

In Commemoration of the 70th Anniversary Victory of China's War of Resistance against Japan

This book is dedicated to all Chinese who lived through the catastrophe

Table of Contents

Preface by Tianchi Zhao i
Author's Note by Zong-Yi Li v
Translator's Note by Christine Yunn-Yu Sun xi

Chapter One: George Wang 1
    From Youth Army to Professor in Petroleum

Chapter Two: Yung-fong Shy 39
    Founding Father of Taiwan's Film Industry

Chapter Three: Florence Lin 79
    From Female Soldier to Master Chef

Chapter Four: Ellie Mao Mok 111
    Singing is a Major Theme of My Life

Chapter Five: Horace Chow 155
    Top student on an Engineer's Road

Chapter Six: Gus Kao 177
    An "Immortal" Practicing Tai Chi Qi Gong

Chapter Seven: David Hsu 213
    An Aeronautical Engineer and His Airplanes

Chapter Eight: Patsy P.H. Peng 237
    We were born to Give Back to Society

Chapter Nine: Ruby Chow 273
    A Dreamer in Science, Music and Art

Chapter Ten: Annie Toy 305
    Bitter-Sweet Life of Early Chinese Immigrants

Chapter Eleven: Shing-yi Huang 317
    From Diplomacy to International Civil Service

Chapter Twelve: Linna Wu 345
    Never about Fame and Wealth

Chapter Thirteen: Peter Sih 369
        An Engineer Facing a Brand New World
Chapter Fourteen: Anna Yang 381
        Such a Fortunate Life
(Listed in order of the number of strokes in their Chinese surnames)

Appendix
Chapter Fifteen: Yen Liang 407
        An Architectual Master's Swan Song
Chapter Sixteen: Hugh & Elsie Chang 419
        A Loving Couple to the Very End

Afterword by Tianchi Zhao   431

China Maps (provinces and major cities)   434

Preface

The author of this book Zong-Yi Li, my wife and I, we moved to Rossmoor, a community in Walnut Creek, California, in late 2012. The early Chinese residents here transliterated Rossmoor to mean "land that favors poetry". A visiting friend once announced that we have chosen a good location. When I asked why, he explained that after exiting Highway 24, one enters Olympic Boulevard, a road that leads to the mountain of immortals. Upon arrival, he found a community of charm and beauty, a hidden and much blessed spot of abundant trees, flowers and birds surrounded by rolling hills.

My friend's comments reminded me of the Olympic National Park in the State of Washington, where we lived before retirement. Within the park is the snow-capped Mount Olympus, named by British explorer John Meares after the home of the Twelve Olympian Gods in Greek mythology. We had visited Mount Olympus on many occasions. So, according to this friend, my wife and I have now moved into the residence of gods! The mountains here in Rossmoor are not as dramatic, but the renowned Tang poet Yuxi Liu already asserted, "No matter how high a mountain, it is the immortals living there that makes its name prominent."

Having moved here, we constantly find this community amazing: A ballet teacher who is nearly 90 years young; an instructor in hula dancing 92; and our teacher in portrait painting also in his 90s. Many of the Chinese residents here belong to a generation before us. Ellie Mao Mok, 93, teaches singing; Annie L. Toy, 93, is a frequent volunteer: Gus Kao, 93, leads us in Tai Chi Qi Gong exercise; Ruby Chow, 92, plays piano for the Chinese-American Association of Rossmoor Choir; Shing-yi Huang, who takes special care of such newly-arrived "young people" as us, is 92; and Patsy P.H. Peng, who is active in our ping-pong club and fitness dance classes, recently celebrated her 90th. All these senior Chinese are healthy, intelligent and young at heart. Not only do they look after themselves and drive everywhere, but some of them also take time to travel around the world. Even more fascinating are their life experiences, which inspired Zong-Yi so much that she wanted to document the life stories of these senior Chinese in our community.

I offered my advice. "It took you up to eight years to produce two collections of essays to commemorate the lives of your parents. You should know how much time and effort it would take to do such a thing for these individuals. If you decided to go ahead, then our lifestyle in retirement, our relaxation in piano playing, singing, fitness exercising, painting, calligraphy writing and traveling, will be totally disrupted." As a matter of fact, I, too, have been there, done that. I recently completed a book of conversations with my uncle, committing more than 400,000 words and four whole years of hard work to document his life experiences and achievements. However, despite my good advice, Zong-Yi would not change her mind. More importantly, the task was rather urgent because these Chinese seniors are already much advanced in age. She immediately started collecting data and mobilizing her contacts to conduct interviews.

It was no easy task to uncover the time-honored memories of these men and women in their 80s, 90s and almost 100. Firstly, to interview them, we needed to gain their permission, affection and trust. Each individual required at least three rounds of interviews. Once each interview was done and recorded, the data was thoroughly checked, with those uncertain bits and pieces being brought up in the next interview to gradually induce more memories and further details. It also took much time and effort to replay and transcribe the recording, and to research and verify the historical events and characters as well as their backgrounds. While the "oral history" here is told from the first-person perspective, that does not equate the role of the narrator to that of a simple tape recorder. Instead, a considerable amount of preparation was required in order for the interviewer to choose appropriate topics, propose suitable questions and take control of the direction of the conversation. The resulting book clearly shows the author's high level of attainment and excellent grasp of history and culture.

The book documents the stories of 14 Chinese couples living in Rossmoor, with another two couples introduced in the appendix who once lived here but had since passed away. Some of these 16 couples are from prestigious families, while others have ordinary backgrounds. They belong to the generation of our parents. Apart from their coming to America, their experiences back in China as young men and women are similar to those of our parents. Their youth had been under a shadow first of the horrifying Resistance War against Japan and later the Civil War between the Nationalist and Communist Parties. Most of these 16 couples continued their studies while escaping from the turmoil of war, eventually leaving their parents behind and crossing the Pacific Ocean, arriving in the United States to pursue further studies and dreaming of one day returning to serve their motherland. They ended up staying here as a result of political changes in China in 1949.

Cut off from contact with their parents as well as their sources of finance at home, these young men and women survived in this foreign land, with only their intelligence and strong will to rely on. They have established successful careers and families. To their parents and families who for decades were isolated on the other side of the ocean, they have tried to offer assistance in every way humanly possible. As soon as political circumstances allowed, they have also returned and visited their home or the graves of their parents to pay respect. Back then, they crossed the ocean alone. Today, many of them have children and grandchildren who, with their prominent careers, form the backbone of this society. Others have descendants who were born in America yet went on to work and live in China. Looking back, this is what they are most proud of and pleased about in their lives – that their offsprings have grown to become successful people who have never forgotten the culture of their motherland.

Also common among the 16 couples introduced in this book is a long and happy marriage. Many of these couples have celebrated their diamond wedding anniversaries; some have even lived together for more than 70 years. A loving and harmonious relationship not only helped them overcome the difficulties of life as new immigrants, but also contributed greatly to the establishment of their careers in the United States. Meanwhile, apart from their remarkable achievements in their respective fields, many of them are multi-talented and have mastered the arts of calligraphy, painting, music, Peking Opera, singing, dancing, bridge (card game), tennis and golf. These talents enriched their lives and make their retirement years active and fun.

As editor of this book, I suggested the title "Whom to Lean On: Out of a War-Torn Country". It was inspired by Tang poet Jiao Meng, who lamented in his poem *War-Torn*, "Everywhere across the Central Plains a scene of devastation / On whom is a feeble vine to lean?" This question well reflects the time and circumstances in which the senior Chinese in this book were situated; however, it also strikes a chord in Zong-Yi and me with regard to our own experiences and perceptions of life. "Whom to Lean On" is a question, to which we believe every reader could find their own answers after reading this book.

– Tianchi Zhao, in his residence
in Rossmoor, East Bay, California, United States
August 28, 2015

Author's Note

Having moved to Rossmoor in Walnut Creek in San Francisco's East Bay Area, I befriended many senior Chinese who are long-term residents of the United States. We refer to each other by our English names, as Americans do. At first I felt awkward and considered this to be rude. However, as time went by, I came to appreciate its benefits in replacing generational statuses and titles with a sense of sincerity. As dear friends, I often heard these senior Chinese chatting about their lives – all sorts of things that are ordinary to them but rather unheard-of to me, things that are absolutely fascinating. What I am doing here is to faithfully collect their life stories into a book.

Each Generation Has Its Own Stories

These senior Chinese lived through a time that is different from ours. As young men and women, they witnessed Japan's invasion of China and the raging fire of the war of resistance. The stories they told me involve a myriad of historical facts about that war, such as their fleeing from calamity to China's vast hinterlands, the bombing, the Youth Expeditionary Army, the "Flying Tigers" American Volunteer Group, the Wartime Cadre Training School, the Women's Advisory Council, the aircraft factory, the rescue of American airmen by Chinese soldiers and civilians after their bombing of Tokyo as the Doolittle Raid, the "National Southwest Associated University", and the retrocession of Taiwan after the victory in the resistance war against Japan. Some of these I had learned from books, but it felt different when they were told by those who had personally experienced them. Our storytellers are neither politicians nor celebrities, yet I believe a record of the personal experiences of those involved in these events will help to illustrate the truth about our history.

What's special about this book is that most of our interviewees arrived in the United States from China in the 1940s. Soon after that, as a result of dramatic political changes in China, they were forced to remain in America. In that era when Chinese still suffered from racial discrimination, they worked tirelessly to earn the status and respect that was due to them. Thanks to their intelligence, diligence and perseverance through hardship, a road was paved for all subsequent Chinese immigrants to follow. Therefore, it is particularly important for this and future generations to comprehend and document the life stories of these senior Chinese, to trace their life paths and the journeys of their hearts, and how they conquered difficulties and successfully settled in America. As there are few accounts of senior Chinese like these in the history of Chinese immigrants in the United States, the stories collected in this book may be seen as a valuable addition.

Each Individual Has His / Her Own Stories

With regard to history, these senior Chinese had indeed grown up in the same macro environment. Most of them studied, sought employment, worked and retired. However, as they came from different families, received different types of education, witnessed different atrocities of war and eventually found work in different fields, each has unique experiences and perceptions of life. Those I interviewed were neighbors on a first-name basis, among whom are an international civil servant, an engineer, a teacher, a singer, a painter, a movie producer, a chef, an accountant and a social activist. Each individual made different choices upon the numerous twists and turns in their lives, resulting in unique yet equally fascinating lives.

The group of individuals portrayed in this book is rather special, thanks to the complex ways in which each is related to another. For example, among them, three studied in Chongqing's Central Chengchi

(Political Science) University; three graduated from Jiao Tong University; five boarded the same ship to the United States in 1947; two pursued further studies in the University of Michigan for the purpose of advancing China's automobile industry; three worked for the United Nations; three led the Women's Association of the China Institute in New York; and, finally, at least six couple accepted Shing-yi Huang's appeal to move to Rossmoor. Also included in this book are two senior Chinese who established their careers in Taiwan and later retired to the United States, as well as one who was born in America. In order to complement the 14 stories of senior Chinese Americans in Rossmoor, we have added two deceased couples: Yen and Dolly Liang, who moved to Rossmoor in the 1970s and started the local Chinese community, and the legendary couple Hugh C. and Elsie L.C. Chang.

My Responsibilities and Work as Narrator

I was born after the victory of the resistance war against Japan. Therefore, the only way I am directly related to that war is through the capture of my father by the Japanese military police in Yenching University in 1941. I remember seeing a photograph of him after his release, haggard and bearded, yet it never occurred to me to ask him about it. It was only until years after his death, when I compiled his writings as a book to honor him that I learned how he suffered at the hands of those savage and hateful Japanese invaders. I felt blessed that he had left many written accounts, which helped me understand the importance of documenting personal history for future generations. I offer this story as an example whenever an interviewee of mine considers it useless to discuss events of the past because none of the young people, including their own children, seems interested in them. Even though our children might not care about such documentation, it should exist in anticipation for the time in the future when they do want to know about it. Should a story not be told, it will forever be covered by the dust of history so that none of our future generations will ever get to know about it.

The stories in this book are told from the first-person perspectives in order to preserve as much of each interviewee's style in storytelling as possible. During their first round of interviews, I was simply a listener, with an occasional question or two about the stories' historical background or details. Then I transcribed the recording and verified the historical characters, events and locations they described. Finally, focusing on their stories and joining together bits and pieces of their memories, I added a historical setting to produce a complete personal biography. Having perused and revised the first draft, we conducted the second round of interviews to discuss and further explore various crucial aspects. The second draft was again closely examined and repeatedly improved until a final manuscript was approved by the interviewee. Throughout this process, some interviewees would confess their lapse of memory about things that happened so long ago. But I told them it's OK, as those stories requiring little reflection are surely most poignant and critical in their lives; once these have cracked open the door to their memory, others will follow. Concerned they might appear boastful, some interviewees would prefer not to have various parts of their stories recorded. This is typical of many Chinese who want to be humble and low-keyed, as the popular Chinese saying goes, "A hero never mentions his past glories." Yet, these senior Chinese have told facts about their lives, things of which both they and I are immensely proud, and I am certain their readers would feel the same way. With their permission, I have preserved as many of these stories as possible in this book. It is my belief that excellent storytelling relies on realistic details. I didn't set out to create a book of inspiration, yet I am deeply touched and further motivated by many stories of hard work and determination under difficult circumstances.

Rossmoor is a community in which only those above the age of

55 can reside. Most of the residents here are above 70, so I had a good collection of senior Chinese men and women as candidates to interview. Initially I only approached those above the age of 85. However, for each person I interviewed, I was told that others have more fascinating stories to tell, so the number of interviewees increased considerably. Each individual's life experiences are worthy of being written as a full-length novel. Due to the limited length of this book, I could only include the stories of those senior Chinese above the age of 90. The stories of those interviewees between 85 and 90 of age will have to wait for the next volume.

The Book Resulting from Everyone's Contribution

My heart-felt gratitude goes to those 14 senior Chinese Americans who gave permission for my interviews and the subsequent publishing of their life stories. To facilitate our conversations, some had prepared photographs and other material in advance, others had rescheduled their medical appointments, and still others had opened their hearts and described those past events they had never mentioned to outsiders. I could only repay their trust by making this book as close to perfect as possible. My gratitude also goes to Pauline Chang who recommended that we relocate to Rossmoor, a move that enabled me to connect with these senior Chinese Americans. I want to thank the children of my interviewees, who provided help, in addition to Changling Hua who expressed interest in this project and helped with our English interviews and the transcription of recordings, and Xuejun Cui and Lily Yang who assisted in proofreading. My special thanks go to Shing-yi Huang and Frank Wang who proposed and facilitated the interviews and offered us much care and support. Shing-yi Huang's newspaper coverage of local Chinese groups and activities provided me with much background writing material. Finally, I am grateful for the assistance of my husband Tianchi Zhao as editor and cover designer, and for his help in improving the structure and writing of this book.

– Zong-Yi Li, in her residence
in Rossmoor, East Bay, California, United States
August 28, 2015

The book's author Zong-Yi Li and editor Tianchi Zhao on stage
in the 90th birthday party of Sheng-Yi Huang and Ruby Chow, October 2013.

Translator's Note

I believe that fate is what we make for ourselves. However, the traditional Chinese notion of *yuanfen* – serendipity – came to mind when I signed on to translate *Whom to Lean On: Out of a War-Torn Country: Life Stories of Senior Chinese Americans in Rossmoor* (2015) from Chinese to English.

I used to work as a freelance translator, before finally settling down in June 2012 to help emerging and established English-language authors, literary agents and publishers to promote their titles as digital and print books to the Chinese World. Still, even with a huge workload (I also help Chinese-language authors both within and outside of China to promote their titles across the world), I often check various websites for their posts of English/Chinese and Chinese/English translation jobs, just to keep in touch with the latest market trends.

On this fine day in March 2016, here in Melbourne, Australia, I happened to browse through the numerous translation jobs posted on a website and bumped into this particular call for a professional translator to translate a book from Chinese to English. This project was unique from the start because the book's author, Ms Zong-yi Li from Rossmoor, Walnut Creek, California, United States of America, included the book's full title and its introduction in the call, precious information that is commonly revealed only after a freelance translator has paid good money to be eligible to bid for translation jobs. As it happened, I was then able to search for details about the book and its author on the Internet.

It took me three hours to locate Zong-yi's email address in a short article published by the online edition of *Rossmoor News* on November 18, 2015. I immediately contacted her to introduce myself and express my willingness to work on the project – and received her response within four hours! In her email, Zong-yi said she was surprised to hear from me, as she had only posted the project several hours before I read it on the aforementioned website. More importantly, Zong-yi said she had been "waiting for someone appropriate to drop from the heavens" for months, as *Whom to Lean On* is not a project that any translator can work on. Not only must the suitable candidate be a highly advanced user of both English and Chinese languages (including a good grasp of classical Chinese literature), but he or she also needs to be able to convey the words and manners of speech of the 14 senior Chinese Americans interviewed in this book.

I knew I was one of the very few translators who could do this job justice, because I majored in Chinese language and literature in Taiwan and am a fluent reader and writer of both Simplified Chinese and Traditional Chinese. Having studied, worked and lived for two years in the United States and nearly 20 years in Australia, my English language is significantly advanced.

Most importantly, I spent seven years researching and writing a Ph.D. thesis on the formation, circulation and standardisation of "Chinese" cultural identity by English-language authors with Chinese ancestry in multicultural societies such as Australia, New Zealand, the United States, Canada and the United Kingdom. In order to understand how these authors identify themselves and/or are identified by readers and critics as "Chinese", I studied the history of Chinese migration and settlement across the world and have always been interested in learning of the latest books published by "Chinese" authors in the West. Whether these were written in English or have been translated from Chinese, what intrigues me is and will always be the many types of "Chineseness" conveyed by the authors and/or expected by Western readers and critics.

As a book of oral history, *Whom to Lean On* is a collection of conversations between Zong-yi, herself a brilliant scholar, and 14 senior Chinese Americans (and their spouses) who retired in the same community of Rossmoor in the San Francisco Bay Area. Also included are the adventures and achievements of two other distinguished Chinese residents (and their spouses) in Rossmoor who passed away well before this book. While these men and women are now in their 90s, they represented the first wave of Chinese immigrants arriving in the United States after the Second World War. They wanted to study in America in order to return home and serve their fellow people, but became stranded in this country after the Communists took over the Chinese Mainland. Cut off from family and friends and forced into survival mode, they worked hard, settled down, and eventually built amazing careers in this migrant nation.

As I read and translated these life stories, I was deeply moved by the youthful ambitions and adventures of these individuals in China and how their dreams were shattered while in America due to the sudden and irrevocable change of Chinese Government in 1949. Grateful for a chance to stay in the United States, this land of opportunity, they struggled to survive while doing their best to give back to American society and its people. Among them were leading experts in petrochemistry, engineering, architecture, singing, painting and Chinese culinary arts, as well as an internationally renowned filmmaker and highly experienced translators for the United Nations. They have contributed much to the American Dream, while serving as role models for later generations of Chinese and other immigrants who seek to serve their adopted country. And when they eventually had a chance to visit China, they did their best to give back to their homeland. These men and women are truly global citizens, comfortable between languages and cultures. They have fulfilled their life's goals and are now keen to help others pursue and achieve success.

I know I have learned a lot from these senior Chinese Americans, as their life stories fill a gap in existing scholarship on the Chinese diaspora in America. They have lived through history and written new chapters based on first-hand experience, enabling readers to comprehend life in China in the 1920s, 1930s and 1940s, as well as the rapid economic growth and dramatic social and cultural changes in America throughout the second half of the 20th century. Most importantly, I learned the nature and significance of the often stereotyped "Chinese" characteristics of hard-working, enduring hardships, modesty, and filial piety. As a matter of fact, these are common features of migrants across our world today, a world that is divided by a myriad of prejudices in every imaginable way. Indeed, these are fundamental characters of all mankind that cannot and should not be distorted, disputed or denied.

I would like to thank Zong-yi, author of *Whom to Lean On*, for this wonderful opportunity to translate a great book. A big thank-you also goes to Mr. Tianchi Zhao, editor of the Chinese edition, whose intelligent and graceful writing is a challenge to translate but serves as an example of genuine traditional Chinese scholarly work. Much of my gratitude goes to Ms Theresa Kuo, editor of the English edition, and Mr. Steve Goschnick, my proofreader and a sub-editor approved by Zong-yi and Theresa, for helping to make my English translation better. Most importantly, I am grateful for the 16 senior Chinese Americans (and their spouses) whose life stories are documented in this book. Thank you for allowing me to convey your inspiring life journeys to the English World.

– Christine Yunn-Yu Sun
Melbourne, Australia, March 2017

George Wang 王季琦
in front of Hillside Clubhouse, Rossmoor
November 2014

    I met George Wang purely by chance. One day I saw a painting displayed at our community activity center which depicted a classical, graceful Chinese lady. George Wang is the artist, but I wondered, who is he? Soon after that, various members of our community grouped together to watch a ballet performance in Berkeley, and I happened to sit next to Mr. Wang. Similar chance encounters kept taking place throughout our association. For example, when my husband Tianchi Zhao mentioned his recent publication *The Epic Quest for Oil in China* on the history of China's petroleum industry, Mr. Wang immediately wanted to read it, as he is an expert in petroleum and has been invited to visit China many times. He donated money as soon as our community's Peking Opera Club was established, and often enjoyed our programs with his eyes closed. When we asked him to perform, he picked a young women's role surprising all with his performance. In our interview, he showed me a photograph taken during the War of Resistance against Japan, in which he and an American instructor stood in front of an army truck. Thus I realized he was part of the Youth Expedition Army and had driven tanks! He described his life as an adventure story. His philosophy is: As long as there's a will, there is always a way. Too much help from others will only lead to dependence and a loss of motivation to improve oneself.

Biography

George C. Wang was born in 1923. His ancestral home town is Yixing, Jiangsu Province. After changing schools seven times in three years while in Junior high school as a result of escaping from the turmoils of war, he settled as a high school student in Jinhua, Zhejiang Province. He entered National Yunnan University in 1942 to study mining and metallurgy. He joined the Youth Expedition Army in 1944 and fought in Burma and India. After the victory of the War of Resistance against Japan when he completed his university studies, he was assigned by the National Government to work for the Chinese Petroleum Corporation in Taiwan in 1948. He came to the United States to pursue further studies in 1956, earned a Master's degree in Petroleum Engineering, and worked for Mobil Oil Corporation. In 1966, he stopped working to pursue a Ph.D. in Petroleum Engineering at the University of Texas, Austin. After receiving his doctorate in 1970, he resumed working for Mobil for three years. To pursue the teaching career, he resigned and taught at the Montana College of Science and Technology and the University of Alabama, serving as acting head of one of the latter's departments, and worked in Saudi Arabia for four years. He moved to Rossmoor, in Walnut Creek in California's East Bay, in 2001.

From Youth Army to Professor in Petroleum

My ancestral home is Yixing, Jiangsu Province. Home was beautiful and peaceful, a region south of the Yangtze River that is densely dotted with lakes and rivers. There were many crescent-shaped stone arch bridges, and all transport was done by boat. My hometown, Ho-chaw, is the local gathering/dispersing center for agricultural and cultural products. Having left home at a young age, I waited more than 70 years before my dream of visiting my hometown finally came true in 2008. Yet the home in my memory no longer exists; the land of rivers, lakes and farmland has turned into noisy city streets. The stone arch bridge, where I as a child had bought sweets from pole-bearing hawkers, is now a structure of concrete slabs full of bustling traffic. Ancient, graceful ancestral homes are replaced by high-rise residential buildings; also gone are the graves of our ancestors. Fortunately, an old family servant gathered and re-buried their remains, thus enabling me to pay respect to my ancestors in front of their new graves.

In China, my grandparents were ordinary landlords. Although the major task in their life was to collect rent twice a year and to purchase more land, they decided to send two boys and one girl, out of their three sons and two daughters, to school. As my grandfather had an elder brother whose scholarly fame had considerably boosted his status within our clan, he felt that some of his children should also be educated in order to glorify his family.

My father Xin-nan Wang was the first in my family to receive a college education. Born in 1887, he studied English and Russian languages and literature at the Shanghai's School for the Diffusion of Languages at the end of the Qing Dynasty. People like him were rare back then, for the Chinese society of the time was very conservative and opposed the intrusion of Western thoughts and cultures. Western-style education transformed his life from that of a traditional landlord to one with dynamic, progressive and modern social views. His conviction in the importance of education had a long and lasting impact not only on his children but also the others in my family. Supported by my grandfather and father, my aunt Zu-yun Wang studied architecture in Germany in the 1920s. My elder brother Bo-chi Wang studied at the University of Paris after graduating from the School of Law at Jiangsu's Soochow University in 1931. Both became renowned scholars in later years.

Living through Wars

My father worked for the Foreign Affairs Bureau in Harbin, Heilongjiang province, in the 1920s. I was born in that city in Northeast China in 1923. Back then the Russians and the Japanese were fighting over control of the region, resulting in frequent battles. My father had once served as a Chinese envoy to Imperial Russia. In 1931, Japan occupied Northeast China and established Manchukuo. I was eight years old at the time, a student in primary school. I remember a Japanese instructor wearing a pair of gold wire-rimmed glasses arriving to teach us Japanese and the "national anthem" of Manchukuo. Refusing to work for the Japanese, my father quit all his government jobs and switched to work for the Russian-operated China Eastern Railway Company. A couple of years later, however, the Russians were forced to sell the China-Eastern Railway to the Japanese. As a result, my father took the whole family from Harbin to re-build his career in Shanghai. He did fairly well, becoming the Administrative Dean of the prestigious Tongji University in just two years. However, our peaceful life in Shanghai was shattered when Japan launched an all-out invasion of China in 1937. Millions of Chinese were driven out of their homes and still millions more died of mass killing, malnutrition and diseases.

Just before the fall of Shanghai, my family managed to escape. Having left our property and land in Yixing to an old housekeeper, my father hired a small boat for us to sail towards the west, since my hometown was densely dotted with rivers and lakes. Our boat sailed day and night towards Wuhu, Anhui Province, which is by the banks of the Yangtze River. Our chance of survival increased as we rowed westward. Indeed, a passenger ship owned by Britain's John Swire & Sons Ltd. had docked in Wuhu to help transport the refugees. Large groups of refugees and my family climbed on board via rope ladders hanging over the ship's side. The ship set sail with a full load of people and arrived in Hankou, Hubei Province, from which we took a train to Changsha, and eventually settled in Lingling, Hunan Province. After the fall of Shanghai, Japanese troops soon captured Nanjing, resulting in the atrocity known today as the Nanjing Massacre. Having lived in Lingling for months, my father was ordered by the Ministry of Transportation and Communications to take charge of Jinhua's telegraph office, causing my family to relocate from Hunan to Zhejiang Province. The part of the province south of the Qiantang River was relatively safe at the time, although all the office clerks and equipment had been evacuated to the countryside because of frequent bombing and machine-gun fire by the Japanese. Three years later, my father died of appendicitis in 1941 due to a shortage of doctors and medicine. He was 54.

    I had changed schools seven times in the first three years of my secondary studies as a result of escaping from the turmoils of war. In sharp contrast, my three years of high school were rather uneventful. This is because the Japanese concentrated on advancing from Shanghai to Nanjing and Hankou. Preferring not to split their forces, they refrained from crossing the Qiantang River, resulting in approximately five years of safety in the part of Zhejiang and Fujian Provinces. Yet, due to constant bombing by the Japanese, even Jinhua High School was evacuated to the countryside. I remember that as a student, I often had to stand up during meal times because of a lack of chairs. There were lots of ponds nearby, so we often had taro, lotus root and locally grown sweet potato and other vegetables for food, of which we grew rather tired. These were cooked with a tiny bit of rapeseed oil, since we didn't even have proper cooking oil. Still every Friday we would have a dish containing meat – one bowl of meat for a whole week. It contained slices of stewed pork belly, what we southerners refer to as braised pork. There were eight slices of pork in the bowl, one for each person. Think about it: One slice of pork for a whole week back then, while people in our modern times eat so well. I mention this to give you some idea of our life and nutrition during the war of resistance. It was really tough.

As students, we didn't have dormitories. All our schools had been evacuated, so where could we live in the countryside? People there couldn't afford to build more houses, so we stayed in their ancestral halls or township offices. Back then Jinhua High School had many branches across the rural area. The whole school owned only one small organ, which had to be carried by two workmen from village to village in order for us to have music lessons. With that said, our school education was of very high quality, as most of our teachers were graduates from Zhejiang University. Wherever we lived and whatever we ate, our teachers did the same.

I graduated from Jinhua High School in 1942. In that same year, a large number of Japanese troops crossed the Qiantang River to advance their invasion southward. This was because the Japanese became aware of the Americans building an airport in Lishui, Zhejiang Province, and were worried that American aircraft could take off from there to bombard Tokyo, thereby casting a threat to Japan proper. As Jinhua is close to Lishui, our graduation was held one month ahead of time so that we could escape from the war.

When Zhejiang Province fell into Japanese hands in 1943, we made our way to Songyang, though my widowed stepmother and my younger siblings could no longer continue fleeing. They were forced to remain there, while I traveled alone to Fujian and eventually contacted my elder brother from Nanping. Having completed his doctorate degree in law after five years of study at the University of Paris, he was then the head of National Yunnan University's Department of Law. He asked me to go to Kunming, the only good way out, as it was still relatively safe inland. Therefore, I embarked on a journey to Kunming.

It was a tough journey, traveling on foot from Zhejiang to Fujian Province, then to Kunming, Yunnan Province. With the railways taken over by the Japanese, including the Zhejiang-Jiangxi line, I could only access country roads and mountain tracks. Completely alone, I managed about 50 kilometers per day. Many residential houses along the way stood empty, whose owners had fled from war and whose doors I took down as base for a bed at night. Occasionally I encountered troops who pitied me as a lonely kid and shared some of their food with me. They also took me across rivers and streams using special equipment, while civilians following behind had real trouble in the water. The journey from Fujian Province to Kunming was equally tough. Risking arrest by the Japanese, I reckon I had marched nearly 2000 kilometers. Sometimes I was lucky to hitch a ride with the "yellow fish", i.e. trucks that ferried produce and goods. Some trucks going my direction would offer a short ride and let me squeeze in among the cargo or sit on top of their carriages. When the trucks stopped, I would try to find another ride. The drivers would ask for a fee, but it wasn't much. In wartime there wasn't any coach for travelers, only the "yellow fish".

I arrived in Kunming safely to enter the National Yunnan University. I majored in Mining and Metallurgical Engineering to learn how to operate mines and make steel and iron. Many youths shared the same ideal, intending to build chimneys and produce steel and iron that empowered the nation. At that time we often had Japanese planes coming from Burma to bombard Kunming, forcing the National Yunnan University to evacuate to the countryside. It was 1942 when I arrived in Kunming where the U.S. Air-force "Flying Tiger Squadron" was stationed. The Japanese bombers were mostly intercepted by the

Americans, either to be shot down or to drop their bombs and leave before reaching the city. The first year of my university studies was spent in the countryside where there was no electricity. We studied at night using lamps burning vegetable oil.

Back then the national university was tuition free. Students lived in dormitories so housing wasn't a problem. And food? All university students had rice tokens, which were cash equivalent of about 15 kilograms of rice. It was a monthly payment, like a salary, which we pooled together to purchase enough food for everyone. Universities at that time operated at public expense, offering not only education but also food and accommodation. I think this was a good governmental service during wartime, helping many youths to receive higher education. University students could also earn pocket money by tutoring, so our life was alright. We didn't expect much material comfort during the War of Resistance. We wore blue cotton gowns but no socks, and one would be relatively well off with a pair of shoes. An occasional cup of tea at the local teahouse was a luxury. Life was indeed tough throughout the war and it was impossible to ask for as much as we do now.

In my second year at the university, we moved back to Kunming. Later, Japanese troops launched the Second Guangxi Campaign in an attempt to attack China's inland area from Burma. Their attack was fierce, soon capturing Guilin and Guizhou's Jinchengjiang District and then marching to Guiyang. Should Guiyang also fall, then they could easily pick their way to either Chongqing or Kunming. In 1944, that was Japan's last attack and a crucial moment for China's survival. Previously the government had denied all student requests at the National Southwest Associated University and other institutions to enlist and fight against the Japanese, as it considered them the future of our nation. However, at such a crucial moment, much expertise in translation and technology was required to operate the aircraft transport route over "the Hump" (the eastern end of the Himalayan Mountains) and the

Stilwell Road (built as an alternative to the Burma Road to ship supplies from India to Kunming), as well as to prepare for a counterattack from Burma. The Nationalist Government planned to utilize all the equipment provided by its American counterpart to assemble a "Youth Expedition Army", a modernized military that consisted of three corps and nine divisions. Chiang Kai-shek, Chairman of the Nationalist Government, proposed "Every inch of our land is as precious as a tiny drop of our blood; a hundred thousand youths are the equivalent of a hundred thousand soldiers" and called for university students to abandon their pens and pick up guns instead, as an attempt to boost the quality of our troops. As a result, some classmates from the National Yunnan University and I enlisted in Kunming to join the Youth Expedition Army. Many university students did so, with more than 1,000 from the National Southwest Associated University alone. All of us were patriotic and willing to sacrifice ourselves for China's survival.

Having trained in Kunming for a couple of months, we, the highly educated, were sent by the government to the U.S.-operated Ramgarh Training Center in India, to learn from American instructors how to drive tanks, trucks and jeeps. We flew there, along that famous route over "the Hump". Our first stop on the way to India was Dinjan, in India's Assam Region, a transfer point for China's expedition army. China, Britain and the United States were allies. Once there, we were required to discard our Chinese army uniforms, shoes and socks and be disinfected, then to change into British uniforms and be catered to with American food and drink. Unfortunately, upon arrival we lost contact with the local troops, and thus had no food or water for a whole day after such a long flight. Our leader, Major General Li Jian, swore not to consume anything when there was nothing for his soldiers. In the evening we received several barrels of dried apricots. We were so hungry that we rushed forward to open the lids and grab the dried fruit, with up to six hands trusting into the barrels at the same time. Having grabbed a handful of apricots, it was difficult to retrieve our fists as the inner edge of the barrels was extremely sharp. Everyone was bleeding from the cuts on the back of their hands, including me. I consider the scar a life-long souvenir.

The next day we flew to the Ramgarh Training Center, our destination in India. Established in 1942, it utilized American equipment in training China's expedition army in Burma in order to "recover Northern Burma and complete the China-India Road". The route was later renamed Stilwell Road, after General Joseph Stilwell of the U.S. Army. After Japan's occupation of Burma, Japanese troops intended to invade Wandin and Longling in Yunnan Province and then attack Kunming. Having been trained by General Stilwell with American equipment in Ramgarh, Chinese troops managed to fend off the Japanese attack after several fierce battles, forcing the Japanese to retreat.

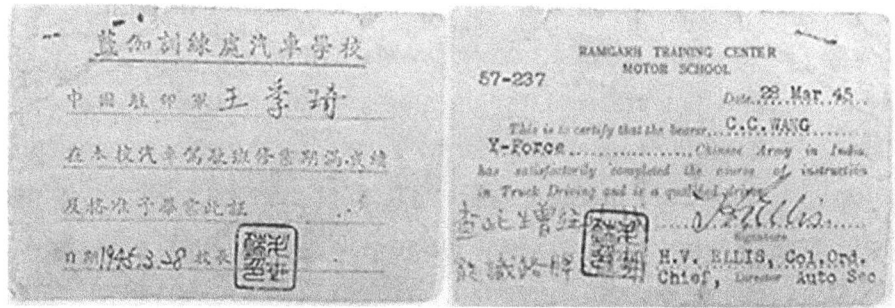

George Wang's Certificate of Completion of Training in Ramgarh, India 1945

About half a year later, having completed training at Ramgarh Training Center, I was sent to a military base in Northern Burma. By then the Japanese troops in Burma already showed signs of losing steam. Our mission was to transfer all the weaponry, ammunition and supplies desperately needed by China's expeditionary army in Burma to complete the Stilwell Road. At that time Japan had blocked all of China's marine and land routes, so that any transport of petroleum, weaponry and ammunition had to be done by aircraft over "the Hump" of the Himalayan Mountains to reach Kunming. A lot of time and effort enabled only a meagre amount of supplies to get through. Should the

Stilwell Road be completed, land vehicles would be able to drive straight from India to Kunming. This is why the Allies were determined to complete the route in order to provide Southwest China with U.S.-supplied equipment. We, who had received training, were the ones who would drive on this road. It is true that Britain had previously stationed troops in Burma; however, they couldn't defeat the Japanese and had to rely on their Chinese counterparts for support in order to safely retreat to India. Back them China's expedition army was really rather famous, and it was with them that I served. Thanks to such famous generals as Sun Li-jen and Wei Lihuang, who commanded China's expeditionary army in Burma in various fierce battles, they were finally able to complete the Stilwell Road. In April 1945, we drove back to China on this road, carrying all sorts of weaponry and equipment piled high in our vehicles. Having passed the famous "24 Turns" in Qinglong, Guizhou Province, we soon reached Kunming.

The dangerously steep Stilwell Road

I belonged to the first convoy of the transport team. Each convoy had 50 to 60 trucks, with each operated by two people taking turns driving day and night. It was very hard work. Upon arrival at Kunming, we handed over all the vehicles, weaponry and ammunition to the army stationed there. While bivouacked with the troops and waiting for our next assignment, we heard rumors that we would be sent to the Philippine to work with American troops in recovering islands occupied by the Japanese. Island-hopping as a military strategy often resulted in high death and casualty rates, as the Japanese refused to surrender, fighting to the very last man. We were all set to go there until a U.S. aircraft dropped the atomic bomb on Japan proper. Back then we had no idea what an atomic bomb was, but those studying science knew that such a weapon is so powerful that one bomb can destroyed a whole city. The Americans dropped one atomic bomb on Hiroshima on August 6, and another on Nagasaki on August 9. After that, the Japanese knew they could fight no more. Their Emperor announced the nation's unconditional surrender on August 15, an end that no one could have foreseen.

George Wang (front row, second from the right) with friends and an American instructor at the Youth Expedition Army, India, 1944

As my university was in Kunming, I applied for discharge from the army and returned to my studies in mining and metallurgy. My service in the Youth Expedition Army disrupted my studies by one and half year. This is the time I made my contribution to our nation. We enlisted out of a sense of patriotism, without caring whether we would live or die. I was only 21 years old.

After being discharged from the Youth Expedition Army, I continued my studies in Kunming and graduated in 1948. Then it was time to look for a job. I was interested in working in steel-smelting facilities, or working in metal or coal mines. Back then you looked for work by yourself with a bit of help from people and personal connections. Since my brother was already in Nanjing, he said he would find me a job at the local coal mine. While waiting, I took some time to visit my sister in Chongqing. A graduate from Tongji University's School of Medicine, she had been working as a pediatrician in Chongqing during the War of Resistance against Japan. I hitched a ride with a "yellow fish" truck from Kunming to Chongqing. However, in just two days after my arrival, I received a letter from the National Resources Commission in charge of the nation's development of heavy industry and mining. In fact, it was the Nationalist Government's highest economic authority during the War of Resistance. According to the letter, I would be working with the Chinese Petroleum Corporation in Taiwan.

Back then I didn't know much about petroleum, as none of China's academic institutions had a department of petroleum. People used to say there was no petroleum in China; however, when an oil field was discovered in Laojunmiao, in Northwestern China's Shanxi Province at the beginning of the War of Resistance, the whole nation was in ecstasy because, as the government claimed, "a drop of oil is as precious as a drop of blood". President Chiang Kai-shek ordered Yumen Oil Field, in Gansu Province, to produce one hundred thousand gallons of petroleum in three months, a goal that they achieved, using an old-fashioned distillation unit. Petroleum was extremely expensive at that time. Instead of petroleum, motor vehicles burned charcoal and were nicknamed "charcoal powered cars". Each of these vehicles had a long, circular stove attached on one side, where charcoal was placed. Before starting the vehicle in the morning, the charcoal was set alight and air pumped into the stove, so that when the coal burned it would produce carbon monoxide. Carbon monoxide can be burned, but not carbon dioxide. The carbon monoxide produced in this way was used to run the vehicle's engine, although it lacked horsepower and couldn't go uphill. To do so, you had to get off the vehicle and push it, before putting wedges against the wheels to keep them still. Then you pushed the vehicle a bit further, then used the wedges again, so on and so forth, until you reached the top of the hill. Such were the "charcoal powered cars", which often broke down and required repairing on the way. It often took days to fix them.

Arriving in Taiwan Alone

The letter I received in Chongqing assigned me to work with the Chinese Petroleum Corporation in Taiwan. As the company had a branch in Chongqing, I enroled there and received a travel allowance to Taiwan. This was truly unexpected good luck – I wondered why such an excellent job came my way. There were lots of mines in Yunnan and Hunan; among the 20 or so classmates who graduated at the same time as me, the majority went to work in those two provinces. I was the only one sent to the Chinese Petroleum Corporation. I could think of two reasons why I got this job. First, those oil fields and refineries recovered from the Japanese were a huge mess as a result of American bombing, so the Chinese Petroleum Corporation required a group of young engineers to clean them up. Meanwhile, I had an excellent academic record at school, and also served our nation in the army.

Mainland China was in total chaos in 1948. Those underground troops cultivated by the Communist Party had now surfaced, and many high-ranking political, army and government officials of the Nationalist Government were revealed as Communists. Also surging were many parades and demonstrations supporting Communism while denouncing Chiang Kai-shek. There was considerable inflation in Shanghai as well. Several of my friends from the National Yunnan University, who had served in the Youth Expedition Army and returned from India with me, were sent to Northeast China to fight in the civil war. However, the government troops there couldn't defeat the Communists and were forced to retreat again and again. I was the lucky one who left the army in Kunming and therefore avoided the civil war. Not only did I complete my studies, but I also gained a good job.

To me, Taiwan was a brand new place. It was relatively peaceful when I arrived, and life was good. The only oil field in Taiwan was a small one in today's Miaoli County. All equipment and dormitories previously operated by the Japanese now belonged to the Chinese Petroleum Corporation. It was here in the mines that I studied, worked and experienced no hardship. I was fortunate to have left Mainland China because in 1949, less than a year after my departure, the Nationalist Government was no longer in power. Shanghai fell and many other regions were now controlled by the Communists, who proceeded to establish the People's Republic of China in 1950. After that, no one could escape from behind the Bamboo Curtain. I counted myself lucky to have been sent to Taiwan. Knowing nothing about politics, I wasn't sure what policies the Communists would have for the future nor how the Nationalist Party would respond politically. I only knew the civil war was fierce.

My wife Helen's Chinese name is Hui-ling Wang, Wang being her maiden name. She didn't adopt mine. She was a 16-year-old high school student when I met her in Kunming. When I arrived in Taiwan in 1948, I wrote and urged her to leave China as soon as possible; otherwise, we would never have another chance to see each other. She graduated from high school in 1949 with plans to study at Cornell University in the United States. Yet, her application for a passport was futile, as our government had been defeated and retreated to Taiwan.

Back in 1949, due to strict border control by the Nationalist Government to prevent Communists from entering, it was difficult to enter Taiwan. Having applied for and received an entry permit for Helen as my fiancée, I sent it to her and begged her to come as soon as possible. Her parents were initially reluctant to let her travel to such a far-off place as Taiwan, for they knew nothing about the island. However, Yunnan Governor Lu Han increasingly showed signs of converting to Communism, while other provinces such as Sichuan had already surrendered without a fight. As Helen's father, a railway engineer in Kunming, also operated a milk factory at home, her whole family was sure to become a target of criticism, humiliation and torture by the Communists. This eventually prompted him to hand over the entry permit with permission for her to leave.

In 1949 I greeted Helen in Keelung, Taiwan, upon her arrival via Guangzhou. As the eldest child, with three brothers and four sisters, she was the only one from her family to leave China all because of me. I recalled how heart-broken I was when I left her behind in Kunming in order to visit my sister in Chongqing. I promised to return to Kunming, but this assignment by the National Resources Commission took me eastward along the Yangtze River to Nanjing and Shanghai, before sailing across the strait to Taiwan. My letters to Helen were full of concerns that the farther I traveled, the less chance we would have to meet again. Who knew, back then, that times and circumstances would change so dramatically, and that both of us would end up in Taiwan. It was truly destiny. Not long after that, the two sides of the Taiwan Strait were cut off from each other. For 30 long years we heard nothing from our families in China. In 1950, the year after her arrival in Taiwan, Helen and I married.

Life-Long Learning

I worked for the Chinese Petroleum Corporation in Miaoli for 11 years (1948-1959). My major was in mining, not petroleum. It's true that I gained some experience in oil development, but my understanding of fundamental theories was still poor. As a result, I acutely felt the need to pursue further studies overseas. With that said, back then I could still be drafted and therefore eligible for mandatory military service. I couldn't leave Taiwan freely; besides, my application for a passport was also rejected. However, in 1955, the Nationalist Government opened up examinations for overseas study, either by government or private sponsorship. This was an opportunity that I took. In 1956, I was admitted to a spot for overseas study by private sponsorship.

I could have left Taiwan that year, but our daughter Lillian was born, six years after the arrival of our boy, Karl. I couldn't leave my wife behind with two young kids and I couldn't leave alone, so I stayed. At that time, we were able to defer our passport application once we passed the government examination. I waited until 1959 before leaving home and coming to the United States alone. My daughter was three years old then. I was 36.

Leaving home wasn't easy, either. Having passed the government examination and receiving permission to study in an academic institution in the United States, the American Embassy had to check not only my English language ability, via face-to-face conversations and oral and written tests, but also my bank savings. I wasn't worried about tests, but money was a serious problem, as there was a US $2,400 deposit requirement for an American visa application. My government salary was low, about US $30 per month. I also owed people money for medical expenses, which further ate into our savings. Nonetheless, our accommodation was free, as the Chinese Petroleum Corporation provided housing and cooking gas to supplement earnings. My income was enough for our daily living, with sufficient food, which was rather nice; but there was never any extra money left. Back then the living standard in Taiwan was low. Any family with the three machines – radio, sewing machine and bicycle – would be considered well-off.

George Wang with wife and children,
before leaving home to study in America, 1959

Because my monthly salary was only enough for our basic living expenses, how could I find the needed US $2,400 for the deposit? It was truly a problem. Luckily, I bumped into a once-in-a-lifetime opportunity. A businessman in import and export, Mr. Fang, often came to Miaoli to handle our company's purchase of various oil-drilling equipments from the United States. He and I were just acquaintances, but often met for business. Somehow he heard that I had passed the examination for overseas study but lacked the money to depart for America. He then proposed to provide the needed US $2,400 with reimbursement upon my arrival in America. So it happened – he loaned me US $2,400 in cash, which I deposited in Taiwan's Bank of China. With such proof of my bank savings, I successfully applied for and received a visa issued by the American Embassy. Such was the favor Mr. Fang had granted me! He helped not only me, but provided monetary assistance to several of my friends. In fact, I didn't know him very well, as I was in charge of engineering, while our company's other departments handled international purchases. Anyway, with this money and an entry permit from an American institution, as well as my passing the American Embassy's English language test, I received my visa. I left Taiwan and arrived in the United States alone in 1959.

George Wang's Certificate of Overseas Study,
issued by the Ministry of Education 1956

I couldn't afford a plane ticket. However, at that time there was a cargo ship departing from the Philippines and sailing to the United States via Yokohama. This required six other Taiwanese students and me to fly to Japan to wait for the ship's arrival. A plane ticket from Taipei to Japan cost more than US $100, a considerable expense. Yet, this was our only option back then, as there was no way to travel by sea from Taiwan to the United States. The seven of us boarded the cargo ship in Yokohama. After 14 days of sailing, we arrived at the port of Tacoma near Seattle.

George Wang (first from the left, front row, holding a bottle of coca-cola) landing in Tacoma, WA with fellow Taiwanese students, August 1959

The other six students had prestigious backgrounds with families being either rich or in government positions in Taiwan. I remember the girl's name as Wanruo Lee (Lily Lee Chen), whose father was a legislator and who later served as mayor in Monterey Park, near Los Angeles. I was the oldest and poorest among us. It was certainly difficult for someone my age and circumstances to leave my family behind in Taiwan and travel overseas. Upon our arrival in Tacoma, we took a bus to Seattle where some of us left immediately on various planes. I was going to the Virginia Polytechnic Institute (VPI) today's VPI University, in Blacksburg, Virginia. Again I couldn't afford a plane ticket, so I took a Grayhound bus from Seattle to Virginia. It was a cross-country journey, from the northern end of America's West Coast to its mid-East Coast. It took me seven days and seven nights where all I could see was the American landscape. Back then these buses traveled straight from the West Coast to the East Coast with various drivers taking turns driving day and night.

It was mid-August then, but we didn't even have a chance to stop for a shower. It was lucky that we had air conditioning. At that time there was fierce discrimination against black Americans. All the seats on the bus were segregated, with the blacks sitting at the back, but I as a Chinese could sit anywhere. Even when the bus stopped for meals, the blacks had to find a separate sitting place from the whites. That was 1959.

Back then the few Chinese students on campus became instant friends when we met. Upon my arrival in VPI, the Chinese students already there took good care of me, inviting me to eat with them and stay in their dormitories until my own place was found. We couldn't afford good housing; instead, we picked the cheapest places that cost only US $20 per month. To save money, many Chinese students lived in basements with only a bed and a small desk, without even a refrigerator. Two other students and I rented one such basement where the landlord refused to turn on the heat since he too needed to save money. Without a refrigerator, how did we store our food? Many houses in America had double-paned windows to insulate from unwanted wind and heat. In winter when it was freezing outside, we placed our meat and vegetables between the two panes of glass, using the window as a refrigerator to preserve our food. When it was cold and there was no heating, we used a small electric stove to boil water and make tea to keep us warm. Because we did not have a bathroom, we showered at the power station's facilities that the university provided its workers. Considering the fact that I had recently arrived from sub-tropical Taiwan, it was truly freezing in Virginia. Back then our life as Chinese students was much tougher than that of other international counterparts. It was our willingness to be assiduous and bear hardship that got us through those difficult years.

I didn't receive government subsidies, loans or food stamps. I had nothing, only myself. Most of the other students were single, but I had a wife and two children in Taiwan. I had to support them and myself, and pay my tuition fees which I had to earn. At VPI I studied oil refining as part of my plan to return to petroleum engineering. I was already familiar with this field, but some work in relevant theories was necessary. I transferred to Oklahoma University of Tulsa after only a quarter in VPI. At that time, Tulsa was considered the "Oil Capital of the World" and the University's program in petroleum engineering was excellent. In order to make up the subjects I missed, I had a huge study load with many units in petroleum engineering to take. Many of the professors in our department were younger than I.

With no car, I had to walk a long way to the University's laboratories to conduct experiments and finish my thesis. Thanks to my experience of working for the Chinese Petroleum Corporation, however, I soon received a teaching assistantship. The stipend was low, and was further reduced because I was a Chinese student. As two Chinese students were hired as teaching assistants, each received only half the amount, about US $50-60 per month. Nonetheless, such a small amount of money contributed considerably to my finance, as I used it to pay my tuition fees, rent and food. While the tuition fees weren't much, I still needed to work during the summer breaks. This is why I always say that if I were able to confront these obstacles and continue marching forward by myself, then other people could do it too. In sharp contrast, international students these days simply demand money from their families, and the government would provide this and that, such as financial assistance and student loans. It was good to be self-reliant. I gritted my teeth and endured until the problems were solved.

While studying for my Master's degree in Tulsa, I rented the smallest and cheapest unit available. Also staying there were several students from Venezuela, who were sent by their government. Coming from an oil-rich country, these wealthy students had the old landlady cook for them and lived quite a comfortable life. In contrast, the University had a cafeteria, but I couldn't afford to eat there. In my attempt to feed myself, I had to wait for the landlady to finish cooking and washing before using her stove, usually quite late and I was constantly starving. A poor young man like me had to cook for himself.

It was only on the day I graduated that I had a meal at the cafeteria. Throughout my studies I also mended my own clothes since I couldn't afford to buy anything new.

In order to support my family and pay tuition fees, I worked summers in large cities. This is something I learned as soon as I arrived in America. On my way to Tulsa, Oklahoma, from Virginia, I stayed in New York City for two weeks. While American universities didn't have winter breaks, there was a two-week period between the end of the autumn quarter in universities in America's southern states and the beginning of the first semester in those in eastern states.

I recall one year, between Christmas and the Chinese New Year, when I stayed near Columbia University with a group of Chinese students who had lived in the United States for many years. In the evenings we gathered to chat about survival and earning money, and it was through such discussions that we became friends. On the next day, two of them took me to a small Chinese restaurant in a town named Little Neck on the outskirts of New York City. The three of us, one female and two males, took care of the whole restaurant's operation that ranged from buying vegetables to cooking seafood. The Chinese chef had jumped ship and smuggled himself into America some years earlier; as a result, he only stayed inside the kitchen for fear that immigration would arrest him. That is where I learned how to cook many Chinese and Western dishes. I learned that Americans eat cereal for breakfast, unlike Chinese people who have rice porridge. What is cereal? It was only then that I realized cereal consists of grains that are processed into various shapes of cooked, dry and crunchy morsels to be eaten with milk. Initially I didn't know which type of cereal to serve – whether it was made with corn, rice or other grains – and had to constantly dash around the restaurant to figure things out.

Throughout those two weeks in New York City, I learned survival from other Chinese students. Back then Chinese restaurants were the only places where we could work to earn money. As for the summer breaks, we had two ways of earning money in New York City: up in the mountains or down by the sea. With the former, it was to find temporary work in hotels in the cool mountains north of the city, as many rich people, including Jews, often went there to escape the heat. With the latter, it was to work in hotels by the beach where many tourists spent their vacations.

George Wang (second from the right) with four friends working for Butler Lodge in summer 1960

Most of the hotels were owned by Jews. Knowing how to make money, they employed a large number of temporary workers when business was good. They liked hiring Chinese students. For example, there was a hotel called "Butler Lodge" in Hurleyville, outside New York City, that catered to Jews. While studying in Oklahoma, we operated the restaurant in the summer. The hotel provided food and accommodation for three months during the summer, so we saved all our salaries and tips for our tuition fees. Many of my fellow temporary workers were students from Taiwan or Malaysia. Unlike us, today's new generation of international students come from rich families.

Instead of working summers, they would rather go sightseeing.

I was a leader back then. I was the oldest in my late 30s, unlike the other students who were recent graduates in their early 20s. I took good care of them. Whenever they couldn't find work in hotels, they would call me to talk to the bosses on their behalf. This is how we worked back then. The Jews trusted us Chinese students because we worked hard and were honest. One of the Jewish bosses even had a Filipino chef cooking Chinese fried rice for us. In one summer we could earn about US $500-600, or up to US $700-800. That was a lot of money back then, enough to take care of a whole year's tuition fees. The fees at that time weren't as expensive as they are now. Furthermore, as students we could also earn some money on campus, by managing equipment in our department or helping professors publish journals. Whatever I could do, I did. After all, life was tough and I had a family to support. Working like this, I was able to study, live, and send money to my family in Taiwan. I sent them US $30 each month, enough for them to live on.

The most difficult aspect of my four years of study in the United States was being away from my wife and children. Such a problem didn't exist for those who were single. Being much older than the others *and* with a family, I had to study while working and earning money; it was really tough. During those four years of pursuing a Master's degree from 1959 to 1962, I never called home nor visited my family. That was particularly heart-wrenching. Back then it wasn't easy to make an international phone call. We had telephones at the University, but my family in Taiwan didn't own one. So, how could my wife answer when I called her? Besides, there wasn't a telephone where I lived. More importantly, I was just an international student. Without a Green Card, I would be asking for trouble if I returned to Taiwan for a visit, as I might never be able to come back to America. Meanwhile, I didn't have money to return home, as a return trip would cost thousands of U.S. dollars. With neither telephone calls nor any chance of getting together, my wife and I could only write letters, which would take a couple of weeks *en route*. Throughout those four years Helen composed 252 letters, while I wrote 186, totalling more than 430 letters. They are all preserved as they were the only contacts I had with my loved ones. Her letters kept me going. Such a problem never existed for those who were single, but people like me were indeed rare. As previously mentioned, if I could survive in the United States, then anyone else could do it too, because their situation would be much better than mine. It was truly tough for me.

Collections of letters George Wang had sent and received while studying in America

Having received a Master's degree in Petroleum Engineering in 1962, I needed a break from studies. America was experiencing an economic downturn then, and many of my job applications were rejected. As my visa would soon expire, I sent an application to Mobil Oil Corporation and was accepted, thanks to my experience of working in the oil industry. They assigned me to work in Lubbock, Texas, with a monthly salary of US $580. This was an important job for me at that time since it solved my financial problems and enabled me to stay in the United States. More importantly, the company sponsored my family so that my wife and children didn't have to wait for a spot in America's immigration quota. I owe my whole-hearted gratitude to President John F. Kennedy for establishing this immigration policy. Having left my family in 1959, I finally was reunited with them in 1963. This was a difficult and unusual story. I will always remember how emotional I became when I saw my wife and children at the airport.

With my family now in America, we had to learn how to adapt to life in this new world. Soon after that, our third child, a boy named Jack, was born. Everything in our life, from food and clothing to accommodation and daily transport, depended on me. It was only after having worked for Mobil for nearly five years in 1967, that we finally settled down. It occurred to me then, that we as immigrants needed something unique in order to compete with the locals. Most people were born and raised here and spoke fluent English. They had properties, relatives and friends, but we had none of these. Worse, we weren't used to their lifestyle and language. This was in sharp contrast to the locals, who started having fun as university graduates, purchasing cars and enjoying holidays. I could only pursue further studies in order to accomplish something great and stand tall in the crowd. I could only compete with them with my academic achievement, something Chinese people generally excelled. In order to secure a prosperous future for my family and a successful career for myself, a Master's degree wasn't sufficient. I needed a Ph.D.

Upon my arrival in the United States in 1959, I was already 36 years old. When I was 44 in 1967, no one believed I would really pursue a Ph.D. at the University of Texas in Austin. It wasn't an easy decision, either. Although our life was relatively comfortable, thanks to my work for the oil company and a steady income, I convinced my family that we shouldn't be content like this – we had to keep on fighting, to endure several more years of hardship. As a result in 1967, I received an extended leave of absence from my work at Mobil to pursue a Ph.D. in Austin, again in petroleum engineering. My plan was in limbo for four years due to my family's arrival. As soon as we had settled down, however, I launched my second plan-of-action.

Doing a Ph.D. was difficult, as I only had a fellowship of US $240 per month. Upon arrival in Austin, I couldn't afford good housing so chose an old dormitory provided by the University for students with families. It was the cheapest, costing US $45 each month; however my fellowship was still not enough to cover my whole family's living expenses. As a result, each summer, I went to Dallas and worked for Mobil's research laboratory in order to earn extra money. Mobil continued to be supportive. They offered me three months of employment during the summers, from which I was able to earn enough money for expenses through the rest of the year. Plus they also sent award grants to my advisor to support my research in Austin. I worked summers for Mobil, but during school terms I devoted all my time and energy to research.

The three years in Austin were hard enough but our spirit was high. We had enough money to survive, and our children received a good education. In 1968, Karl finished high school and was awarded a full scholarship by the prestigious Rice University. Later he completed a Ph.D. from the Massachusetts Institute of Technology (MIT). Lillian did equally well in high school. After university, she earned a Doctorate of Medicine from the Baylor School of Medicine. Jack was only four years old then and required looking after. He went to study at the University of Houston, receiving Bachelor's and Master's degrees in science, plus a Master's degree in Business Administration. I myself completed my Ph.D. in 1970 after three years of hard work. This is why I often say that as long as you are willing to succeed, there is always a way. Too much help would only make you dependent on others and reluctant to move forward.

George Wang (right), aged 47, receiving his PhD degree from University of Texas in Austin 1970

My Teaching Career

Soon after my graduation, I returned to Mobil, working at its Midland Division in Texas. In order to better use my training and experience, in 1973 I resigned and switched from industry to education. My first teaching position was in the Department of Petroleum Engineering at Montana College of Science and Technology. I was the first and only Chinese professor there, so that upon arrival, I was interviewed by a local journalist who later published a newspaper article titled "Dr. Wang in Pursuit of Freedom".

In this interview, I discussed my experiences in China and those after my arrival in the United States. I also mentioned the fact that I had lost contact with my China-based brother for more than 20 years. Even after President Nixon's visit to China and considerable improvement in diplomatic relations between the two countries, I still feared that any communication between us would cause him trouble. America, being democratic and free, had provided my children and me with the best education. It remained my hope that China's political environment would improve, as it is human nature to pursue freedom and liberty.

Local newspaper coverage of George Wang, first Chinese professor in Montana
1974

Montana is one of the most beautiful places in the world, where the renowned Yellowstone National Park is situated. While there, we as a family often went hiking and fishing. However, Montana's winters are very cold, full of ice and snow. Having arrived from the hot climes of Taiwan and Texas, we couldn't stand the extreme Montana weather. I only taught there for a year before suggesting to my wife that we transfer to somewhere warmer.

In 1975, I accepted a position as assistant professor at the University of Alabama's Department of Mineral Engineering, which brought our family to Tuscaloosa. Back then the Department had two research streams, mining and petroleum. As I specialized in petroleum engineering, this position in the University represented a new challenge as well as an opportunity for further development. In fact, my experiences and connections in the oil industry paved the way for the growth and improvement of the Department's petroleum program. I built up contacts, developed research projects, and secured donations from oil corporations. In 1984, through my work for the Department of

Land and Natural Resources in San Francisco, I established contact with various people in charge of the San Francisco Energy Research Laboratory and later provided consulting work for them. This made it much easier in subsequent years to apply for government funding for the University's research projects. We received research funding from federal and state governments, organized research topics, constructed new laboratories, designed and developed new courses, enrolled many students, and published many papers, all of which helped boost the Department's teaching and research capacity in petroleum engineering. As a result, in 1980 I was promoted to Tenured Full Professor and served one year as Acting Department Head. I was also the first faculty member in the Department to win an Outstanding Teaching Award. Those years in Alabama were the most productive and enjoyable of my life.

While teaching in Alabama, I worked twice in Saudi Arabia for about four and a half years. It was an interesting experience. An Islamic country and the "Kingdom of Oil", Saudi Arabia has abundant oil reserves. The Arabian-American Oil Company (ARAMCO), the largest oil corporation in the world back then, was established with assistance from the United States. In 1936, the Americans discovered oil in Saudi Arabia and provided the country with geologists, engineers and architects, as well as all the necessary equipment and material. To strengthen friendship between the two countries, President Roosevelt, who recognized the importance of crude oil, even gifted an airplane to the old king of Saudi Arabia in 1940. Thanks to its oil, Saudi Arabia did and still does maintain close relationship with the United States. America initially controlled 75 percent of ARAMCO's shares, with the remaining 25 percent belonging to Saudi Arabia. This ratio gradually became 50-50, with Saudi Arabia eventually purchasing all the shares in 1980 and turning the company into a state-owned entity. However, many Americans remained in the country because of a lack of local professionals. As Saudi Arabia cultivated its own talents, the number of

Americans there slowly decreased although it was the Americans who had helped to build up their riches in the first place.

I taught at the University of Petroleum and Minerals in Saudi Arabia, where everyone spoke English. I spent two and a half years developing new courses and applied for research funding for them. Later they invited me back for another two years. By then our children had fully grown, with one graduated from university, the other getting married and the youngest a university student in the United States. As a result, I went to Saudi Arabia with only my wife, who was willing to accompany me everywhere I went in the world. She considered our two trips to Saudi Arabia both a true adventure and an interesting opportunity to broaden our horizons.

The local people prayed five times a day during which all the doors were shut, even at meal times. So what could we do in the middle of a meal? Being Korean, the boss of our restaurant would close all the curtains until our meals and the local prayers were both concluded. The same applied to my teaching, as my students would leave the room and pray on their special mats outside. They would wash their hands and feet and pray faithfully before returning to class. Despite our different religious beliefs, I had truly pleasant working relationships with my colleagues and students there.

While working in Alabama, I also visited China several times. In 1980, the Chinese Government invited a group of seven or eight American experts, including engineers, geologists and myself to investigate the potential of oil exploration and production in China. I went to Daqing oil fields in Northeast China and Shengli oil fields in Shandong Province. Because China had just opened up, everything we saw, from their equipment to technologies and methods of oil exploration, were from 1950s Russia. They were ancient, rusted and broken. Meanwhile, representatives of the Ministry of Petroleum Industry accompanied us from Beijing to Northeast China, then to Shandong, Jiangsu, Guangxi, Guangdong, and finally to the Hainan

Island, to explore potential locations for future oil discovery and development.

After 13 years of teaching at the University of Alabama, I retired in August 1987. The Board of Trustees expressed in a resolution its appreciation for and recognition of my services as "a sincere, devoted and masterful engineer and teacher, providing an ever-ready source of scientific, analytical, as well as practical knowledge and inspiration to his students and colleagues alike". Eight years after that, in 1995, as a result of my research in the University of Alabama, I was again invited to China to give a seminar on Enhanced Oil Recovery at the University of Petroleum. It is there that I met an assistant professor who was smart and well-accomplished in digital modelling. I later helped him to pursue a Ph.D. at the Texas A&M University. Now he works for Chevron.

Painting as a Hobby

Having retired, I moved from Alabama to Houston because most of my friends were in Texas. In 1994, a friend and I launched the Western-style Painting Club for Amateur Chinese Artists. I had always been interested in painting, having done so before and during my university studies. During the War of Resistance against Japan, I would paint portraits of movie stars and sell them to subsidize my daily living expenses. While it was never a professional pursuit, I started painting earnestly and frequently after arriving in Saudi Arabia where there was less work and more leisure time. Having established the club, painting became a serious hobby. Because we had one exhibition every year – I had to push myself to paint often. I mainly do oil and acrylic painting and pay specific attention to combination and arrangement of colors. I like portraits as well, but enjoy natural, still life even better.

Since our son worked in San Francisco's Bay Area, he asked us to move closer to him. As a result, in 2001 we moved to Rossmoor, in

Walnut Creek, California. Ours had been a life of running around. After our arrival in the United States, moving was constant as a result of my switching schools, conducting research projects in summer holidays, and, in particular, working for oil companies that assigned its employees wherever necessary. We are different from most local Americans – they stay in one place, with a permanent house and many relatives, and become increasingly reluctant to move as time goes by. If we needed to leave Houston behind, then that would be that. I chose to move to Rossmoor, an excellent community with a professional art studio and a painting club. Many of the residents here are professional artists, so I, too, devote much time to painting.

George Wang's acrylic paintings (originally in color) of tree shadows and California oaks

After my wife Hui-ling Wang (Helen) passed away, I painted her portrait as a tribute. Last year, our painting club chose it for display at the community activity center. All our exhibited paintings were juried by professional judges from outside the community. Meanwhile, because painting requires a good search for background scenery, and because I am too old to paint outdoors, I picked up photography in order to transform my photographs into paintings. Earlier this year I took a photo of a sunset. As the colors and composition resemble those of the German national flag, I posted it to the German Embassy, which in turn sent it Germany. When Chancellor Angela Dorothea Merkel saw it, she loved it so much that she sent me a personal letter and an autographed photograph of her portrait. This story was later published on the front page of our community newspaper Rossmoor News.

George Wang's oil painting "My Wife" 2014

Nowadays, apart from painting, I live an active life by practicing Chi Gong and attending musical concerts.

George Wang was singing a female role in Peking Opera Club.
September 2015

Our Chinese community launched a Peking Opera Club, with Mr. Qian Qiming, renowned for his previous service at the Beijing Peking Opera Theater, playing the *Jinghu*, a classical two-stringed Chinese musical instrument specifically for accompanying the Peking Opera singing. Most of the time, I would enjoy the club's programs with my eyes closed. On the rare occasions that I hummed along, others insisted that I should perform. Back in my youth I did enjoy performing; however, now that I was in my 90s, I had not attempted singing Peking Opera for nearly 70 years. Still, upon earnest requests from friends, I agreed to perform an aria sung by Yu the Beauty, the leading female character in *Farewell My Concubine* – and surprised them all.

From my point of view, my life has been extraordinary and rather successful. Not only did I earn the highest academic degree, but I also achieved an academic position of the highest level – a tenured full professorship. Now, as a professor emeritus, I have written a short autobiography, "Our Roots". It is an attempt to explain to our children where I came from and how I lived my life from the earliest days in my hometown to those later as an educator.

As we have no more direct relatives living in China, I never considered returning there throughout the years. In 2008, however, 70 years after my departure, I finally revisited Ho-chaw, my hometown in Yixing, Jiangsu Province, and received unexpected greetings, assistance and respect from the remaining members of my clan. Ho-chaw, famous in the region south of the Yangtze River, is a rich land that has fostered numerous great men, including artists Wu Guanzhong and Xu Beihong and scientists Zhu Hongyuan and Tang Aoqing. When I visited the Wang family home, I discovered that the building had long disappeared, apart from a black marble tablet standing where the backdoor used to be. Etched on the tablet are the words "Home of Professors", with a paragraph explaining that the town has fostered more than 500 professors. I think I am one of them. Also belonging to this list is my elder brother Bo-chi Wang, an expert in civil law. He later moved to Taiwan and served as a law professor in both National Taiwan University and Soochow University. With his life-long devotion to education and numerous academic publications, he deserves to have his name etched on this tablet. Both of us have honored our family. It is truly a case of a great place fostering many great people.

Now that I look back at my life, it has been an exciting story of adventures, hard work and accomplishments. The loss of my parents at an early age made me exceedingly independent and self-reliant. The long and destructive wars taught me how to survive and bear hardship with fortitude. These are my unique life experiences. Furthermore, the Chinese traditional virtues of moderation and humility have given me guidance on how to work with people in harmony, and values I have inherited have also formed the foundation upon which all my dreams have come true. The greatest accomplishment of my life, however, is that my wife, Hui-ling Wang, and I have raised three wonderful children. We brought them to this land of freedom and opportunities, and I remain convinced that future generations who live and grow up in this great country will always flourish and be blessed with the best in their lives.

Yung-fong Shy 沙榮峰
In his residence, with a Cannes Film Festival Award Certificate
December 2014

To mark the 50th anniversary of the establishment of Rossmoor as a community in 2014, a series of celebrations were launched, including a week-long international film festival that showcased famous international movies of the 1960s. When *Dragon Inn* (1967) was recently selected as one of 22 Cannes Classics in France, it became the best choice to represent Chinese film. Released by Union Film Company in Hong Kong, the movie was produced by Mr. Yung-fong Shy. As I knew little about the early history of Taiwan's film industry, this was the first time I heard Mr. Shy's name. It was also then that I realized he is a member of the Chinese-American Association of Rossmoor. He gladly accepted my invitation for an interview. He even prepared relevant documents for delivery to me by his daughter. Facing such a rare opportunity of meeting Mr. Shy, one of the founding fathers of Taiwan's Mandarin language film industry, I carefully studied his book on the establishment and evolution of the Union Film Company. While not in perfect health, Mr. Shy was full of energy and excitement throughout our conversation about movies. With a heavy Jiangsu accent, he recalled years of hardship at the beginning of his career and the later triumphs of the Union Film Company, as well as many behind the scenes movie stories.

Biography

Yung-fong Shy was born in a farming village of Zhouzhuang in Jiangyin, Jiangsu Province, on February 7, 1921. After graduating from primary school in his hometown, he entered Jiangsu's Nanjing Senior High School, but dropped out at 13 due to changes in his family's circumstances. He apprenticed at a cotton shop and eventually launched his own company at 19. In 1947, he relocated from Shanghai to Taipei. In order to promote Mandarin and Chinese culture in Taiwan after the end of the island's 50 year occupation by Japan, Shy and three friends shifted their career focus to the film industry, and in 1953 formally established the Union Film Company in Taipei. For years he served as the company's chairman, devoting time and effort to make films in Mandarin. Not only did he produce many popular and internationally renowned movies and cultivate numerous talents in the industry, but he also founded the International Film Production Co., Ltd. and the Motion Picture Studios Association of Taiwan. As a founding father of Taiwan's film industry and an outstanding contributor to its development and prosperity, Mr. Shy received a Special Contribution Award at the 28th Golden Horse Film Festival and Awards in Taiwan in 1991. He owns a condominium in Rossmoor in Walnut Creek, California and currently lives in Lafayette, California with his daughter.

Founding Father of Taiwan's Film Industry

With the Yangtze River to its north and Lake Taihu to its south, Jiangyin is a transportation hub in the lower reaches of the Yangtze. Back then Jiangyin had three satellite towns to its southeast that were rather prosperous – Houcheng, with Zhouzhuang being five kilometers to its south, and Huashu further to the south and beyond Mount Sha. A town of strategic importance in Jiangyin, Zhouzhuang is connected to Jiangyin and Wuxi with canals and land routes and boasts a convenient transportation system. Blessed with the typical topography of lakes and rivers, it featured farm fields, villages and hard-working men and women. Today, the town of Houcheng has been integrated into the newly developed metropolis Zhangjiagang, while Huashu was rename Huashi, with its village of Huaxi calling itself the "Number One Village of the World". Zhouzhuang, too, has become prosperous with highly developed local businesses and all kinds of industrial parks.

It was impossible for me to trace the origins of the Shy Family. Our ancestors appeared to have fled from Sichuan Province to Jiangyin, where a small number of them eventually settled. Two of my ancestors served as government officials during the Qing Dynasty. They were respected in our town for their honesty, fairness and generosity. My father, Xizhang Shy, owned a fabric shop in Shanghai. Having escaped from the turmoil of war, he set up a towel factory in our hometown. He died in 1934 at the age of 43 from overwork. My mother came from a family of medical doctors. She worked extremely hard to raise the five of us as a single mother.

I went to a large and famous grammar school in Zhouzhuang. My class instructor, Rongting Chiang, taught the fifth and sixth grades. A well-read and highly sophisticated person, Teacher Chiang was capable of explaining profound literary thoughts and theories in simple terms, and treated all students as his own sons and daughters. I will always remember him as my first great teacher because of his huge impact on my life. Back then we had a comprehensive assessment program for all primary school graduates. All my classmates had performed well, topping the list across the whole Jiangyin region. I was accepted by Jiangsu's Nanjing Senior High School, a prestigious institution that cultivated such renowned people as educator and politician Jack C.K. Teng, sociologist Wu Wenzao and author Wang Zengqi, among many others.

A Nanjing High School's tradition was to sing the school anthem at weekly assemblies. One sentence from the song's lyrics considerably influenced the ways in which I conduct myself as a person: "Uphold loyalty, forgiveness, diligence and thrift as distinct instructions, while abiding by orderliness and solemnity as strict standards." At the age of 13, as a result of my father's death and changes in my family's circumstances, I had to drop out of school. My aunt recommended me as an apprentice at a cotton shop in Jiangyin. I studied under Mr. Wang, my second pivotal teacher, who enlightened me with a wide range of insights and experiences in the cotton industry during the day. At night, he taught me calligraphy and explained all kinds of lessons from poetry and literature, as well as how to live with others in harmony in this world.

Leaving Home for Society

After bidding farewell to my teacher eight months later, I followed my cousin, Shoukang Liu, to Shanghai where he was the manager at the Huacheng Textiles Company. Under my cousin's instructions, I started from the bottom: from receiving and examining raw materials and organizing product transport and delivery, to preparing accounts and documents, receiving clients, and tidying accounts and overdue receivables. Through hard work, I gradually learned how to handle everything, while gaining respect from my cousin and other colleagues. He further encouraged me to enroll in night school and to keep studying while working. Back then we did not have photocopiers, so I had to manually write and keep a copy of all the company's business correspondence. In cases where clients did not respond, we had to send out follow-up inquiries. This included keeping a detailed record of all the Chinese New Year greeting cards the company sent to its clients across the nation at the end of each year. This kind of management relationship contributed considerably to the long-term development of our company's business. Later, this experience was also beneficial to launching and leading my own company.

When I was 19 in 1942, I established my own firm, Dingsheng Textiles Company in Suzhou, Jiangsu Province. With business expanding rapidly, I branched out to Wuxi and Jiangyin the following year while negotiating further business opportunities in Shanghai. I was also in charge of the Minsheng Cotton Mill in Suzhou. In early 1943, relatives introduced me to Miss. Xue-e Cao, daughter of a famous dentist in Wuxi. In the April 8th of lunar calendar, 1944, we were married at the Shanghai YMCA and settled in Suzhou.

A Life-Changing Point

After the victory in the War of Resistance against Japan, several friends from Jiangyin relocated their businesses to Taipei. According to them, Taiwan's gentle climate and beautiful natural scenery were indicative of a good place for business investment and development. In 1947, I found the place to be nice but lacked commercial activity, as there was not even a source of material to make clothes. Still my friends urged me to move to Taiwan and take advantage of its ample business opportunities. After that my wife, infant son and I stayed in Taipei for a month in order for her to check it out. We toured many places to understand the local market. After 50 years of Japanese occupation, Taiwan lacked basic goods and supplies, causing my wife to consider life there to be poor and miserable. However, we thought there were business opportunities. We would find a way to live, grow and prosper with a business there. While in Hsinchu County after an evening meal, my son who was learning to walk, suddenly let go of his mother's hand and took several steps forward by himself. Both my wife and I were thrilled, marking this as a good omen for relocating our business to Taiwan. Consequently, we decided to set up a branch of our textiles business in Taipei the following year with goods and supplies shipped from Jiangsu and Shanghai. I arrived in Taipei in 1948 ahead of my family, unsuspecting then that it would be such a life-changing moment for all of us.

After the Nationalist troops lost the Battle of Hwaihai in southern Shandong Province to the Communist People's Liberation Army, the situation in neighboring Jiangsu Province rapidly deteriorated. I urged my wife to come to Taiwan, but she was reluctant to travel alone with children. I would have gone back to Jiangsu, but my father-in-law insisted that my wife leave China instead of my going back under such urgent and dangerous circumstances. Then, in early 1949, as Shanghai came under threat by the communist, my wife fled to Taiwan with our two-year-old son and two-month-old daughter; we settled in Taipei. I remember the day that they arrived was February 8. Traveling by sea was extremely risky at that time.

A little earlier the SS Taiping had sunk on its way from Shanghai to Taiwan's Keelung Harbor; all crew and passengers drowned. In addition, there were so many people trying to leave China that it was nearly impossible to get tickets for any ship. Fortunately, my father-in-law knew the captain of a ship that was already full of passengers. He was willing to offer his own cabin to my wife and children. None of us had foreseen that upon our arrival in Taiwan, it would be another 50 years before we would see China again. My wife arrived in February. In

May, the Communist troops entered Shanghai. My businesses and properties in China were lost, forcing me to start a new life in Taiwan from scratch. It was before Chiang Kai-shek and his troops arrived there. After the fall of Shanghai, all transport and communications ceased between the two sides of Taiwan Strait. Having sold all our existing stock in Taipei, we started bringing in goods and supplies from Hong Kong. In 1950, I established Youxin Woolen Goods Department Store in North Yanping Road in Taipei. As there were very few department stores back then, we did relatively well. It was also the year our second son was born.

There is Always a Way

In 1951, Weitang Xia, Taoran Zhang, Jiuyin Zhang and I discussed movies. Since Xia and I came from the same hometown, we had known each other for a long time. He operated a textiles business in Nanjing while I managed mine in Shanghai. Xia had a friend from Hong Kong who used to work in the film industry in Shanghai. He suggested that Xia introduce some China-produced movies to Taiwan. Xia thought it was a good idea, as did his housemates, the aforementioned Taoran Zhang and Jiuyin Zhang. Knowing that such an endeavor would require a capable manager, they enlisted my help. In our days-long discussion, we discussed the cultural gap between local Taiwanese and those arriving from China. As a result of 50 years of Japanese occupation, generations of Taiwanese people were influenced by the Japanese language and culture, to such an extent that they knew very little about China's culture, language and lifestyle. Meanwhile, with no knowledge of the Taiwanese dialect, those arriving from China continued to rely on their own regional dialects, resulting in a linguistic gap and much confusion in daily communications. Also ineffective was the government's promotion of Mandarin. Therefore, in our view, it would be useful to promote Mandarin dialect films to achieve the dual purpose of introducing Chinese culture and encouraging the use of Mandarin or *Guoyu* as our nation's official language. We established a company to distribute Mandarin movies. It was risky to give up our own successful businesses and take on the film industry, something with unknown future and of which we understood very little; but we felt it would be a career worth pursuing.

A different profession is like something on the other side of a huge mountain. As businessmen in the textiles industry, we had seen many movies, but possessed none of the knowledge and experience of working in the film industry. We did not even know where to start to acquire such information. Fortunately, someone introduced us to Jianguang Zhou, manager of Hong Kong's Kin Wah Film Company; he explained the essentials of film making in great detail. That was when we became determined to leave the textiles industry and devote ourselves to films. We sent Xia to Hong Kong to search for and purchase films, and to engage Kin Wah Film Company as our local representative. We learned by doing.

After learning some valuable lessons, the four of us put together two million Taiwanese dollars in 1953 to purchase a building at Number 4, Alley 34, Section One of Taipei's Kaifeng Street, as the headquarters of our newly launched Union Film Company. Each of us had an equal share of the company, with Xia serving as its chairman and official spokesperson, Taoran Zhang being stationed in Hong Kong to purchase films and invest in new productions, Jiuyin Zhang looking after the finances, and, finally, me working in Taiwan to distribute and promote our films. We trusted each other and worked hard, discussing and making all decisions together while doing our best to complete our own tasks. Though we started as outsiders, within a few years, Union Film Company grew to be a "monopoly" in Taiwan's film industry. We focused on practical issues and avoided unnecessary expenses while working in Kaifeng Street for 25 years. From 1953 to the end of the venture in 1978, we produced 31 Mandarin language films and distributed more than 720 Mandarin language films made by such companies as Hong Kong's Shaw Brothers Studio, Motion Picture & General Investment Limited (MP&GI) and Yung Hwa Motion Picture Industries Ltd. On top of that, we represented more than 100 films produced by studios in Japan, Britain, Germany, Italy and the United States. In short, we were the largest film distribution company in Taiwan.

When the Union Film Company was launched, business was tough because Taiwan was dominated by Japanese and Western films. I was convinced of Taiwan's film market potential, but the key issue was how to develop it so that the audience would enjoy watching movies in Mandarin. As I was in charge of marketing, it occurred to me that in order to survive in a market dominated by Japanese and Western films, our audience had to understand Mandarin; the locals did not! In the beginning, only three or four people attended each session, disastrous for business. Then I tried slides beside the movie screen with written characters, but that did not work either, because the audience did not have time to switch between the slides and screen while enjoying the film. Eventually I inserted subtitles at the bottom of the screen summarizing the characters' conversations. Once our audience understood what was said in the movie, they were able to follow the plot and gradually appreciated the whole story. Even those who only knew a little Mandarin could enjoy our films as well as learn the language from the subtitles.

In the 1950s, Mandarin language films entered the stage where "no movie should be made without songs" since radio stations constantly aired theme songs from popular movies. In order to familiarize themselves with the lyrics, many fans repeatedly went to the theater and turned themselves into movie buffs. The fact that subtitles helped people learn their favorite songs contributed to the promotion of these movies, which in turn added to the popularity of Mandarin language films in general. Producing the subtitles was labor intensive.

However, as the number of people watching Mandarin movies increased, I suggested and then insisted that MP&GI, Hong Kong's major producer and distributor of Mandarin language films, should start inserting subtitles directly into the copies of their products. Though production costs were high, they complied after witnessing how subtitles enhanced the popularity of Mandarin movies. Not long after that, Hong Kong's Shaw Brothers Studio also started producing subtitles for their films.

The first ten years of Union Film Company were devoted to distributing Hong Kong-made Mandarin language films. When there were only a few available films, we produced our own. Apart from working with Hong Kong investors, we collaborated with Changfu Shen's troupe of acrobatics – which was extremely popular in Southeast Asia at the time – and made a movie of their prowess. It was the first of our films bearing the name "Union Film Company". In order to promote the movie in regional Taiwan, where many had yet to adopt the nation's official language, we distributed it in both Mandarin and the Taiwanese dialect with huge success. So, step by step, we established the International Film Production Co. Ltd. on January 27, 1956, with Xia being its chairman and me serving as general manager. With this company specifically representing the movies distributed by its Hong Kong counterpart, we were increasingly busy with both Mandarin and Western films.

We started distributing Mandarin language films in Taipei, Taiwan by recommending Mandarin language films to movie theater owners throughout the city. However, they often stopped showing these movies after only two or three days because of limited audience. These people originally from China lived in military communities, had low purchasing power and rarely visited movie theaters in city centers. Consequently, I spent much effort persuading smaller, regional movie theaters to feature our Mandarin language films, but they still lacked sufficient patronage. Eventually I became convinced that we needed a movie theater of our own, dedicated to promoting Mandarin language films in the long run to cultivate an audience. So from 1954 I spent years negotiating long-term contracts with theaters to specifically showcase Mandarin language films until we gradually established a group of ten theaters across the Greater Taipei area. Once we had achieved this, I proceeded to patiently and diplomatically take care of such issues as scheduling films for different movie theaters, resolving conflicts of interest among the movie theaters themselves, as well as dispersing profits shared between distributing companies and movie theaters.

Back then the production costs of mandarin language movies were relatively low. While movies made in China and Hong Kong lacked customers, it was cheap to purchase rights for showing them. However, importing them remained expensive for two reasons. First, copies of films had to be made in Tokyo instead of Hong Kong. Second and more important, Taiwan's customs duty on imported film copies was particularly high. With movies being considered part of the entertainment industry, up to one third of our marginal profits were taxed, making it impractical to import many film copies. Consequently, a lack of available copies forced us to use the same copy of a movie in two or three theaters with only twenty minutes between their show times. At that time, each movie was divided into several rolls of filmstrips. As soon as a theater completed the showing of one roll, a capable young man would cycle it to the next theater. Every second counted! Most theaters had their projection room on the third or fourth floor. In order to save time, they would dangle a rope outside the projection room window to hoist the roll of filmstrips as soon as it arrived. On rare occasions when a train ran between two movie theaters, the delivery man could only wait anxiously for his crossing. His lateness disrupted showing the movie, resulting in an angry audience though audiences in Taiwan were reasonable and quiet most of the time. Many of the supporters of Mandarin language films were soldiers from China.

After organizing the theaters in Taipei, we expanded to other cities though with difficulty. By then we had a theater in every regional city from Taipei in the north to Kaohsiung in the south. Most of the theaters already existed and signed long-term contracts with us to showcase Mandarin language films, but Tianle Theater in Taoyuan County was among those we built.

There were two theaters in Taoyuan owned by a soy sauce maker. No matter how good your movies were, he would only give up to 5,000 Taiwanese dollars for the showing rights. The deal was off if you dared to refuse it, leaving no one in Taoyuan to show your movies. With deals like that, the man made a lot of money. Later, when our distribution increased with none shown in Taoyuan, we decided to build a theater there ourselves. It was difficult to find a vacant lot. However, we eventually located one to establish the 1,200-seat Tianle movie theater. Plus it was the county's first air-conditioned movie theater. However, the soy sauce maker did everything to stop the government from issuing an operating license. He even registered a complaint that our theater was located within 1,000 meters from a primary school. Hence, our project died, as the county government disallowed all entertainment venues to exist within 1,000 meters of a school.

Frustrated, we went up a level and approached the provincial government. One of the high-ranking officials there was the former commander-in-chief of Taiwan's air force, whose good friend was my associate as well as the calligrapher who created major signs for the Tianle Theater. We informed him about this case, including the fact that based on professional measurements, our theater stood more than 1,000 meters away from the primary school in question. In spite of getting a permit to build the movie theater, the soy sauce maker pressured the Taoyuan county government not to issue us a licence to operate it. After half a year of argument and delays, in September 1959, the provincial government finally overruled its county counterpart's decision and ordered the theater to be opened. I was then able to relax. It shows that as long as there is a will, there is always a way. It was tough at that time to negotiate with people like this.

In the end, Union Film Company secured exclusive deals with more than 30 theaters across Taiwan's counties and cities, including six or seven that we built and operated ourselves. We were the only distribution network of Mandarin language films in Taiwan with the most integrated distribution network in general. Even the overseas distribution of movies produced by the government-operated Central Pictures Corporation (CPC) had to rely on the assistance of our privately-owned Union Film Company.

By 1957, though Union Film Company had established a distribution network of Mandarin language films and covered more than 300 theaters in Taiwan, we faced the problem of a dearth of movies. Although we handled all of the Mandarin language films produced in Hong Kong at the time, it was still difficult to meet the demand. Consequently, Union Film Company managed to re-record into Mandarin quality Cantonese movies from Hong Kong, including those featuring martial arts, and to supply four such motion pictures per month to Taiwan's film market.

When we started out as a distributor of Mandarin language films, it was a relatively smooth process as there was no competition. All the Mandarin language films and their distribution were handled by Union Film Company. After eight years of hard work, we had removed all obstacles in the distribution of Mandarin language films, including the construction of new theaters and refurbishing existing ones, as well as establishing a powerful distribution network across the whole island. This considerably benefited the whole film industry, but gave rise to copycats who quickly fought over available movies. We deserved credit because throughout the history of Mandarin language films in Taiwan, Union Film Company was a pioneer and a significant contributor to our government and nation. We persevered even though we often lost money in our attempt to promote Mandarin language films since we relied on earnings from Japanese and Western movies. I still maintain that the success of a film's distribution depends on the quality of its promotion.

In February 1959, I launched the *International Films* magazine and served as its publisher and general manager until 1976 when it closed. In 1963, I was elected a board member and team leader of the Republic of China Magazine Business Association. In February 1971, I established *Contemporary Films* magazine, which published four issues before closing in December that year. While working for Union Film Company, I looked after and financed everything, from planning and implementing the packaging and advertising of each film, to monitoring the scale and effectiveness of its promotion. Whether we dealt with movie posters, pamphlets or leaflets, however much they cost, we did our best to deliver them to every corner of every city and county town. To distribute and promote movies, one requires insight into market demand. One also needs to be innovative in the process, specifically showcasing explicit aspects of a movie such as genre, storyline, director's style, cast of stars, theme songs, and special effects, etc., so that there is always something fresh for the audience. The foundation of my success was the notion "efficiency comes from diligence". As the boss, I worked 15 hours each day, which was hard for my subordinates to match.

Bridging Hong Kong and Taiwanese Film Industries

When we first started Union Film Company, it was rather difficult for independent filmmakers arriving from China to make a living in Hong Kong, as they were oppressed by the left wing majority. Consequently, in addition to helping these filmmakers distance themselves from the leftist campaign, we also invited their collaboration in order to strengthen our film production. As United Film Company had a long-established branch in Hong Kong and had won the trust of filmmakers, industrial unions and the local government, it was no surprise that we became a bridge between the three parties.

At that time actors and others working in the Hong Kong's film industry could not easily traval to Taiwan. Each case required a separate application process and permission by the authorities. Even individuals receiving honors at Taiwan's Golden Horse Film Awards ceremony needed guarantees from Union Film Company. Consequently, we not only handled their arrival and departure from Taiwan, but also looked after them during their sojourn. Because all actors were fully aware of their own importance, it was hard to make them feel as well-treated as they felt they deserved.

Our last actress arriving to work in Taiwan from Hong Kong was Gong Qiuxia, a famous singer and movie star and one of China's most celebrated young actresses. Since she was highly admired by the leftists, it was difficult to direct her enthusiasm to a politically conservative Taiwan. However, once she did arrive in Taiwan, there was no production in which she could act. I eventually found Yi Wen, a renowned Hong Kong director, to write a script specifically for her, which resulted in the film *The Decisive Battle* (1971). It depicted the life of Yue Fei (1103-1142), a heroic military general in the Southern Song Dynasty whose mother, played by Gong, tattooed the words loyalty and devotion on his back as an inspiration and reminder for him to serve the country. Meanwhile, we also assisted many Taiwanese filmmakers to work in Hong Kong by creating some impact on the movie industry there. In the 1950s and 1960s, Union Film Company further invested in collaborative productions between Hong Kong and Taiwan with *Nobody's Child* (1960) and *Liang Hongyu* (1962).

Working with Li Han-hsiang

Taoran Zhang, Union Film Company's representative in Hong Kong, was the mastermind behind the proposal and implementation of the plan to encourage the renowned director Li Han-hsiang to leave Shaw Brothers Studio and work as an independent filmmaker in Taiwan in 1963. Zhang used an ordinary proverb to lure Li: "A commoner will never stand out in the crowd; neither can those animals laboring at others' command. A good sail should be fully raised whenever there is wind, as one without wind will forever remain unused." Li had always focused on quality instead of quantity. At that time, his eight-year contract with Shaw Brothers Studio was about to expire, with 11 movies yet to be made. From Li's point of view, one popular and award-winning film was the equivalent of two, but they disagreed; such disagreements made Li want to be his own boss rather than continue to work for others. As soon as Shaw Yat-fu, owner of Shaw Brothers Studio, heard of this, he tried to retain Li with various incentives, but it was too late.

Supported by Loke Wan Tho, owner of Hong Kong's MP&GI and Sinagpore's Cathay Organization, Li established Grand Motion Pictures Co., Ltd (GMP) in Taiwan under his wife's name. Loke proposed that Union Film Company shoulder half of GMP's production costs to which we agreed. In fact, GMP's name in Chinese is *Guo Lian*, with the character *Guo* coming from Loke's Cathay Organization (*Guo Tai*) and the character *Lian* from Union Film Company (*Lian Bang*). All films produced by GMP were represented and distributed by our company.

Li left Hong Kong without completing *A Maid from Heaven* for Shaw Brothers Studio. As a result GMP's first movie in Taiwan was a remake of *A Maid from Heaven*, which became a fierce competitor against the movie of the same title that was completed by Shaw Brothers Studio after LI's departure. The two films premiered at almost the same time.

In order to attract the audience's sympathy and support, I arranged daily newspaper coverage on how a big corporation such as Shaw Brothers Studio oppressed Li as an independent filmmaker. As an innovative strategy, I also had GMP's *A Maid from Heaven* featured by Xinsheng Theater that specialized in showing A-class Western films, instead of relying on our usual theaters that were known for Mandarin movies. I visited the owner of Xinsheng Theater late at night to negotiate this deal, and asked him to keep it as a secret. Consequently, although GMP's *A Maid from Heaven* premiered five days later than its counterpart by Shaw Brothers Studio, its earnings were far greater in comparison.

Li was well respected in Taiwan's political and cultural circles. I fully supported him, both because I had always valued talent and because of Union Film Company's sponsorship. Li signed up to produce 18 films in Taiwan. However, because he cared little about money, he spent more than 20 million Taiwanese dollars on one film, *Xi Shi* (1966). Having exhausted the budget, he abandoned the project and launched another in order to receive a new injection of money, ignoring the convention that one should only begin a new production *after* two-thirds of the old one had been completed. Such an approach was akin to consuming tomorrow's food today and lacking sustainability, but Li hardly cared, taking money from both Cathay Organization and Union Film Company.

Meanwhile, we had to pay the copyright royalties in advance, for both of these productions and on behalf of Cathay Organization in Singapore. This was a huge expense, with absolutely no return for our investment until the film production was completed. Worse, according to the contract, Union Film Company could not finalize its accounts with GMP until Li produced 18 films. Abiding by my principles of honesty, trust, benevolence and righteousness, and to show my support for Li's career, I never pressured him. However, he misunderstood my kindness as malice and launched a lawsuit against us in 1970 with the excuse that Union Film Company refused to finalize its accounts with GMP and had supposedly snatched much of his money from the earnings of films thus far. Throughout the following year or so, we went to the Taipei District Court numerous times and spent countless hours cooperating with the court-assigned public accountant who had been approved by both prosecution and defense to examine our company's accounts. The results indicated our accounts were clear, and it was GMP that owed Union Film Company a considerable amount of money. The court granted us a "promissory note of debt obligations", which we could use to claim back our money at any time. But I never did out of my concern for Li's reputation and personal circumstances.

In the end, Li returned to Hong Kong, but was unable to work for Shaw Brothers Studio again. In 1983, when China adopted the "reform and open" policy, he set up the New Kunlun Film Company to work there with the initial capital supplied by Macau billionaire Ho Yin. In China, Li produced *The Burning of the Imperial Palace* (1983), *Reign Behind a Curtain* (1983) and *The Last Emperor* (1986), making a lot of money. That remains a story to be told.

Establishing Our Own Studio

The 11th Asia Pacific Film Festival took place in Taipei in June 1964. It was the first time this renowned international event was held in Taiwan. Loke Wan Tho, the aforementioned owner of MP&GI and Cathay Organization, led a group of Malaysian and Hong Kong representatives to attend the festival. Unfortunately, after visiting a branch of the National Palace Museum in Taichung, their plane crashed on its way back to Taipei, killing all on board, including our chairman Weitang Xia who had accompanied Loke and his group. Consequently, our board of directors elected me to replace Xia to shoulder the vital responsibilities of policy making and client relationship management *on top of* my own tasks of film distribution and promotion. The loss of Xia, my fellow countryman and dear friend, with whom I had launched a career and worked side by side for so many years, saddened me deeply. His death had a profound impact on my subsequent career as I vowed to serve my community and society, and make the best of my life. After several months of deliberation, I became convinced that our mission to promote Mandarin movies was solid. Our job from now on should be to cultivate new talents in film directing and acting, acquire the latest lighting and recording equipment, train technical staff for film production, and develop a sense of moral conduct among all actors and employees in order to uplift the professional standards of the film industry in general. I focused on continuing Xia's legacy and directing our effort to film production and processing.

A bird's-eye view of the International Film Studio in Danan, Taoyuan County

In 1965, I toured the United States and Japan to study their film industries, and to fulfil a dream of establishing a modern studio for film production and processing. After searching Taiwan for several months, I found a suitable site of approximately 49,600 square meters in Danan, Taoyuan County, on which to build the studio. From ground breaking, road building, laying the electrical cable and arranging water supply and sewerage from early 1966 to its completion, it took a total of 380 working days to construct our modern "international film studio". Facing such a once-in-a-lifetime project, I spent much time and effort and insisted on top quality down to every tiny detail. The studio was equipped with the latest filming, lighting and stage operating facilities from the United States and Germany, with one large and two interconnected, smaller soundstages, all of which were well-equipped. Later we also built a recording laboratory and a film-processing factory. From that moment on, Taiwan had a first-class, fully equipped film production site. In March 1968, I was elected an executive council member of the Motion Picture and Drama Association, Republic of China.

Dragon Inn (1967) Producer: Yung-fong Shy, Director: King Hu

Dragon Inn (1967) was the first movie produced in this international film studio by Union Film Company. According to King Hu, the famous director we invited from Hong Kong, there was no shortcut to make a good martial arts film. While famous actors could act well, their ability to practice martial arts was limited by their age. Hence we auditioned young actors and had them trained by experienced martial artists. More than 1,000 responded to our newspaper advertisement for regular actors. With a famous playwright, a renowned film director and me as auditioners, and after preliminary and secondary tests and a final screening, we signed six-year contracts with Feng Xu, Lingfeng Shangguan, Juan Shi, Ying Bai and Peng Tian. Most of them were 16 or 17 years of age, with neither experience nor training in performing arts. But they were very, very smart.

Being ordinary looking, these new actors were not considered by many within and outside the film industry to have a bright future. However, I was and still am of the view that superficial beauty cannot lead to success. Good actors need to be able to express emotions through their eyes, have distinct facial features, and are quick-witted and resourceful. More importantly, my focus has always been on the result. No matter what people say, I stick to my plan; at the end we can discuss whether or not the results are appropriate.

These new actors went through four months of training. In the morning they had lessons on pronunciation, singing, dancing and performing classes, as well as professional ethics and conduct. In the afternoon they studied and practiced martial arts under professionals instructors that we hired. Most of them had never learned martial art before. Facing real physical fighting on the set, with no computer generated imagery, they had to learn how to handle all types of weaponry. Despite their moaning and groaning throughout training and filmmaking, the completed films fully displayed the excellent skills and breathtaking actions of these young men and women. Under our care these actors worked hard toward a bright future and never caused any trouble for our company. All of them achieved much in subsequent years, which confirmed our vision and effort to cultivate new talent.

Premiering in October 1967, *Dragon Inn* received positive feedback from the audience. Critics thought it spearheaded a new generation of martial arts films. It featured a sense of history while symbolizing the spirit of the time, with emphasis on natural setting and character development plus fast-paced, awe-inspiring actions that together, helped to create a poetic sense of theatrical aesthetics. Also impressive were the movie's box office earnings. After that, via the many costume dramas and a few art films produced in our international film studio at Danan, Union Film Company cultivated many new talents. A good example is Shangguan Lingfeng, who, after being selected as the female lead in *Dragon Inn*, not only worked extremely hard in her martial arts training in our studio, but also sought private instructions in karate. In 1968, *Dragon Inn* won awards for Outstanding Feature Film and Best Screenplay at the Golden Horse film festival and Awards organized by the Ministry of Education's Bureau of Cultural Affairs.

A Touch of Zen (1970) Producer: Yung-fong Shy, Director: King Hu. Actors: Feng Xu et al.

Another influential film produced by Union Film Company was *A Touch of Zen* (1970), adapted from a classic story collection in *Strange Tales from a Chinese Studio*. Feng Xu as the female lead deserved all her fame. She had studied the screenplay so thoroughly that she memorized other people's lines. When filming involved others on the set, she quietly stayed nearby to learn from their experiences and skills. When it was her turn, she insisted on filming even with injuries. It is fair to say that *A Touch of Zen* as a film was more influential than *Dragon Inn*, because it received the Technical Grand Prize at the 28th Cannes Film Festival in 1975. It was the first Chinese movie produced in Taiwan, Hong Kong or mainland China to be honored by one of the world's five prestigious film festivals. Director King Hu worked hard on this movie, introducing a sense of *Zen* to motion pictures about martial arts. The film looks fascinating even today.

In 1973, Brigitte Lin acted as the female lead in her first film *Outside the Window*. As a result of a rights disputes caused by Chiung Yao and her mother, from whose story of the same title the movie was adapted, it was not allowed to be shown in Taiwan. Later I met Lin when songwriter and filmmaker Chia-chang Liu accompanied her to my office to discuss this issue. The first time she debuted on the Taiwanese big screen was in *Gone with the Cloud* (1974), her first movie for Union Film Company. My contribution to the film's success was to mobilize the media with large-scale promotions. In addition to a full month of previews and advertisements featuring Lin's name and 300,000 pamphlets introducing her as an actress, there were also advance screenings and press conferences that helped to make the movie a household name before it even premiered. After *Gone with the Cloud*, Union Film Company went on to produce *Moon River* (1974) and *Misty Drizzle* (1975), with the latter featuring a full list of famous movie stars to support Lin as the female lead. A highly attractive individual, Lin's remuneration as an actress had increased more than tenfold by then.

Having distributed and produced films for decades, I firmly believed that the key to quality movies rested on processing techniques and had long planned to establish a modern factory to process color films. Previously, after producing a movie, we had to send filmstrips to Japan for time-consuming processing. Now, with our own factory, we could process and assess a film as soon as it was produced and proceed to immediately re-make unsatisfactory sections, thereby making our work highly efficient. More importantly, not only did it help to reduce our expenses, but it also enabled us to hold onto our nation's cultural assets. In 1974, we formally established the International Film Processing Co., Ltd., another milestone in the history of the Union Film Company. Starting with Brigitte Lin's *Misty Drizzle*, we no longer sent filmstrips to Japan for processing.

Misty Drizzle (1975), Producer: Yung-fong Shy, Director: King Hu. Actors: Brigitte Lin et al.

Working with King Hu

Both Union Film Company's classic films, *Dragon Inn* and *A Touch of Zen*, were directed by King Hu. Indeed, another achievement of Taoran Zhang, our representative in Hong Kong, was to invite Hu to work in Taiwan. Hu's talents were not fully recognized by Shaw Brothers Studio, which as a commercial entity, did not agree with his focus on quality instead of quantity. While we had long noticed Hu as a gifted filmmaker, we signed him up only after his contract with Shaw Brothers Studio had expired. By then Hu still owed them six movies, an issue that was supposed to be handled between themselves. However, Shaw Brothers Studio elected to take the unreasonable approach of banning in Singapore and Malaysia all films that Hu produced for Union Film Company, as if the money we lost there could be used to repay Hu's debts to them.

Worse, in order to retain Hu, Raymond Chow, then head of publicity and the production chief of Shaw Brothers Studio, mobilized his university friend Shen Bin to contact the Nationalist Party (Kuomintang) Central Committee in Taiwan. As a result, Division Six of the Party's Political Committee in charge of overseas Chinese affairs, invited me for an "interview". It was revealed that Division Six was currently investigating Hu based on an informant's letter, and would either send his case to public security officials for further assessment or issue an order to prevent him from working in Taiwan's mountainous areas. As we were then halfway through shooting a mountainous outdoor scene for *Dragon Inn*, to stop filming would incur a huge loss of time, manpower and capital. Eventually, our company's shareholders decided to accept Division Six's advice: that Union Film Company should sell to Shaw Brothers Studio the rights to distribute to Hong Kong, Singapore, Malaysia and Brunei the four movies that Hu would produce under our two-year contract. Because the selling price of these movies was calculated according to their estimated production costs, and because the accumulated production costs for *Dragon Inn* were more than twice the estimated amount, we ended up losing a considerable amount of money in Hong Kong, Macau, Singapore and Malaysia. This accounted for two-thirds of our Mandarin language film market. The record earnings the film generated in Taiwan partly compensated our losses.

As a result of this deal, millions of Hong Kong dollars generated by *Dragon Inn* went to Shaw Brothers Studio. Meanwhile, although Union Film Company received nothing, it was easy for those outside of the deal to assume otherwise. This included Hu, who became upset that we did not offer him a bonus from these "profits". In fact, not only were we unaware of the misunderstanding, we also signed another two-year contract with Hu, despite the fact that he had produced only one, not four, movies for us by 1967.

As a director, Hu had very high standards for costumes and settings. For the production of *A Touch of Zen*, for example, we built a permanent set that was the equivalent of an ancient city. From pavilions, pagodas, ponds and courtyards to shops, houses, terraces and mansions of all different sizes and shapes, everything was there, built on top of solid foundations. Instead of just one simple layer of paint, all the pillars, posts and window frames had been spray-painted, then baked using a hand-held flame gun, and then carefully polished with sandpaper to produce an exquisite appearance. Indeed, it took us one and a half years to complete the whole set. After that, in order to create a ghostly atmosphere around the military general's mansion in the film, we planted many reed flowers among the weeds on the set. When the flowers withered under 200,000 watts of spotlight, we had to plant additional reeds and wait for them to flower, taking several more months.

A conceptualization of the set built within the International Film Studio in Danan, Taoyuan County, for the filming of *A Touch of Zen*.

The production of *A Touch of Zen* was slow and lacked planning, making it difficult to execute the budget. This gravely concerned me because my job as producer was to control both the film's budget and the production schedule. I tried to discuss it with Hu, but he claimed to be too busy to see me. Worse, he proposed dividing the movie into two parts, which he knew I would not accept. As much as Hu tried to postpone everything and asked others to persuade me on his behalf, I was aware that based on his slow schedule, there would be such a long interval between the two parts of the movie that part two would not have a good reception. With that said, there was nothing I could do but to accept Hu's proposal – and pay him for the production of two movies instead of one. Consequently, production of *A Touch of Zen* commenced in 1967, with part one completed in 1969 and part two in 1971. A total of five years and 30 million Hong Kong dollars were spent on this movie, approximately ten times the budget of a movie produced in Taiwan. Understandably upset, our shareholders worried our company would become bankrupt if we continued to support Hu.

Within the terms of the two two-year contracts signed by Hu, he should have produced eight movies for Union Film Company, but managed only two – *Dragon Inn* and *A Touch of Zen*. It was fortunate that we could afford it, thanks to our earnings from film distribution and other movies we had made. Otherwise, we could not have handled the significant delay that Hu had caused. Still, he had done a great job as a director. For example, the battle in a bamboo forest in Ang Lee's Oscar-winning *Crouching Tiger, Hidden Dragon* was in fact inspired by the scene in *A Touch of Zen* in which our heroine leaped through a bamboo forest with a sword in her hand. Similarly, many special effects in *A Touch of Zen* were nothing special at all. Without computer generated imagery, all the actions – leaping, falling, fast forward and slow motions – were done by editing frame-by-frame, with 50,000 meters of filmstrips cut to only 2,000 meters in the end. It had been tough for Hu, whose talents and hard work I truly admired. With that said, I do not think any other film company would have been as tolerant as we were, allowing him to spend three years and three films' worth of budget on the making of one single movie.

Those years were the golden age of Mandarin language films to which our Union Film Company was a leading contributor. In 1970 Shaw Yat-fu invited me to a meeting in Japan to discuss the possibility of appointing me as General Manager of Shaw Brothers Studio. I was deeply moved by such recognition and support but politely declined this offer to boost my personal fame and fortune. I simply knew I could not abandon those career partners who had worked hard with me for the past twenty years. Later in 1972 I also turned down a request from the Kuomintang's Central Committee for me to take charge of the Central Pictures Corporation.

Mandarin Language Films on the World Stage

Dragon Inn marked the moment when Union Film Company entered the global film market. The film was distributed to 28 countries on five continents with record earnings in Chinese communities across the world. While it was common back then for theaters to schedule at least one week for each movie on general release, *Dragon Inn* was shown for three weeks in New York and two weeks in Los Angeles, with repeat showings that same autumn. In 1968, *Dragon Inn* premiered in Hokkaido as the first Chinese film officially shown in Japan with much more audience feedback than Bruce Lee's *Enter the* Dragon (1973). When the film was shown in Korea with Korean subtitles, its earnings even surpassed those of the James Bond movies. *Dragon Inn* further boasted record earnings in Southeast Asia. It performed particularly well in Hong Kong, where 14 first-run theaters showed the film for three weeks, grossing 2.1 million Hong Kong dollars or approximately 14 million Taiwanese dollars. The film was even shown in South America, much to the delight of local Chinese communities. In short, the success of *Dragon Inn* was a breakthrough, demonstrating the achievement and the advances made by Mandarin language films in their production and distribution.

In 1975 *A Touch of Zen* was nominated for the Palme d'Or and received the Technical Grand Prize at the 28th Cannes Film Festival. In 1978, thanks to this film, Hu was chosen by the International Film Guide in The United Kingdom as one of the year's five outstanding international filmmakers. Back then the European distribution rights to *A Touch of Zen* were sold to one of Cannes Festival's selectors for the low price of US $20,000. Still, whatever its gains and losses, the movie helped to boost the name of Chinese cinema in Europe and attracted much attention from film industries around the world. With such an achievement, all the disputes and disappointment that occurred during the filmmaking process were thoroughly forgotten. The only regret left was that many international critics considered *A Touch of Zen* to be a Hong Kong production.

Rectifying the Name of the Film Industry

In Taiwan, film production and distribution had always been categorized as part of the entertainment industry, where the rate of the "amusement tax" charged for films was much higher than tax for the other industrial products. On top of that was an extra three-percent tax as duty stamp, compared to less than one percent for the other industries. Consequently, for any movie ticket sold for ten Taiwan yuan in Taiwan, only four yuan were left as after-tax earnings for film producers and distributors. Facing such an unreasonably high tax rate, I was convinced that the only way to sustain the film industry was to reclassify its name to a "cultural industry" to qualify for the low tax rate shared by other industries. For this, I campaigned vigorously.

In 1968, when the Ministry of Education's Bureau of Cultural Affairs was launched, I discussed this issue with director Hongjun Wang who agreed with my view. However, because filmmaking was considered part of the "entertainment industry" and placed outside of the bureau's jurisdiction, he had no way of changing relevant laws. I then contacted the Director General of Budget, Accounting and Statistics under the Executive Yuan and the Bureau of Industrial Development within the Ministry of Economic Affairs. Both authorities insisted that filmmaking could not be considered an industry because it entertained the public. The officials in charge came from China and were now so old and stubborn that they refused to listen

Consequently in 1971, I applied for the establishment of a "Motion Picture Studios Association of Taiwan", i.e. if one company was powerless, then this organization could serve as a union to represent all our industrial colleagues and to fight for our rights. Members of our union consisted of post-production technicians in fields such as film processing, recording and special effects, all undoubtedly industrial professionals. From my point of view, such an industrial union would be highly useful in our long-term campaign to recategorize filmmaking as a cultural industry.

On March 10, 1973, as a result of our hard work, the Ministry of the Interior gave its approval for the establishment of the "Motion Picture Studios Association of Taiwan". An inaugural party was held at the Freedom House in Taipei on April 30 where I was elected director, a position I served for three terms in a row. Why did we choose the word "Taiwan"? Obviously it referred to the Taiwan area and excluded China, as this was a union designated specifically for professionals working in Taiwan's film industry. Among its six members were three government-owned entities: Kuomintang's Central Pictures Corporation, the Ministry of National Defense's China Motion Picture Studio, and a studio owned by the Taiwan Provincial Government. The other three members were privately owned studios, including our International Film Studio.

Our union continued to negotiate with the government to identify filmmaking as a cultural industry. As director, it took me more than five years to achieve this goal of reducing taxes charged for our products. It fully demonstrated how success favors those who seize opportunities. Meanwhile, the then premier Yun-suan Sun called for a meeting of filmmakers at the national level, to be organized by the Council for National Construction and Development. Yat-fu Shaw, Raymond Chow, Yejun Dong and King Hu from Hong Kong, and Hsing Li, Yung-hsiang Chang and myself were invited from Taiwan. At the meeting, I urged all attendees to consider filmmaking as an industry with multiple functions. I asserted both verbally and in writing that film production and distribution should be seen as a cultural industry, and that it was unreasonable to place films in the same "entertainment" category as public baths and prostitution. Noting this argument, Premier Sun promised to consider it. He later accepted my advice to propose a bill to officially designate the term "cinematic cultural industry". Thanks to another ten years of hard work by the Motion Picture Studios Association of Taiwan, the *Motion Picture Act* finally passed the legislature and became law in 1983.

However, an affirmation from Premier Sun was not enough. In order to officially transfer filmmaking from the "entertainment industry" category to that of "cultural industry", Shutong Chen, deputy head of the Cultural Work Commission that was in charge of the film industry under the Kuomintang's Party Central Committee (and the younger brother of Bulei Chen (who was personal secretary of former president Chiang Kai-shek), organized a meeting of all the ministries and bureaus involved. With so many government departments related to "entertainment" and/or "industry", not a single conclusion was achieved by the end of several meetings. But I did not give up. In our last meeting, I invited officials from all the ministries and bureaus involved in films, cultural affairs, entertainment and industrial development to sit in the meeting room at our International Film Studio in Danan, Taoyuan County. I introduced the complex process in which movies were made. I explained that filmmaking was an industry because we utilized a wider range of equipment than ordinary manufacturers and worked for longer periods of time than those in other professions. All attendees then toured our studio. Afterwards, everybody claimed they had never realized movies were made in this way, and promised to further investigate the relevant issues. Eventually they all agreed to transfer filmmaking from the "entertainment industry" category to that of "cultural industry".

Without our spacious meeting room and without this excellent film studio built by Union Film Company, this crucial meeting would never have been possible. The establishment of the Motion Picture Studios Association of Taiwan and the recognition of filmmaking as a cultural industry were an important chapter in the history of Taiwan's film industry. From then on, we were able to apply to the Ministry of the Interior and Ministry of Finance for tax deduction in our imports of equipment, filmstrips and other items required in filmmaking. We could also campaign for a fair and reasonable working environment to support the production and distribution of movies, which in turn benefited a great number of independent filmmakers and talented actors in their careers.

Our International Film Studio occupied a large piece of land. A portion was set aside for a cinematic arts college to cultivate talent in this field. Convinced that education is the foundation for long-term professional development, I discussed my plans with a relative named C.K. Teng, who was then deputy head of the Ministry of Education. I explained a specialized college would facilitate students to learn and intern in the film studio, and provide in-service opportunities for those already working in the film industry. Teng countered with two concerns. First, we did not have enough instructors in Taiwan, and it would be too expensive to appoint foreign professionals. More importantly, the Ministry of Education would not support a specialized college if there were insufficient jobs for its graduates.

With that said, according to Teng, there were ample opportunities for me to invest in education by providing financial support for specialized technical courses in a secondary school in Toucheng, Yilan County. This in turn would help enhance the educational environment in Eastern Taiwan. Consequently, some friends and I established the private Fu-Hsin Institute of Technology (today's Lan Yang Institute of Technology), with a department specifically dedicated to films, which has cultivated many technical talents since then. While I did not get to launch a specialized college in cinematic arts, my part in setting up the Fu-Hsin Institute of Technology fulfilled my wish to contribute to education. I served on the school board until 1988 when I retired and relocated to the United States.

The best example I can use to teach and inspire future generations is my lifelong pursuit of learning. I was forced to drop out of school at 13. Starting as an apprentice, I established my own career, experienced much frustration and the turmoil of war, journeyed from my hometown in Jiangsu Province to Taiwan, and finally settled in the film industry, a highly complex and developing profession full of conflicts and disputes. A firm believer in the ultimate importance of education, I have always focused on learning. Starting from my youthful days as an apprentice, I studied whenever opportunities arose at work. These included a series of business administration courses at the National Chengchi University in 1971, my attendance at the Sun Yat-sen Institute of Policy Research and Development in 1973, and my appointment as a member of the Institute's Management Steering Committee in 1982.

A Classic at the Cannes Film Festival

The introduction of popular Western movies had a profound but adverse impact on locally produced films. The birth and popularity of video cassettes also made it increasingly difficult to work in the film industry, but I never stopped dreaming as a filmmaker. After the fame of *A Touch of Zen* subsided, many of our shareholders considered filmmaking a useless profession. This led to Union Film Company's decision to suspend its film production in 1974, even though up to 300 films had been produced in our International Film Studio in Danan. These accounted for nearly half of the movies made in Taiwan up to that point.

While our studio offered the best equipment for the lowest price, the rent we charged only covered the utilities and salaries for some of our staff, but not our equipment costs. Some saw it as running the business at a loss, which in my opinion was probably the major reason why our shareholders forged my signature and sold our film studio to a property developer in 1977. They took advantage of my being in the United States. Without my permission, they rationalized that the land would be more purposefully used for housing development. However, no housing was ever built there, as other companies continued to rent the studio for their film production. Indeed, with its first-class facilities and exquisitely designed and constructed soundstages and outdoor settings, our film studio in Danan was peerless in both Taiwan and Hong Kong. Had it not been sold then, it would have been worth trillions of Taiwanese dollars by now. The demolition of the studio several years later was a huge blow to Taiwan's film industry. It was an incomprehensible decision. Nonetheless, despite my anger and frustration, I followed my lawyer's advice to remain calm. In order to maintain decades of friendship and collaborative relations with our shareholders, I chose to accept the results of their illegal behaviors instead of litigating.

Later I tried but failed to start over again. Although I left the film industry, I still supported the preservation of our cinematic cultural heritage and offered long-term sponsorship to the Chinese Taipei Film Archive (today's Taiwan Film Institute). In 1991, I authorized filmstrips, soundtracks, subtitle cards, film copies and promotional materials from all 22 movies produced by Union Film Company to be shipped back from Hong Kong and permanently preserved by the Chinese Taipei Film Archive. As both commodities and works of art, these internationally recognized films would last forever. In 2005, the Hong Kong Film Awards Association Ltd selected the 100 best movies to mark the 100th anniversary of the birth of Chinese Cinema. Both *Dragon Inn* and *A Touch of Zen* were among the top ten on the list.

In 2014, *Dragon Inn* and 21 other international films were featured as Cannes Classics in France. This section of the Cannes Film Festival has always been a battleground for the world's restored classic movies. To be selected, not only should a film be recognized by generations of international audiences, but its restoration should be in the standard 4K ultra high definition, with the digital copy's horizontal resolution on the order of 4,000 pixels. With technological and financial subsidies from the Ministry of Culture, the Taiwan Film Institute had already been restoring classic Chinese movies since 2013. To support the ministry's fundraising activities, I donated 500,000 Taiwanese dollars to the project with many other donors following suit. Old films may be digitally restored to various degrees. The higher the quality and resolution the more technological skills and equipment are required.

In the restoration of *Dragon Inn*, the filmstrips were sent to Italy's Cineteca of Bologna, a world-class center for film restoration. The filmstrips were scanned, 24 frames per second, as digital files. They were then restored frame by frame, some by computer algorithms but mostly manually. With Taiwan Film Institute collaborating with the Cineteca of Bologna, it took a whole year and more than three million Taiwanese dollars to fully restore *Dragon Inn* to the 4K UHD standard.

As one of Union Film Company's representative films, *Dragon Inn* was the first Chinese movie to be selected as a Cannes Classic and will be permanently preserved as part of their museum's collection. More importantly, the timing of *Dragon Inn* receiving this honor coincided with the 60th anniversary of the establishment of Union Film Company. To mark this milestone, the College of Sound and Image Arts of the Tainan National University of Arts, sponsored by Taiwan Film Institute and the Tainan City Government's Bureau of Cultural Affairs, organized a special exhibition to review 60 years of history of our Union Film Company. Following in the footsteps of *Dragon Inn* being honored at the Cannes Film Festival and thanks to a donation of 5.1 million Taiwanese dollars from Feng Xu, the actress who played the female lead in *A Touch of Zen* for its digital restoration to 4K UHD, it, too, was selected as a Cannes Classic in 2015.

Looking back, I had the fortune of introducing Mandarin language films in Taiwan. You can say I spent my whole life supporting, promoting and witnessing the development of Taiwan's film industry. In 1980, I was presented with a certificate by the Kuomintang Party's Central Committee listing my lifelong contributions to Taiwan. These ranged from my establishing a network of movie theaters, a production studio and a modern film processing factory, to my launching the Motion Picture Studios Association of Taiwan, and my long-term campaign to uplift the standards of locally made films and develop foreign markets and finally to my constant encouragement for overseas Chinese filmmakers to contribute to our nation, and my continuous efforts to support our men and women in the military services.

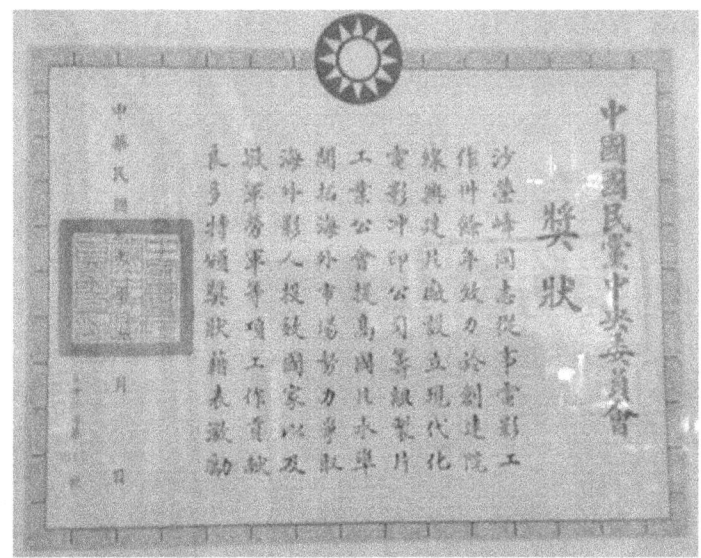

Certificate present to Yung-fong Shy by the government 1980

Unexpectedly, in 1991, more than a decade after I left the film industry, I received a Special Contribution Award from the Motion Picture Foundation, Republic of China, at the 28th Golden Horse Awards. My wife Xue-e Cao and I returned from the United States to attend the award ceremony. That was the most glorious moment of my life as they not only detailed my personal achievements but also organized a special exhibition to review the films produced by Union Film Company. There was even a series of press conferences with me in the spotlight. As someone who had worked tirelessly behind the scenes, I never expected to become a media celebrity.

Thanks to my wife I was able to concentrate on my career throughout the years. She took care of our family and children and left me with neither worries nor fears. When our children were little, she often went to school with them in order to repeat the teachers' instructions at home. For example, my daughter used to be so stubborn that she refused to answer the teacher's questions. Consequently, my wife would accompany her to school every day until she had fully adjusted to her surroundings. Back in Taipei we held parties during the Chinese New Year holidays to entertain journalists covering films and theaters. With dozens of people partying throughout the night, my wife played the perfect hostess before retreating with our children to a separate building in the backyard to resume our normal routine.

Yung-fong Shy and wife Xue-e Cao at the 28th Golden Horse Awards Ceremony 1991 and his Special Contribution Award

Our children have established their own careers, and we have been blessed with many grandchildren and great-grandchildren. Unfortunately, right before the showing of the digitally restored *Dragon Inn* at the Cannes Film Festival on May 16, 2014, my wife Xue-e Cao passed away in our California home due to deteriorating health. One week prior, we had celebrated our 70th wedding anniversary with our many children and grandchildren. No words can describe the pain in my heart.

Among the numerous condolences I received was a sympathy card from the members of the Chinese-American Association of Rossmoor in Walnut Creek where I live. To express my gratitude I wrote the following words in my response. "Dear President, Board Members and My Fellow Members and Friends from Taiwan, Hong Kong and Mainland China, on both sides of the Taiwan Strait: I regret to inform you that my wife Grace Xue-e Shy (nee Cao) died peacefully in her sleep in the early hours of May the 15th. She is in heaven now. With all my heartfelt thanks to your sympathy and kind words, I hereby offer all of you, my best wishes for your health, happiness and peace. Sincerely Yours, Yung-fong Shy."

Florence Lin 沈鵬俠
Receiving the "Milestone Award" from the International Association of
Culinary Professionals
San Francisco, April 2013

Soon after our relocation to Rossmoor, I had a chance to taste Florence Lin's candied orange peel and found it utterly delicious. My own attempt at the dish was not as good, and having heard this Florence drove me to her place for a personal demonstration. She had all the ingredients and equipment ready, and commenced the cooking process with detailed explanation of every step along the way. Her moves were so swift and precise that I could not believe she was already 93 years old. Nor did I realize that before her retirement, Florence had taught Chinese cooking in New York for many years, published six popular books on Chinese culinary arts, and received the Lifetime Achievement Award from the Asian Culinary Arts Institutes.

Knowing how much I enjoy cooking, she often allowed me to

observe her in action and ask crucial questions. I am fortunate to have learned from such a master chef, with her being so kind to even consider us as friends across generations. Apart from our culinary discussions, she also shared her life experiences with me. She said it was happenstance that favored her with various opportunities, as demonstrated by the Chinese saying "Heroes emerge in troubled times". However, I feel it was the courageous decisions she made in the face of such opportunities and her determination to see them through to the end that truly mattered. The following story arose from a Q&A session about her heroic-sounding Chinese name, Peng-xia. While "peng" is a giant bird in Chinese mythology that is akin to the mythical creature in Arabian folklore, "xia" is often associated with the Western notion of a chivalrous swordsman or noble knight.

Biography

Florence Lin, whose Chinese name is Peng-xia Shen (originally Han-ju Shen) and whose ancestral home is Zhenhai, in Ningbo, Zhejiang Province, was born in 1920. She lived with her father, a businessman, in Wuhan, Hubei Province, since the age of seven. While in high school she participated in the Anti-Japanese and National Salvation Movement that were popular among youths. In 1938 she enlisted as a female soldier in the First Division of the Wartime Cadre Training School established by the Nationalist Government's Military Committee, which later moved to Chongqing, Sichuan Province. In 1947, she travelled to New York to marry Kuo-yung Lin and settle there. As a result of various twists and turns in her life, she started teaching cooking at the China Institute in New York City and introduced Chinese culinary arts to mainstream American society through her writing. In 1995 she relocated to Rossmoor in Walnut Creek in the San Francisco Bay Area.

From Female Soldier to Master Chef

Think about this first if you want me to share the stories of my life throughout the past 95 years. From a traditional farming family in rural China, I became a silk merchant's daughter enjoying all the luxuries of a big city. Then my life changed againdue to the impact of war and influences of new friends and new thoughts. I became a soldier in China's War of Resistance against Japan; then I taught Americans how to cook Chinese dishes after my arrival in the United States. Don't you think I have many, many stories to share about my life?

Getting to the City

My ancestral home is in the outskirts of Ningbo, a rural area of Zhejiang Province. My ancestors were generations of farmers, part of the middle or lower class, apart from families of scholars. Back then it was difficult to travel, so you remained a farmer in the countryside if you were born there. My father was lucky to have an opportunity to travel to Hankou, Hubei Province, to learn a trade. Otherwise, he would have been a farmer, and I in turn would have lived my life as a rural person.

My father, Zong-Yin Shen, worked as an apprentice in a silk shop in Hankou for many years. We referred to this as learning a trade, which means you have an opportunity to work for a master by doing everything under his guidance and observing how things are done in his field. You start by serving your master, including pouring him a cup of tea. Then you gradually learned to shoulder more and more responsibilities.

My father finally established his own silk shop in Hankou in

1920, the year I was born as the third daughter in our family. Because my father was in Hankou when I arrived in this world, I was named Han-ju ("ju" being chrysanthemum). My father considered my birth a symbol of his fortune and had me live with him between the ages of seven and ten; indeed, his business boomed during those years. I was the only one staying with him in Hankou while the rest of our family remained in the countryside.

Florence Lin's father Zong-yin Shen, mother and second brother

At that time many businessmen left their wives and children behind in rural areas where the living was cheap. My father didn't go home to Ningbo very often, only two or three times a year, while my mother remained in the countryside throughout her life. There were many children in our family. I had two older brothers, two older sisters and three younger sisters. Among them, two (my second brother and second youngest sister) died at a young age. It was only after my father's business prospered and a house was found nearby that my family gradually relocated to the city. Initially my second older sister had to stay behind, as the house in the city wasn't big enough to take in all the kids at one go. Among all my siblings, I lived in the city the longest.

Every time my father came home to Ningbo, the first thing he did was to pay his respect to my grandmother in her room. I remember he talked far more to my grandmother than to my mother. Here's something interesting about my family. When my grandfather, the oldest son in his family, was ready to marry, he insisted on having a wife with unbound feet. A farmer himself, he wanted his wife to also work hard in the field instead of being looked after at home. Back then many girls had their feet bound so that they grew up with small feet resembling the "three-inch golden lotus"; otherwise, no one would want them as a wife. As there were very few girls with unbound feet, our family had to find one from the countryside. Consequently, my grandmother thumped around with her big feet at home and in the field, an extremely rare sight during that era. It sounded really funny when I first heard this story about my grandmother.

Imagine this: I'm already in my 90s, and these are people from two generations before my birth that we're talking about! I can't even figure out how long ago that was. Anyway, later, as my family prospered, my father married my mother who had bound feet. As for my generation, my father had the common sense to prevent my mother from binding my sisters' and my feet. As soon as he came home and saw my mother binding my oldest sister's feet, he would tell her to stop. I think this is because my father had been a man of the world in the city. This was the era when foot binding slowly lost its appeal as a custom, so my sisters and I never suffered it.

My mother was a Buddhist and would recite the Heart Sutra in her small chapel every morning. It looked like reciting, but she had memorized every word by heart. Being illiterate, my mother would ask us to read the sutra out loud so that she could commit every single syllable to memory. This is despite the fact that as kids, we didn't really know all the words and would often make things up. My mother was a vegetarian and would prepare her own meals even after our family hired a cook. As children we loved my mother's vegetarian dishes.

In Hankou, my father's business was located in a four-story

building. The shop was on the ground floor, while the second floor consisted of the tailors' workshop and various residential units, including one for my father and me. The third floor was for storage of all kinds of silk and dress-making materials, and the top floor was full of sewing machines and other equipment. Also living in the shop were a servant and a cook who cooked for everyone. The cook had to prepare various special dishes for my father who enjoyed them with a bit of wine in the evening. Meanwhile, my father often held parties and hosted his business associates.

On various occasions when we were invited to dine out, my father would take me along whenever circumstances allowed. Back then Chinese men rarely brought their wives to business functions, as if women were less qualified for things like that. Hence it was highly unusual that my father took me with him; no one had ever heard of a man doing business with his daughter in attendance. One of his business associates suggested girls could help doing things, but I was too young then to be of any use to my father. It was always he who looked after me. I think he just needed a companion.

In Hankou we always had good food at parties, so I had ample opportunities to experience all kinds of excellence dishes, a seed that later budded and blossomed into my career as an instructor of Chinese culinary arts. Furthermore, as a result of my frequent encounters with adults, I built up a bit of knowledge on how to conduct myself around people. You can say I had experienced a little bit of the world. My sisters often commented how lucky I was, as they never had such opportunities in the countryside. The only disadvantage of staying with my father was that he didn't know how to look after me when I was sick. For example, I always got seasick whenever I went on a boat accompanying him on his business trip.

Back to the Countryside

My life and that of my family changed in 1931 when Japan invaded China. At that time anyone who had associations with the Japanese would be in big trouble, which included my father as some of his goods were imported from Japan. I remember at one stage he had to hide in a hospital with my mother and me. A year after that, when I was 12, my father passed away at the age of 49. While my oldest brother took over our father's silk business, he also assumed the position of the head of the house, looking after our grandmother and mother as well as all the siblings. When our mother became sick, he sent her to the outskirts of Ningbo to live with our grandmother. We had relatives there, but they thought it would be nice for a daughter to come along and accommodate our mother's daily needs. That was how I moved back to the countryside at the age of 15, still a high school student.

Once there, I saw some boys flying kites outdoors and wanted to join them but was reprimanded by my paternal grandmother. Being traditional and conservative, it was my grandmother's view that girls should stay indoors and behave, and that was that. But my maternal grandmother didn't mind these things. I remember she always gave me a bowl of longan soup whenever I visited her. Her feet were extremely tiny. I still have a pair of her petite shoes as keepsakes.

I didn't go to school for a year but my relatives didn't care, dismissing the importance of girls receiving education. Apart from looking after my mother, I learned many things in the countryside in Ningbo, as my relatives expected me to marry soon and therefore wanted me to know everything about running a household. The first thing they taught me was embroidery. I embroidered ten pairs of pillow cases as part of my dowry, which I still keep today. Every day I learned needlework, cooking and other "women" skills from these relatives. As my aunt cooked for the whole family, I spent a lot of time helping her in the kitchen. It was hard work preparing meals in rural areas. Whenever one was cooking on the stove, someone else had to stay behind it, keeping the flames alive with straw.

Dinner was the most important meal of the day. We normally ate simple dishes, using only a big pot on the stove. Into the pot went rice and water, then a wire shelf, on top of which were placed three or four bowls. In the bowls were various dishes, a bit of salted fish or meat with vegetables and a soup made of pickled cabbage. The whole pot was covered by a bamboo lid and heated from below by fire. By the time the rice was cooked, all the dishes were done. After the meal, we would scatter some grass and grain husk over the hot ashes to keep the flame alive throughout the night. That small amount of heat was enough to cook a pot of beans or porridge, which would be the next day's breakfast. It was akin to today's slow cooker.

These were our daily meals, with pickled cabbage being a constant dish that required no cooking. If there were birthday celebrations or visitors, we would go to the nearby town to buy meat, fish and vegetables for extra dishes. Interestingly, on the birthdays of our ancestors we would offer dishes to their spirits, an important ritual in the eyes of my relatives. From my point of view, it was an opportunity for everybody to have a good meal, as we often made such offerings on the birthdays or anniversaries of their deaths. I remember they once purchased a rare food item to celebrate the birthday of my then deceased great-grandfather, and ended up eating it themselves.

So, to cook rice where did we get the water? We had wells in the countryside, but not enough ground water. Instead, we used "sky water" that is raindrops running down the roof and collected in a huge urn. This water was specifically reserved for cooking. For washing, we had to walk two or three hundred meters, the distance of two or three blocks, to wash our vegetables, rice and clothing in a river. Now that I think of it, it was truly horrifying. While one was washing clothes in one spot, nearby would be someone else washing their rice and vegetables. Our family even had a small pond outside the back door for washing dirty clothes, as we were not supposed to take our soiled clothing directly to the river. They had to be cleaned first in this pond. Also, back then we didn't have electricity in the countryside. We used oil lamps with the glass covers blackened by smoke by the end of each evening. My job was to clean the glass during the day.

I was used to city living and had only gone to the countryside for a short visit each year. Now that I had lived in the countryside for more than a year due to my mother's illness, I learned a lot about life in rural areas. This was good since I had then experienced both styles of living. People of the same era as my grandparents and those of my own generation lived like that in the countryside not only in China but also across many parts of the world.

A Rebellious Youth

I was 16 when my mother passed away. As there were no schools in the countryside, my eldest brother and his wife took me back to Hankou to resume my studies. My father had saved a lot of money as a result of his successful business operations. However, after my brother became the boss, he started spending, splashing money over things such as hiring a man to pull our family's rickshaw with bell, taking my sister and me to the movies, and feeding us chocolate as snacks. Our family soon ran out of money.

I like meeting people and have always had many friends, even in the army. I had a good friend called Peng-fei Wang, a classmate in primary school in Hankou that was operated by my fellow countrymen from Ningbo. The only child of her family, she had many unconventional thoughts and ideas that profoundly influenced me. For example, in our second year as primary school students, she gave herself the name "Peng-fei" ("giant bird flying") while asking me to change mine to "Peng-xia", so that we could be sisters. These names demonstrated how two little girls aspired to achieve all they could.

After that, no one called me "Han-Ju" any more. Apart from some old friends, no one knew the name "Peng-Xia" ever since I came to the United States, married and became Florence Lin.

After my mother passed away, when I returned to Hankou, I spent much time with Peng-fei. It was during the War of Resistance against foreign invasion that I as a teenager gained a bit of knowledge and the idea of being rebellious.

My brother planned to marry me off the following year when I was 17. The man I was supposed to marry also lived in Hankou and was from a family in the money-lending business. He had seen me before I went to live in the outskirts of Ningbo. The man's father had already passed away by then. When he mentioned me to his mother , she thought it would be nice to have someone to help with the house chores. Hence she asked a matchmaker to send a wedding proposal to my brother, which he accepted, as he thought it would be advantageous to be connected with such an affluent family. So they arranged my engagement with this man in Hankou in my absence, and sent the engagement certificate to me in the countryside. When I saw the certificate in Ningbo, I refused to accept it, not because of that man, who was indeed a decent person, but simply because I didn't want to be married off like this. At that time, many women were married via arrangements by matchmakers, including my sisters. My second sister, who was two years older than me, didn't have any choice. She obeyed our family's decision and became someone's wife, just like that. In sharp contrast, my life was different, as I had been educated in Hankou and influenced by friends with new thoughts such as Peng-fei Wang. I knew I could resist if I didn't want this marriage. I didn't have to get married just because my family said so.

Thanks to my unconventional knowledge and life experiences, I reversed the whole arrangement. By then my brother had already set the time for the wedding and told the man's family that I would be there. However, as I had made up my mind to rebel, I visited the man's house and announced I wanted to cancel the engagement. His mother, a very capable woman who had long been used to running her house, was so upset that she invited several elderly relatives from her clan to evaluate this issue. Five old men sat there on one side, saying what I did was wrong, while I sat on the opposite side, insisting on cancelling the engagement and making all of them mad as hell. I don't remember why my brother was not there. Anyway, I told them my decision to cancel the engagement and formalize it via the media. Unless both sides were willing to cooperate, that was the only way to dissolve a wedding arrangement back then. I was so stubborn that as soon as they were notified, I formally proceeded to cancel the engagement by announcing it in our local newspaper. It sounded like a tough thing to do, but I had my friends supporting me, who believed that whatever I did, I should only do it out of my own free will. I had the courage to do what I did only because I trusted my friends. If it were just up to me, it most likely would not have happened. Worse, if I had stayed in the countryside all along, then I would never have had such an idea or opportunity to do it. Both timing and friends were crucial factors.

Friends matter a lot. Back then we didn't have modern communication tools such as e-mail, iPad, etc. Nor did we have convenient transport and mass media, so it was difficult to keep in touch with the world outside. It was only due to war, as well as my association with friends whose thoughts were ahead of their time, that I had the courage and opportunity to resist an arranged marriage. Otherwise, I would never have been so brave. I really, really valued my friends.

Peng-fei Wang had many crazy ideas. We had planned to enlist in the army together to fight the invading Japanese, and to pursue further studies in the United States. However, it was I who achieved these goals, not her. I lost contact with Peng-fei after leaving Wuhan. I returned to China in 1978 and searched for her in Wuhan, but to no avail. In 1980, I finally found her and was heart-broken to see her living in a tiny apartment unit with her husband and daughter, having to burn coal for cooking and heating, and lacking such basic utilities as water and toilet in her daily life. I paid her another visit after that, but two years later, in my attempt to contact her, I discovered she had passed away.

A Female Soldier

The Japanese occupied Northeast China and then expanded southward, burning, killing, robbing and looting along the way. These horrifying acts were well known among the people in big cities, but those living in remote and poor regions had absolutely no idea. I was 17 and still a student when the Marco Polo Bridge Incident took place. Finding it unbearable that our nation was being invaded by Japan, I participated in the Anti-Japanese and National Salvation Movements and joined other youths to raise public awareness of this national tragedy in the countryside. We spent six months putting up posters and conducting singing and theatrical performances, trying to encourage the crowds to support our speeches on fighting the Japanese and saving our nation. It was during this period that I received much training in writing, public performing and speaking.

Now that I think about it, however, such activities might have been a Communist campaign to attract young students. They did it subtly, nothing obvious or straightforward. Some of them contacted me privately, asking if I wanted to go to Yan'an, then the center of the Chinese Communist movement in Shaanxi Province; but they soon stopped, perhaps shifting their focus to older and more experienced students. It was lucky that I didn't join them or my life would have been ruined. Anyway, when Chiang Kai-shek realized the risk of our young students being attracted to Communist Yan'an, he set up the Wartime Cadre Training School in early 1938 to cultivate talent for the Nationalist Government. He further appointed himself as the school's director, military commander Chen Cheng as deputy director, and army general Yong-qing Gui as superintendent of education and training. After Nanjing was captured by Japanese troops, Wuhan in Hubei Province became our nation's temporary capital and the center of our War of Resistance against Japan. Wuhan consisted of three districts: Hankou, Wuchang and Hanyang. The Wartime Cadre Training School was headquartered in Wuhan University in Wuchang,.

From Hankou I crossed the Yangtze River to Wuchang with two other female classmates whose families were relatively affluent. When the three of us young ladies arrived for registration, people in the school said to us, "Are you aware how tough life is here? Do you really want to join?" They probably thought us unlikely soldier material. Anyway, before our training commenced, one of my friends changed her mind due to family pressure. My brother also tried to talk me out of it, but I refused to go home; I wanted to fight the Japanese invaders.

At that time, the Wartime Cadre Training School attracted many young people, who might or might not have realized it was the equivalent of a military school with vigorous training and substandard living conditions. I belonged to the first class within the first division, which consisted of many female soldiers. We were trained separately from the males. We conducted military exercises during the day and slept on an icy cold concrete floor at night with everybody crowded together for warmth. We ate brown rice, supplemented by a large bowl of cabbage and several slices of pork fat. I had never tasted anything like this before and found it hard to swallow at first, but soon learned to accept it because there was nothing else to eat.

After the initial three months of training were completed, another friend was ordered home by her father. My brother tried again to get me out of the army to return home but I refused. It was lucky that I didn't obey him, or I would have lived a considerably different life. Later, seeing that three months were too short a period to cultivate a soldier and that Wuhan was still free from the Japanese, the authorities decided to enforce another three months of military training upon our school. These extra months were mainly for physical drills which were so rough that our shoes wore out. General Yong-qing Gui saw our misery and ordered the school to give us shoes, but they were made of straw; oh my god, they were so ugly. Anyway, it took me three months to learn to fire a gun, but I became pretty good at loading and unloading due to daily practice. That gun weighed four kilograms and was genuinely impressive, but they were unable to provide us with real bullets for practicing. We were allowed only one real bullet each to get the feel for it. That was the only time in my life that I fired a gun. The recoil was truly astonishing.

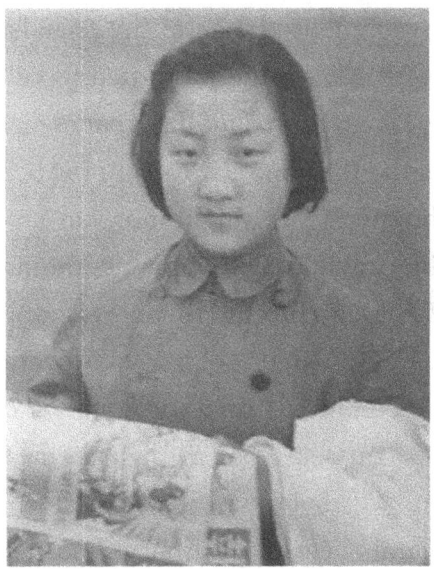

At the Wartime Cadre Training School 1938

When I graduated in July that year, Wuhan was on the brink of falling into the hands of Japanese troops. The authorities decided to shift all of us young men and women who had completed six months of military training to Chongqing as soon as possible. We took the boats from Hankou, all of us crowded together, each carrying a small bundle containing our personal belongings and a sleeping mat, which we spread out on the deck at night. It was truly miserable. Those boats did not seem to contain cabins. Even if cabins existed, they would have been for our superiors.

In Chongqing, we suffered daily bombing by Japanese warplanes and had to evacuate to various shelters during air raids. Twice I witnessed the destruction of the place I stayed where everything was destroyed, apart from me, the lucky one. At one stage, an enormous air-raid shelter collapsed as a result of fierce bombing, suffocating thousands of people inside. Worse, after that tragedy, we were sent to count the bodies. From that moment on, I harbored deep hatred toward the Japanese. Many years later I had a dinner party at home in New York. One guest among my husband's business associates was a Japanese about my age. I could not bring myself to speak one word to him. He was an enemy in my mind.

In Chongqing we were administered by the Political Department of the Nationalist Government's Military Committee. Upon our arrival they immediately assigned us to train the university students there. Apart from leading these students in military exercises, we ourselves were trained by one unit after another within the Political Department. For example, I learned accounting in one unit and combat casualty care in another, where I gained a bit of knowledge on how to apply bandages. The head of the unit where I studied accounting also spent time teaching me how to use an abacus, conduct surveys and create various types of graphs. I also had to learn calligraphy, which I enjoyed and in which I already had some basic training.

Despite the fact that I didn't complete high school, I had the opportunity to study accounting in a school in the countryside and acquired skills such as reading classical Chinese Literature, using an abacus and basic bookkeeping. Life was tough in rural areas, with my sleep constantly disrupted by insect bites such as bed bugs and fleas. In spite of this, I had learned enough there to enter a profession. For a period of six months, I even studied statistics at Nanjing University, which had been relocated to Chengdu, Sichuan Province, because of war. After graduation, I was finally out of government-sponsored schools. My family arranged a job for me working for a company that promoted locally made goods. An excellent user of the abacus, I worked as an accountant for that company for about three years. The head of their accounting department was Kuo-yung Lin, my future husband. We met, befriended one another and became engaged in Chongqing without my family's blessings, as my brother still remembered that affluent family to which I was promised and which I ended up rejecting.

How should I explain this? Should I have obeyed my brother, married into that rich family, and most likely ended up with a nice life? However, it would have been a completely different life where I would have been a housewife and given birth to some kids but nothing else. I would never have encountered all the opportunities given to me, all the things that I learned and experienced, such as studying and a career. Ultimately, it was a time in which circumstances were constantly changing. China had changed so much as a result of war.

Going to America

China was in constant chaos at that time. Many young people wanted to go to America, but very few of them could make it. My fiance, Kuo-yung Lin, was a nephew of the renowned scholar Yu-tang Lin. With his book *My Country and My People* (1935) published in New York, Mr. Lin introduced Chinese people and culture to the West, thus greatly enhancing China's reputation around the world. Because of this, Chang Kai-shek invited Mr. Lin to visit China in the hope that he would write about Japan's invasion of China. In 1944, Mr. Lin brought his family to Chongqing and subsequently visited places such as Baoji, Xi'an (Shaanxi Province), Chengdu (Sichuan Province), Guilin (Guangxi Province), Hengyang and Changsha (Hunan Province). I got to meet him in

Chongqing. Mr. Lin planned to bring his eldest nephew back to the United States for further studies, but ended up choosing another, Kuo-yung, instead, as the former was getting married and wanted to remain in China. Thanks to Chang Kai-shek's help in the rapid processing of his passport, my future husband arrived in America with Mr. Lin and became a student. We kept in touch via letters. Three years later, Kuo-yung managed to get me accepted by New York's Syracuse University as an international student. Otherwise, I would never have had such an opportunity to get a visa and come to the United States.

SS General M. C. Meigs - the ship bearing 300 Chinese students from Shanghai to San Francisco, January 4, 1947

SS General M.C. Meigs, the ship bearing Florence Lin and 300 other Chinese students from Shanghai to San Francisco. January 4, 1947

Still, it was difficult to get to America. I needed to purchase a ticket for a ship *and* study English. I remember spending 150 U.S. dollars on a steerage passenger ticket for the S.S. General M.C. Meigs, which departed from Shanghai to San Francisco via Hong Kong in January 1947. However, as a result of a dockers' strike, several passages were cancelled, forcing an unusually large number of people to board our ship. Worse, I had my lifelong problem with seasickness. As I lined up for my first dinner on the ship and given a huge tray of food, I took one look at it, and went straight to the lady's room to throw up. For the next two weeks or so at the sea, I remained in my bunk, getting up only to vomit in the toilet. It was lucky that a Chinese cook on the ship took pity on me and the other seasick Chinese students by preparing rice congee for us; otherwise, I would have been unable to eat anything else. I lost ten pounds of weight on that voyage. When I finally arrived in San Francisco, the first thing I saw was the clock tower on Pier One where our ship moored. I then saw Kuo-yung Lin standing there. He had spent three days and four nights on a train from New York to San Francisco to pick me up.

There were more than 300 Chinese students on our ship, with the majority staying together in a huge cabin. On the day before our arrival in America, I met Wan-ching Chiang (see the Chapter on Linna Wu), who was also going to New York. We exchanged addresses, but lost contact with each other after saying good-bye in San Francisco. It was only after 1995, when both of us had retired and relocated to Rossmoor, in San Francisco's Bay Area, that we saw each other again.

This was my first trip out of China. Armed with very little English, I suddenly was in New York. I stayed in an apartment in a four-story building for two months. While I needed to learn English and adapt to my surroundings as soon as possible, we also wanted to get married. It was Uncle Yu-tang Lin and his wife Cui-feng Liao's view that we should have a Western-style wedding ceremony. So in March that year, Kuo-yung found a small apartment on the west side of Central Park and purchased an emerald ring. He even booked a brand new Studebaker. I put on my white wedding dress in his uncle's apartment and we were married at the Riverside Church on the east side of Columbia University. A tea party was then held at the Columbia Faculty Club.

Kuo-yung and Florence Lin in their wedding car 1947

By the end of that year, our first daughter was born. Later I worked as a volunteer at her kindergarten. I enjoyed this so much that I wanted to set up a similar school myself, but this was stopped only by my poor English proficiency. At that time, Kuo-yung received his Master's degree in Business Administration from Wharton School of the University of Pennsylvania and commenced working for Shanghai Commercial Bank in New York. Throughout that year, my first in America, we planned what to do after returning to China. It was only later that we realized we might not be going back.

Instructor in Chinese Culinary Arts

I had always loved cooking, and often hosted dinners for my husband's business associates at our home. After our second daughter was born in 1953, I became even more interested in this field and would always inquire how people prepared their dishes, what ingredients they used and how much, etc. Still, most of the time, I just managed my own cooking at home. I had never considered teaching Chinese culinary arts.

So, how did I end up teaching cooking at the China Institute? It's an interesting story.

I enjoyed baking the most, and would often compare my results with those of my friends to find out how my techniques could be improved. At one stage I shared my curry puffs with a group of friends. One of them, a former student of Cornell University's Department of Food Science, informed me that Western people adopt a scientific approach to cooking, both within and outside of academia. Western people are highly precise in the amounts of ingredients to be used in each dish, unlike Chinese recipes, which only indicate "a little bit of this" or "an appropriate amount of that". He said I should look into this issue which I did. I conducted various experiments and the results were ideal. As long as I used exactly the same amounts of ingredients each time, my dishes would taste the same every time I cooked them. It was such an inspiring idea.

I presented my curry puffs at a Chinese community event at the Riverside Church in 1960. One of the participants at the event was K.Y. Ai, organizer of community courses for the China Institute. Having tasted my curry puffs, he insisted they were so delicious that I *had* to teach Chinese cooking for them. That was at least half a century ago, which began my 35-year career as an instructor in Chinese culinary arts at the China Institute. It was the right opportunity encountered at the right time. It sounds like happenstance, but my meeting with people like Ai had much to do with our family's social circles.

Beginning in 1930 the China Institute in New York City launched a series of popular community courses on Chinese language, culture, arts and history. By attending these courses teachers from New York's primary and secondary schools received credits formally certified by the Department of Education plus a pay raise. Hence there was a great demand for instructors in Chinese language, history, calligraphy, painting and cooking. The Chinese cooking class was particularly popular because it cost only US $8 for a credit, and you also got to taste all that delicious food! This created huge amount of pressure on the two existing instructors. One was Grace Chu, wife of General Si-ming Chu (an army officer and politician in the Nationalist Government) and a graduate of Wellesley College. As wife of a military attaché at the Chinese Embassy in Washington, D.C., Chu often held parties and was a great public speaker. Having published a series of books on Chinese cooking, she was a widely celebrated instructor in Chinese culinary arts. The other instructor was Dorothy Lee, a graduate of Cornell University's Department of Home Economics who had studied nutrition. Compared to them I was hardly qualified.

As an educational organization the China Institute had a great tradition of appointing excellent instructors. While I had never taught anybody before, I accepted the appointment and worked extremely hard, learning everything along the way. In order to face all the American students, I spent much time preparing for each class by trying out all the dishes in advance, recording their corresponding recipes, and practising my English. The actual teaching was even more difficult. I had to start by showing all the American students how to hold and use a Chinese cleaver. We also had an enormous mirror hanging at an angle from the ceiling so that students could observe my movements.

Grace and I became very good friends when I went to her courses where I learned a lot. Coincidentally, it was also during that period around 1963, that Craig Claiborne, the renowned restaurant and food critic, became a food editor for *The New York Times*. He wasn't that famous then; however, as the paper's first ever male food editor, he felt he needed to do something special. Aware of the fact that most Americans were rather conservative with what they ate, Claiborne placed an emphasis on recommending Asian and Mexican cuisines in his articles and eventually discovered the China Institute. He happened to encounter my curry puffs, which was a dish well known in the West. As a result, he published a significant feature about me in *The New York Times* with a follow-up article in 1965, which made me famous. That was pure luck; he needed something unique while I required exposure, so we suited each other's purpose perfectly. I was lucky. Luck played an important role in my life.

Thanks to unexpected good luck, another established publisher Time Life Books approached me. In 2014 for the first time in the nation's history, a series of five stamps featuring famous chefs was published in the United States to mark their contribution to American food and drink culture. One of the stamps featured Joyce Chan, who established the first Chinese restaurant in New England near Harvard University in 1958 and introduced Northern Chinese cuisine to Americans. In 1967, *the* Time Life Books planned to produce a series of books called "Foods of the World Recipes". In need of a Chinese expert for the book "The Cooking of China", they tried to engage Chan, who was already famous for her restaurant and Chinese cook books, as a consultant. However, Chan was too busy to travel from Boston to New York for this job and so my friend Emily Gus, who owned a Chinese restaurant and knew the publisher well, recommended me. She even put in a good word about me as an instructor in Chinese culinary arts etc. Opportunities like this were certainly fortuitous for me.

Consequently, Emily invited me for a meal with the publisher. One of their staff sat next to me and listened as I explained how to prepare the Drunken Shrimp dish. Shrimp from China's West Lake measured about an inch and a half with the edible flesh being only an inch. Having harvested the shrimp from the lake, you cut off their big feelers with a pair of scissors and placed them in a pot full of liquor. You then covered the pot with an upside-down bowl with the live shrimps inside. To eat them, you picked one out with a pair of chopsticks and dipped the live shrimp in a sauce of sesame paste mixed with soy sause. When you bite into the shrimp, it and the sauce move around in your mouth, and you have to learn how to shell it and mix its flesh with the sauce. Impressed by this, the publisher arranged a formal interview with me, which led to their engaging me as a consultant.

This opportunity with Time Life was originally Chan's, but became mine as a result of my being geographically closer to the publisher than she. A few months after that, Time Life published their first cook book. It was truly lucky that the first in the series was on Chinese cuisine instead of French or Italian, as a Chinese person happened to come along and accommodated their lack of experience in publishing this type of book. I might not be as qualified as other Chinese chefs, but such an excellent opportunity helped generate more precious experience for me in this field.

Time Life Books had ample money to fund the project. We had beautiful Chinese ceramic dishes to use in the kitchen, a professional photographer, someone to observe the cooking processes and translate them into recipes, and another person to wash all the dishes. It took them three days to photograph the Peking duck, which became rather unpalatable by the time the process concluded. My own books that published later didn't cost as much because many of the illustrations were hand-drawn.

Although it was a good opportunity involving much hard work, I was unable to handle some of the intricacies because of my poor English. Still, it was done. It remains my view that in order to succeed, one needs not only luck but also much courage. This well received book was published in 1968 and was a breakthrough in my career and helped secure my position in the traditional Chinese culinary arts. After that many established food manufacturing factories and companies engaged me as a consultant in Chinese cooking. When DuPont attempted to raise the profile of their non-stick cookware, they hired me to promote both their pots and pans *and* my book in New York's various department stores. Apart from the China Institute, I was approached to teach Chinese cooking in places such as New Jersey, Washington and Atlanta. Furthermore, I published many newspaper articles on Chinese culinary arts.

While I was busy pursuing my career, I discovered a lump in my right breast in 1971 after reading an article in the Readers' Digest about breast self-examination. After an operation to remove the cancerous growth, I couldn't even raise my right arm, which was absolutely crucial for a chef. I practiced every day, trying to lift my arm inch by inch, and was finally able to raise my hand above my head after several months. It took me two years to get truly back to normal. It was a huge challenge for me, but somehow I managed to defeat cancer and go back to my normal, busy life.

Some of the Chinese cooking books published by Florence Lin

In 1974 Hawthorn Publishing invited me to write a book of Chinese recipes, which I thought should include China's four famous cuisines. With Kuo-yung's help I conducted much research, studied many existing titles and incorporated many of my own experiments at home. This book, *Florence Lin's Chinese Regional Cookbook*, was published in 1975 and was selected as the cook book of the year. I travelled all over America to promote and sign the book and was very surprised at the passion of my readers and how they were influenced by this book. I was a truly lucky person.

Unfortunately, my husband was suddenly diagnosed with Parkinson's disease. We made long-term arrangements and hired a nurse to look after him at our home. I spent as much time as possible with him while trying to accommodate a busy schedule of teaching and traveling. Approximately a year and a half later both my husband and his uncle, Mr. Yu-tang Lin, passed away in 1976. My husband was only 61. I felt I could only ease my sorrow and find peace through work.

I continued to teach at the China Institute with more organizations across the nation trying to appoint me as an instructor in Chinese culinary arts as a result of the impact that *Florence Lin's Regional Cooking of China* had made. Meanwhile Hawthorn Publishing signed a contract with me to write three more books, which were published between 1976 and 1979. I wanted to have a break after five titles, but one of my students was married to an editor in the William Morrow Publishing Co. This publishing company wanted me to help publish recipe books. Hence I did more experiments and composed *Florence Lin's Complete Book of Chinese Noodles, Dumplings and Breads*. It was the most difficult thing I had ever attempted in my life, as their editor disliked my writing and insisted on having it re-written. They remained fussy even after I spent US $8,000 on a re-write. Nonetheless, this title became highly successful; even the re-prints soon sold out. Today, a copy of it would cost a couple hundreds of dollars on Amazon.com if available. Many Chinese restaurants approached me for consultation, but I never wanted to have my own restaurant business. I once said, "I would be in financial trouble if you ever found me running a Chinese restaurant." I was lucky not to have such a chance.

People asked whether I had many famous chefs as students. Some of them, like Julia Child, had indeed participated in my class and I befriended many of them. However my class was never for famous chefs. Famous chefs studied in restaurants and thus mastered their way of cooking, something that we were unable to learn at home or school. Nevertheless, people could always find good dishes when they went to restaurants with me. Many chefs were my friends and were willing to tell me the secrets of their cooking. While we might have different approaches to creating a flavor, there was still much insider's information to discuss and debate. Why were these chefs so nice to me? When I taught cooking, my students always held graduation parties and invited families and friends as guests, and would book more than a dozen tables at these restaurants. I would sometimes recommend specific restaurants, which these students would also frequent in later years. There was much mutual dependence between restaurants and people like me, as their chefs and I were willing to help each other.

People also asked where I learned my cooking skills. My father had a chef in Hankou when I was little, but I always sat ate at the table with my father, without even once stepping into the kitchen. After that, what was available in the countryside? We would be lucky to have a chance to buy some meat from the nearby town. My subsequent days of serving as a soldier in the army involve no kooking. In short, I acquired my culinary skills not from study and practice but from eating. To be able to create good dishes, it is important to have seen and tasted the good stuff so you get to know the flavor. Once you know the flavor, you only need to work out how to create it. My hard work in this field received much affirmation and encouragement. For example, in 1992 I became a Lifetime Honorary Member of the New York Association of Cooking Teachers. In 1995 I was awarded a Lifetime Achievement Award by the Asian Culinary Arts Institutes Ltd. as an affirmation of my protection, comprehension and appreciation of culinary arts around the Asia-Pacific Region. Even better, in 2013, more than 20 years after my retirement at the age of 93, I was awarded a Milestone Award by the International Association of Culinary Professionals, which recognized those professionals who had permanently and widely influenced the development of America's culinary arts. Thanks to my daughter and the luxurious limousine she hired, I went in style to San Francisco to receive this award.

Florence Lin attending award ceremony in San Francisco
with daughter and son-in-law 2013

Setting Up the Women's Association of the China Institute

Apart from teaching cooking, I also helped to set up a Women's Association at the China Institute and later served as its president. Initially, the China Institute was funded with Boxer Rebellion indemnity money, a payment from China that was used to promote Chinese education and culture in the United States. Later, as the money ran out, one of the important responsibilities shouldered by the Institute's second chairman, Chih Meng, was to raise additional funds. The organization was situated in a four-story stone building on 65th Street on New York's East Side. The building was donated by Henry Luce, former president of Time, Inc. Born in China, Luce's father was a missionary who spent much time promoting Christianity in Shandong

Province and had much respect for Chinese history and culture. Operating such a large organization required a lot of money, so where could Meng raise his funds? Aware that many senior American men and women living in New York's Park Avenue were interested in China and willing to spend money on everything Chinese, Meng knew there were opportunities to be cultivated. He asked them for donations, and one time took me along on his visit to an enormously rich family there. Rich Americans were truly rich and were untroubled about the small amount of money we requested. Nevertheless, we still needed to raise our own funds.

In 1965, Meng came to me to propose establishing a Chinese women's association in the United States similar to the one in China during the War of Resistance against Japan. He asked me to organize it. I invited a group of influential figures, including Grace Chu (wife of General Si-ming Chu) and Cui-feng Liao (wife of Mr. Yu-tang Lin) and others, for lunch. All of them supported the idea, so a Women's Association of the China Institute was established.

The most important event in that first year was the Chinese New Year celebration, which was held in a restaurant with a plethora of joyful and auspicious decorations. Everybody put on traditional Chinese clothing and enjoyed many interesting performances, such as how a Chinese bride and groom in the olden days were dressed and presented at the wedding ceremony with a piece of red silk connecting them. The children also wore traditional Chinese gowns. Our American guests found this lovely and were willingly to participate in our celebrations and give donations. Apart from the Chinese New Year, we also organized similar celebrations for the Mid-Autumn Festival and other traditional Chinese festivities. Later, we organized bazaars for many, many years, raising funds by selling all sorts of things people donated. Everybody had fun helping to present these items. Even better, we raised a considerable amount of money every year and would donate it to whatever important causes that were in need of financial support. Indeed, as a fun-loving yet well-operated unit, our Women's Association raised a lot of money for the China Institute.

Retirement in Rossmoor

By 1995 with my daughters married, I was living in New York on my own. One day I received a phone call from my friend Theresa Chow (see the chapter on Horace Chow) in California who suggested a suitable house for me in Rossmoor, where she lived. My daughters thought it worth a look, and I happened to have a plane ticket to the West Coast, so I flew to California from New York the following day. Upon arrival I found the community lovely with a nice natural environment and many good old friends living there. So I bought the apartment the next day. Now we have four female residents at Rossmoor who served as president of the Women's Association of the China Institute, including Theresa Chow (see the chapter on Horace Chow), Patsy Peng (see the chapter on Petsy P.H. Peng), Alian Ong and me. Lily Chang, also living in Rossmoor, served as the China Institute's deputy head.

Since my relocation to Rossmoor, I have spent 20 wonderful years with my friends playing ping-pong and mahjong, attending theatrical performances or simply gathering together for fun. Interestingly, I also met Wan-qing Chiang (now called Linna Wu) here, who came to America on the same ship as me. In 1997, while preparing to mark the 50th anniversary of our arrival in the United States, we discovered three more residents in our community who had come to this country on that particular ship. The five of us celebrated the event at my place and had a great deal of fun. Later, the event was featured by our community newspaper and attracted further attention from people who arrived in America on that ship the same day. Even more of a coincidence, this land, where Rossmoor as a community was established, was perchased from the proprietor of Dollar Ocean Liners that owned the ship that ferried us to America. You can't find happenstance like this even in novels.

I have been lucky all my life, having encountered many good opportunities and making the correct decisions about them at numerous crucial moments. You can say it is good timing, or traditionally, we called it fate. As an old Chinese saying proclaims, "Heroes emerge in troubled times." I took the opportunity to run away during Japan's invasion of China and ran all the way to America. Had I stayed in China, I would not have had a chance to teach cooking. My daughters and their children were born and raised in the United States with a love for Chinese food. My oldest daughter and her husband worked in the food industry as well. They specialized in food packing to be specific, and are now retired. My second daughter is a veterinarian. While her husband loves my spring rolls, their daughter, my granddaughter, has even learned from me how to make *zongzi*, a traditional Chinese food made of glutinous rice stuffed with different fillings and wrapped in bamboo leaves.

Florence Lin teaching her granddaughter how to make *zongzi*, 2009

At Rossmoor I was always independent, driving myself around the community and helping to cook vegetarian dishes at a nearby Buddhist temple on a weekly basis. Whenever my friends became sick, I would cook and deliver various dishes to revive their appetites.

However, concerned that I was living alone in my 90s, my daughters urged me to move closer to my second daughter's place in New York. Considering the fact that I could go and make new friends as a healthy person instead of becoming sick and being carried there, I eventually agreed to the move.

People at Rossmoor held a huge farewell party for me. My friends and I performed various comedies on the stage. A couple of my fellow countrymen from Ningbo also told some jokes, but apart from ourselves, I don't think anybody else understood what was so funny about those anecdotes. My neighbor, contemporary dancer Yen-Lu Wang, dedicated a dance she choreographed herself. She invited more than 20 friends to perform the dance at my place and asked my young friend Zong-Yi Li to sing the renowned Chinese folk song *How Can I Not Miss Him?* by Yuan-ren Zhou as background music. Using my recipes, Zong-Yi made delicious snacks for everybody to enjoy and referred to them as her "homework" for me.

Florence Lin and the author Zong-Yi Li, September 2013

In the fall of 2013, I moved from California to a senior-citizens' apartment complex in Syracuse in Upstate New York to be close to my daughter. You might recall it was Syracuse University that I went to when I first arrived in America with a student visa. What a big circle I had gone through, and now I was back to the starting point of my life in the United States. The first person I met here was a chef with pretty good skills. These days I have my own kitchen but would only cook for fun when my granddaughter and other relatives visited. In our apartment complex, we have many professors from Syracuse University and nearby Cornell University. There are two or three Chinese people in their 80s as well, but I don't associate with them much because they always ask me the same questions and talk so slowly that I can't stand it. Apart from attending various seminars and other activities here, as well as going swimming and playing sports, I practice my calligraphy on a small desk on my own with the brushes, ink and papers all set up. I still write in the style of Gong-quan Liu, a famous Chinese scholar from the Tang Dynasty, which I had practiced much in the past. I also take walks outside when the weather is good. With my legs still relatively strong, I walk fast and powerfully like a soldier doing military exercises, unlike the people in Shanghai who take their time.

Ellie Mao Mok 茅愛立
At her residence in Rossmoor, September 2014

Ellie Mao Mok and my mother, Ping Wang, were classmates 阿± Yenching University in 1938. We often visited her after we moved to Rossmoor. I call her "Aunty Mao". The first time we met, I was impressed by her vitality and the force in her voice, an individual in her 90s who was much more confident and dominant than most people her age. As we conversed, she suddenly pointed out that my husband spoke from a shallow spot in his chest instead of utilizing the strength in his abdomen. This is the observation of an expert, a professional singer. Now 95 Aunty Mao still manages her own life, driving to visit her doctors and friends and shopping at the supermarket. Continuing a tradition of 70 years plus, she still instructs singing with ten regular students. I am lucky to be one of them, learning much while helping her to summarize the essentials in vocalization for professional singers. She has shared with me many stories of perseverance. Her motto: "Pursue your dreams. Whatever it is, either you choose not to do it or you persevere until it is done." It is this disposition of never giving up, of offering either all or nothing that has helped her establish and maintain her lifelong career.

Biography

Ellie Mao Mok, whose Chinese name is Ai-li Mao, was born in 1920. Her ancestral home is Licheng, Shandong Province. In 1938 she entered Yenching University's Department of Music, embarking on her journey in this field. After the outbreak of the Pacific War, she arrived in Shanghai in 1941, received a Diploma in Education from St. John's University, fled the turmoils of war, and experienced a wide range of difficulties on her way to Chongqing, Sichuan Province. She went to the United States for further studies in 1947, arriving from such renowned Chinese institutions as Yenching University and the Shanghai National Conservatory of Music (today's Shanghai Conservatory of Music) to enroll in the most prestigious music academy in America. She also studied music in Vienna in 1954, and, after much hard work and perseverance, became a famous soprano with solo performances across Europe, Asia and the United States. Apart from teaching vocal music and Chinese at the university level, she played a major role in introducing Western-style vocal music education in China. She settled in Rossmoor, Walnut Creek in San Francisco's East Bay in 1995, and continue to work in vocal music education and the organization of musical activities for the local community.

Singing is a Major Theme of My Life

My ancestral home is Licheng, Shandong Province. My father Zhen-dai Mao was born in 1888. With both parents dead, he grew up with his grandfather, a high-ranking government official in Chengdu, Sichuan Province. My mother Jun-ling Xiao was from Tianjin, Hebei Province, and the younger sister of one of my father's classmates. I was born in Tianjin in 1920 but moved to Beijing when I was three months old. Having studied the German language, my father loved the name Elli from a German novel so much that he nicknamed me Ai-li. After my graduation from primary school in Beijing, our family relocated to Qingdao, Shandong Province, because my father was transferred from the Ministry of Transportation of the Beiyang Government (author's note: the government of the Republic of China from 1912 to 1928) to the Jinan Railway Bureau. The Bureau supervised the railway between Qingdao on the east coast of Shandong and Jinan, the provincial capital.

After graduating from the Qingdao Municipal Girls' High School, I passed the entrance examination and entered Yenching University's Department of Music, embarking on a lifelong journey in this field. I have two younger sisters, Yi and Hao, and a younger brother, Yuan. The formal name my family gave me as a high school student was Yun, but I never felt like a Yun Mao. I preferred Ai-Li Mao instead, as the three Chinese characters seemed to contain a certain sense of music.

An Initiation to Music

I was born with a love to perform. My music initiation began with Peking Opera. One of my father's uncles from Sichuan Province was Yan-heng Chen whom we referred to as Grandfather Chen. Every year he came to Beijing to spend spring and summer with us staying in the South Wing which was relatively isolated from us in the North

Wing. There was a door separating the two buildings. Chen was a highly regarded musician in Peking Opera, often respectfully called "a divine Huqin player". He was also a scholar and reformer of Peking Opera. As a result, whenever he came to stay with us in Beijing, our South Wing would be crowded with opera singers in the evenings. These included such major stars as Lan-fang Mei, Xiao-yun Shang, Ju-peng Yan and Shu-yan Yu, as well as renowned Huqin (Jinghu) player Lan-yuan Xu and a series of drummers. While these opera singers proudly displayed their talents, various musicians would also take turns to show off their skills. I was so proud of having these people as our guests that I insisted on sitting next to my father to enjoy their performances. I would try to sing along with them while imagining myself as part of the future world of Peking Opera. That was a great feeling and could be considered as my earliest musical education.

Ellie Mao Mok with her younger sisters and brother, 1933
(from left) Yuan, Hao, Yi and Ellie

When I was six years old, my family took me to Tianqiao, the famous market district in Beijing that was popular among the people with its diverse range of street performers and bustling musicians. Once there, I immediately saw a girl singing the traditional "drum song", a form of story-telling accompanied by rhythmic drum beating that was unique in Northern China. She was a bit older than me with bows at the end of her two long braids and a slightly transparent black silky jacket dotted with golden buttons over her summer gown. She was so beautiful and admirable in my eyes that I wanted to be like her and sing her songs. Once home, I insisted on having everything she had, forcing my father to buy a drum and my mother to produce clothing that was exactly the same as hers. Then I learned how to perform drum songs from a record, and gathered all our relatives and servants as my audience. I would beat the drum and tell my tales, fulfilling my desire to perform and enjoying it.

If I had been born into a family like my own today, my parents would have encouraged me as a child to study music and attend a music academy. However, when I was little, my family merely considered me to be a funny kid and ignored my musical talents. After the age of six, I attended a private Catholic school, the Bacon Elementary School, today's Fuyoujie Primary School in Beijing's Xicheng District. Situated at the northern end of Fuyou Street, it had annual fundraising events in the auditorium of Peking Union Medical College Hospital that was funded by America's Rockefeller Foundation and the like.

Having realized that I had a great voice, and could sing and dance, teachers often sent another classmate and me to fundraising events. We both wore tutus and danced, and I would sing children's songs composed by Jin-hui Li, including *The Butterfly Girl, The Grape Fairy, Qiu-Xiang the Poor Girl* and certainly the famous *Bright Moon Song*. At that time, Li's songs were extremely popular among adults and children alike. I wonder why people stopped singing them. Anyway, I spent a lot of time singing and dancing for our school, especially during the parent-teacher gathering at the end of each school year. I would be the proudest performer. I still recall how I played the role of the kid in the children's opera *The Sparrow and the Kid*. That was a lot of fun for me, as I always loved performing.

As a high school student in Qingdao, I stopped performing children songs. One of our teachers was Zi Gao, who had studied dancing in Russia. She taught us Russian folk dancing and would often ask another classmate and me to perform. Another teacher in music was Yun-jie Wong, who later established an orchestra for the Shanghai Film Studio and composed many songs for movies such as *Red Flag over Green Hill* (1951), *Gate Number Six* (1952), *Nurse's Diary* (1957) and *The Opium Wars* (1959). Teacher Wong's family owned pedicabs and hired them out to laborers eager to earn a living by ferrying people around. He despised his father for exploiting those tricycle pullers and was determined to rebel, insisting on learning music and studying piano when his father disallowed them.

Though he studied piano at the National Conservatory of Music in Shanghai (It was called the National Training School of Music then), he told his parents that he was studying painting. At that time there was a Russian bakery in Qingdao whose owner had a piano. Teacher Wong paid the baker to practice on that piano. As we lived nearby, he would come to our house and teach me to play piano too. One day he said, "I think you have a great voice. You should study vocal music at the university." While I didn't know what vocal music was, his words stayed in my mind. At school he would try to get me to perform in concerts. He loved Franz Schubert's *The Trout Quintet* and would insist I sing the song so that he could have fun playing the accompaniment. I ended up with absolutely no idea what I was singing, nor did I understand the German lyrics. I could only sing a song by ear with the melody played on the piano. In short, Teacher Wong was the only one in high school who pushed me towards singing. He even suggested to my father that I should study voice in the future, to which my father gave no reply.

As a matter of fact, my father enjoyed music too. He played the erhu (a 2-stringed bowed Chinese musical instrument) well, and studied violin from the renowned violinist Shu-zhen Tan in Qingdao for a couple of years. Sometimes he would play Schubert's *Serenade* at night after we had gone upstairs to bed. Whenever there was a modulation from one key to another, he would fail to find the correct tonic notes, which would annoy me so much that I couldn't sleep. This was likely to have resulted from the lack of chromatic scales on the erhu.

Yenching University

I graduated from high school in June of 1937 with every intention of following Teacher Wong's footsteps and sitting for the entrance examination for the Shanghai National Conservatory of Music. However, in July Japanese warplanes commenced their bombing of Shanghai and the renowned Great World amusement arcade. The entertainment complex was reduced to an enormous hole in the ground. After the National Conservatory of Music in Shanghai closed its doors, I lost contact with my family causing great concern for my parents. With luck I managed to find a boat to Qingdao.

In 1938 I took the entrance examination for Yenching University which consisted of the usual subjects and an IQ test with a series of odd questions. I was lucky to pass it. Established by John Leighton Stuart in 1919 with the motto "Freedom through Truth for Service", Yenching University had the most beautiful campus in the world. Its lake and pagoda remain beautiful today, but the campus was taken over by Peking University in 1952, with its "ambience" and "spirit" permanently altered. Back then, one-third of Yenching University's professors were Americans and many courses were taught in English. Teachers and students enjoyed equal status which generated much discussion in class. Students unable to pay the tuition found part-time work on campus. Both the character and atmosphere of Yenching University were similar to American liberal arts colleges. I spent three years and 100 days there, plus the summer of the last year for further studies. The relaxing, carefree student lifestyle was the happiest and most unforgettable period of my life.

My family did not try to stop me from studying music in Yenching University, not that I would have listened to them even if they had. The Department of Music was headed by Mr. Bliss Wiant, an American professor. Our motto was "Help students express themselves through music while leading them to help others in like manner."

Our first year focused on a series of interdisciplinary subjects in science and humanities, such as psychology and mental health. I formally started in the Department of Music in my second year with four or five other classmates. This was just the right number, as the university ruled that a department could not exist with less than five students. We all had some training in music and had to demonstrate our piano skills to the head of the department. We studied the fundamental subjects of Western-style musical education including music theory, harmony, counterpoint, ear training, music appreciation, chorus, conducting, vocal music and piano. Yenching University further promoted "using Western musical techniques to promote the beauty of traditional Chinese music".

Initially I wanted to study piano, but shifted my focus to singing after a teacher praised my voice. My first instructor in vocal music was Mrs. E.K. Smith, a graduate from Oberlin College in Ohio. It was said that she was once an excellent alto but lost her voice after the birth of her second daughter. I never heard her sing, not even to demonstrate. As I was new to singing, she carefully helped strengthen my voice through gentle vocal exercises and various simple songs. This had a profound impact on me and is a method that I still use to teach my own students today. Prior to that, I never realized I had a good voice that ranged almost three octaves from the F below Middle C to High C that is two octaves above the Middle C. She was really nice to me, showing me photographs of her past concerts and giving me ice cream as a treat after class. When she discovered later that I suffered from frequent bouts of flu and colds, she introduced me to Professor Yin-xiang Xu, a renowned otorhinolaryngologist at the Union Hospital, to have my tonsils removed. This reduced the number of flu and colds while enhancing my vocal tract resonance which considerably benefited my singing.

Ellie Mao Mok in singing practice at Yenching University, 1939

Every Christmas Yenching University's professors opened their homes to students. We hired a donkey cart to ferry an organ for Mr. Wiant to play, and walked to these professors' residences for carolling and treats of tea and snacks. Our last stop was the president's house. If Mr. Stuart was home, he provided us with excellent refreshments. We had a great time singing and eating.

The Christmas tradition at Yenching University was to perform George Frederic Handel's Messiah at the administration building on campus and the Beijing Hotel. All vocal music students were required to lead other departments in the choir. Mrs. Mildred Wiant sang solo with a voice so pure that it was akin to music from heaven. She presented superb techniques and perfect resonance in her performance.

Having heard her sing, I very much wanted to study with her, but I didn't want to offend Mrs. Smith who was really nice to me. One day, I summoned the courage to visit her and expressed my gratitude for her teaching the past two years. However, it was my sincere wish that she would allow me an opportunity to study under other teachers before graduation, as this would enable me to learn from their respective strengths. Having heard this, Mrs. Smith became very upset. She was mad at both me and Mrs. Wiant, who she thought was trying to steal her student. Even Mrs. Smith's daughter was on her side and drove me away.

When I explained this incident to Mrs. Wiant, she was surprised but told me not to worry. While we conversed, I decided to leave quietly by the back door after discovering through the window that Mrs Smith was coming to see Mrs. Wiant. Under these circumstances I could no longer study under Mrs. Smith. Although this issue caused a fair bit of unpleasantness between the two ladies, it gave me an opportunity to learn from Mrs. Wiant for more than a year. She helped stabilize my vocalization and gain better control of my voice. In order to study more from her, I didn't even return home that summer. I further befriended Xiang Shen, her student from the Department of English Literature who was two years younger than me. He took his required courses there and his electives in the Department of Music. Shen eventually became a famous tenor and educator of vocal music in China.

While in Yenching University, we had many opportunities to perform, including monthly concerts for students. I gained much experience in 1940, singing solo in a concert dedicated to Johannes Brahms and also serving as a soloist and lead singer in Joseph Haydn's *The Creation*. In 1941, after my third year at the university concluded, I also gave a concert at a Jewish hotel in Tianjin City with Xiang Shen, bass singer Nai-qun Qi and piano student Yuan-yuan Chi. Shen was rather naughty back then; though a good student in class, he imitated the styles of the world's famous tenors. Whenever we had a concert, Mrs. Wiant worried, wondering what kind of trick Shen would play this time.

One year during my studies at Yenching University, I decided to spend the winter holidays at home. One of my family's visitors was from Germany, a physician who also enjoyed singing baritone. We took turns singing accompanied by my younger brother Yuan, an excellent pianist who sight read straight from sheet music. The German doctor later suggested to my father that with my talent I should study music in Italy, but my father remained silent, sitting and smoking his cigarettes. I knew then that my father would never send me to Italy since he didn't have the money; but even if he had had the funds, he would never have allowed it. I realized that, if I wanted to study overseas, I had to rely on myself financially.

While I studied at Yenching University, Beijing was already occupied by Japanese troops who did not disturb the institution because it was sponsored by American churches. However, on December 8, 1941, in my last year as a university student, Pearl Harbor was attacked and the Americans declared war against Japan. At the outbreak of the Pacific War, Japanese troops immediately surrounded Yenching University. After entering the campus, they gathered us in the administration building and announced, "All of you must leave within 24 hours and never come back." That night we lit a fire in the courtyard of the girls' dormitories trying to burn everything written in English. We burned many English documents, photographs of our English teachers, and all our English certificates, identity papers, books and letters. We spent all night doing this without sleep. Otherwise, we would have been beaten up by Japanese soldiers at the city gate's checkpoint if they discovered our identities as students from Yenching University. Suddenly I recalled leaving a book of sheet music on a shelf in the piano room of the Department of Music. My friend Yuan-yuan Chi also forgot hers, something that neither of us wanted to leave behind. Having dashed back there, we found Japanese soldiers guarding the front door. We managed to get in through the back door and retrieved our books. It was lucky that no one caught us in the dark.

At that time I happened to have a fever and a sore throat, but there was no alternative.

The next day, we pushed two bicycles carrying all our belongings from Yenching University to the city gate. After the university closed its door I stayed with my uncle's family in Beijing. In order to purchase a train ticket home, I needed a citizen's ID (I had burned my student card) and would be qualified to apply for one after two weeks' stay in the city. To kill time, my friends and I often gathered at the home of a classmate, Le-shan Lu, to discuss our next step and the future. My decision was to return and find a teaching position in Qingdao.

Qingdao and Shanghai

As I sat at the back of a carriage on the train to Qingdao, many Japanese soldiers boarded our carriage at one stop. Two of them were so drunk that they immediately started harassing the girls sitting at the front. Seeing this, I dashed into the toilet and locked the door from the inside, and remained there until they finally left about half an hour later. How miserable it was to live in an occupied country and be enslaved by the invaders!

Upon my arrival in Qingdao, I was immediately engaged by the Sheng-Kung Girls' High School as a music teacher. As the American nuns who taught English and music at the school were imprisoned at Japanese-operated concentration camps after the attack on Pearl Harbor, I taught nine classes across the junior and senior sections, the equivalent of today's seventh to twelfth grades. Apart from teaching music theory and choir, I also had several piano students after school. One was a tall girl named Jin-wei Li, who later became a soprano and married Xiang Shen. Furthermore, as the school suffered from a lack of staff, I recommended several of my classmates from Yenching University to teach Chinese Literature and languages, including English. I enjoyed my job and the income was good.

However, after only one semester, Qingdao fell into the hands of Japanese soldiers. One day, when my cousin and I were on our way home from a movie, two Japanese soldiers chased us with their big guns and hard boots, saying, "Girls, girls, slow down, slow down." We ran as fast as we could, desperately trying to evade them. We arrived home and thumped on the door until my younger brother opened it. I yelled at him to bolt it after we entered and to remain quiet. The Japanese soldiers soon arrived, shouting and knocking on the door for more than twenty minutes before finally giving up. After that I said to my mother that I could no longer stay in Qingdao as incidents like this would keep happening. Initially reluctant to let me go, my mother gave her consent after realizing how difficult it was for young girls to remain safe. In the end, I decided to continue my studies in Shanghai.

After Yenching University closed its doors many of my classmates went to Shanghai. We stayed in the Shanghai International Settlement which was free from Japanese disturbance. The British, French and Americans established their enclaves when Shanghai was opened to foreign merchants under the terms of the Treaty of Nanjing after China lost the First Opium War (1839-1842). In 1942, I enrolled in Shanghai's St John's University to study education. Since I already had credits for subjects studied at Yenching University, such as psychology and the theory and practice of education, it took me only two years to receive a degree.

Meanwhile, I also studied under Vladimir Shushlin, a renowned bass singer from Russia who was then teaching at the National Conservatory of Music in Shanghai. Because he already had the required number of students, he announced no new students would be accepted. I then insisted he should listen to me sing an aria from the opera *Madame Butterfly*. After I finished singing, he went quiet for a while before telling me to enroll immediately and start free lessons at his studio. I was so excited.

The National Conservatory of Music accepted my credits from Yenching University which were sufficient for a degree. All I needed was to attend choir lesson every Thursday where I reunited with my university friend Xiang Shen. The two of us spent a lot of time together discussing breathing and vocalization and became really good friends. We even got quite a reputation performing the famous duet *Libiamo ne' lieti calici* from the opera *La Traviata* accompanied by the St John's University's student orchestra and were invited to many evening parties after that. I also became friends with other classmates, such as De-lun Li and Zhong-jie Han from the National Conservatory of Music. We often sang and played music for stage plays around the city. Shen later became a prestigious tenor and educator in vocal music with several of his students with various voices winning major awards in international competitions. Each time I returned to China from America, I brought many books, reference materials and records and discussed the latest methodologies in vocal music with him.

My other friend, Zi-ying Lu, a year younger than me, studied education at Yenching University. While studying together at St. John's University for a degree in education, her mother invited me to stay at their home in order to improve my living conditions. Their house was so big that I occupied the whole third floor and cycled to school with Lu every morning. We became very good friends.

The Shanghai Conservatory of Music originally was The National Training School of Music. It was renamed after being taken over by Jing-wei Wang's collaborationist regime. It became a puppet institution controlled by the Japanese. The school was then headed by Wei-ning Li, who insisted on having Xiang Shen and me perform a concert in Nanjing. As the concert marked the occasion in which money "donated" from people in Japanese-occupied regions was presented to Wang's regime to purchase warplanes and "save the nation", I refused to go. I also stopped attending school from that moment on. Li searched for me everywhere but could not find me.

One day I went to a concert at the Lyceum Theater and bumped into Li at the entrance after parking my bicycle. He grabbed me and said, "Ai-Li Mao, after all these wild goose chases, I've finally found you. Now you have to do me a favor and sing at this concert in Nanjing. *Miriam's Song of Triumph* in Schubert's *Song of the Sea* requires a range from G below Middle C all the way to High C. Only you are capable of this." I knew my own capabilities, but still refused to go. When he asked why, I said I refused to participate in such a blatant attempt to sell out our nation. I further said, "Let me tell you this, Mr. Li, don't you do it either, or your reputation will be forever tarnished." He responded, "Are you lecturing me! Fine, I have a brother working for the Ministry of Foreign Affairs in Chongqing. He can help me." I said, "Great, let's wait and see. Whatever you do or say, I definitely won't go." He was so angry that he retorted, "Then I'll expel you!" The next day the school put up a big poster to announce the expulsion of both Xiang Shen and me.

Interestingly, one day after my relocation to America, as I sat in the corner of a subway train in New York, a man boarded the train and stood in front of me. It turned out to be Wei-ning Li. I said, "Mr. Li, do you remember me, Ai-Li Mao, the student you expelled?" He couldn't even look at me, shying away and mumbling, "Why mention those old things now?" As soon as the train came to the next stop, he left. It was a typical case of enemies crossing each other's path.

Two days after Wei-ning Li expelled me, my friends and some former students of Yenching University helped me give concerts at two local theaters to raise money for my travel expenses. Then I left Shanghai for Chongqing.

108 Days of Fleeing from the War

On May 29, 1944, I left Japanese-occupied Shanghai with Zi-ying Lu and two male classmates from St. John's University. One of them was short and stout, so we called him Little Melon. The other was called Elephant because of his long nose. Initially we followed five or six traveling salesmen, but they, like us, had no idea how the war was going, where the Japanese were located, etc. With everything so confusing, we took a train from Shanghai to Hangzhou, Zhejiang Province, and visited the renowned West Lake as if we were ordinary tourists.

While admiring the famous tidal bore at the mouth of Qiantang River, we heard that on the other side of the river was Chinese-controlled territory, but the trick would be to cross a bridge guarded by the Japanese. It was said that Japanese soldiers would change shift about eight o'clock every evening. If we sneaked through after one group of soldiers left and before the next group arrived, then we would see Chinese soldiers soon. Having learned this trick, we waited at the riverbank in the evening and saw the Japanese soldiers marching off with their guns at eight o'clock. Then the locals signalled us to dash over the bridge. As time was tight it was highly dangerous. Once we crossed the bridge, we shook hands with the Chinese soldiers who met us. It was only then that we were able to relax. We were in Chinese-held land again.

As far as I can remember, one of the traveling salesmen led the way. We followed him along the narrow banks separating the rice fields, trying to find temporary shelter in local farm houses to spend the night. The banks were wet and slippery, particularly when it rained. The men ahead of us were always in a rush. Zi-ying and I were so slow that we couldn't catch up, often losing our footing, falling into the rice paddies and becoming covered in mud. There was nothing else we could do but to stand up and keep going. When we finally found shelter at a farmer's place, we washed and dried our clothes and squeezed onto their *kang* (earthen platform heated in winter by fires underneath and spread with mats for sleeping) for a rest. One day there was no shelter available, apart from a family who had recently lost a member. They told us to stay where the coffin was placed since that was the only spare room they had. At night there was no light, and as we laid there, our hair would stand on end whenever there was a tiny sound. That was a horrible night.

With no previous experience in fleeing from the turmoil of war, we carried a fair bit of luggage. One day, as we walked on a steep path along a river, the wheelbarrow pusher we hired lost his balance and both of them went into the water. He managed to rescue himself and our luggage, but everything was wet, including our clothing. After we reached Shangrao, Jiangxi Province, the salesmen departed leaving the four of us alone. A common way of traveling back then was to hitch a ride with a "yellow fish" truck, but, in our case, it was difficult to find a truck going the same direction and with enough room for all of us. Having nowhere to go, we remained in Shangrao and tried to dry our clothing, but many of the items were so moldy that they had to be discarded. It was so stupid for us to bring so many things. Anyway, with very little money left we stayed at a so-called inn.

Our biggest problem was going to the toilet since it was just a bucket in a corner of our room. Even with a lid, it smelled terribly as no one bothered to remove the overflowing contents. Consequently, we went to the riverbank at night where we weren't alone. People simply squatted to do their "business" while chatting. At that moment I realized our life had become the same as people living in the countryside. That is, the people squatted to do their "business" at night and washed their clothes during the day in the same river. You can imagine how clean those clothes would be!

While in Shangrao we met a couple from Suzhou, Jiangsu Province. We found the man rather talkative and funny because he mentioned many of his own love stories to us. One day on our way to buy eggs as part of our routine to cook for ourselves, we realized the man was an expert bargainer. However, when we returned to the inn with ten eggs each purchased at a fairly cheap price, he came to show us the many eggs that he had stolen from the seller by sneaking them into his sleeves and pockets. We knew he had done the wrong thing, but we also considered him to be capable, witty and amusing. Now, guess what? He left with his wife ahead of us. Several days later, when we were ready to leave, Zi-ying and I realized that he had stolen all our valuables. That's the kind of person he was, a thief. We had no idea who he was. We couldn't even track him down since we didn't have his address. It was our bad luck. We were so naive back then that we were easily cheated.

One day we had to flee because the Japanese troops were only ten kilometers away from Shangrao. The locals had run away at night, carrying their luggage of all shapes and sizes and their children in baskets. Luckily for Zi-ying and me, Elephant had found a tiny flat-bottomed wooden boat that was used to ferry rough straw paper. While it was rather soft and warm as we lay there, the boat moved so slowly that it took three days for us to cross a distance of little more than ten kilometers. After we heard rumors that Japanese warplanes would bombard the area, we kept the boat close to the riverbank in order to climb out and hide under a tree in the event of a bombing. And they did come, we were so scared we couldn't breathe. Though the bullets from the warplanes hit the ground around us, it was only pure luck that none of us were hit. After they left, we rushed forward in our little boat, only to take refuge elsewhere as the Japanese troops approached. As a result, Zi-ying and I starved for three whole days.

Following our boat, Little Melon and Elephant walked on the riverbank but somehow the former got separated. Little Melon ended up spending one night alone at a local temple. He burst into tears as soon as we were reunited, perhaps because he felt reliefed. Indeed, he was so thin and haggard that he looked like a ghost himself. Those days were truly tough, but we comforted ourselves with the thought that one day, should we look back at this period of our lives as old men and women, we would surely consider everything to be funny and unique.

It was this thought that kept our spirits up.

Finally, we reached Ganzhou, Jiangxi Province, and found a sizeable inn called *De Chang* – virtue and prosperity - a good omen, perhaps? By then Zi-ying and I had used up all our money except for forty cents among the four of us. While we were enjoying our "spiritual meal", imagining ourselves sharing such wonderful dishes as sweet and sour fish, barbeque pork, roast chicken and beef, etc., one of the patrons at the inn came to ask whether we would like to have some of the extra rice that he had cooked. We were so happy. We spent all forty cents for peanuts and side dishes; that was one of the best meals we had ever tasted in our lives. We thought about pawning our clothes and watches when things became desperate. However, there was no pawn shop in Ganzhou under the policies of the "New Life Movement" that was administered by Ching-kuo Chiang, then local governor and the oldest son of Kai-shek Chiang. Luckily, Little Melon remembered a secret compartment under his trunk that contained several piece of gold foil. He kindly lent them to us with the promise of future reimbursement, so we managed to exchange them for some money.

The scenery was good all along our "yellow fish" ride, especially in Qujiang, Guangdong Province, where the rivers were absolutely amazing. From there to Yangshuo, Guangxi Province, was a series of winding mountain roads, with steep cliffs on one side and a deep, sharp gorge on the other that was gouged out by rapid river currents. As our truck was pretty old, at any moment the driver could lose control, tumbling all of us into the river below. It was very dangerous. Still, we were so naive then that everything was fine, including watching the scenery even though we were starving. Upon our arrival in Yangshuo, we greedily fed our eyes with the fascinating landscape. A famous Chinese saying quips, "The scenery in Guilin is the best in the world, but that in Yangshuo is even more fantastic." We could only compare the two after reaching Guilin.

When we reached Guilin we were truly penniless. Hungry, tired and dirty, we were just like homeless people on the street. Seeing the Chinese Travel Agency and its attached hotel in the city, Little Melon suggested approaching the manager, as there was a good chance he would know Little Melon's brother, who was in charge of a branch of the agency in the other town. Because all four of us were as filthy and shabby as beggars, the guard at the hotel entrance refused to talk to us. Somehow we persuaded him to contact the hotel manager, Mr. Xiang-sun Wu, who immediately agreed to take us in. He even arranged a suite for us which included two bedrooms, a living room, and a bathroom with a shower. We were so excited that we immediately took turns to wash. After that, we dressed to the best of our abilities, as Mr. Sun had invited us for dinner. Both Zi-ying and I looked rather pretty in our dresses, and Little Melon and Elephant even put on their suits and ties. The guy at the hotel entrance must have found it strange that we looked so different in a matter of minutes.

At dinner Mr. Wu lent us money with our promise that we would repay him later. He also suggested we stay in his hotel and tour Guilin while waiting for our relatives in Chongqing to send money for us to travel there. So, while waiting for the money, we visited various renowned scenic spots in Guilin, including the Great Karst Cave, the Seven Star Crag and the Reed Flute Cave while sampling a series of delicious local snacks. The scenery in Guilin was indeed fascinating, but I felt that Yangshuo's was better. When money arrived from Chongqing, we repaid Mr. Wu and thanked him profusely for his generosity. We were truly lucky to have met him. Later we became close friends with Mrs. Wu, his wife and daughter.

We took a train from Guilin to Guizhou Province. It had two engines, one to push from the back and the other to pull from the front. The train went through various tunnels that were dug in sulphurous rock cavities. The air smelled so bad that I never ever wanted to go there again. Imagine what would happen if the train were to break down inside the tunnel! A popular Chinese maxim describes Guizhou as a place where "there are never three sunny days in a row or three square inch of level ground, nor do the people even have three cents in their pockets."

It was raining hard on the day we arrived, but we were lucky to find a social service centre that was perhaps sponsored by the government. It was a huge room containing rows and rows of clean beds with mosquito nets. Men and women slept on these beds, too exhausted to care much about gender differences. It was also the first proper bed I had slept on since leaving Shanghai, apart from Guilin of course.

Speaking about a proper bed, I recall that we arrived at a local school in Jiangxi Province where we were allowed to sleep in a classroom on students' desks with straw as our bedding. The students had yet to return to school for the new semester. The desks were very clean but the straw was full of fleas. As a result my body was covered with flea bites that I kept scratching until they became infected. The staff told me to drink the so-called "snake wine" after reaching Qujiang, Guangdong Province. The wine with a snake preserved in it looked terrifying, but only a small cup of it was enough to take care of my infection then and other sores and pains later.

From Guiyang, capital of Guizhou Province, we hitched a ride on a truck to Chongqing, the very last stop before our journey ended. The driver, originally from Guangdong Province, told me to sit at the front between him and his young assistant, while Zi-ying, Little Melon and Elephant sat in the back with our luggage and the cargo (empty oil drums). Halfway through one of the narrow, dangerous winding mountain roads, the old and rusty truck with no cover over the back broke down. The driver announced he would hitch a ride to the next town for help to fix the truck, leaving his assistant to watch over us and the cargo. Suddenly, something went terribly wrong with Zi-ying; a high fever took hold of her and turned her blind. While Elephant took her and hitched a ride to find a hospital in the next town, Little Melon stayed alone in the back of the truck. Before long he too decided to leave. Consequently, only the driver's assistant and I remained in the truck.

That assistant was only a boy in his late teens. As evening arrived, he said, "Miss Mao, let me tell you something; We would be in danger if the weather remained dry, because wolves could come to eat us." I was so scared that I prayed it would rain, and it did, buckets of rain not just outside the truck but also through the leaky roof. Eventually, having discovered the truck carried piles of old newspaper besides the empty oil drums, we spent the night trying to keep ourselves dry by blocking the leaks here and there with page after page of paper. When it was finally dawn, Elephant returned with the news that Zi-ying had malaria but was feeling much better. He was willing to stay with the truck and our luggage, so I hitched a ride to the next town to be with Zi-ying and little melon. Elephant arrived in the truck that evening, so the four of us were together again after a whole day of trouble. Luckily, from then on we traveled safely to Chongqing with no more glitches.

From Shanghai to Hangzhou, Zhejiang Province, then through Jiangxi, Guangdong, Guangxi and Guizhou Provinces before finally reaching Chongqing, Sichuan Province, we had spent 108 days walking and struggling in and out of a series of boats, trains and "yellow fish" trucks. Since we were in our early 20s, not much bothered us throughout the journey, making it a once-in-a-lifetime experience.

Music and Songs in Chongqing

Having parted ways with Little Melon and Elephant in Chongqing, Zi-ying lent me some of the money her family sent her. The two of us stayed in a shabby inn where we heard heavy footsteps at night. After turning the light on, we discovered that the sounds were made by several giant rats. The next day we tried our best to seek classmates and friends who might be able to help us. One was Ying Xu, president of the Yenching University Alumni Association, who was full of energy and passion. We called her "Big Sister". She proposed that the alumni association set up a concert to raise funds for me. I needed to practice singing and required a piano accompaniment.

One day Big Sister took me to a social gathering where I met a Sichuanese-lady, Ms. Ruo-hua Zhu from the Ministry of Foreign Affairs, who informed me that only seven pianos existed in the whole of Chongqing. While I already knew this, she mentioned one of those pianos was located in their ministry and asked me to contact a man called De-chang Mok who held the key to that instrument. Now, do you remember the De Chang Inn in Ganzhou, Jiangxi Province, that I mentioned earlier? I imagined this De-chang Mok (whose first name in English was Robert) to be an old man, but he turned out to be around my age and highly interested in music. Knowing that I was from Shanghai, he immediately asked many questions, whether I knew this or that person and what I thought about this violinist or that pianist. A typical music fanatic, I thought, but I tried to tell him everything I knew because I needed a piano. He then insisted that I should sing at an evening concert to be held by the Ministry of Foreign Affairs to which I agreed for the sake of the piano. He even asked me to sing the famous art song *Three Wishes of the Rose* by Chinese composer Zi Huang so that he could personally accompany me with his violin. I was fine with every one of his requests. Furthermore, he found a colleague called Wei-e Li to play the piano accompaniment. This is how I met and befriended Mok and Li.

At that time Zi-ying and I stayed with my sister Yi, who was working for the Nationalist Government's Resources Committee. We occupied a room upstairs and would often share our meals with other classmates from Yenching University, including Liang-yi Zhu and Xiu-yuan Shan who lived downstairs. Wei-e Li visited me often, always mentioning his brother Wei-guo Li, who appeared to be a high-ranking official at the Ministry of Foreign Affairs. He had another brother, Wei-ning Li, the man I mentioned earlier who expelled me from the Shanghai Conservatory of Music, a puppet institution controlled by the Japanese. It was Wei-e Li's business to be proud of his brother, but his frequent mumbling of "my brother" this and "my brother" that nearly drove me crazy.

Meanwhile, Robert Mok also visited me frequently, offering his assistance for all sorts of things, from organizing a band to accompany my singing to selling tickets for my concerts. We shared the same interests and had much to talk about, so that became the beginning of our romantic relationship. After two concerts in Chongqing, I was appointed professor of vocal music at the National Music Academy (today's Central Conservatory of Music) in Qingmuguan, a suburb of Chongqing. I gave two lectures each week in exchange for a monthly salary of one *dan* of rice, approximately 50 kilograms, which was rather considerable then. I went to Qingmuguan on Thursdays and stayed overnight in a room called "Mao Yue-li" at the Academy. The floor planks at one end of that room would lift upward if two or more people stood at the other end.

With Yenching University operating again in Chengdu, Sichuan Province, the alumni association arranged a concert for me in the Rong Guang Theater in the summer of 1945 which was attended by many teachers and former students. A meeting was further held after the concert by university officials, with the conclusion that I deserved to receive a certificate of graduation. They agreed because I had already studied for and received more credits than those required for a degree; plus I sang in concerts held in Beijing, Tianjin, Qingdao, Chongqing and now Chengdu. Consequently, a diploma was sent to me in Chongqing from Yenching University's Department of Music, despite the fact that I never asked for it. Still, I was very excited, as I now had two bachelor's degrees, one in music from Yenching University and the other in education from St. John's University.

After Chengdu I was invited to perform in another concert in

Kunming, Yunnan Province. While our alumni association in that city had managed to sell all the tickets, I arrived in August 1945, to the news that Japan had surrendered unconditionally. With the war now coming to an end, many of the ticket holders were eager to return to Beijing and Shanghai. Others, as traders of gold, U.S. dollars and stock shares throughout the war, now lost much money. While a few of them committed suicide, the rest had lost interest in such entertainment as a concert. Consequently my concert in the Nan Ping Theatre was warmly received by only a small audience, despite the fact that it was sponsored by the wife of Long Yun, governor of Yunnan Province.

I have been financially independent since my days as a student in Yenching University in Beijing. Since I had given concerts in Tianjin and Beijing, a relatively rare kind of event back then, people considered me a great performer and paid a lot of money see me sing. While my father didn't support my career in vocal music, he thought I was successful and took pride in all the concerts I had given. In spite of this, my father never praised me. An introvert with few words or facial expressions, he withheld his emotions all his life. Nonetheless, I was able to raise enough money through concerts to study in the United States and to cover my own travel expenses, tuition fees and living allowance. You could say I am a self-made person who worked long and hard to achieve my goals.

Career and Family in America

By then Robert Mok had been working as a secretary at the Department of East Asian Affairs in the Ministry of Foreign Affairs. A position had become available as a cultural attaché in the Chinese Embassy in Argentina, but there was also news that the Secretariat of the United Nations (UN) Preparatory Committee was to appoint Chinese translators through an examination. This committee was set up in London after the Second World War as various Western powers proceeded to establish the UN. In addition to English, French, Russian, Arabic and Spanish, Chinese would be an official language used by the international organization when China became one of the Allied Nations and hence a permanent member of the Security Council. Because Robert was uncertain whether he should sit for the UN examination or pursue the position in South America, I encouraged him to choose the former as there would surely be other opportunities in the future to work overseas.

Meanwhile, we became engaged on my birthday in 1945 to culminate our long-term relationship. Thanks to Robert's capacity to translate from either English or French to Chinese, he passed the UN examination and went to London via India and Egypt at the end of 1945 before arriving in New York with the Preparatory Committee. For the next 34 years he worked for the UN Secretariat until his retirement in June 1980. Anyway, after he left Chongqing, I concentrated my efforts on applying to American schools and was admitted to both the Juilliard School of Music in New York and the Oberlin Conservatory in Ohio; the latter was even willing to provide a scholarship.

Ellie Mao Mok's concert at the Shanghai Municipal Council prior to leaving for America, 1946

Before leaving for the United States in 1947, I was able to give concerts in Beijing and Tianjin with the help of Yenching University's alumni associations. In Shanghai, thanks to the support of former students from both Yenching University and St John's University, I performed in concerts at the Shanghai Municipal Council as well as the Lan Xin and Da Hua Theatres. As a result, I raised enough money to cover my passage on a ship to America plus living expenses there for a whole year.

Before I purchased my ticket, Robert informed me in a letter that, according to the UN's regulations, I could have a first-class ticket on a ship as a UN employee's fiancée if I agreed to marry him within the following six months. I responded that I was willing to marry him in the United States, but I refused to tell people that I would be married in six months' time. I loved my freedom too much to be restrained in this way, preferring to purchase my own ticket for a third-class cabin. After all I could well afford such a ticket, which cost about US $150 at the time. However due to a dockers' strike, it took several months for a ship to become available. On January 2, 1947, my sister Hao and I finally boarded the SS General M.C. Meigs (owned by Dollar Oceanliners) and embarked on our 18-day journey to America.

Because Robert worked and lived in New York, he was keen for me to enter the Juilliard School of Music. However, I chose the Oberlin Conservatory because of their willingness to give me a scholarship and commenced my studies there in February 1947. While the winter in Ohio was unbearable, what truly bothered me was the instructor in vocal music, a recent alto graduate with neither experience nor desire to teach. As all she wanted was to advance her own career, there was no need for me to waste my time with her. In sharp contrast, I learned a lot from a Professor Hall whose subject was about the appreciation and analysis of opera as an art form, including famous pieces by Italian and German composers such as Wilhelm Richard Wagner. Still, with the arrival of summer, I transferred to the Juilliard School of Music in New

York. It's not that one institution had a better reputation than the other. Instead, the key issue was and had always been to improve my singing techniques under the guidance of a good teacher. Whatever fame they possessed, no academic institution could keep me as a student if they didn't have capable teachers.

My instructor at Juilliard was a former piano accompanist who had assisted a famous singer in student supervision. With neither singing lessons nor actual experience in teaching vocal music, she never demonstrated how to sing. When I expressed a desire to change instructors, I was warned about the impact this might have on my examination because it would be judged by all the teachers. Besides, my options were limited as all the teachers there had their own issues. One instructor was said to have such a bad temper that he would smash books on students' heads while another, a tenor, might not have the necessary knowledge and skills to teach female vocalists.

At the end of 1948, I stopped going to the Juilliard School of Music and transferred to Columbia University's Teachers College which allowed students to take core subjects outside the university and recognized all resulting credits. More importantly, I felt that in teaching vocal music a Master's degree in music education might be far more useful than one from Juilliard. Later someone introduced me to an excellent instructor named Emma Zador from outside the university. A strict and patient teacher, she corrected many of my problems in singing techniques and helped to establish the foundation of my vocal music. I admired her so much that I studied under her guidance for the following 20 years until she passed away.

When my money was nearly used up, I found a part-time job at the United Board of Christian College, the sponsor of both Yenching University and St. John's University, where I learned to type. While going to school in the morning and working in the afternoon, I attended all kinds of concerts with Robert in the evening to learn from famous singers and musicians. On June 5, 1948, we married at the Riverside

Church near Columbia University.

A musical couple: Ellie Mao and Robert Mok, 1948

In the summer of 1949, I received my Master's degree in music education from Columbia University. I remember the graduation ceremony was held in an open space with a temporary podium. More than a thousand students sat in a large tent with the tassels of our caps on the right side. The moment we moved our tassels to the left signified the recognition of earning degrees. It was a lot of fun.

After that I returned to the Juilliard School of Music to tackle subjects I needed, focusing specifically on repertoire. They had a famous teacher, Sergius Kagen, who was such a heavy smoker that his students kept all the windows opened during class. The teaching and learning environment were unbearably noisy due to underground trains emerging onto the street. Kagen specialized in interpreting German and French songs, and would often curse at those not up to his standards. However, I participated in the master class with more than 40 other students where everyone competed to sing for and be cursed at by him.

Eventually I had a chance to sing three of Schubert's songs in his presence accompanied by Anna Mi Lee. He said, "Miss Mao, your pronunciation of the German language is not often accurate. It's like swatting flies – sometimes you get them and at other times you don't." He proceeded to criticize Anna's piano accompaniment and scared the hell out of her. Still, while his words might be unpleasant, I found there was much truth in them. After that masterclass, I asked Anna whether she would like to take private lessons from Kagen; both of us ended up paying for another semester of studies at his studio where he cursed less often. Anyway, in art songs, especially those from 19th-century Germany, singing and accompaniment enjoy equal status and complement each other. I continued to work with Anna, a fast sight reader, for the following 40 years or so until my retirement at the age of 70.

Ellie Mao Mok (right) and Anna Mi Lee (left)
taking a break after a performance at the China Institute 1953

Having concluded my studies under Kagen, I gave my first solo concert in America in New York City Hall in the spring of 1954. Herold Schönberg, a famous critic, gave me a thumbs-up, praising my clear pronunciation, especially in Italian. However, he further pointed out I needed to improve my German songs. Adding his review to the aforementioned comment from Sergius Kagen that my singing ability in German was like swatting flies, I was determined to improve my pronunciation in this regard. I told Robert that I had to go to Vienna, as it was the birthplace of so many German composers, from Franz Schubert and Robert Schumann to Johannes Brahms, Johann Strauss Jr. and Gustav Mahler, whose works are among the world's most important art songs. Only after I had mastered the German language would I be able to precisely express the depth and intensity of these masterpieces.

A poster of Ellie Mao Mok's first solo concert in America 1954

Advanced Studies in Vienna

In autumn 1954, I boarded the RMS Queen Elizabeth to Vienna via the Atlantic Ocean. While Austria was then free from Nazi rule after the Second World War, it was still occupied by the Allied powers (the United States, the Soviet Union, the United Kingdom and France) and in considerable poverty. Having no one to rely on there, I had to establish a new life by myself, buying things and taking public transport with the little bit of German language I had learned from my two years of studies at Yenching University and the songs I had sung. Once, at a restaurant, I wanted to order a hamburger, the only item I recognized on the menu. It turned out to be such a huge dish that I had to ask other patrons to help eat it. Meanwhile, I found places to live by checking the "Rooms to Let" noticeboard outside the branch office of American

Express in Vienna. However, I had to relocate several times because the landlords were either stingy or trying to steal from me. Eventually I rented a room from a nice couple whose house was only two blocks away from a Chinese restaurant. It was very convenient.

It was my intention to study at the Vienna Conservatory (today's University of Music and Performance Arts, Vienna). What bothered me were not the institution's old and shabby buildings but its president. As soon as he heard I was from America and wanted to study German songs, he dragged me to his residence and tried to talk me into learning from his wife. When we arrived, she was in the middle of a rather barbaric music lesson where she forced her student to lie on the floor. Then she placed a pile of books on his stomach and then put her feet on them, which in my eyes was a shocking way to teach breathing. Worse, she demonstrated singing with a loud, wild voice that was akin to that of a roaring beast. I immediately announced I had other appointments and escaped from that place. Afterwards I dared not return to the Vienna Conservatory.

Eventually, I decided not to search for an institution, as I had acquired enough knowledge and skills in vocal music. Instead, what I needed was a teacher. The most famous instructor in this field in Vienna at that time was Eric Werba, a piano accompanist for many renowned European singers and a specialist in German art songs. From him, I learned a series of 19th-century German lieder and other poetry-based repertoires.

While I was in Vienna, Robert sent me about US $150 each month. As one U.S. dollar was the equivalent of approximately 26 Austrian schillings back then, I was pretty rich. It was therefore perfectly understandable why musical experts such as Eric Werba enjoyed teaching students from the United States. While local students paid US $1.50 per lesson, people liked me paid US $ 4.00. Throughout the two years of my studies there, I learned a huge repertoire from Werba.

My other instructor was Hanrich Schmidt, an expert in Johann Bach's *Christmas Oratorio* who also charged US $4 per lesson. Not only hid I learn so much from these teachers, but through Schmidt I also had a chance to give a solo performance at the local Bach society where I was accompanied by a small ensemble renowned for their presentation of Bach's music. In fact, almost all of my concerts in Vienna and Saltzberg were accompanied by Eric Werba, a very nice person. Interestingly, as I sang in Italian and English in addition to German, he asked me to teach him non-German songs. In an attempt to expand his professional capacity, he was keen to listen to my instructions on how to accompany these songs on the piano. Several years later, when Werba visited New York, Robert and I hosted a lunch for him at the Delegate's Lounge in the United Nations. It made him very, very happy.

Ellie Mao Mok at her solo concert, the Wiener Musikverein 1955

To be a musician, one has to attend concerts as frequently as possible to learn from your peers. While in Vienna I spent every evening enjoying either an opera or a concert. I attended so many concerts that my repertoire expanded considerably. More importantly, because I was exposed to German every day, my capacity to use the language improved a great deal. That period was indeed very rewarding as I also made many friends, including many from America. After concerts we often gathered at the Gloria Cafe to chat about all sorts of pleasant things. It was truly one of the happiest and most comforting times of my life. Whenever Robert came to visit me, we toured cities such as Venice, Munich and Saltzberg while attending more concerts and musical festivals.

U.S.-China Arts and Cultural Exchanges

Having concluded my studies in Vienna, I returned to the United States in 1956 to start a family after eight years of marriage. In order to give our forthcoming daughter Gwendolyn a healthy living environment, we moved from an apartment in central New York City to a residential area in suburban Queens that the United Nation had built for its employees. The community itself was a tiny U.N. with people from every country around the world living together.

I continued practicing singing and preparing for my first concert since returning to America. In my ninth month of pregnancy, I drove a car with manual shift to the city for classes at Emma Zador's house, only to receive this announcement from her: "This will be your very last class. I can't teach you anymore. I don't want you to hit a high note and give birth to your child here." Perhaps as a result of my constant singing during pregnancy, Gwendolyn was born with plenty of musical talent. When she was only four months old, I held her in my arms while singing Brahms' *Lullaby*. I was surprised to find her staring at me, trying to sing in harmony.

As I continued practicing after her birth in March 1957, I was able to give a concert at the Carnegie Recital Hall in 1958. Thanks to my two years of studies in Vienna, my pronunciation and interpretation of German songs was greatly enhanced, winning critical acclaim from the *New York Times*, *Herald Tribune* and other print media. Subsquantly I hired an agent to manage my performing schedule. It was a very active period of my life. Apart from my own concerts, I also presented at the WNYC Radio Station's musical broadcasts, performed in museums, and participated in chamber music concerts. As my daughter was still little, most of these opportunities were situated in New York and surrounding cities. At one juncture an opera house inquired whether I would perform the main character Cio-Cio-san in *Madama Butterfly*. While I had no desire to play this role, I emphasized my interest in other operas, only to receive their response that "no Asian faces are required for the other pieces." I rejected them straight away.

In October 1959, I gave a concert with the Honolulu Symphony Orchestra in Hawaii. With my husband and daughter by my side, I realized we were already halfway to China. It would be a good chance to try to get there. After much negotiation in Hong Kong, the three of us were allowed entry into China using Robert's U.N. passport. As this was the first time I had returned since leaving China some twelve years earlier, we wanted to reunite with family, but all foreigners were kept in government-authorized guesthouses. Worse, we had to wait for government approval of our application to meet people, whether they were family members or not. In less than two days my two-year old daughter caught a cold because our guesthouse provided heating only early in the morning and late at night. Still, we fought hard and they finally allowed us to move out of the guesthouse to stay with my family.

After that government vehicles showed us around the capital in an attempt to immerse us in the new and dynamic atmosphere of New China so that we could promote it back in America. Thanks to my brother Yuan, a composer for the Central Opera House Theater, and his wife Ke-yu Li, a costume designer for the National Ballet of China, we had many opportunities to attend concerts, operas and ballet performances in Beijing. Because both Robert and I were overwhelmed with gratitude, we wanted to contribute further to the music of New China. However, my mother suggested that we should be patient and try to visit China a few more times before making our decision. We accepted her advice, thus avoiding the Cultural Revolution that thrust China into turmoil in 1966.

In 1961 our son Kenneth was born. We hired a nanny so that I could perform in places farther away from home. Once, when Anna Mi Lee and I attended a concert in Georgia, we were surprised to see one ladies room labelled "Colored" and the other one "White". We wondered which one to use before entering the "White" ladies room, and found a black woman who was there to clean the facilities but not permitted to use them. That was America in the early 1960s.

In my concerts, apart from lieder and operatic arias in German, French, Italian and English, I always sang Chinese art songs and ballads of various styles as a finale. In 1963 Folkway Records published my *28 Chinese Folk Songs* as a cassette tape and later as a CD which are still for sale today. I still teach my own students these Chinese art songs and ballads. In one incident, when Zu-qiang Wu, former president of China's Central Conservatory of Music, visited the United States, he heard one of my American students sing the Chinese song *Swallow* that he himself had adapted from a ballad of Xinjiang Province in remote northwest of China. It made Mr. Wu very happy.

In the summer of 1963, I gave a concert at the Hong Kong City Hall and invited my father and father-in-law as guests. As my father could not attend the event, we decided to visit him in Beijing, only to realize he had developed hematological purpura due to an allergy to insecticide on fruit. My father was very pleased with my new cassette tape because its cover featured one of his Chinese paintings. He had been a famous artist in his younger days in Qingdao, meticulously depicting flowers in great detail. He held my son and marvelled how much they resembled each other. The next day we sent him to the hospital where he died after a failed attempt to save his life with a blood transfusion.

After President Richard Nixon's visit to China in 1972, relations between the two countries gradually improved with many universities across America starting to provide courses in the Chinese language. I found a full-time position at the City University of New York teaching Chinese to adult students. Like teaching children, my method was for them to learn speaking before recognizing the characters. It required a familiarity with *pinyin*, a romanization system for standard Chinese, which was used in conversations. It was my view that language has as much rhythm as music. I even added music scores to *pinyin* textbooks in order for my students to understand the rhythm and tempo. For example, when one pronounces the phrase *you ren shuo* , "people say", the three Chinese characters would be in different length, with *you* and *ren* being a quarter note each and *shuo* being half note that is twice their length. Another example is *wo shuo ta* - "I say he..." - with *wo* being a quarter note that is twice the length of *shuo* and *ta* as eighth notes. One would instantly recognize a foreigner trying to speak Chinese when attempting to pronounce these three characters in equal lengths. Only by pronouncing them with my method can he or she learn to appreciate the rhythm of the Chinese language.

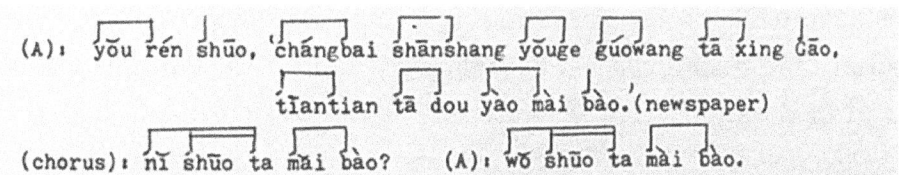

Pinyin with a musical score in *Hanyu (Chinese Language) for Beginner Students*, which reads:
(A): People say there's a king in Changbai Mountain whose surname is Gao. Every day he has to sell the newspaper.
(chorus): You say he buys the newspaper? (A): I say he sells the newspaper.

I started working as a professor in vocal music at the City University of New York's Queens College the following year. In addition to these two teaching positions, I also attended and organized various concerts and arranged singing and musical performances for the university. During summer breaks I would be either participating in research seminars on vocal music education or looking after two kids at home. Life was busy but full of fun,

In 1981 with an invitation from China's Ministry of Culture, I led a group of 12 American musicians to give master classes in piano, violin, clarinet, trumpet and French horn in Beijing and Shanghai, with me providing singing lessons in art songs. Also in Beijing we collaborated with the China Symphony Orchestra in a concert conducted by De-lun Li at The Cultural Palace of Nationalities. That was my first concert in China after 34 years of living overseas. The audience cheered endlessly rendering me overwhelmed with fierce emotions. It was the most unforgettable performance of my life. I would have loved to sing the duet *Libiamo ne' lieti calici* with Xiang Shen one more time, but he was no longer a singer after the Cultural Revolution ruined his health.

Thanks to my one-year sabbatical, I was able to remain in China after the others returned home. Through the Ministry of Culture's arrangement, I taught at music academies in Sichuan Province and cities such as Xi'an, Beijing and Tianjin, where the students were talented and worked hard. However, I found that as a result of China's long-term isolation from the world, these students were only capable of singing a limited number of operatic arias. It remained my hope that the music scores and recordings we brought them would help to broaden the horizons of all Chinese musicians. Indeed, after many years of development, Chinese music academies enjoy very high standards today.

An interesting episode happened in 1983 when I accompanied another group of American musicians to conduct cultural exchanges and sightseeing across China. While I was introducing the scenery in

Guilin, Guangxi Province, someone caught my attention by yelling "Ai-li Mao". I turned and was surprised to see Liang-yi Zhu, a classmate from Yenching University and one of the downstairs neighbors during my stay in Chongqing in 1944. Thinking a tour guide's voice sounded similar to that of his old friend, he thought it unlikely to be me but wanted to give it a try. We immediately gave each other a big hug. An expert in instrument and meter engineering, at that moment he was showing a group of fellow scholars around. That was coincidence for you. Serendipity.

Life in Retirement – Never Give Up

In 1990 I retired from the City University of New York at the age of 70. In 1995, I relocated to Rossmoor, Walnut Creek, in San Francisco's East Bay. At our golden wedding anniversary ceremony on June 20, 1998, our whole family performed on stage, with my daughter presenting the piano accompaniment, my son playing clarinet and me singing. As he had done so many years ago, my husband Robert played the violin for me to sing the art song *Three Wishes of the Rose*. You can see the important role music has always played in our family.

At the concert marking Ellie Mao and Robert Mok's Golden Wedding Anniversary, (from left) Kenneth, Gwendolyn, Ellie and Robert

After we moved here, I spent a lot of time looking after my husband, but unfortunately he passed away in November 1998, several months after the aforementioned concert that marked our golden anniversary. Encouraged by our children, I started learning computer. Starting in 1999, I spent two years writing my 236-page autobiography *This is My Life*. It was written in English because I felt my children and following generations of our family should understand what my life was like and what I went through to accomplish my achievements today. That was 16 years ago, and I am still adding contents to the book.

I served as vice president of the Chinese-American Association of Rossmoor for two years, then as its president for another two years. In fact my biggest contribution for our Rossmoor community is the organization of all kinds of concerts. I remember Mr. Brian Pennobaker, then newly appointed to our Recreation Department, helped with my 80th birthday concert. He has been my career partner since then assisting me in the organization of three to four concerts every year. Our tasks have ranged from inviting famous Chinese American musicians to sing or perform in Rossmoor, preparing flyers, translating lyrics to arranging post-concert receptions and seating lists. I am working on this even today. Up to the present I have organized a total of 74 concerts for our community.

My family lived in a small compound in Beijing with flowering Begonia trees growing in a small courtyard that was surrounded by one-story rooms on three sides. It was situated near the back entrance of the Beihai Park next to a small alley that leads to the Lotus Market at the back of the Rear Lake, a very good location indeed. When the Red Guards raided our house during the Cultural Revolution, my mother was so scared that she burned all of my belongings, including my graduation certificates and photos. She had a stroke after the first raid, but the second stroke caused by the second raid eventually led to her death. These days my brother Yuan and his wife Ke-yu Li own that place, which is where I stayed in 1981 when I taught a series of master's classes in Beijing. My sister Yi lives near Washington, D.C. Having worked as one of the teachers for the Voice of America's *900 English Sentences* program in the 1970s, many Chinese youths back then would have heard her voice. My youngest sister, Hao, used to live in Rossmoor before moving to New Jersey to be closer to her daughter.

Now, at the age of 95, I enjoy an independent life and drive myself to all sorts of nearby places. My brain still functions well. Whenever I am awake at night, I sing songs in Italian, German, French and Chinese that I have long kept in my heart. My daughter often takes time out of her busy career as a professor and performing pianist to travel from Berkeley to see me. My son, a television and movie producer, also takes his children to see me from time to time.

There is one thing special about me: whatever I want to do, I will definitely do it. Whatever people say, no matter how difficult it is, if I feel a goal can be achieved then I will keep fighting until it is done. Take the National Centre for the Performing Arts in China as an example. In 1966, Robert and I saw a television interview of Chinese-American architect I.M. Pei in front of the Musée du Louvre in Paris. Pei mentioned a series of architectural designs around the world, including the many libraries and theatres he had built. Wondering why he never built anything in China, I wrote a letter urging him to do something as a Chinese. Robert thought my inquiry was useless, but I knew Pei would definitely read it. Indeed, Pei later called me to say that China had never asked him to do anything. More importantly, it would be difficult to work in China as there might be insufficient financial resources. When I asked what he would do with an invitation from China to design a building there, his response was to wait and see, as he wasn't sure of his capabilities at the age of 80.

Now, it was my wish that Pei build a theatre in China. Consequently, I wrote a letter to Ze-min Jiang, then the President of The People's Republic of China, a ridiculous idea in the eyes of my husband Robert and brother Yuan. I asked Yuan to deliver my letter to the State

Council. When he asked me how? I said, "I don't care whether you try the front door or the back door or by air mail or snail mail. You have to deliver it for me." I wondered how he did it, but my letter later reached Mr. Zheng-ming Wang of the Construction Committee of the National Centre for the Performing Arts. Thus we established contact followed by many international telephone calls and letters.

I raised approximately US $20,000 to install seats in the building. I recall an interview with Mr. Dong Shi from the Chinese-language Bay Area Metro Radio's *Conversing across the Horizon* program. We discussed those seats for the National Centre for the Performing Arts while setting up an international telephone interview with Mr. Wang. Wang described me as a very determined person and said that my efforts were truly admirable. He had much praise for our successful collaboration. After that, when I visited China, Wang invited Yuan and me for lunch at the National Centre for the Performing Arts where there was a bronze plaque on the wall of a walkway that record the names of all the donors of the building's seats. While I was capable of achieving this goal, which took me a total of nine years, others would have given up long, long ago.

I am a caricature of what is known as determination. Whenever something needs to be done, either I choose not to do it, or I persist until it is done. I never give up, where others may abandon a task simply because it's too hard. In my dictionary there's no such phrase as "giving up". Instead of giving up, I choose to fight until the end. My motto is "You have to pursue your dreams, rather than leaving them on the shelf. Pursuing your dreams but failing is still better than abandoning them on the shelf." These are the words I taught my children. Both of them have indeed achieved their goals and succeeded in their career paths.

When people ask me what's the secret to longevity, I say the first tip is to be optimistic about life, to look forward and work for the community instead of always thinking about your own age. The second tip is to work with young people. With my ten students, I am able to keep busy every day. Finally, as a professional singer, I am lucky to maintain the habit of breathing by diaphragmatic contraction. The diaphragm is a muscle located horizontally between the thoracic cavity and abdominal cavity, used for what Chinese physicians refer to as deep breathing or abdominal breathing. Singing, taking in and expelling air are done through diaphragmatic breathing, which is highly beneficial to my health. Even today my voice remains loud, as it is supported by *chi*, the energy force of my body. I have given several breathing classes in our community in hopes that it will be of some use to everyone.

Ellie Mao Mok demonstrating diaphragmatic breathing during class at home, September 2014

Ellie Mao Mok with the author after a students' recital, August 2015

Horace and Theresa Chow 周鶴, 王仁霖
At Home in Rossmoor, October 2014

In conversation Horace Chow is conscientious and orderly, typically of an engineer. He outlines his life in a clear and logical fashion. Not just his work experiences but the addresses of all the places he has stayed across America throughout the past 60 years are listed down to the specific street number. I asked him to share some interesting anecdotes which he did in his usual sober and serious manner. Luckily, these were complemented by many vivid and fascinating details provided by his wife Theresa. From primary school to graduate studies, Horace was always a straight-A student. Although he was forced to remain in the United States due to the turmoils of war and political turbulences in China and consequently failed to fulfill his dream of launching an automobile industry there, he was able to fully utilize his talents as an engineer and industrial inventor. Supported by Theresa, he started out as an ordinary engineer and ended up the chief technical officer of a multinational corporation. He is a role model for all the Chinese engineering students who remain in America to pursue success in life and career.

Biography

Horace Chow, whose Chinese name is He Chow, was born in 1924 in Changshu, Jiangsu Province. After graduating from Shanghai's Zhonghua Vocational School, he entered the National Chiao Tung University. In 1947, having passed the national examination for overseas study, he chose the University of Michigan with the plan of returning to China to establish an automobile industry. In 1948 he received a Master of Engineering Science (MEngSc) degree and started working for the China Motor Corporation in New Jersey. He continued working as an engineer on the American East Coast until 1989 when he retired. After that with his wife Theresa he relocated to Rossmoor, Walnut Creek, in San Francisco's East Bay.

Top Student on an Engineer's Road

In 1924 I was born into a big family in Changshu, Jiangsu Province. Situated to the northwest of Shanghai, Changshu is a land of abundance, renowned for the production of rice and cotton. The Chows had a sizeable estate in Changshu with three courtyards separating five large buildings occupied by my grandparents and the households of their three sons and other relatives. Back then my family was relatively affluent and employed servants and cooks. Our estate was named "Rang De Tang", which literally means the hall that honors humility as a virtue.

The Chow Family paid tribute to the Great King of Zhou as their ancestor. This renowned leader of the Zhou clan during the Shang Dynasty (circa 1600-1046 BC) fathered three sons. Upon his death, the Great King left the throne to his eldest son, Taibo, who humbly declined, as did the second son Zhongyong and the youngst Jili. Even after Jili became the king, Taibo chose a life in exile and twice refused to take over the position. Hence the term "Rang De" derived from this remark by Confucius: "Humility is the ultimate virtue." Three times Taibo humbly turned down the offer of the throne. People couldn't find words to describe such modesty. The name "Rang De Tang" was used in our family's genealogical charts, studios and libraries, halls and chambers, and rituals and finance books. It was even marked on our daily utensils and the lanterns for Chinese New Year festivals.

My father Liang-ru Chow was the eldest son in his family of three brothers and two sisters. My mother, being warm-hearted and easy going, was the peacemaker among all the relatives. When I was three, my father died of appendicitis at the age of 38. My grandfather was a textile merchant who shipped cotton to Fuzhou, Fujian Province. It was said he also operated a private bank though without much success. My grandmother was a great woman. Although her feet were bound to resemble the so-called "three-inch golden lotus", she was a pretty fast walker. Upon my grandfather's death when I was five, she single-handedly managed our family's 400-*mu* rice field (approximately 26.7-hectares) and 4,000-mu cotton field (approximately 266.7-hectares) without relying on her children. After the Communists came to power, none of our family members (such as my mother, uncles and aunts) was labelled a "landlord' in the agrarian reform movement except my grandmother, who suffered a great deal as a result. After my father passed away, my grandmother gave 400 *mu* of land to my brother as both the first son and the oldest grandson in our family. Consequently, he too, was categorized a landlord and suffered greatly.

The Chow Family: Mother (fourth from the right),
Horace Chow (fifth from the right) and grandmother (first from the left) 1928

A Straight-A Student from the Chow Clan in Changshu

As the youngest child in our family of three children, my sister and brother were respectively four and two years older than me. I was a very naughty kid. Our family accountant and other servants learned to avoid me because I would punch every one of them whenever I returned home for lunch from the primary school in Changshu and saw them having their meals. After primary school at the age of 13, I entered the Zhonghua Vocational School in Shanghai. My mother came from a family of scholars and wanted the best education for me, but she wasn't sure which school I should attend. As my father had already passed away, she discussed the issue with relatives. One of them, a graduate from the Zhonghua Vocational School, recommended it, so it became my school as well.

After the Marco Polo Bridge Incident on July 7, 1937, Japan launched a full-scale assault on China. To flee from the turmoils of war, my mother took us on a boat that sailed along the Yangtze River from Changshu to Shanghai. I still remember that the ship was so crowded with people that my sister had to drag me forcefully aboard from the ferry boat. The Chow clan had a house in Shanghai where each family used one of the rooms. Later while my mother and brother traveled to the countryside near Dongting mountain, west of Suzhou, Jiangsu Province, my sister and I stayed in Shanghai with my uncles. Throughout the following six years of studies in Shanghai during my separation from my mother, it was my sister who helped me a great deal.

Founded by educator and industrialist Yan-pei Huang, the Zhonghua Vocational School was a five-year institution starting from what is now considered to be Year 7. I was a very good student and graduated as the No.1 student of the school. Instead of entering a university, the majority of students from our school found employment after graduation. However, one of the teachers said to me, "A student like you should not start working straight away. With your academic achievements, you really should go to university." As a result after graduation I worked for a very short period of time for a company called Yong Fa. I was assigned by our school to work there and I helped to improve their accounting system. Soon after that, I passed the National Chiao Tung University's entrance examination to study mechanical engineering. One's life can truly change for the better if he or she is lucky enough to encounter a good teacher.

I worked really hard at the National Chiao Tung University. As a result of having a vocational school background, I didn't study many of the subjects required for high school students such as chemistry and Chinese literature. I studied so hard that, by graduation in 1946, I was top of my glass with an A for every subject except for German. After that, I worked as an assistant to Professor Shu-pei Huang, who was in charge of our department. I also worked for the Shanghai Municipal Council's technical department headed by Zeng-yu Zhao, a graduate of the National Chiao Tung University.

Horace Chow (middle of front row) graduating from the National Chiao Tung University, Shanghai French Concession 1946

Further Studies and an Innovative Career Overseas

A year later on July 30, 1947, I passed the Ministry of Education's examinations for overseas study by private sponsorship. Zeng-yu Zhao, the aforementioned head of our technical department and a graduate of the National Chiao Tung University, served as a guarantor for my finances. While Zhao offered only his name, it was one of considerable political-social status and afforded me the opportunity of getting an American visa. Knowing that China lacked automobiles at the time, I was determined to return home after my overseas studies to launch an automobile manufacturing industry. Hence I wanted to choose an academic institution close to Detroit, America's Motor City, and so ended up choosing the University of Michigan at Ann Arbor, turning down a scholarship offered to me by the Massachusetts Institute of Technology (MIT).

One month after the examination, I fulfilled my wish and

entered the University of Michigan to study Automotive Engineering. Indeed, it seemed to be the wish of many other Chinese students studying in the United States, including Tian-yi Yang, husband of my old friend Anna Yang. Having graduated from the National Chiao Tung University five years earlier than me, he and his wife were also students of the University of Michigan (see the chapter on Anna Yang). As I was studying by private sponsorship, throughout the first year or so I was financially supported by the US $150 my mother sent me each month. While this covered my tuition fees of US $100 per year, the University of Michigan also offered various stipends and teaching assistantships. While at the university I was able to complete my Master of Engineering Science (MEngSc) degree in a year, receiving top scores in all the required subjects. At the graduation ceremony in 1948, I was presented as one of the university's Honor Students.

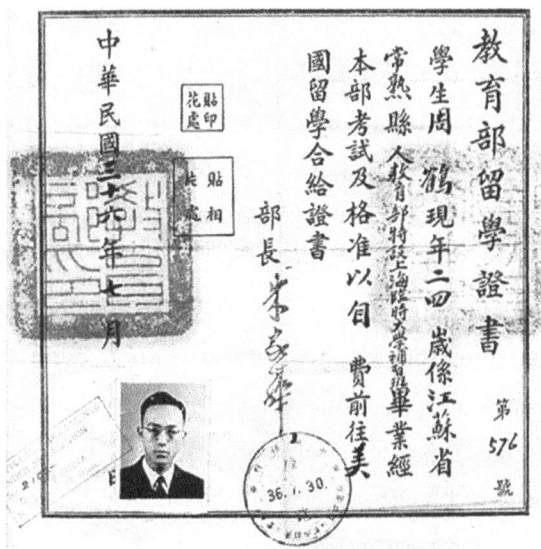

Horace Chow's Certificate of Overseas Study,
issued by the Ministry of Education, 1947

In the early 1950s it was difficult for Chinese students to find employment in America, especially those studying liberal arts. My first ten years after graduation were the toughest as I changed jobs five times.

Fortunately, I never stopped working and was always able to secure a new position before the old one terminated. Even better all five positions involved industrial design. I had much more luck than students who had to serve and wash dishes in restaurants. Many American companies were reluctant to consider Chinese graduates as potential employees, but we worked hard to earn their trust. This was a crucial chapter in the history of Chinese immigration and settlement, enabling us to integrate more fully into the United States. From then on American industries and academic institutions gradually recognized the intelligence and diligence of the Chinese and became willing to engage their services. I was one such example.

After graduation I worked for the China Motor Corp in New Jersey hoping that the experience I gained there would contribute to my ambition to establish an automobile manufacturing industry in China. Headed by Chinese American David H. Huang, a graduate of MIT and an expert in aeronautics, the company produced a three-wheeled vehicle for promotion in China. However, the political changes in China in 1949 made it impossible for me to return home and fulfill my dream. The company also lost its business there. After trying to rent out its factory and certain machinery to another company, the China Motor Corp eventually closed for business with numerous debts including several months' salary owed to me. As a graduate student I wasn't supposed to be working in the United States, even for a company owned and operated by a Chinese American. When the Immigration Department located me later on and questioned why I worked for the company, I pretended to know nothing about it. Still, I was fortunate to receive a work permit in June 1949.

While working for the China Motor Corp., I was accepted by New York University's Department of Mechanical Engineering as its first Ph.D. candidate. It was quite a tough period for me, working during the day and studying at night. I often napped on the subway after work before arriving at the university for research. After three years of hard work and passing the qualifying examination as a Ph.D. candidate, I had to terminate my studies in 1951 because my supervisor, a recent graduate from Brown University, wanted me to take over his research project there. Before I had a chance to complete my research, a Ph.D. student from Brown University published his thesis on the same topic. I had to start a new project. With that said, financially, it would have been impossible for me to give up my job and spend two years working on a thesis for my supervisor.

Horace Chow driving a three-wheeled vehicle produced by
China Motor Corp., 1948

In 1948 the American Congress passed the Displaced Persons Act to allow entry and settlement of people from Europe who were oppressed by the Nazis during the Second World War and also those who could not return to their countries after the war due to their racial, religious and/or political circumstances. This policy was later expanded to include migrants from Asia. After 1949 many students from China had difficulty surviving as they could neither receive money from home nor find employment in the United States. The American Government considered the Chinese people here to be without a nation or home due to the Communist takeover of China, so it granted them an opportunity to remain in the United States. All Chinese students could apply for permanent residency with the American Government providing tuition fees and a monthly subsidy for living expenses. As a result of the educational subsidy, many Chinese students chose to remain in academia to pursue a Ph.D. This group of Chinese students cultivated by the American Government later formed a burgeoning group of Chinese professors within American universities. A good example is Chen-ning Franklin Yang who achieved great success. He is one of 1957 Nobel Prize laureate in physics. In 1951 I too qualified as a displaced person and received a monthly subsidy of US $150 for nearly two years. Without the Displaced Persons Act, a Chinese person like me could never have remained in the United States.

In 1951 I helped develop an electric Chinese-language typewriter for a company called Interworld Industries Inc. Headed by a former student of the National Chiao Tung University, the company based its development on a system of arranging/combining distinct radicals (i.e. partial characters) to form Chinese characters, a technique devised by the famous Chinese linguist and literary scholar, Yu-tang Lin. The project later failed because the company lacked funding to create a prototype. It was years later that I learned the project was sponsored by Lin himself. Lin had spent so much money on the development that he nearly went bankrupt. Both a renowned scholar and an inventor, he eventually came up with a prototype and was issued a patent six and a half years later.

Also in 1951, I was lucky enough to meet Theresa, my future wife, in New York. Without her all aspects of my life would have been considerably different from what they are now; nor could I have achieved everything I did. One day I had lunch in New York with an old friend from the University of Michigan. After lunch, I accompanied him to visit Theresa's brother-in-law whom I knew as well. It was there that I met Theresa who happened to be holidaying at her sister's place away from her studies in North Carolina. At that time there were so very few Chinese women studying in the United States that for every female in the Greater Manhattan Area, there would have been ten males vying for her attention. This is why I consider myself a lucky man.

Later, a large group of female Chinese pilgrims travelled to Germany under the leadership of a priest surnamed Mao who worked for Cardinal Yu Pin. Upon their arrival in the United States, all of them were sent to study in Catholic girls' schools. As these women remained in America, Chinese communities soon experienced considerable change.

After we met, Theresa moved to New York to work for Columbia University and a local publisher. At that time, America had become involved in the Korean War and was fighting against the Chinese. Working for the Bank of China in Hong Kong, Theresa's father, Zhen-fang Wang, suggested that we wait to see how events turned out before deciding to return to China. In 1953 Theresa and I married in New York. We soon had a boy and a girl.

Horace and Theresa Chow with their daughter and son at home, 1964

Everything I did after graduation was related to industrial design. After the project on Chinese-language typewriter failed, I started working for a company called Consulting and Designers, Inc. Usually, before any manufacturer started mass producing a product, they needed to acquire a series of specific tools for their factory. My job was to illustrate and design the manufacture of these tools.

About two years after that, in 1954, I started a company called Westchester Technical Corporation with two other graduates from the National Chiao Tung University. One of my partners was Hsue-chu Tsien, cousin of Chinese rocket scientist Hsue-shen Tsien (or Xue-sen Qian) and father of Chinese American biochemist Roger Y. Tsien, the recipient of the 2008 Nobel Prize in Chemistry. Tsien and I were very good friends. I was one of three partners in the company and again we were making tools. Eighteen months later I also joined a famous company called Celanese in New Jersey where my job was to design textile machinery. I left this job in 1958 when the company decided to relocate its factory to the south.

Having found a new position in Melnor Industries, a major manufacturer of gardening tools, I received my licence as a professional engineer in 1960. One year later my boss informed me that, if I had had a Ph.D., the company would have considered me to be over-qualified and refuse to hire me. Indeed, since my entry into the Zhonghua Vocational School at the age of 13, I have been studying engineering all my life. I have always enjoyed working in the industry. I think it's rewarding – it gives me a sense of achievement. Had I received a Ph.D., I would have become a university professor. Instead, for someone like me who enjoys inventing and designing machinery, it is better to remain in the industry and work for companies.

I love brainstorming. In our company my specialty was to research, develop and manufacture new products to meet the specific needs of our clients. From 1955 to 1989, I applied for and was issued more than 60 patents, many of which were for our company's products. Among my own patented inventions was a Walking Sprinkler, which involved a structure that drew out and then rolled up the gardening hose as it sprinkled water over a designated area. By the time the hose was fully rolled up around the tap, all the plants in this area would have been watered. Another invention was a Timer which turned a piece of machinery on and off automatically. Such a device is rather common these days, but it was quite rare back in the 1960s when semiconductor technology was undergoing development and very few electronic devices were automatic.

While working for Melnor Industries, I went on leave-without-pay in 1967 to launch my own company and promote my own patented products. My company Link Age manufactured a linkage ball joint I invented, which could be used in air conditioning and many other types of machinery. I designed the product and distributed a catalogue. Tian-yi Yang, my aforementioned old friend from the University of Michigan (see the chapter on Anna Yang) , used this linkage ball joint when his company installed air conditioning in the Lincoln Center for the Performing Arts. It was rather easy to assemble such a joint, so I set up a factory at home using US $60,000 that friends invested. We installed a machine in our basement so that Theresa and other ladies from the neighbourhood could monitor it throughout the day. As they assembled the parts together for the linkage ball joints, Theresa often grabbed our son, who was then a primary school student, and asked him to pile up the completed products. It was a job he truly hated. Meanwhile, whenever the trucks made their deliveries, the drivers refused to go down the steep ramp next to our house for fear that the trucks would not be able to make it up again. When they abandoned all the parts in huge boxes on the street, I had to go and move them by myself. It was such a physically challenging job that I hurt my back in the process.

While I manufactured this product, my American partner Simon promoted it. His company was involved in a Federal Government project to produce a type of air nozzle for rockets. I was engaged to manufacture some tools for them. It was a difficult project, as each nozzle was required to handle at least 500 pounds of air pressure.

Further complicating the issue was the fact that the outside layers needed to be produced before the inner ones. When the project was successfully completed, Simon was so happy that he later came to support my newlyestablished company. Anyway, in order to manage our finances, I worked at another factory during the day and apportioned half of my earnings to Simon as his salary. In the evenings I worked for our own factory at home. Simon used to live a rather comfortable life, even owning a private airplane. Later it was said that his wife divorced him because he was often away from home on business but lacked a stable income. His airplane was eventually sold.

Theresa worked with me for our company without salary or complaints. Apart from caring for the kids, we were able to save money by working at home. We didn't even have a car at that time. Prior to her arrival in America, Theresa was never required to do any chores at home. When she moved into a dormitory in the United States as a student, she didn't even know how to make her bed with the sheets and blankets provided. In sharp contrast since we married, she had to cook, take care of our children, paint the walls, sew the window curtains and couch covers, perm her own hair, and even manage a factory for me. I am truly grateful for her unconditional support in every aspect of our life throughout the past 62 years.

Eventually an opportunity came up: an air-conditioning company in Philadelphia wanted to buy another one of my products, a "door linkage closer" used in air conditioners. While their engineers tested and praised the quality of my product, their superiors turned down the deal since they already had a factory manufacturing something else. They said it would be impossible for them to shut down the existing production line and switch to manufacturing my product no matter how good and cheap it was. Initially I thought my product would sell well because it was good, but things didn't work that way. It was only then that I realized marketing is as important as manufacturing. To operate a company in the United States, it was crucial to have enough capital and to ensure that products closely follow market trends. My own company existed for a total of 16 months, but it felt much longer than that, perhaps because to run it was truly hard work. Later, I sold the company to my major competitor who purchased all my patents. I received US $60,000 for my patents and equipment, enough to compensate the capital invested in the first place. That was a lot of money back then.

In American manufacturing and industries, the Chinese often faced a "glass ceiling". It seemed that even though you performed well, you would only promote to a certain level, and that is that. No matter what you did, you would always remain at the lower level as an engineer. Fortunately, at Melnor Industries my boss appreciated my talents and hard work. An engineer himself, he promoted me to be the company's chief engineer as well as the deputy director of the products department. Hence I entered the management level and broke through the "glass ceiling" in 1968.

In 1986 when Melnor Industries acquired Beatrice Foods, I became a major shareholder of the company. In 1988 when Melnor Industries further acquired Hunter Fan Co., it was actually several members of the management group who did the acquisition and later sold it for a profit. This is what I consider to be the unfairness of capitalism. Those at the top level skim off all the fat while those at the bottom level can rely only on their salaries. We could have survived on my salary alone, but our lives would never have been as comfortable and free of financial concerns. Starting in 1968 I worked for Melnor Industries for the following 31 years. After my retirement at the age of 65 in 1989, the company had to hire two people to do what I did on my own.

While I was busy working, my wife Theresa studied elaborate-style Chinese painting while devoting herself to voluntary work. At one stage she also served as president of the Women's Association of the China Institute in New York.

Giving Back to Family and National Chiao Tung University

Despite the fact that I had left home long ago, I always maintained a close relationship with my family in China. Since my graduation from college, I sent money to them every month as a financial subsidy. At that time there was no direct communication between China and the United States and not way to send money. We sent US $150 every month to my mother in Shanghai via someone in Hong Kong that my father-in-law introduced to us for a total of ten years.

My brother had six children, three by his first wife and three by his second. As the first three kids were looked after by my mother, our payment was mainly for her to purchase nutritious food for the family. Most of the Chinese children back then lived a tough life with hardly anything to eat. Those three kids knew that the money was from their uncle in America to give them a better life. In 1995 I sponsored my sister's family to migrate to the United States. In 1962 she and I went through the process to enable our 73-year old mother to relocate from Shanghai to America. However, she decided not to undertake the journey from Hong Kong because in her view it would be both difficult and risky at her age.

After China opened its doors to the world in the early 1980s, I also sponsored my nieces and nephews in their pursuit of higher education in the United States. All have now established successful careers and settled well in America. It pleases me to see our family prosper here. While there was only me in 1947, by 2003 the Chow Family had 42 members in the United States with a total of 53 relatives attending our Golden Wedding celebrations that same year. Now we have even more family members here.

Having arrived in America as a student in 1947, I returned to China for the first time 26 years later in 1973 when I was invited as a member of a group of American professors, experts and IBM engineers.

My daughter, then a recent graduate of architecture from MIT, also participated in the trip. Not many people returned to China at that time. Having just opened its door to the world, there were many misconceptions about America, with many people still shouting slogans like "Down with American imperialism." Still, they treated us like honored guests after our entry to China via Hong Kong. At universities and in cities around the country, we gave speeches on China's future development, but we were unable to visit home due to our busy schedule. It was only in 1978 that my family and I were able to visit my mother and brother in China. When we returned to Changshu, Jiangsu Province, the locals followed our car everywhere around the village because they had never seen people from America.

That was the first and last time for our whole family to be together since I left home some 31 years earlier. It was also during that trip that I learned that my grandmother passed away at the age of 100. She could have lived longer than that. However, during the Cultural Revolution, when my grandmother lived in Shanghai, the Red Guards accused her of having gold hidden under the house, and tore apart both the floorboards and the walls. When they found nothing, they tried to force her to hand over the gold, something she never possessed. So she hanged herself that night. Later, my mother and brother stayed in the same room in a hospital in Shanghai in 1980, and they died two days apart from the same disease. After that, we only went to China for sightseeing as there was no more family to visit. We have been to China many times since then, the last time being in 2010 to visit the World Expo in Shanghai.

Throughout my life I have received help from many graduates of the National Chiao Tung University. Indeed, at my alma mater we always celebrate the tradition of giving back to those who have helped us. Back in 1978 when China just started to open its doors to the world, a group from Shanghai's National Chiao Tung University arrived in Washington, D.C., via Paris for a 47-day visit. During their journey through 20 American cities, there were always local alumni associations to welcome and look after them with passion. In New York, for example, our alumni association hosted the group at the restaurant on the top floor of the World Trade Center.

After my retirement I served as the chairman of the Chiao Tung University Alumni Foundation in America from 1992 to 1999. I organized numerous fundraising activities to donate money to the university's five branch campuses in China and Taiwan. During my tenure as chairman, a total of 671 former graduates like myself, including the aforementioned Zeng-yu Zhao and Chinese-American computer engineer An Wang, raised more than 1.3 million U.S. dollars in funds. Also in 1996 on behalf of the foundation, I attended and gave a speech at the ceremony in Shanghai that celebrated the 100th anniversary of the establishment of National Chiao Tung University. Even Zemin Jiang, then the Chinese president, greeted me in person.

In 2000, I donated US $10,000 to set up the ZXJZ Scholarship Fund at the university in Shanghai in the name of my mother (Jin-zhi Zhou, née Xu). The scholarship is mainly given to academically excellent students in need of financial resources, but part of it may also be awarded to teachers. In short, I dedicated 10 years of my life serving the National Chiao Tung University's various alumni associations. In 2011, I was named an honorary chairman of the Chiao Tung University Alumni Foundation in America.

Busy Life after Retirement

We had many friends in New York, who wanted to live near each other after retirement. None of us particularly wanted to depend on our children. In fact we couldn't, partly because our children had yet to settle down and would often relocate. Another reason is that our children were highly Americanized with different ideas about life. They would likely feel a lack of privacy if we insisted on living with them.

With that said, as old men and women, we are also Americanized individuals who do not feel the need to be supported by our children. More importantly, although we have lived in the United States for many years, we still enjoy Chinese food. It would be lovely to have a huge kitchen and employ someone to cook Chinese cuisine for us.

I dreamed of setting up a retirement village. I had even written a detailed proposal and designed an application form, but the project was neither easy to implement nor fully supported by our friends. Later some friends recommended that we relocate to Rossmoor, in Walnut Creek, California. Apart from having no one to cook for us, everything else about this community suited our needs. So, one major reason why we moved here from the East Coast in 1989 was to be with our friends in retirement. Another reason was to be near our daughter, who worked at the University of California at Berkeley.

The "Sharing Life's Journeys" bus shelter donated by the Chinese-American Association of Rossmoor

When we came to Rossmoor, there were about 40 Chinese residents. Some of us from New York, including Peter Sih, Shing-yi Huang (see the chapters on these two friends) and me, thought that we could gather everyone together to achieve our goals. Hence the Chinese American Association of Rossmoor (CAAR) was established in 1990 with Sih as the first chairman. I served as the association's second deputy chairman and the third chairman from 1992 to 1996.

Several projects were completed during my tenure. First, when the CAAR was established, we proposed building a bus shelter in our community. The completed bus shelter was inscribed with the Chinese characters of "Sharing Life's Journeys". Second, since our association's membership register listed only English names, I added Chinese names. I also issued a certificate to the 100th person joining our association. Third, for friends living nearby who wanted to join CAAR's activities, I set up a system of Associate Membership. Fourth, I proposed that our association should have annual reports and records of activities to promote our achievements. I don't know whether they still keep such reports these days. Finally in 1991, my wife and I launched the Mahjong Club as a subsidiary to CAAR. With more than 80 members, we presently play mahjong every Friday afternoon.

I have always been busy. This did not change after my retirement since I continued to organize fundraising activities for the Chiao Tung University Alumni Foundation in America. I also spent two years scanning and indexing all of our family's photographs as computer files. In addition I helped relatives manage their family trust funds.

One of the relatives was my cousin Chun-hua Li, a physician in the United States and four years older than me. In the last year of his studies at St. John's University's medical school in Shanghai, his family arranged his marriage to the daughter of a famous gynecologist. In 1948 he came to America without his wife and son who was then only one month old. He also served as the best man at my wedding. Though he spent his entire life as a physician in America, he was very frugal. He drove an old car, read newspapers at the library instead of subscribing to them, and used all his money to purchase shares in the stock market. Even his Chinese language capacity was greatly reduced as a result of his reluctance to socialize with others. We occasionally met him.

In 1997 a friend called to inform us that this cousin had passed away in his apartment. No one knew about this. His neighbors reported the death to the county authorities who in turn held a funeral for him, gathered his personal belongings, and were in the process of searching for his family and/or relatives to claim his possessions. This is what's great about America. The county authorities requested the Post Office to deliver his mail to the county government to research his identity. Because my cousin graduated from St John's University, the alumni association in New York sent him a notice about their forthcoming social activities. When the Post Office delivered the notice to the county government, the authorities immediately contacted the alumni association in New York about my cousin. The person in New York in turn directed them to the president of the alumni association in California, but it was another dead end.

One day this president in California mentioned the matter in conversation which was overheard by a friend of mine. My friend immediately announced that he knew this person. Better yet, he knew this person's cousin, which was me, and so he contacted and informed me about this issue. Others advised me not to get involved, but I felt it important to transfer to my cousin's wife and children all the money he had earned after more than 30 years of hard work. Otherwise, if I didn't get involved, the county government would have taken all the money. The county authorities were genuinely helpful. They had processed and indexed all my cousin's personal belongings and photographs. When we arrived at the county office, they recognized us and were convinced of our identities because they had seen our faces in the photos. Things became easier when the authorities discovered the name of his wife that we had supplied from one of my cousin's tax returns.

For the following 15 years, I spent much time managing his trust fund which was such a highly rewarding experience that my daughter helps now. We even managed to send to my cousin's wife all the letters they had exchanged in the past. His son, my nephew and an honest man, was so grateful for this that he promised to come to America and look after us in our old age. I wondered, whether his good wishes would ever be fulfilled.

On my 70th birthday I mentioned that all my good friends referred me as "Little Chow". Now after another 20 years, I am 90 years old. No one would call me "Little Chow" any more. All my life I have been a fortunate man, having been cared for by my family, especially my sister, throughout my childhood. After my wife and I married, she has helped me on every front. We have a happy family with our daughter working as a professor in architecture at the University of California at Berkeley and our son serving as a physician in Florida. These two excellent children are my fountain of joy. Even better, I have five grandchildren. Obviously I also want to give thanks to my friends Sheng-yi Huang, Anna Yang and her husband Tian-yi Yang, because it is they who suggested and encouraged us to relocate to Rossmoor upon retirement (see the chapters on Sheng-yi Huang and Anna Yang). Rossmoor is the reward for my many years of hard work, as we spend our days dancing, playing golf, ping pong, mahjong and traveling around the world. Such is our happy life in retirement.

Gus Kao 高銓
At the author's home in Rossmoor, September 2014

Gus Kao described how he fled from the turmoils of war from Shenyang, Liaoning Province in Northeast China, to Tianjin, nearly 140 kilometers southeast of Beijing in Hebei Province, and then boarded a ship from Qingdao, Shandong Province, to Taiwan. His story reminds me of some of the historical events portrayed in Taiwanese author Ying-tai Long's 2009 book *Big River, Big Sea: Untold Stories of 1949*, but the difference is Mr. Kao personally experienced them. Born in the 1920s when warlords battled each other for power, he felt the pain as a member of the conquered people in Japanese-occupied Northeast China, and, after victory in the War of Resistance against Japan, bore witness to the civil war between the Nationalist and the Communist armies. He further experienced the fierce storms of political change while contributing to the launch and take-off of Taiwan's numerous industries. Now he lives in beautiful Rossmoor, in San Francisco's East Bay, leading his friends to practice *Tai Chi Qi Gong* every day. Watching his silver hair and youthful face moving slowly and gently along with the music,

I recall a song called "Immortal" by Chinese singer Quan Dai. Here are the slightly modified lyrics:

"The wind carries me to a place

Where an immortal says to me:

Relax, breathe in, relax, breathe out.

Life rushes by, short as a moment.

But if you closed your eyes,

You can see even the distant paradise."

Biography

Gus Kao, whose Chinese name is Quan Kao was born in 1922 in Shenyang, Liaoning Province. His ancestral home was Shandong Province. Having graduated from Shenyang's Wenhua Junior High School and the Beijing Huiwen Middle School, he received his Bachelor's degree from Fu Jen Catholic University's Department of Western Languages and Literature in Beijing in 1945. After graduation, he was assigned a position in the Nationalist Government's Office of the Commissioner of the Ministry of Foreign Affairs in Shenyang to oversee the handling of international affairs in Northeast China after the victory in the War of Resistance against Japan. In 1949 he fled from the ravages of war from Shenyang to Tianjin, Qingdao and finally Taiwan, and worked for Taita Chemical Company, Ltd. until his retirement. Since his relocation to Rossmoor in San Francisco's East Bay in 1988, he has been actively contributing to activities of local Chinese communities.

An "Immortal" Practicing Tai Chi Qi Gong

I was born in my grandmother's home in Shenyang, Liaoning Province, in 1922. While my ancestors came from Liaoyang, also in Liaoning Province, my ancestral home was actually Shandong Province. My ancestors migrated from Shandong to Northeast China and had settled there for generations. I don't know much about my grandfather, except for a story told by my father. When my uncle was attending the Qing Dynasty's imperial examination, my grandfather purchased firecrackers but hid them in case of his son's failure to achieve anything. The firecrackers were lit when the news came that my uncle passed the examination and was officially pronounced a scholar. He was one of the Qing Dynasty's very last scholars, as the title became useless after the imperial regime was replaced by the government of the Republic of China. Indeed, one of the games I used to play as a child was *Shengguantu*, a traditional gambling game in which a throw of the dice promotes you through imaginary government ranks arranged in a chart. It was certainly fun to envision yourself passing the national examination and rising to be a top-ranking government official. I still keep a set of the game today, but not many people know how to play it these days.

My father Li-yuan Kao was once the head of the Bureau of Commercial Ports in Liudaogou, Jilin Province. Although a small place, Liudaogou had everything, including a Japanese consulate. A series of commercial ports was also established there near the end of the Qing Dynasty. Liudaogou was later renamed as Longjing Village though Longjing is now a city in Jilin Province. The primary school in Liudaogou that I attended was sponsored by my father. However, due to a lack of educational resources there, I was later sent back to my grandmother's place to receive further education in Shenyang. My family had always been affluent. With that said, as the young master of the house, I was never a spoiled brat.

In Shenyang I entered Wenhua Junior High School, an affiliate of the Dongguan Church that was built by Scotland's United Presbyterian Church using Boxer Rebellion indemnity money. The school, situated outside the East Gate on the north side of the Hun River, was so far away that I took a bus and walked 30 minutes to get there. I commuted to school during the summers, but had to board in the winters because it was impossible to walk in the fiercely icy wind, not to mention the snow that was so deep that you couldn't even get out of the front door. Ours was a Western-style school that offered regular middle school subjects, besides courses such as English, natural science, physical hygiene and ethics among others. Yet because our school catered only to students in their junior years, what are now considered to be Years 7 to 9, I had to go to Beijing to find a high school.

At that time my father was under constant surveillance by the Japanese. He was such an efficient public servant that they came to "interview" him each week. It was only after my father informed them that he knew their boss while studying in Tokyo, Japan, and showed them various photographs as proof that they stopped harassing him. Otherwise they would have continued to scrutinize his every move for fear that he might escape. Escape to where was unclear, as we were right on the China-Korea border? Instead their real concern was my father's possible contact with his friend Zhan-shan Ma, the famous Chinese-Muslim general who commanded 3,500 guerilla fighters against the Japanese in Northeast China.

My father did a lot for the region, especially in the development of local industries, such as the telephone, roads, the supplying of electricity in 1924, and the introduction of tap water in 1934. To help the locals improve their living standards, my father directed them to establish power stations, set up telephone connections, build roads, operate long-distance buses for public transport, and raise cattle, sheep and even bees. It was a time when government officials collaborated with local businesses for the latter's success and prosperity, unlike today where the two sides often collude with each other for their own profits. When the Japanese arrived, they threatened to imprison my father if he refused to continue his work. To look after our family, and to serve his fellow people, my father agreed to keep working. Two years later he finally found an excuse to retire and return to Shenyang. I recently found many of these historical events in Northeast China discussed by Taiwanese scholar and author Bang-yuan Qi in *The River of Big Torrents* (2011), also translated as "The Great Flowing River". To me they have great meaning indeed.

Further Education in Beijing

In 1938 after the Marco Polo Bridge Incident on July 7 and the floods in Tianjin in late August, I traveled with my uncle from Shenyang to go to high school in Beijing. I was 17 years old. My uncle, a smart young man only a couple of years older than me, was a graduate of Beijing Huiwen Middle School. Then a student in journalism at Yenching University, he promised to look after me in Beijing. We left Shenyang because we wanted to be free of Japanese occupation as no one knew then how long their domination would last in Northeast China. We could only wait and see.

Due to the floods in Northern China, I arrived too late to start the autumn semester at Beijing Huiwen Middle School. As a result, I had to study at a private school near the Xuanwu Gate in the city's southwest. Operated by my fellow people from Northeast China, the school was situated near the French Language School that was part of the Roman Catholic Church of the Virgin Mary. It wasn't until the beginning of the following year during the winter holidays, that I passed Beijing Huiwen Middle School's entrance examination and formally enrolled as a student. Having left home at an early age, I was used to living on campus at my junior high school, senior high school and later university. This is why I still live an independent life at the age of 92.

Beijing Huiwen Middle School was operated by the Methodist Episcopal Church from the United States, and therefore, free of Japanese control. I had a great time there as all our classmates loved reading, especially on extracurricular topics. Most of the books we enjoyed were banned by the Japanese. However, the bookstall owners knew us well and would let us know whenever a shipment of banned books arrived. Back in our dormitory, which had two people per room, we would curtain the windows with bedsheets and read these books by candlelight at night. Among the many titles we consumed was the *West Wind* magazine edited by renowned translators and brothers Jia-de Huang and Jia-yin Huang, as well as the famous scholar Yu-tang Lin. The magazine was similar to the *Reader's Digest* in America, with common sections such as coverage of and comments on current affairs, war and social news, serialized literary works, biographies, reports on scientific, natural, psychological and educational trends, famous quotations, extracts from Western books, literary and artistic notes and comics. Reading them was fun, thought-provoking and provided much knowledge. We also read a lot of English books.

As for Chinese titles such as Ba Jin's Torrents Trilogy – *The Family* (1933), *Spring* (1938) and *Autumn* (1940) – I had read them as a junior high school student back in Shenyang. Such radical reading was often done secretly since these titles were banned by the Japanese but embraced across China. As students, we would sneak a title around until everyone had a go and the book nearly fell apart after so much use. It was lucky that there weren't many traitors back then to report us to the Japanese, or we would surely have been in big trouble. Indeed, when Beijing Huiwen Middle School held drama performances such as Yu Cao's *Thunderstorm* (1937) and *The Wilderness* (1937), students like me had more fun watching them than getting directly involved in the productions. One of my classmates was interrogated by the Japanese as a result of his role in *The Wilderness* and had to pretend he didn't know about the play's anti-Japan undertone. Life was incredibly harsh for those of us living in Japanese-occupied areas. The movies were another example because any image of the Chinese national flag was prohibited. Still, whenever there was a glimpse of it on the screen, the audience erupted with cheers and applause like crazy.

Some of my classmates liked Peking Opera. Instead of learning how to perform it, I would either playfully hum along or go to a show or two with my friends, such as *Farewell My Concubine* performed by Shao-shan Jin and Su-qiu Wu. Back then the actors used their real voices to reach the audience sitting at the theater's outskirts, unlike these days with the use of mini-microphones disrupting and distorting the "flavors" of the voices. One of the four rising stars in Peking Opera at that time was Shi-fang Li, a great performer who was only a couple of years older than us. We chatted with him during his stay at my friend's place. He had a rough voice, but, on stage he was able to sing in the thin, high-pitch voice of a young girl. I myself tried an aria from *The Qingding Pearl*, also named "Fisherman's Revenge", at the Rossmoor community's Peking Opera Club last year. That was the first time in my life that I sang along with jinghu, a traditional Chinese musical instrument commonly used in Peking Opera. It was more than 70 years after my playful humming along with high school friends.

While I studied at Beijing Huiwen Middle School, my uncle was a student at Yenching University. As a result of his frequent suggestion that I get tutoring on campus, I knew the place pretty well until 1952 when it was taken over by Peking University. Back then the Japanese did not disturb Yenching University because it was sponsored by the Americans. However, there were all sorts of divisions on campus, from the Kuomintang's supporters and those backing the Communists to those leaning toward Japan and the United States. We often saw all kinds of slogans splashed across the walls in the bathrooms by anonymous authors. I also remember a restaurant outside the university's rear entrance selling sweet pastries with sesame filling and ground pork stir-fried with "thousand year eggs". They were the only source of these dishes that I knew of. The sweet pancakes were so delicious that I still remember the taste today.

Something else happened during my life in high school. I had an operation on my appendix requiring a stay at the Union Hospital for a week. Because the hospital was founded by the Rockefeller Foundation, all of its machinery and equipment came from America and used 110v. The rooms were beautiful and spacious with two occupants per room. When you needed an X-ray, they would bring the machine to your bed. Even the nurses were beautiful and pristine, wearing tiny caps on top of their heads. All the high-ranking nurses had graduated from Yenching University's preparatory nursing school prior to their studies and work at the Union Hospital.

While I was there, one night a patient was moved into the other bed after a hernia operation. He claimed to be a carpenter who had worked on the construction of the Union Hospital. He said the hospital was built on the former site of a mansion owned by the descendants of Prince Yu, the 15th son of the Qing Dynasty's founding emperor and a famous war hero in 17th-century China.

During the construction, someone found a secret cellar full of silver coins. Soon the workers on the site started smuggling the silver coins out after their shifts ended. One day a couple of them tried to carry so many coins that the weight forced them to bend over. When the inspector saw this, he became concerned about their stooping as a sign of potential sickness and inquired about their health. As soon as he checked them out and discovered the attempted smuggling, the site was shut down and construction halted. The authorities turned the site upside down and further discovered a set of armor made of pure gold near the chimney of the today's hospital. That was all found on the site. Later it was said that the Union Hospital was built with the best and most expensive materials and in accordance with the highest construction standards because there was plenty of money to splash around. Besides the funds from America, there was also money from the silver found in the cellar. Thus, they could afford to build a fancy building using polished bricks and lots of top-quality material.

Having graduated from Beijing Huiwen Middle School, I passed the Fu Jen Catholic University's entrance examination and enrolled in the Department of Western Languages and Literature. Situated near the rear part of a scenic lake called Shichahai in Beijing's Xicheng District, the university was established by the Benedictines of St Vincent Archabbey in Latrobe, Pennsylvania at the request of the Holy See. Its campus consisted of the former sites of the mansions owned by the descendants of two Qing princes. The boys' school was the reconstructed residence of Prince Tao Dai, the 15th son of Emperor Kangxi. The buildings there were grand and lordly, a bit like those in Vatican City. The girls' school was even larger in size, occupying 100 mu or approximately 6.68 hectares of land dotted with ancient buildings, gardens and forests, which were beautiful and highly sophisticated. Dingfu Street ran between the two schools. Fu Jen Catholic University was one of four famous academic institutions in Beijing with the other three being Peking University, Tsinghua University and Yenching University. Meanwhile Beijing Normal University could be the fifth. When I was studying there, Fu Jen Catholic University was operated by the Society of the Divine Word in Germany. The institution was taken over by the Beijing Normal University in 1952. Because it was considered a religious organization, its operations were repressed until it practically ceased to exist. When I visited the campus again in 1994, all I could see were weeds growing on top of the glazed roof tiles. Even the buildings among the gardens, where priests from the Society of the Divine Word used to reside, were now messy compounds occupied by a myriad of families. They were no longer beautiful and clean.

I was interested in the Department of Chemistry. I had been interested in chemistry since my days as a student of Wenhua Junior

High School in Shenyang. Our school was small but had good standards which allowed us to use high school-level textbooks in our chemistry class. We also got to do all sorts of chemical experiments, a rare chance at that time, as there had not been a single chemical experiment conducted in my high school in Beijing. Our chemistry teacher at Wenhua Junior High School was a very nice person from Guangdong Province. Later he became a researcher at the chemistry section of the National Academy of Peking, the equivalent of today's National Academy of Sciences, near Beijing's Beihai Library.

Anyway, although I received a good score at the Fu Jen Catholic University's entrance examination, it wasn't enough to enter the Department of Chemistry. Why? Because their laboratory was so small, the department could accept only 30 students each year. Facing such fierce competition, those of us with good scores but no chance to enter the Department of Chemistry resorted to other majors. I chose the Department of Western Languages and Literature because I had been studying English since Year 5 at the primary school. It was a good thing that I changed my major because there were more girls studying in the College of Arts than in the College of Science.

Initially, it was relatively cheap to study back then. However, later, due to inflation, it became impossible to calculate our tuition fees in terms of money; we had to do so in terms of bags of flour instead. One of the priests from Germany was in charge of the university's finances. Indeed, someone had to keep accounts on money spent for food, drink, electricity, telephone and water that were used by the university's thousands of students every day not to mention trying to make money for the institution. The Society of the Divine Word owned dozens of trucks in China which were used to transfer food and other goods between Shanghai and Tianjin in an attempt to raise funds to support the university. That priest lived in Tianjin and was highly capable of managing these issues.

On December 8, 1941, Japan launched an attack on Pearl Harbor, signaling the start of the Pacific War. Both Yenching University and the Union Hospital ceased operations because the Japanese troops' occupation of the campuses. They shut down so suddenly that my uncle didn't even have a chance to pack his personal belongings except for some books. The Fu Jen Catholic University also closed its doors but for only one day. We were able to quickly resume our classes since our institution was sponsored by the Germans, a fellow Axis power with the Japanese. Indeed the Germans managed to reopen the university by placing a courteous telephone call to their Japanese counterparts. On the day the university shut down, I rode my bicycle out of the campus but had nowhere to go. I didn't even know where I could sleep at night. It was only in that evening when the dormitory opened its doors again that I was able to return.

With that said the Japanese maintained a firm grip on our university's operations. One night, a student in our dormitory turned off his light and went to sleep as usual but was arrested and taken away by the Japanese in the middle of the night. There was a place called "Shatan" in Beijing that was central to all traffic and transport between the city's eastern and western sections. Situated there was Beijing University's renowned "Red Building", where Japanese military police and secret agents were stationed at that time. Many Chinese people were killed there. With constant cries and screams coming from within, no one dared to go near it. Once taken there, it would be impossible to get out. I was only there once, after the victory of the War of Resistance against Japan.

I spent five years at the Fu Jen Catholic University. It should have been four years, but in my second year I had to remain at home due to typhoid. My attempt to return to the campus was dashed when I became sick again during mid-term examinations, so I went on leave of absence for the rest of the year. After that I met my wife, Ru-qian Zhao; the character "qian" meant "pretty and sweet". She was one year younger than me. However, after taking one year off, I shared the same class with her in the Department of Western Languages and Literature. Taking a year of sick leave was worth it because it gave me the opportunity to meet her and she was an excellent woman.

Anyway, my wife's uncle was a sinologist doing research at the Beijing Library. He encouraged her to study a lot of Chinese books, so she was far more knowledgeable about Chinese literature than me. By comparison I focused more on Western knowledge as most of the schools I attended from Beijing Huiwen Middle school to the Fu Jen Catholic University were Western-style academic institutions.

Back then we didn't have many girls on campus. The classes were co-educational, but male and female students lived in separate dormitories. Female students could attend classes designed for their male counterparts, but some of the classes were held at the girls' school where entry by males was forbidden. Under strict control we had to first call on the gatekeeper of the girls' school before trying to talk to any of the girls there. Their two-story building at the back of a huge garden was said to contain ninety-nine and a half rooms. Everybody could hear the gatekeeper yelling, "Miss So-and-So, there's someone outside looking for you!" This was a lot of fun. We had to offer tips to the gatekeeper on public holidays and festivals, or he would refuse to pass on our messages to the girls. He claimed it was his "shoe money", for he had worn out many pairs of shoes trying to locate the girls in the building on behalf of the male callers.

I had always enjoyed sports. Inspired by the long jump athletes at the Olympic Games, I dug a sand pit in the backyard of our house and practiced every day. At university I played mainly ballgames and would watch all sorts of related competitions. I remember a girl called Tong-yun Chen from the Department of Sociology who was not only a great volleyball player but also very beautiful. We watched her and other teammates when the volleyball games were held outside the university entrance but were disappointed when they played only at the girls' school. Chen is now more than 90 years old and a famous physician in Traditional Chinese Medicine. She still treats patients and discusses health and cosmetology on television in Beijing.

There's also Ellie Mao Mok at Rossmoor, an accomplished soprano, whose younger sister Hao was my classmate at the Fu Jen Catholic University (see the chapter on Ellie Mao Mok). Their younger brother Yuan, then a high school student, often came to visit Hao, but he was only a little boy in our eyes as university men and women. I even attended an Ellie Mao Mok concert at Yenching University one Christmas Eve. We had to ride our bicycles 45 to 50 minutes to get to the campus outside of the city and sometimes more than an hour if it was windy. It's so hard to imagine events now about things that happened more than 70 years ago. In our dormitories we had many students from Tianjin. Those from Beijing preferred living at home where conditions were far more comfortable than in school.

My wife's family was also in Tianjin. My mother-in-law was from Southern China, spoke fluent Shanghainese, and made superb flour-based dishes. My father-in-law once studied in the United States. His Master's degree in Business Administration from Northwestern University was useless at that time in China due to the turmoil and chaos of war, so he managed to find work at the Beijing Railway Bureau. After that, he secured a professorship in Beijing University's School of Law and finally a position in the United Nations Relief and Rehabilitation Administration (UNRRA). This was the United Nations proposed by U.S. President Franklin Delano Roosevelt and announced by the United States, Britain, China and the Soviet Union at the Tehran Conference in 1943, not the one supported and launched by 50 countries in San Francisco in 1945.

The UNRRA was established to support countries which suffered the most throughout the Second World War. Among those receiving help was China, while those providing assistance included the United States, Britain and Canada. The UNRRA's Chinese counterpart, the CNRRA, was administered by the Executive Yuan. The UNRRA provided funding for major projects, and their representatives stationed in China helped the CNRRA with its distribution. The Americans made generous donation, which used to help those in need. People from the Department of Sociology were in charge of selling truckloads of donated clothing, and some of the pockets often contained five, ten or even twenty-dollar bills donated by the Americans. Back then the CNRRA was truly dedicated to getting things done. No one thought of keeping any of the donated goods for themselves.

Here's something else for you: after the victory in the War of Resistance against Japan, the Minister of Education Li-fu Chen delivered a speech at our university in Beijing. That evening while visiting the Dong An Market, I saw Minister Chen buying shoes at a stall. As he lifted his feet, I saw that the soles of his shoes were completely worn out and full of holes and he was a high-ranking government official. Some people are truly admirable.

After the outbreak of the Pacific War, as the only university free of Japanese control, Fu Jen Catholic University was considered to be the premier educational institution in the Japanese-occupied areas across China. However, even our university was in chaos as all the professors from Britain, America and Holland were either arrested or driven away. Only a few Chinese professors and German priests remained on campus. Among them was our principle Yuan Chen, an old man from Guangdong Province with a tiny moustache. He knew every student in our university and kicked people out of his class if they were not among his registered students. His walls at home were pasted with sheets of white paper on which he recorded whatever ideas he happened to think of. In this way he had famously found a section missing from the *Twenty-Four Histories*, the Chinese official historical books covering the period from 3,000 BC to the Ming Dynasty in the 17th century.

Whenever Mr. Chen met Mr. Jia-xi Yu, then head of the Department of Chinese Literature, they didn't to talk to each other. Because they both were so knowledgeable and so well read, neither wanted to bring up something to cause conflict. Mr. Yu was a linguist from Hunan Province. An old man with a beard, he often wore a Chinese skullcap resembling the skin of half a watermelon. His son-in-law Zu-mo Zhou, also a linguist, was then an associate professor at the Department of Chinese Literature. I had also taken his class. All of these scholars were truly excellent. They genuinely wanted to teach you everything they could without holding back or keeping anything secret. But they were also very strict. They would order you to re-write an essay or poem if it was not up to their standards.

Having a great teacher is highly beneficial. Even a single word from them at the right moment can have a profound impact on your life, which is why I often refer to them as "one-word teachers". Another one of our teachers, surname Yen, had studied in Britain and specialized in English rhetoric and composition. However, his favorite topic was Peking Opera. A huge fan of superstars like Lan-fang Mei and Xiao-lou Yang, Mr. Yen discussed Peking Opera with far more enthusiasm than he did English subjects. He had also been in Japan.

After the war he became head of a department in Shenyang's Northeastern University. I recall the novel *Gone with the Wind* was newly published then. When he bought a copy and pointed out the typographical errors throughout the pages, I wondered whether he was capable of writing something as great as this book. Indeed, the book's English writing used American spelling while he was a scholar in British literature. although he complained the book was too full of errors to be read, the movie version was great. At that time a movie ticket in Tianjin was so expensive that you needed more than a bag of flour to purchase one. So who could afford a trip to the movie theater? Mainly the filthy rich textile merchants who knew nothing but speculation and profiteering. In sharp contrast, poor students like me could only wait until the price of a movie ticket dropped. We could afford only the cheapest tickets and were forced to take the farthest seats from the screen.

Back to Shenyang

After graduating from Fu Jen Catholic University, I found a position in the Office of the Commissioner of the Ministry of Foreign Affairs in Shenyang. My work commenced on January 1, 1947. Soon after that my wife and I married at the Grand Hotel des Wagons-Lits (today's Hua Feng Hotel) in Beijing. It was situated in between our families in Tianjin and Shenyang, making it fair and easy for everyone to travel there in war time. I played a couple of songs on the piano at the wedding. After that, my wife accompanied me to live with my parents in Shenyang.

The Nationalist Government's first commissioner to Northeast China was Ching-kuo Chiang, the oldest son of president Chiang Kai-Shek. Since he never reported for duty, the real commissioner was a so-called Russian expert named Jian-fei Zhang. The Office of the Commissioner was established in response to Russia's occupation of Shenyang and its further attempt to control the whole of Northeast China after Japan's surrender at the conclusion of the Second World War. As if people hadn't suffered enough at the hands of the Japanese, they now had to endure the "big-nosed" Russians.

After the Meiji Restoration in Japan in 1868, as a result of Emperor Meiji's desire to permanently take over the rich resources in Northeast China, the Japanese had constructed a series of warehouses, roads and industrial buildings. After the Japanese surrendered at the end of the war, the Russians also wanted to capture this region. Having taken Harbin, capital of Heilongjiang, China's northernmost province, they proceeded along the Chinese Eastern Railway and reached Dalian and Lushun on the Liaodong Peninsula at the southern tip of Liaoning Province. The Russians took these strategic cities and the surrounding areas to compensate for their lack of ports on the eastern side of their own territory. However, what distinguished them from the Japanese was their intent to grab everything for themselves. Even the Chinese railway was re-constructed to match the Russian track width. According to one of my friends in Changchun, Jilin Province, the Russians took anything and everything they could lay their hands on – pots, pans, bowls, spoons, toilet seats, bath tubs, and even windows and doors. It was akin to experiencing a hurricane where everything was blown away, leaving only the basic framework of a building. This was unprecedented in human history.

Numerous lives were ruined at the hands of the Russians. A well-known case involved a father using an axe to attack the Russian soldier who was raping his daughter, killing her as well in the process. And that would be trivial when you consider the fact that every female in Shenyang at that time shaved their heads and hid indoors in an attempt to avoid attracting the Russians' attention. It was useless as the Russians broke into their houses with guns. Everyone was frightened of them. Even my two nieces pretended to be men by shaving their heads, painting their eyebrows black and thick, and wearing men's clothing whenever they went out.

And here's another weird story from official records for you: The Japanese had built many warehouses and stored a lot of food in them. When the Russians arrived, they announced that all the citizens in Northeast China could come and take this food for free as they were now free of Japanese oppression. When the happy Chinese people arrived, they were directed along a specific route to pick up and drop off the bags of produce they desired. Eventually they realized it was a huge circle. All the food they thought they had taken was now returned to the warehouses leaving them left with nothing. All of this was a big show used to produce a film to demonstrate to the Allied Powers how generous the Russians were and how they were willing to share their food with the local Chinese because they truly cared about them.

Indeed, back in the days of the Russo-Japanese War (1904-1905), the two sides fought each other on Chinese land. The local Chinese residents were forced to adopt a special currency issued by the Russian

Red Army Command Center for use by their troops in the occupied areas. The paper money was nearly five times the dimensions of a U.S. one-dollar bill but worth absolutely nothing, particularly after the Russians left. It would be a beautiful wall paper, though. Those "big-nosed" Russians were indeed crazy.

Because my major was English at university, I was assigned a position in the Office of the Commissioner's second section, which handled issues relating to Britain and the United States. The office's first section focused on Russian-related issues, the third section on the Japanese, and the fourth on general affairs. However, with the Russians being too dominant and snobby to be bothered with us, and with the Japanese having already surrendered to the Allies, our section was the only one that was busy with work. Our main task was to liaise with the Americans, to improve our friendship with them and with the British, and to arrange the repatriation of German citizens to their home country. I had personally escorted various groups of German people by train from Shenyang to Tianjin and then to Shanghai, where they boarded an American airplane destined for Germany. At that time, those of us working for the Office of the Commissioner were all young and hard-working. We would get together after work to study, taking turns to teach each other English, German and Russian. Back then I majored in English and minored in French, but three years of French lessons were wasted on me; I have long forgotten how to use that language.

A colleague of mine, surname Zhang, was sent to Changchun to set up a temporary branch office. Before he left, the two of us managed to produce a special communication code by changing the first letter of each word in telegram code. As there was no one else capable of secret coding back then, I now wonder how we managed to be so clever. When the Communists attacked Changchun, Zhang managed to retreat by boarding the last airplane back to safety. Because there wasn't any room for luggage, he had to put on many layers of clothing, such as two suits, several pairs of socks, etc. When we went to pick him up at the airport, he looked absolutely huge in size.

While working for the Office of the Commissioner in Northeast China, I also had a chance to serve as a translator for Albert C. Wedemeyer, the replacement for Joseph Stilwell as the commander of U.S. military forces in China. At Wedemeyer's field office, I was ranked a lieutenant colonel, but with the salary of a major.

It was around that time that people who worked in the local office started retreating from Shenyang to Beijing. As China Airlines was still non-existent, we had to rely on the Central Air Transport Co. (CATC) and a Far East-based American company called the Civic Air Transport (CAT). I knew CAT pretty well since several of my friends from university days were working there and had insider information about the availability of passenger tickets. Among the dozens of people I helped to escape, quite a few asked me to get tickets from CAT. After I sent a request, the tickets arrived a couple of days later without extra cost.

By the time the staff at the Office of the Commissioner was due to leave, we had to wait for our turn to board the chartered flights. We waited and waited. after several weeks had passed, the head of the office got on a flight and left everyone else behind. Prior to taking off, this guy even destroyed all the personal papers that identified him as a member of the Nationalist Government. I decided not to work for the Ministry of Foreign Affairs any longer. According to the rule, as if they had to let employees go, then it should have at least given each of us a passport and US $500 as compensation. But they did not give us anything and only told us to wait and see. Half a year later we were all dismissed when the communists arrived. We had lost our jobs. I was further shocked to discover that the person who took over my job was also a former student of Fu Jen Catholic University. He had abandoned his studies after only one year on campus to go to Yan'an, then the center of the Chinese Communist movement in Shaanxi Province. Now he was arrogant and rude, propping his feet on the desk while talking to people like me. It was only then that I realized the secretary to the head of our office was a communist himself. He was tall and always friendly but suddenly looked like a different person to me with my new knowledge. I forgot which province he came from.

I had always been on good terms with the American consulate in Shenyang. After the Office of the Commissioner was shut down, the consular director asked me to work in his office. At that time the communists had yet to arrive though the locals had started retreating. One day, having received the director's permission, I drove the consulate's jeep everywhere to find out what was going on. Now that I think about it, what I did that day was truly dangerous as anyone could have attacked me sitting in that fancy American jeep with the American flag flapping in the wind. Indeed, the following day I found the American Consulate guarded by soldiers from the People's Liberation Army. I quietly parked the jeep in the garage and slipped away. No more risky driving!

After that I moved to my grandmother's house, a sizeable compound now occupied by my parents. My maternal great-grandfather was one of the Qing Dynasty's two high officials in charge of the security of the capital cities, called "Jiumendudu". He was stationed in Shengjing, the Qing Dynasty's capital from 1625 to 1644 and today's Shenyang, while the other official looked after Beijing, the capital of China since the 12th century. My great-grandfather's position was the equivalent of today's capital garrison commander, one of the highest ranks. My maternal grandfather was also successful as the governor of Tongzhou at the northern end of China's Grand Canal (today's Tongzhou District in Beijing).

After the Communists arrived, they wanted to set up a police station at our house. After they occupied my aunt's medical clinic at the front, they insisted on taking over the rest of the compound by kicking us out. Our glass wardrobe was too big to be moved, so they smashed it into pieces. They had no wood to light their stove, so they burned all our family's cypress furniture and commented on its good smell. When I tried to move our heavy stove with a friend, the police chief was happy to lend a hand because the weight was nothing to him since he used to be a night soil collector.

Here's something funny for you: All of the communist soldiers had a strip of red fabric attached to their guns, whether they were rifles, muskets or pistols. They claimed it was to fend off evil spirits, but how could any communist be afraid of spirits if he or she didn't believe in them?

All the Way to Taipei

By May 1949 Shenyang was controlled by the Communists. I became unemployed and alone after my wife returned to her family in Tianjin to prepare for the birth of our first child. I wanted to go to Tianjin, but needed a travel permit to purchase a train ticket. My permit identified me as an "employee of the Bogus Ministry of Foreign Affairs". Somehow I got hold of a ticket, but it was still unnerving to face interrogation by Communist guards at the Shenyang Station. Some people were forbidden to board the train even with valid tickets.

By June of that year, the Communists had captured Nanjing in Jiangsu Province forcing the Nationalist Government to relocate its capital to Guangzhou, Guangdong Province. Having reunited with my wife in Tianjin, we were supposed to go to Guangzhou as well. However, there was neither transport nor a way to contact anybody representing the government there. As my in-laws had already gone to work in Taiwan a year earlier, I decided to take my wife, our one-year-old daughter and one of my wife's sisters to that island.

There was no ship sailing from Tianjin, so we had to travel to Qingdao in Shandong province to find one to Taiwan. The trip by truck from Hebei Province to Shandong Province took more than a week. All along the way there was saline-alkali soil from which not even a blade of grass would grow. At night we slept in a tent. We dug 12 inches into the ground and used that as a floor and rolled out a mat on the earth's surface and used it as a bed. Traveling southeast to Shandong Province, we passed a place called Mount Liang, known as the stronghold of the 108 legendary bandits of the classic Chinese novel *The Water Margin*. Then it was Yueling, famous for its jujube fruit, and Changyi, a production center for textiles. Finally, it was Weifang where a concentration camp was set up by the Japanese at the start of the Pacific War to hold enemy personnel from the United States, Britain and Europe. While running to catch a ferry to cross the Yellow River, I accidentally dropped my eyeglasses and broke one of the two temple end pieces, and had to find a string to tie the frame to my ear.

We felt miserable sitting on the truck. However, while crossing the Yellow River, we saw many Nationalist soldiers walking, limping, crawling, or carrying one another in their arms or on their backs. Some had become so desperate that they commited suiside by hanging. When they saw us sitting on a truck, the look of envy in their eyes was truly heart-wrenching. These people didn't know where they were going except to keep surviving. What more could they do? They had lost the war.

Along the way we passed through many check pointss. The one outside of Tianjin was managed by young communist students who were rather polite and friendly. Then it gradually worsened. Prior to our trip, my wife's grandfather took a gold ring from his finger and gave it to me to exchange for money should our circumstances become dire. He would not let me hide it, so I wore it to show my gratitude. Then at a check point in Shandong, a female communist guard wanted that ring and threatened to imprison all of us on the truck. I had no choice but to hand it over to her. After she put it on her own finger, she kept me in detention for half a day and confiscated the other people's valuables as well. Indeed, we lost everything on that trip.

We hardly had anything to eat. The so-called noodle soup for a whole week consisted of a bowl of water, a couple of thin noodles and several cabbage leaves. It was only after we arrived in Weifang that we tasted chicken. Another place we passed was the Lan Village in a town called Jimo, about 50 kilometers from Qingdao. It was there that we found two U.S. one-dollar bills in my wife's purse. We immediately burned them over an oil lamp. Otherwise, anybody ay any check point could accuse us of being involved with the Americans and arrest us.

On the last day before our arrival in Qingdao, from dawn to about four o'clock in the afternoon, my wife and daughter rode in a wheelbarrow, I walked by their side. There were so many Japanese warplanes with their machine guns flying overhead that people urged us to turn our daughter's bright red jacket inside out to avoid any unwanted attention. A couple of soldiers, who were also fleeing from the war, assured us that machine gun bullets from warplanes wouldn't be able to get to us; instead, our real concern sould be mortar shells. Anyway, I had been walking for so long that the soles of my shoes fell off, and I had to hold them in place with rope. Luckily, a generous passer-by gave me a pair of cloth shoes to wear.

When we finally reached Qingdao, which was still under control of the Nationalist troops, only one of us was allowed to enter the city to find a guarantor and submit our identity papers for processing. I contacted one of my father-in-law's friends there, whom I had never met before, while leaving my wife and child waiting by the roadside outside the city gate. My contact was shocked by my appearance: a pair of broken eyeglasses bound on one side of my face with string, a messy beard, an old hat, a blue cloth jacket full of holes, a pair of threadbare velvet pants, and a dirty pair of cloth shoes. I looked truly shabby and miserable. He immediately took me to a police station, signed up as our guarantor and had our identity papers stamped. I was further warned that I needed to bring my wife and daughter into the city before the gates were shut at six o'clock in the evening. I managed to gather my family a couple of minutes before six, and somehow brought along another woman with her two daughters. That woman carried a hot water bottle everywhere she went claiming to have milk in it for her children. It was only after we had safely entered Qingdao's city gates that she confessed she had gold hidden in that bottle. It was truly scary now that I think about it. Anyway, we finally reached Qingdao, had a shower and changed into clean clothes. That was the toughest week of my entire life, but we made it. Luckily, nothing like that ever happened to us again.

Due to inflation the price of postage went up considerably every day. Later the Nationalist Government issued such ridiculous currencies as the "gold dollar" and "silver dollar" certificates both of which were practically impossible to use. Only the silver coins issued in the early stages of the Republic of China with the image of Shi-kai Yuan's head, the notorious Chinese general, politician and self-proclaimed emperor, managed to keep their market value. Back in 1948 and 1949, one such silver coin was worth the equivalent of two U.S. dollars. However, after the communists captured Qingdao and the American troops retreated from the city, even U.S. dollars lost their value with two of them being barely worth the equivalent of one "Yuan's big head" silver coin.

After a week's stay in Qingdao, we finally boarded one of the ships in a fleet led by Admiral An-qi Liu, commander of the Nationalist Government's 11 Pacification Zone. The fleet consisted of dozens of ships, including two ships of more than 10,000 tons called the Freedom and the Victory. Our tiny vessel of 180 tons was so slow that it only managed eight knots per hour compared to the big ships with speeds of dozens of knots per hour. We slept in cabins where all sorts of goods were stored. Having passed the Zhoushan Archipelago and reaching the mouth of the Yangtze River, we bumped into one of the many Nationalist navy ships that had defected to the communists. It was lucky that they didn't attack us.

Our captain had no knowledge of English nor any of the navigation charts required for sailing. We tried to follow the other ships in the distance but ended up getting lost. One of the sailors on our vessel was in charge of telegrams. As he understood the machine but not the incoming English telegrams and weather charts, I ended up translating them from English to Chinese and became a highly valuable person in the eyes of our captain. He even let my family sleep in the telegram room where only the aforementioned sailor and his machine stayed. We were also able to purchase food from that sailor which was rice porridge for every meal. While my wife was too seasick to eat anything else, I had only some flat bread and pickled vegetables for food, which I had carried all the way from Qingdao. One day a woman on our vessel begged me for some food, so I shared a piece of our bread with her. She was so hungry that she immediately ate it, despite the fact that the bread had long gone stale and moldy. Life was truly miserable then. By the time we reached the Geelon Port in Taiwan, people rushed out of the cabins in their attempt to leave the vessel as soon as possible. Some fell into the water when our vessel bumped into another boat. Others drowned when they tried to jump onto the dock.

Ours was the last ship leaving Qingdao. I remember it was June 1, 1949, amid the celebrations of the Dragon Boat Festival. My wife had been upset that I brought along half a dozen beers for the occasion, but I ended up drinking them during the trip because there was no water on our vessel. We were among the last group of people leaving Shandong Province, part of the famous Great Retreat from Qingdao in 1949. The day after that, Qingdao was captured by the People's Liberation Army.

Report to Duty in Guangzhou

Having arrived in Taiwan, my wife and I had exhausted all desire to travel. Where could we go anyway? My wife even made a joke that it would be easy to commit suicide by drowning because the island was surrounded by the sea. I approached the Nationalist Government, who told me to report for duty at the Ministry of Foreign Affairs in Guangzhou. What else could I have done to earn money to purchase food for my wife and child except to return to the Chinese mainland for work?

In August, 1949 when I arrived in Guangzhou, the Americans issued the "White Paper on United States Relations with China" which ended all military aid to the Republic of China without formally recognizing the People's Republic of China. It was weird going to Guangzhou, as we flew in one of the "air palaces" that were newly purchased by the Central Air Transport Co., airplanes with jet engines, propellers and a speed of more than 300 miles per hour. Having traveled from Taipei to Guangzhou, we took a bus from the airport to the city. The Ministry of Foreign Affairs had a hotel rented for our temporary stay which was near Shamian, a place I had heard of but knew nothing about. It turned out to be an artificial island where only Westerners were allowed to reside, like a designated area for foreign embassies. Another time while walking in Guangzhou, I was sprayed with DDT the insecticide which left numerous spots on my white shirt.

Upon reporting for duty in Guangzhou, I was told to go on leave of absence and given only a US $300 travel allowance. When I complained it was far less than the amount of money I had spent fleeing from Tianjin to Taiwan via Qingdao, they said rules were rules.

At that time there were 72 employees working at the Ministry of Foreign Affairs. The renowned scholar Shih Hu was assigned to be minister by acting president Zong-jen Li, but Hu never took the position. Instead, the ministry was directed by George K.C. Yeh who later fled to Taiwan. Most of the high-ranking government officials arriving in Taiwan were competent. It was lucky there were some honest and capable people there; otherwise, the Nationalist Government in Taiwan would have collapsed long ago.

Back in June 1949 when I left Qingdao, Shanghai had already been lost. The People's Liberation Army managed to cross the Yangtze River before the Dragon Boat Festival, leaving the Nationalist Government to control only bits of land in Northwest and Southwest China. People at the Ministry of Foreign Affairs told me that if I really wanted to work, they could find me a position in Kunming, Yunnan Province. I said, "No thank you." There was a funny saying back in Northern China that one could move from a pit containing urine to one holding shit. But I refused to do it. If I had agreed to move to Kunming, then I would never, ever have a chance to leave China. It was lucky that I didn't go as the Nationalist Government relocated to Taiwan soon after that. I started working for the Ministry of Foreign Affairs in 1947 and left in 1949. That was the end. I refused to work for them for free.

Life in Taipei

So, with no money from the Ministry of Foreign Affairs, what could I do next? I returned to Taiwan to find a job. I stayed in Taipei where our life was relatively uneventful. Because I knew some English, I was able to work for a company that imported and exported electric appliances. Ten years later when the company re-grouped, I switched to work for the Formosa Plastic Group. Another four years later, when the corporation's various partners established theirown businesses, I started at Taita Chemical Company and remained there until I retired. Considering the fact that I wanted to study chemistry at a young age, it was interesting that I ended up in the chemical business.

At that time Taiwan experienced an economic boom with all sorts of industries witnessing rapid development. It was during this period that America helped Taiwan to set up a "productivity center". It collaborated with the Taipei Institute of Technology to organize a series of evening classes on topics related to industrial engineering. Finally, I had a chance to study industrial and business administration. For three years non-stop, from seven to ten o'clock every evening, I went to these classes after work. That was the most diligent, hard-working period of my life. I studied for and received more than 140 credits from all the courses required for a university degree in industrial engineering. More importantly, all the instructors were genuine industrial professionals with practical work experience. They were proactive and enthusiastic teachers while students like me were equally passionate about learning.

There was never a boring class. Take quality control as an example, a concept that only became popular after the Second World War. It was a brand new idea during the early stage of Taiwan's development of modern industries. Our instructors worked with us to produce a series of textbooks based on what actually happened throughout the manufacturing processes at various factories, and they also established the Chinese Society for Quality Control (today's Chinese Society for Quality) in 1964, with some of its members arranging meetings periodically for decades until they retired. Now that I think about it, in that period I had learned much new knowledge and made many friends from all walks of life. It was a truly rare opportunity. Later I also had a chance to teach various classes at the Taipei Institute of Technology. The institution was upgraded and renamed the National Taipei University of Technology in 1997. It is now one of the most prestigious technical universities in the world.

At Taita Chemical Company, my busiest time was spent in the procurement division where I had considerable power and responsibility managing the import of raw materials while monitoring the export of finished products. I worked hard and gave them all I had, never complaining no matter how exhausting my tasks were. Fortunately, everything was successfully done and my boss appreciated my efforts. Indeed, I was exhausted every day working from eight-thirty in the morning to nine o'clock in the evening. With no canteen in the factory, we had to ask a maintenance worker to make a special trip on his bicycle to purchase meals for us. Even taxis were not widely available then, so we had to go a long way to find a restaurant whenever there were clients to entertain. Today there are lots of restaurants.

As Taita Chemical Company expanded, it set up factories in Singapore, Malaysia and even the United States. I think they have a total of 12 factories now, four of which produce raw materials while the others do processing. One of our branch companies, the China General Plastics Corporation, ended up making so much money and being so big that it became a major rival to Yung-ching Wang's Formosa Plastics Corporation.

The Taita Chemical Company was also quite profitable, attracting the attention of Mobil in the United States who sought to produce chemical materials and plastics with us. However, it was an extremely slow process as the U.S. Government disapproved of many of our collaborative projects. But the truth is, back then the Americans had yet to enforce many environmental protection regulations as they do now. They only pretended to want to work with us, while managing to secretly get everything done in their own backyard. They called us "honey" while working with us side by side, but as soon as they departed they ceased being sweet. To avoid paying taxes, they invested capital in the name of a company in Panama and transferred all their earnings to a bank in that country as well. Later, our boss in Taiwan decided to sell off all of our factories. It was a smart move, but getting to a position of success, realizing it was probably time to sell, and being capable of making such a tough decision was even harder. I believe it is what they called "from small things big things grow".

Upon our arrival in Taiwan, my wife was invited to teach at the National Taiwan University. She chose not to accept the position because she was about to give birth to our youngest child. Instead, she later became a high school teacher. In my opinion, teaching high school students is much more difficult than teaching their university counterparts. A high school teacher has to make sure all the students have truly learned the lessons while university students can choose whether they want to accept the knowledge or not. Anyway, my wife taught English and had thousands of students at two high schools. She began with three classes but later expanded to supervising two of their experimental classes in what is now considered to be Year 12. It was in these experimental classes that innovative teaching methods were tried with a focus on cultivating the special talents of students.

Ru-qian Zhao and students of the experimental class at the Affiliated Senior High School of the National Taiwan Normal University Taipei 1962

My wife was such a dedicated teacher that she gained quite a reputation. One of her students, Jian-lu Wang, contributed an article to the website of one of the schools describing her as the perfect speaker of both Mandarin and American-style English. Her pronunciation was as beautiful as the way she looked: She always wore her hair in a bun but changed the style and color of her Chinese cheongsam every day. Her appearance was both dignified and graceful and much prettier than Hong Kong movie star Maggie Cheung in her 2000 film *In the Mood for Love*! To pay tribute to her achievements as a teacher, her students donated money to set up a "Ms. Ru-qian Zhao Scholarship" to provide financial subsidies to poor but talented students.

Something else interesting happened while I lived in Taipei. One day while waiting for a bus to go home after work, I saw a long row of military trucks rushing past. The next day the local newspaper reported that the construction of the National Palace Museum was completed and that all sorts of cultural and artistic relics were now being transferred from Taichung to Taipei. Tons and tons of these priceless relics used to be stored in boxes and hidden in a cave in central Taiwan survived numerous journeys over land and across the sea,. After they were safely moved to Taipei, my wife and I often visited the extensive exhibitions at the National Palace Museum.

We lived in Taipei for more than 40 years. The oldest of our four children was the daughter I mentioned earlier, the girl who wore a bright red jacket as we fled from the turmoil of war in China. The other three boys were born in Taipei.

I am a Catholic. Both my junior and senior high schools were sponsored by Christian churches, and I had joined a Bible study group back in my days as a junior high school student. Even Fu Jen was a Catholic university. The thought of being baptized never occurred to me, nor did my wife, who was a Catholic herself, ever try to talk me into it. However, after many years of being near the religion, I finally chose to follow it. I consider myself to have been a good Catholic throughout the past 60 years. I have my wife to thank for that; it was she who led us into the door of genuine religious faith.

Retirement in America

Having completed her studies in the United States, our daughter married, settled down and wanted us to relocate there. She even had all sorts of application forms and supporting material prepared on our behalf, but I refused to go. What would I do in America? We couldn't just depend on our daughter's support. Then in June, 1986 when our company was about to be listed on the stock market, I purchased many shares in response to my boss' open request. My intention was for this to be an investment, but the company did well and the price of its stock rose rapidly. This led me to sell my shares making me a rich man overnight. I never thought that things would turn out that way, but my boss considered it a reward for my more than 20 years of hard work for the company. As for myself, I tend to think of it as a sign of good luck, part of my destiny, and a gift from the heavens. Otherwise, with no money of my own, I would never have decided to come to the United States. It is true that we were now capable of supporting ourselves, but there is no denying that our children would always be happy to look after us.

We moved to America in 1988 after I retired. Soon after that, a friend of mine recommended that I look at Rossmoor, Walnut Creek, California. I liked the fact that it is so quiet, convenient and safe here that you can lock your door and travel for months without worrying about being robbed. With that said, after we moved here, my daughter and her husband were assigned to work in the Philippines and left us here. Most of the residents here are American, but there are no communication issues because both my wife and I speak fluent English. Upon our arrival here we knew not a single person, but we soon met a Chinese man, surname Zhang, who quickly introduced himself as a former graduate from Fu Jen Catholic University. Back then Rossmoor only had a few dozen Chinese residents, but the number soon expanded considerably. I even reunited with some of my old friends here.

Gus Kao and wife Ru-qian Zhao in their retirement

I have lived in this community for more than 26 years. I was 67 years old when we moved here, but soon after that my wife became ill and returned to Taiwan for an operation. The doctors claimed to have done a good job and it indeed sustained her for another seven years. Initially her health was good and she was taking Chinese medicine. Her red blood cell count was back to normal and we were able to travel together to many places around the world. Once we spent a week attending a class on nutrition and organic food therapy that was organized by a Japanese in Sacramento. We visited some scenic spots nearby including a town called Oroville where a Chinese temple was built in 1863. During the gold-rush days, there were more than 10,000 Chinese laborers working in gold mines across California. In this particular temple there was a board horizontally inscribed above the front door that was bestowed by the Empress Dowager Cixi. Numerous Chinese gods and deities were also worshipped there including the Three Purities of Taoism (Lord of Primordial Beginning, Lord of the Numinous Treasure and Lord of the Way and Its Virtue), Matsu the patron goddess of all seafarers, Lord Guan the God of War, and

Confucius the Divine Teacher, among many others. With such a compendium of Chinese gods and deities on display, the temple also served as a museum. We had a lot of fun there, visiting a nearby river and fishing at a lake.

Indeed, for decades – no, for nearly two hundred years – our fellow Chinese people hardly lived a good life for one day. That is, to count from the tumultuous and chaotic days of the Opium War and the Taiping Heavenly Kingdom, right? We are poor Chinese as a people.

My wife passed away after seven years in this blessed community. I am alone now, but there are many activities and friends here to have fun with. It is also enjoyable to share these life stories with anyone who will listen. I have such a wonderful life here that I hardly ventured outside the community the past ten years. I have practiced *Tai Chi* Qi Gong for more than 20 years. Initially there were only a few students but now I have dozens. From Monday to Thursday, in the morning, I lead our community members in *Tai Chi* Qi Gong practice for an hour. Many people consider this to be highly beneficial to their health. Then after that I dance with friends or go for a meal. For example, I drove a couple of ladies in their 90s to sample Chinese dumplings only two days ago. I have no problem driving on the freeway. As a major residential area for people working in San Francisco and Silicon Valley, the East Bay boasts many one-direction freeways with six lanes each. There are many, many cars driving at high speeds.

Gus Kao leading community members in *Tai Chi* Qi Gong practice

My daughter long ago returned to the United States and is now working on the East Coast. Two of my sons are in Taiwan while the third lives in Thailand. Every year during the Chinese New Year holidays, I visit and stay with each of them for a while. I have much free time now, but they are too busy working to travel. Once at an airport the staff of an airline company checked my passport and looked at me in amazement. I tried to convince them that I was more than 90 years old. A woman even asked me, "If you're truly in your 90s, then how come you're not in a wheelchair?" I stretched my arms and legs and responded, "Do you think I need a wheelchair?" A man has to be in good spirits. What fun would it be if he simply hunched his back and used a cane to help him walk?

David Hsu 徐宗華
At the Great American Music Hall, San Francisco, 2014

    I ha long heard the story of a man called Zong-hua Hsu at Rossmoor who went to Taiwan to take over Japanese-operated airlines after the victory of the War of Resistance against Japan. He responded politely to my invitation for an interview, and recalled many of the events in the distant past with the assistance of his son Chivay Hsu. What he helped to take over was not an air carrier, it was all the machinery, equipment and production-related materials used by the Japanese in its airplane manufacturing factories in Taiwan. The move was to prepare for the production of aircraft trainers by the Chinese Air Force. It was right after Japan's surrender that he arrived in Taiwan at the age of 25. The record below can help readers understand his ancestors' life experiences as well as his own story. His recollections ranged from his fleeing the turmoils of war to witnessing large-scale Japanese bombing in Chongqing, Sichuan Province, where he was studying aeronautical engineering, to taking over the Japanese factories in Taiwan, and finally to his making airplanes for the Chinese Air Force and, after his retirement from air force, to his contribution to the early development of Taiwan's civil aviation industry.

Biography

David Hsu, whose Chinese name is Zong-hua Hsu was born in Nanjing in 1920 His ancestral home was Changshu, Jiangsu Province,. He went to Chongqing as a student of the Affiliated Experimental Senior High School of the National Central University at the start of the War of Resistance against Japan. Having graduated from that university's Department of Aeronautical Engineering in 1944, he joined the Air Force and commenced working at the No. 3 Aircraft Manufacturing Company in Chengdu, Sichuan Province. In 1945 when the war ended, he was assigned to Taiwan to take over the Japanese aviation industry. He then took charge of technical and administrative operations of the No. 3 Aircraft Manufacturing Company after it was relocated from Chengdu to Shuinan, Taichung County, Taiwan. After being discharged from the Air Force in 1959, he served as the director of China Airlines' aircraft maintenance plant before relocating to the United States in 1977 to work for a company that supplied aviation equipment. He retired and moved to Rossmoor, in San Francisco's East Bay in 1988.

An Aeronautical Engineer and His Airplanes

My ancestral home was Changshu in Jiangsu Province, but I was born in Nanjing in 1920. My father Bao-chong Hsu graduated from the Nan Yang Public School, the first university in modern Chinese history and today's National Chiao Tung University. He worked for the Nanjing Electric Lighting Plant, a power plant constructed in 1910 during the reign of Emperor Xuantong, commonly known as Henry Pu Yi, the last emperor of the Qing Dynasty, to provide electric lamps to Nanjing. By the time the Republic of China was established, the plant had become a public power station operated by the Jiangsu Government. Today it is known as the Nanjing Xiaguan Power Plant. My mother Bao-ying Wang was a housewife. We all lived in Nanjing back then.

My ancestral home was in the countryside outside of Changshu. We seldom went there except for an occasional short stay during the summer holidays. It used to be a land of abundance criss-crossed by waterways where all transport was done by boat. My grandfather, a physician of traditional Chinese medicine, set up his clinic on a small vessel. His private boatman would row to village after village where my grandfather would receive patients on the boat and dispense medicine from it. The patients would then throw a certain number of coins as payment into the boat's rear cabin. I recall that every day, upon my grandfather's arrival at home, one of our family's long-term servants would go to the vessel to collect the coins.

My father later joined the Chinese Army's wireless communication operations. I don't know when he enlisted, but among the documents kept in Taiwan's National Archives is a report that my father presented to the then president Chiang Kai-shek. Titled "Observation of Instructions to Conclude and Transfer All Operations to A.D.C. to the Chief of the Army Staff", the report hints at an order given by Chiang, perhaps to assign my father to a different position. My father remained in the army until his discharge after the victory of the War of Resistance against Japan. When I was in kindergarten, because my mother had to look after my baby brother and sister, my father left my older brother and me in the care of an uncle who was teaching at the Affiliated Experimental Primary School of the National Central

University. As we were both little, this uncle in turn let us stay in the dormitory of a female teacher that he appointed to care for us. With all of us taken care of, my father was able to devote his life to his work. Meanwhile, I started living on campus as a student of the Affiliated Experimental Kindergarten of the National Central University. I went on to study at the affiliated experimental primary and middle schools of the institution before becoming a university student there.

Studying and Fleeing from the War

In August, 1937, I was a high school student. As our experimental school in Nanjing's Sanpailou District was destroyed by Japanese warplanes, I traveled westward with the teachers in September to resume our lessons in Tunxi, Anhui Province. Later, as Anhui Province was also in danger of being captured by the Japanese, we relocated again to Changsha, Hunan Province. When Changsha, too, became a dangerous place and I became sick, my father who was then in Chongqing, Sichuan Province, came to pick me up. We then returned to Nanjing and took the whole family to Chongqing by boat. At that time there were many, many boats sailing along the Yangtze River to the vast hinterlands. Most of the passengers were employees of schools and government organizations who had to retreat by boat because there was no more space on trains.

As my father worked for the army, traveling with him was certainly easier than going with our school. Upon our arrival in Chongqing, Japanese warplanes had yet to arrive as they had to capture Hankou first in order to take off from Hubei Province to attack us. Still, the bombing of Chongqing began in early 1938 and was both frequent and fierce. Initially our own pilots were able to fight back, but they were soon demolished. The poor Chinese Air Force had no way of competing against the Japanese in terms of both the number of their warplanes and their flying and fighting skills. The bombing destroyed many important government organizations, industrial facilities, urban and economic centers, schools and civilian residential areas. Our citizens suffered heavy casualties.

Having graduated from the Affiliated Experimental Senior High School of the National Central University, I then failed to pass the Chinese Air Force's entrance examination to train as a pilot. Instead, hoping to one day make airplanes for our nation, I decided to study aeronautical engineering at the National Central University. Our campus was situated in Shapingba, a district of Chongqing and a strategic point at the junction of Jialing and Yangtze Rivers. Right beside the rivers, a series of solid bomb shelters were dug into the hills. In 1941, Japanese warplanes twice targeted the National Central University, Chongqing University and Fudan University, and destroyed all major buildings on these campuses. Whenever they came, we would dash into nearby bomb shelters. We were safe but exhausted due to frequently running back and forth. The Japanese pilots, surveying over the Jialing and Yangtze Rivers, were flying so low that we could see their faces. They could see us clearly as well and would often waved their hats and scarves to taunt us. We really hated them, but there was nothing we could do. They were able to show off as much as they wanted because there were only a few anti-aircraft guns in Chongqing.

Taking Over Japanese Aircraft Factories in Taiwan

In 1944 I joined the Chinese Air Force as a university graduate. After receiving some training, I was assigned a position at the No. 3 Aircraft Manufacturing Company in Chengdu, Sichuan Province. Our factory mainly copied Western trainer aircrafts and gliders. We also copied the Russian Tupolev SB-3, a high-speed twin-engine three-seat monoplane bomber. In August 1945, soon after the Japanese surrendered, the Air Force Command Headquarters sent an urgent note ordering our factory to take over all Japanese aircraft manufacturing machinery, equipment and production-related materials in their factories in Taiwan. Our director, Major-General Duo Yun, arrived in Taiwan in early September with his deputy and chief engineer. Meanwhile, I was transferred to our factory's Shanghai branch to prepare for my trip to that island. Major-General Yun and his people inspected two Japanese factories in Taiwan – No. 61 Aviation Factory of the Japanese Imperial Navy in Gangshan, Kaoshiung County, and No. 5 Field Army and Aircraft Maintenance Plant of the Japanese Imperial Army in Pingdong County. It was discovered that, in an attempt to avoid U.S. bombing, these two factories had dispersed much of their equipment and machinery across Taiwan. Consequently, Major-General Yun and his people had to fly around the whole island in a Japanese military airplane and visit many locations in order to organize the takeover by our people in Chongqing.

I departed for Taiwan on October 5, 1945. To receive a travel permit, I had to report to the U.S. Air Force at an airport in Shanghai before taking one of their airplanes to Taipei. Back then we had yet to re-establish our own air force flight transport and had to rely on the U.S. Air Force's support. As I was an aeronautical engineer from the No. 3 Aircraft Manufacturing Company, they were happy to issue me a handgun and send me as a single person from Shanghai to Taiwan to take over all the Japanese aircraft manufacturing equipment, machinery and production-related materials. I was only a lieutenant, a low-ranking officer from the Air Force, a 25-year-old recent university graduate. As the Nationalist Government had yet to relocate to Taiwan with its troops, the whole island was still under the Japanese. Indeed, Japanese officials had managed Taiwan for decades, using it as a military base in their invasion of the Chinese Mainland. At that moment they still had more than 200,000 troops and hundreds of thousands of other personnel stationed there.

As soon as I boarded the airplane to Taiwan, I discovered a group of Nationalist Government representatives sitting in front of me.

Among them was Chia-kan Yen, then the Ministry of Transport's special commissioner who later rose in the hierarchy to be the Taiwan Provincial Government's Minister of Finance, the Premier, Vice President, and President of the Republic of China after the death of Chiang Kai-shek. Now I find it hard to comprehend that back in 1945 I was traveling to Taiwan in the same airplane as this famous person. Upon our arrival in Taipei, Yen and his people got off first to be received by a couple of Chinese people in suits.

However, things were completely different when I got off. The first person to receive me there was a Japanese colonel as indicated by his name card. As I stepped off the airplane, I was shocked to see a large group of Japanese soldiers, pilots, air force officers and even generals lining up to salute me. It was akin to a marching band welcoming an honored national guest. What's going on here? I had to ask exactly whom they were expecting. It was only after I heard them reading out loud the written instructions from their superiors which specified my name David Hsu that I dared to enter their military vehicle.

As the Japanese driver was able to speak English, I hassled him with questions such as from which department he was sent and exactly what orders he had received. Finally, certain that the person they wanted was me, I relaxed. But it was such a funny feeling as if I had reached the sky in a single bound. I was only a low-ranking officer, a lieutenant. I was given such a courteous reception only because our nation had won the war! So I travelled with them in a daze from the Songshan Airport to downtown Taipei. All along the way I was well treated by the Japanese and ended up staying in one of their military guest houses. The next morning an old Japanese army officer picked me up and accompanied me to board a train to take over their factory in Taichung. Judging by his uniform, his rank could have been as high as lieutenant general. I had previously studied Japanese uniforms in order to understand their titles. I needed to know who my opponents were.

As the war had just finished, life was still not normal. People had only started to try to recover. Take that train trip as an example. It was about eight o'clock in the morning, and seated in all the carriages were young students on their way to school. As soon as that Japanese lieutenant general and I boarded the train, all the students jumped to their feet. They remained standing even after the general had spoken to them in Japanese, so I thought they must be too afraid of Japanese people to sit down. Then he asked me to take a seat, which made me highly embarrassed. How could I sit when all the children were standing? They refused to sit even when I asked them to. While they recognized me as a fellow Chinese because of my Chinese Air Force uniform, they had no idea who I was. They were afraid to sit down because all they knew was they were in the presence of a high-ranking Japanese military officer and that he was standing. Anyway, I ended up taking a seat, but all the other seats in that carriage remained empty. Even the Japanese lieutenant general remained standing by my side throughout the train journey from Taipei to Changhua County's Yuanlin Station on the other side of Taichung County. That was a 200-kilometer journey which would take at least three hours even with today's fast trains. He simply stood there, neither moving nor eating. This was after the Japanese surrendered. From that incident I was able to understand a little bit about the relationship between the Taiwanese and the Japanese.

By the time we arrived, nearly all of Japan's aircraft manufacturing factories in Taiwan had been destroyed by American bombing. Although the Japanese did not base their aviation industry in Taichung, they had transferred much equipment and machinery into the mountains of Yuanlin, a small county that felt like a country town to the south. Anyway, upon my arrival in Yuanlin, there was nothing remotely like a take-over ceremony. Instead, the Japanese prepared a detailed list of the items waiting to be transferred to my authority, and that document was as thick as a book. While I could only get a rough idea of the numerous items they had shown me throughout the area's many different sections, I was somehow pleased by what I saw. The Japanese spent decades building an aviation industry in Taiwan, and now all of it was going back to the Chinese. It was such an emotional issue. Born and raised on the Chinese mainland, I had never had a chance to visit Japan or Taiwan. Now all of a sudden we had won the war and were faced with a brand new world. I had never imagined there would be so many things waiting to be transferred back to the Chinese. It was like a gift from the heavens that I felt ill prepared for.

All the people I talked to in Yuanlin were Japanese who paid me much respect. Because I didn't speak Japanese and they didn't speak Chinese and because I didn't want any Taiwanese-speaking local person to serve as middleman and further complicate the situation, I proposed conversing with those among the Japanese who could speak English. They came up with several, but their English was pretty rough. Still, I ended up staying in Yuanlin among these Japanese soldiers for six months. Considering we were enemies only a short while before, it could have been an unnerving experience, but it wasn't like that at all to me. What was there to be nervous about? They were the ones who lost the war. If I had been afraid, I would never have gone there.

David Hsu (front row in the middle) and a group of Japanese soldiers, Taiwan, 1945

The repatriation of all Japanese personnel in Taiwan began in 1946. Both soldiers and civilians were transported to Geelon by train and then sent back to Japan by ship. Still, in our establishment of a branch aircraft manufacturing factory in Taichung, we employed many Taiwanese laborers who used to work for the Japanese. One of them had a Japanese girlfriend and wanted to keep her in Taiwan. Besides she did not want to leave, so the two of them found a place to live in our military camps. Unfortunately, our military police arrested and imprisoned both the Taiwanese laborer and his Japanese girlfriend, before sending her to Geelon and finally back to Japan. Ultimately, having ruled Taiwan for 50 years, all the Japanese in Taiwan had left in just a couple of years. That was very strange indeed.

The so-called Japanese aviation industry in Taiwan mainly consisted of a series of plants for maintenance and repair but not manufacture. Initially I only knew we were to take them over. Upon my arrival in Taiwan, however, I realized our takeover was only part of a very important mission which was to produce all kinds of aircraft for the Chinese Air Force. Back in 1944 with the prospect of winning the War of Resistance against Japan, the Nationalist Government set up plans to develop China's aviation industry. The goal was to achieve the capacity of building 1,000 airplanes in four years, including trainers, pursuers, bombers and transporters. Our No. 3 Aircraft Manufacturing Company began relocating from Chengdu to the Shuinan Airport in Taichung which was once a base for the Japanese Imperial Army and their Mitsubishi A6M Zero fighter aircraft. During my six months in Yuanlin, I supervised the transport of all Japanese equipment, machinery and aircraft-related materials to the Shuinan Airport. Then the construction of the No. 3 Aircraft Manufacturing Company in Taichung began followed by the gradual arrival of all the workers and their families from Chengdu. Using the equipment and machinery from Chengdu along with those collected from Japanese factories across Taiwan and some others from Europe and America, we established a large aircraft manufacturing factory in the Shuinan Airport. The 1,200-plus workers produced aircraft trainers and handled maintenance and repairs.

Getting Married

In August, 1946, after nearly a year of staying in Taiwan, I took some days off to return to Nanjing to get married. My wife's name was Jin-yun Zhang. Her father, Ye-Lu Zhang, was my father's boss during the war, and the two families had been living side by side as neighbors since our days in Chongqing's Hualongqiao District. My father-in-law was the deputy head of the Transport Division under the General Army Office of the Chinese Armed Forces. Under the Transport Division were various departments such as design, electronic communications and transport. My father worked for the army's wireless group under the Department of Electronic Communications.

David Hsu and wife Jin-yun Zhang outside of their residence in Taichung, 1946

As the oldest among her siblings, my wife was a very capable woman. Back in 1937 when the War of Resistance against Japan first started, her father was too busy working in Chongqing to take care of his family in Nanjing. With the Japanese approaching, my mother-in-law and her three children had some army orderlies to help pack and transport everyone and everything, but somebody needed to take charge and organize it. As my mother-in-law had bound feet and was not capable of doing much, it was my wife and her younger sister who directed the relocation of the whole family from Nanjing to Chongqing. She was 14 year old at that time, her sister 11. Upon their arrival in Chongqing, their father was still too busy to look after them. My wife began managing the household from then on.

Later, after graduating from the Chongqing Nankai Secondary School, she studied statistics at the Central Chengchi (political Science) University (today's National Chengchi University) in Chongqing and was in the same class as Xiao-xia Fang, wife of Shing-yi Huang (see the chapter on Shing-yi Huang). After that, she worked at a paper factory in Chongqing and lived locally for eight years. By the time I went back to China in 1946, her family had returned to Nanjing. After the wedding, I returned to Taichung. My wife soon arrived to stay with me in Taiwan.

My Father-in-Law

My father-in-law Ye-lu Zhang's ancestral home was Shaoxing, Zhejiang Province, but his family lived in Yangzhou, Jiangsu Province. With his father being a physician of traditional Chinese medicine, they were rather affluent. As a young man, my father-in-law joined the Baoding Military Academy in Hebei Province and specialized in artillery due to his excellent study scores in English and mathematics. After that he went to Shanxi Province where my wife was born; hence the character "Jin" in my wife's name, a short-hand reference to that province.

According to my father-in-law, one day he and other soldiers went through a storm of mortar shells and bullets heir battalion's horse riding commander was wearing a woolen uniform that was common among army officers in Northern China. All of a sudden an aide yelled out, "Sir, you're injured!" It gave the commander such a fright that he fell off his horse. When the whole battalion stopped to check on the commander, they realized there was no injury at all. A bullet had hit the commander's water bottle so that liquid leaked out and soaked his woolen uniform. The commander was so embarrassed that he pulled out his pistol and shot that babbling aide on the spot.

After that traumatic incident, my father-in-law gave up being a soldier. Instead, he picked up a lucrative job in Mongolia as a broker of army horses for the warlord Xi-shan Yan. It was said in my family that when my father-in-law returned to Yangzhou, Jiangsu Province, he had to hire a team of mules to carry the brokerage fees he had earned from that job. It was this money that he used to marry my mother-in-law.

So, instead of serving as an artilleryman, my father-in-law started handling transport and supplies for the army. Prior to the War of Resistance against Japan, the Chinese Army ordered 700 trucks from the German car maker Mercedes-Benz. On top of the shipment of 700 trucks, the Germans also included 10 sedans. Somehow my father-in-law received one which he drove around in Chongqing. Soon after that, on July 17, 1937, Chiang Kai-shek held a government meeting at Lushan, Jiangxi Province, and delivered the famous "Lushan Proclamation" to announce armed resistance against Japan. As a high-ranking army official, my father-in-law was even present at that historical meeting that was attended by numerous important people.

However, one unfortunate incident happened to him bringing everlasting sorrow to our family. Back when Nanjing was about to fall into the hands of the communist army, my wife managed to relocate our two families to Taiwan. But my father-in-law insisted on staying in China as he needed to look after his son who had just entered Fu Dan University in Shanghai. Then in 1949 the communist troops captured Nanjing and held a welcome ceremony for themselves. For some reason my father-in-law, who had already retired by then, decided to attend the ceremony in his full Nationalist military uniform with all of his medals. He was immediately arrested. Despite the fact that he was discharged from the army right after the victory of the War of Resistance against Japan and had never fought against the communists, they accused him of being a war criminal and locked him up at a detention house for war criminals in Fushun about 50 kilometers east of Shenyang in Northeast China's Liaoning Province. Also imprisoned were Japanese prisoners of war as Pu Yi, the last emperor of Qing Dynasty and the Japanese-assigned ruler of the puppet state Manchukuo in Northeast China and Inner Mongolia, and various high-ranking officials from the Nationalist army.

In 1986 when the ban on cross-strait traveling was finally lifted in Taiwan, my wife visited many former prisoners-of-war in China in an attempt to find information about her father. We heard that after 1959 Chairman Mao of the Communist Party had gradually pardoned the so-called "war criminals" across China. Many of them returned home alive, but my father-in-law had died in the detention house in Fushun. Later, when my wife visited the city of Fushun, someone gave her an item that was said to have belonged to her father. It was a undershirt riddled with gaping holes. Unable to confirm whether or not that piece of clothing really belonged to my father-in-law, my wife brought it back to Taiwan and gave it to her younger brother, who had married and settled on the island. He later buried that undershirt with the ashes of my mother-in-law.

The February 28 Incident

When I first arrived in Taichung, I often saw people wandering around the streets, with three letters "POW" (prisoner of war) written in English and Japanese on their shirts. These were POWs who had returned from Southeast Asia, local Taiwanese who were conscripted by the Japanese Imperial Army to serve as laborers, guards and even soldiers after the outbreak of the Pacific War. Many of them had fought on the frontlines across Southeast Asia but were now prisoners of war after Japan lost the war. Seeing them in Taiwan was a very strange thing indeed.

In 1947 the February 28 Incident took place in Taichung, which signified local people's direct resistance against the Nationalist Government that had taken control of Taiwan. By then the construction of our No. 3 Aircraft Manufacturing Company was already completed. One of the local leaders of the resistance was a woman called Hsueh-hung Hsieh (Xue-hong Xie in Hanyu Pinyin or Soat-hong Sia in Taiwanese), a rather famous figure. She came to the factory trying to persuade the director, Major General Duo Yun, to surrender to her guerrilla force based in Taichung. She didn't threaten us. Instead, in tears she tried to talk us into handing over all matters pertaining to the defense of the Shuinan Airport. On that day I stood guard outside the director's office and heard the whole conversation. Hsieh was an excellent negotiator. Although a Taiwanese, she spoke perfect, clear and logical Mandarin and was highly pleasant to listen to. She wanted our director to promise not to get involved in this confrontation between the locals and the Nationalist Government. In return her militia forces would not bother us. I don't remember her exact words, only the feeling at that moment that our director had no other choice but give in to her demands.

On March 4, 1947, Major General Yun held a peace talk with the local guerrilla force and handed over weapons on behalf of our factory. By transferring our guns to them, we practically announced our intention to surrender and avoid armed conflicts. With that said, it was only a small number of guns. I further played a part by removing some small parts from the guns so that they could not be fired. Not being soldiers, the local people knew nothing about using, maintaining and repairing guns nor did they know why the guns would not work. After that the factory's workers and their families went into hiding at the Shuinan Airport.

I recall returning home and bursting into tears in front of my wife. Because of this February 28 Incident, Major General Yun lost his job and was recalled to Nanjing. Later, when the Nationalist Government formally relocated to Taiwan on the eve of the Communist troops' arrival in Nanjing, some chose to stay there. Among them was Major General Yun, who ended up joining the Communists. I on the other hand decided to remain in Taiwan to pursue opportunities in making airplanes.

Building Aircraft Trainers

During the war many of our airplanes came from the U.S. Air Force. The Chinese factories were mainly for maintenance and repair, but occasionally they would build one or two aircraft for our own air force. At that time we were unable to mass produce anything. The airplanes we built were only to cultivate talent in this field, as one who understands how to build an aircraft is more knowledgeble to know buyer. After the victory of the War of Resistance against Japan, the Air Force Academy was moved back to its original site in Jianqiao, in Hangzhou, Zhejiang Province, only to be greeted by a completely destroyed campus. For the Chinese Air Force to cultivate pilots and for their existing personnel to resume flight training in Hangzhou, a good number of aircraft trainers needed to be built as soon as possible.

In 1945 the Nationalist Government launched a plan to build primary-level aircraft trainers in Taiwan using Japanese machinery and equipment that we had taken over. This mission was assigned to our No. 3 Aircraft Manufacturing Company. In June 1946 the Chinese Aviation Committee established during the war was regrouped to become today's Air Force Command Headquarters. Having been given the responsibility to negotiate with the Boeing Company in the United

States, they purchased the rights to manufacture 100 PT-17 Stearman planes as primary trainers. However, because all the Japanese hangars in the Shuinan Airport had been destroyed by American bombing, we had to construct a brand new manufacturing plant. Worse, much of the machinery and equipment that we had taken over from the Japanese were useless in our attempt to work with the specifications and design of an American airplane. Instead, we had to purchase all the necessary machinery, equipment and production-related materials from the United States including all the parts and some of the machinery.

After all the hangars were constructed, production lines established, equipment installed, and workers recruited and trained, we witnessed the arrival of aircraft production-related materials from Boeing. We commenced manufacturing by the end of 1947, and by February 1948 the first PT-17 Stearman primary trainer built by our No. 3 Aircraft Manufacturing Company successfully completed its test flight. While the aircraft's model was set as "PT-1", it was nicknamed "Man-Ping" after the child of one of our colleagues. As young officers like me were all having newborns at that time, our factory decided to name our airplanes after these babies in chronological order of their birth dates. It was a lot of fun. Indeed, the sixth airplane built by our factory was named "Chivay", after my son.

"Chivay" the PT-17 Stearman Primary Trainer, Shuinan, Taichung, 1948

All of our primary trainers were built to the highest standards. They were of perfect quality and didn't encounter any problem during the test flights. Whenever they conducted a test flight, I would ask the pilot to take me along. Indeed, PT-17 Stearman as a primary trainer was fairly easy to control. With the pilot sitting in the front and me in the back, both of us had to wear flight masks in order to communicate with each other. I would observe the pilot's every move until I had mastered all the required maneuvers. Later, when the pilot expressed doubt that I could conduct the test flight, I assured him that I had learned everything he knew. He ended up allowing me to sit in the front, with him in the back keeping control of the airplane. Once we were in the air, he would let go of the control and give me a chance. He ended up trusting me fully allowing me to take over the test flight and fly the trainer in whatever way I liked for more than 30 minutes every time.

Another time I said to the pilot, "I'll bet you that whatever maneuvers you're required to do for the test flight, if you just do it once, I can master it." Unconvinced, he challenged me with aerobatics, but I assured him that I was capable of it. Indeed, when we did the test flight, whatever loops, rolls and other feats of spectacular flying he managed to do, I was able to do it in exactly the same fashion after him. Soon he stopped being arrogant and giving orders on how to conduct a test flight. Instead, I told him to simply describe what needed to be done and I would understand because the principles of flying are exactly those on which airplanes are designed. Eventually he agreed with me and was glad of my help as an additional test pilot. Indeed, I did so many test flights that I was in the air almost every day. But I didn't tell my wife about it in case she might become worried.

By July 1948 we had completed building 108 primary-level aircraft trainers. As our contract had specified only 100, it was obvious that we had used up all the extra equipment and materials purchased as spares. Having such a large number of airplanes manufactured within a year was unprecedented in the history of the Chinese Air Force. Indeed, on the day that these primary trainers were completed, all the instructors and students from the Air Force Academy arrived in the Shuinan Airport to fly them back to Hangzhou. That was a spectacular day with 108 airplanes taking off from Taichung on their way to the Chinese mainland in perfect formation.

David Hsu (left) undergoing training in the United States 1953

David Hsu (second from right) at Chinese New Year in America 1953

Leaving the Air Force and Joining China Airlines

Having produced the primary trainers, I never had another chance to build aircraft for the Chinese Air Force. After the Nationalist Government relocated to Taiwan, our factory was mainly responsible for maintaining and repairing various aircraft purchased from the United States as well as American warplanes arriving from the Korean War. I started out as a lieutenant in the Air Force. From there I slowly rose through the ranks and was sent to America for advanced training in 1953. I dedicated a total of 15 years to the Air Force and was discharged in 1959 as a lieutenant-colonel/aeronautical engineer. In fact, knowing that I would have no future in the Air Force as a technical personnel involved in production and management, instead of a pilot participating in battle, I was eager to leave. Back then, the way to leave the armed forces was to have a series of sick leaves and then to negotiate with your physician. If the doctor was willing to issue a medical certificate stating you were unwell due to whatever sickness you claimed to have, then you could be discharged.

I was still young when I left the Air Force. As there was yet to be any decent industry in Taiwan, the only thing available at that time was handicraft – handmade items like souvenirs and small items for daily use. It was akin to what people do in today's Third-World countries and other underdeveloped regions still requiring assistance from the United Nations. Anyway, I was recruited by the government's Center for the Development of Handicraft to promote various useful crafts and skills. Considered quite a good job back then, it even involved frequent negotiation with foreign consultants. Hence I accepted the position.

When I left the Air Force in 1959, the government in Taiwan had just started preparing for the establishment of China Airlines. They approached me several times without success as I felt it was too risky a business to get involved in. It was only after China Airlines was formally established and in need of a specialist to take charge of maintenance and repair work that I agreed to join them. Later, when that department was expanded into a full-scale maintenance plant, I assumed the position of its director. That was in the midst of the Vietnam War. After gaining a license to maintain and repair all the transporters owned by the United States Air Force, China Airlines witnessed a boom in its operational income. It was with this increased income via our maintenance plant that the company was able to purchase its first passenger jet and establish an air route between Taiwan and America.

Interestingly, prior to that, I had always worked at factories where all sorts of aircrafts were manufactured using aluminium alloy. Having become accustomed to the smell of aluminium, I experienced quite a bit of physical discomfort in the year or so after leaving the Air

Force. Even repeated medical tests at hospitals could not explain what was wrong with me. Then, as soon as I started working for China Airlines, the discomfort disappeared. The same experience was also shared by various former employees of the Air Force that I had recommended to come and work for the company. All of us felt much better physically after our return to an aircraft maintenance and repair plant. It was almost like we were destined to work in this field.

(left) David Hsu receiving Ms. Mei-ling Song, wife of then president Chiang Kai-shek, and Ms. Xiang Tan, wife of then vice president Cheng Chen at China Airlines 1965
(right) David Hsu accompanying foreign guests in a tour of the maintenance and repair plant at China Airlines 1962

Soon after I joined China Airlines, I traveled to Hong Kong where many good-quality China-made tools were being sold. As those Chinese tools were of similar quality to those made in the West but considerably cheaper in price, I wondered why we shouldn't purchase them for use at our maintenance plant. Politically though, how could we even think of buying things made in China? Could we purchase any equipment or machinery from the communists? Impossible! Instead, we continued buying everything from the United States.

Over the years I had been sending money to my family in China via a relative in Hong Hong. Even these days, my nephew often comments on how miserable their lives would have been if it weren't for the money I sent to his family. However, all the letters written by our relatives in China were confiscated when they arrived in Taiwan via Hong Kong. According to my wife, many of her former classmates at the Central Chengchi (Political Science) University ended up working for the government in Taiwan in areas such as mail checking. In my own case, having been questioned many times by the government's intelligence units, I would never dare to make any direct contact with anyone on the Chinese mainland.

Work and Retirement in the United States

I left China Airlines after 18 years of work there. As a semi-public organization, all the higher-rank positions were taken by people from government. Knowing that I would never get a promotion higher than my current position, I refused to work for the company any longer. Hence I retired at the age of 57. Fortunately, because China Airlines had been buying aircraft from the Boeing Company, one of the related American businesses expressed an interest in employing me. As a result my role changed from a buyer of equipment and machinery on behalf of China Airlines to a representative of the supplier. I relocated to the United States in 1977 and lived in White Plains, NY, about 50 minutes by car to New York City. Our house in Taipei was then taken over by our son who had then returned to teach in Taiwan after the conclusion of his studies in America.

At that time the U.S. Government had just established diplomatic relations with China. With the two sides beginning to communicate with each other, China also started buying airplanes from America. Apart from selling aviation equipment and machinery to Taiwan, our company sold many products to people in mainland China. Back then the Americans often confused the Republic of China in Taiwan with the People's Republic of China on the mainland. It was just one more word in English, but the U.S. Post Office often got things mixed up and sent letters meant for China to Taiwan instead. People used to be highly sensitive about this, so we were always expected to write "Republic of China" when sending letters. Things are different now. No one cares about it anymore. These days even people like me use the name "Taiwan" much more often than the nation's formal title.

Both my wife and Shing-yi Huang's (see the chapter on Shing-yi Huang) wife had studied statistics at the Central Chengchi (Political Science) University. They were classmates back in Chongqing and would often visit each other after our relocation to New York. On the eve of my retirement from the aforementioned American company in 1988 we moved to Rossmoor, in San Francisco's East Bay. Thanks to a recommendation by Huang, who had moved there one year earlier with his wife. Life here has been so relaxing. Many of Rossmoor's Chinese residents moved from New York and other places across America, and were former students intending to study here but were unable to return to China after 1949. We have similar life experiences and work as a team to organize all sorts of community events. We also travel together as well.

Since the 1980s my wife often took trips to the Chinese mainland. As previously mentioned, my father used to work for the nationalist army but retired after the victory of the War of Resistance against Japan as a technician in wireless communications. He chose to stay in China in 1949 and passed away after the Cultural Revolution in his 80s. I have since visited his and my mother's graves at Shangfang Mountain in Suzhou, Jiangsu Province.

I have lived in this community for more than 26 years. Many of my dear friends have since passed away while others have grown old. My wife died in 2014. I have lived alone since then, but my daughter who lives nearby often visits me. My son who lives in the state of Washington also comes and stays with me every once in a while. We have a breakfast gathering here. A group of old friends, seven of us in our 80s and 90s who have lost our wives, meet at our community restaurant on Saturday mornings and have breakfast together.

My granddaughter Eyee Hsu is an experienced broadcaster on Beijing's English-language television channel CCTV-9. She once hosted *Up-Close*, a popular television show featuring interviews on cultural topics. Now she is the host of *Crossover*. As for me, although I no longer return to China due to limits in my physical strength, I often feel much comfort watching my granddaughter on television.

(This chapter is written with assistance from Chivay Hsu, son of David Hsu.)

Patsy P. H. Peng 陳珮兮
2014

When I first met Patsy Peng, my husband and I were still indecisive about moving to Rossmoor. With Peng being her late husband's surname, Patsy's Chinese name is Pei-hsi (nee Chen), which sounds like Patsy. She urged us to move to Rossmoor as soon as possible, as we were then still young enough to use all the facilities in that community. As for herself, Patsy played ping-pong with friends at 6:30 in the morning, followed by tennis, golf, dancing and mah-jong throughout the day. I often wondered how she could be so full of energy in her 80s. However, two years later when I visited Patsy after our relocation to Rossmoor, I hardly recognized her. As a result of injuries she suffered while playing golf, Patsy was a changed person both physically and spiritually. All the electric appliances at her house appeared to be broken, but it was only because her fingers lacked strength to push the buttons. Under such difficult circumstances, Patsy still lived an independent life. I witnessed her determination in the following two years: with medical treatment and constant exercise, she had straightened her back and returned to dancing classes and table tennis. Her life story had a profound impact on me, but this didn't make it easy for her or me to use words to document her experiences. Still, we discussed this chapter many times in order to make it perfect. According to Patsy, despite the many hardships she had suffered throughout her life, she never stopped to complain. Instead, she worked hard to conquer all obstacles – such is life. It's almost like she lived through more than one lifetime's worth of difficulties.

Biography

Patsy Peng, whose ancestral home was Fuzhou, Fujian Province, was born in Beijing in 1925. She relocated to Chongqing, Sichuan Province in 1937, after the Marco Polo Bridge Incident on July 7, a battle between Chinese troops and the Imperial Japanese Army that marked the start of the Second Sino-Japanese War (1937-1945). After graduating from high school, she worked as an English secretary for Lieutenant-General Wang Shuming, director of Chinese personnel involved in the operations of the Fourteenth Air Force stationed in Hanzhong, Shaanxi Province. After the war she arrived in the United States in 1948 to study at Mills College in Oakland, California, where she received her Bachelor's and Master's degrees in education. In subsequent years she looked after her family while building a career in education and social welfare in New York. In 1990 she moved to Rossmoor, Walnut Creek, in SanFrancisco's East Bay and has remained active in such affairs as community management and assisting in the development of her alma mater.

We Were Born to Give Back to Society

Both of my parents came from Fujian Province where my grandfather was said to be a magistrate in Fuzhou. I was born and raised in Beijing. We had a large courtyard where I remember a manservant who used to sit under a tree and tell stories to my older siblings and me. My father's given name was Puxian Chen; his courtesy name was Bosheng. With a degree in economics from Tokyo's Waseda University, he served as editor for *The Morning Bell* newspaper in Beijing and raised public awareness of current affairs. The newspaper was later renamed *The Morning Post* with my father as editor-in-chief. After *The Morning Post* ceased publication in 1928, my father worked for Zhang Xueliang, the "Young Marshal", in Northeast China. He returned to Beijing in 1930 to serve as director, chief editorial writer and editor-in-chief for *The Morning Post* when it resumed publication. Thanks to loading such an influential newspaper, my father was a famous figure in media circles then.

I was the youngest child in my family of two brothers and four sisters. My mother died when I was three. As my father worked late everyday writing and editing newspaper articles and also had frequent overseas trips, no one looked after us. There was once a prestigious family willing to marry their daughter to my father, but he refused because he was concerned that six children would be too much work for her. More importantly, he had never met her – men and women back then didn't date each other like they do today. Later the wife of my father's friend Wen-kan Lo (Wengan Luo) (author's note: an important figure in the Nationalist Government) agreed to look after us until my father remarried. Hence Luo and his wife became our godparents until eventually we did have a stepmother.

War Escape and Studies

In 1936 my father was sent to Tokyo to set up and manage the Japanese branch of China's Central News Agency. The following year Japanese troops occupied Beijing after the Marco Polo Bridge Incident. In 1938 when my father was ordered to serve as editor-in-chief of the Central News Agency in Chongqing, Sichuan Province, my two oldest sisters fled Beijing to China's hinterlands. It was a tough journey with the roads in awful and chaotic conditions. They hitched a ride with a "yellow fish" truck carrying steel pipes. While my second sister sat next to the driver, my big sister was out on the truck's bed where her leg was hurt by tumbling pipes. They were even robbed of everything before finally arriving in Chongqing. My big brother died while in high school. My stepmother took my second brother, third sister and me to Shanghai to consider our next move. Despite the fact that Japanese troops already occupied the city at that time, most people didn't expect the war to become large scale and long lasting. On rare occasions my father would ask people to smuggle some money for our use, but often we would have no income for months with only tofu and vegetables for food. I could not receive an education in Shanghai. Eventually, we decided to go to Chongqing to be with my father. We dressed as ordinary country people. I remember one morning at five o'clock, we had to cross a river in the dark. Japanese soldiers stood on both riverbanks with bayonets fixed to their guns. Knowing that Japanese people loved sardines, my brother gave them two packs in exchange for our passage. They allowed us to board a boat, but it was so full of people that as soon as we squeezed onto it – splash! – two other people fell into the river on the other side. Lucky were those who managed to stay alive.

Not far from Shanghai was a place whose real name I can't remember. It was referred to as "no man's land", as the Nationalist Party, the Communist Party and Japanese troops paid no attention to it. Once we arrived, it was relatively safe to travel to the hinterlands. We also went through a place in Hunan Province. For security reasons we would search for a place to hide before sunset and be on the road before sunrise in the same way that ancient poets described their long and difficult journeys. We would stay in crumbling, rustic houses in the countryside with absolutely nothing to eat. On those rare occasions where a food vendor or two were found, everything was covered in dust, but there was nothing we could do but eat the dusty food. I don't like talking about the hardship we suffered while fleeing from the war. It saddens and frightens me to think about it as there were many times we nearly died. I can never forget those events. That was perhaps the most difficult period of my life.

Without family in Chongqing, my father stayed with two colleagues who were also famous in the media industry in a three-storey house. Upon arrival we squeezed in and stayed in the rooms between the upper and lower levels. The frequent bombings by Japanese warplanes caused us to flee at the sound of sirens. We could escape from one end of the air raid shelter if the other end was blocked by the bombing, but people would suffocate when both ends were destroyed. Many people died during the Japanese bombardment of Chongqing, yet I attended high school there. Wanting to study law, I would work under candlelight at night when there was no electricity. I studied hard but my results were average.

Air Force Hero in the War of Resistance against Japan

In 2005 on the invitation for my 80th birthday party there was a photograph of 18-year-old me standing on the wing of an airplane. Painted on the plane were the words Patsy Angel, "Patsy" being my English name. At the party there were two American gentlemen who served as pilots for the First American Volunteer Group of the Chinese Air Force, who recognized the plane in the photograph as a Curtiss P-40. When they asked, "Patsy, what's going on in this photo?" I didn't answer. They said, "Someone would have carried you onto the wing?" still no reply from me. Finally they commented, "This plane has your name on it!" I didn't say anything, for it was a heartrending story too painful to tell.

Patsy Peng on the wing of a Curtiss P-40 fighter aircraft operated by the "Flying Tigers" First American Volunteer Group in Hanzhong, Shaanxi Province, 1943

It was not that I worried people would know about it. It was just something I wanted to keep to myself, not share in public, as I didn't know who could fully comprehend the anguish and significance. What if people misunderstood its importance? For more than 70 years it has been an untouchable memory, securely locked in a corner of my heart. I didn't want people to probe, nor did I need their sympathy. However, after another ten years I was 90 with a better capacity to examine past events.

So, on the 70th anniversary of the victory in the War of Resistance against Japan and the 70th anniversary of his death for our country, I am willing to share his story as a permanent tribute to him, a man who has been and will always be the love and pride of my life.

During the toughest part of the War of Resistance against Japan, at the crucial moment determining our nation's survival, when I was 18 and full of youthful passion, I was both loyal and courageous not only for my husband but also for our nation. Under those circumstances we all had suffered, yet we kept on marching forward without fear. I will always cherish that marriage as a precious part of my life. I have kept many photographs, but I hardly look at them because I am an emotional person and it hurts so much to do so. I now wonder how I was so brave back then. Even after such a long life full of ups and downs, twists and turns, if I were able to experience that journey all over again, I most likely wouldn't dare to do it.

When I was in Chongqing as a high school student, the U.S. Fourteenth Air Force was stationed in the countryside. Thanks to my father's fame and the fact that hardly any educated girls still living in Chongqing could speak English, the Chinese pilots in the air force would often invite my three sisters and me over for a visit. Having been hand-picked by the Air Force and trained in the United States, these pilots looked particularly proud and handsome in their uniforms; they were excellent dancers as well. Yet at the beginning of the war, with fewer and inferior aircraft, they could hardly rival the Japanese. Nonetheless, each and every one of them was fearless and had shot down many Japanese planes. Some of them even ended up smashing their blasted and burning aircraft against their Japanese counterparts so that both sides perished together. All those Chinese pilots who sacrificed their lives were honored in a state funeral held by the then president Chiang Kai-shek.

With that said, after 1941 with assistance from their American peers, the Chinese Air Force was finally able to compete against the Japanese. All the pilots were trained by the aviation school, where a great number of young men had applied for a spot but only a handful were chosen as candidates. Many of these pilots had studied in or graduated from renowned academic institutions. Some of them even came from prestigious families overseas and were determined to serve their nation when it came under attack.

The pilots from the Fourteenth Air Force would drive us to their headquarters where we spent several weekends visiting and getting to know them. Being only sixteen or seventeen then, I really didn't know much. Later, a pilot named Hongjiu Zhong would often request to see me, and eventually he proposed. Initially my father said I was too young for marriage. Yet when some friends suggested that Zhong as a pilot could die at any moment and I would end up suffering as a young widow, my father changed his mind. While being in the air force was indeed a dangerous profession, his friends' words had helped to convince my father that risking one's life and even dying for one's nation would be a great service! Consequently, Hongjiu and I married at the air base in Chongqing's Baishiyi on October 23, 1943. We chose an American-style ceremony with my father and sisters among the guests. Our wedding was highlighted by tradition with members of the squadron lined up on both sides of the church steps and their swords criss-crossed above us as we came out as a couple. It was very impressive!

After the wedding my husband was sent to the airfield in Hanzhong, Shaanxi Province while Ms. Luo, my godmother, asked me to stay with her in Guilin, Guangxi Province, for several days. When Guilin came under threat of Japanese troops, my husband came to arrange my relocation before returning to work. When I traveled to Hanzhong by myself, the train left and returned to Guilin several times as a result of Japanese bombing. There was no seat on the train, so I stayed in a freight car crouching in the tiny space between piled-up cargo and the ceiling. As the train moved out and back into the station over the following hours, I could only jump off from the top of the carriage to go to the toilet. Once I crashed to the ground on my knees. Even today, bits and pieces of gravel still remain in the scar. I took the train to Guiyang, capital of Guangxi Province, then switched to a "yellow fish" truck to Hanzhong. It was a difficult journey with one section of the road nicknamed "Devil May Cry". Every time we stopped on that steep road, the driver had to block the wheels with rocks to stop the truck from rolling backwards. Having narrowly escaped death several times ourselves, we saw a number of cars that had tumbled down the mountain. I often say that I experienced more than one lifetime's worth of difficulties. Indeed, I feel I have survived many lifetimes' worth of hazards.

The Fourteenth Air Force stationed in Hanzhong was what is known today as the First American Volunteer Group (AVG) or the "Flying Tigers". Chinese and American pilots operated both Curtiss P-40 and B-25H Mitchell bombers. The aircraft with my name painted on it was a single-engine, single-seat Curtiss P-40 Warhawk with my husband as its pilot. Commanded by Clare Lee Chennault, the AVG was stationed in a newly-built airfield just outside of Hanzhong. Lieutenant-General Wang Shuming, commander of the Chinese Air Force's Third Group and a pilot himself, directed all Chinese personnel and ranked the same as Chennault in the AVG. He was short but majestic-looking, so the Americans affectionately nicknamed him "Tiger Wang".

At the airfield as a pilot's wife from the hinterlands who could speak some English, I worked as one of Wang's secretaries. We received all government officials and pilots at the office before they met Wang. As he had studied in Russia rather than America, I acted as his interpreter whenever he spoke to the Americans. I was only 18 then, but rather fearless with my Pidgin English. On occasions when Wang flew to Chongqing, he would let me come along to visit my father. Later he was promoted commander-in-chief of the Air Force. In 1960, when Wang served as leader of the Republic of China's delegation to the Military Staff Committee (MSC) of the United Nations, he visited my family and me in New York and gifted us a painting by renowned artist, Junbi Huang. As Huang's eyesight had been deteriorated back then, the painting was in the splash-ink style.

The pilots of the Fourteenth Air Force were young but brave, ready to die for our nation. They often said, "Every flight could be our last flight. Every time we go out to battle the Japanese, we don't think of coming back!" As wives of the pilots, we watched our husbands take off every morning. Every evening we counted the number of warplanes that made it back. Whenever a plane went missing, we immediately knew which one among us had lost her sweetheart. It was truly miserable. Still, back then we were all so patriotic that none of us complained about injuries or deaths.

Hongjiu Zhong, a hero from the War of Resistance against Japan in his air force uniform, wearing medals awarded by the Nationalist Government's Military Committee and the American Government.

My husband had been through numerous battles in the air. As deputy leader, he was responsible for leading the P-40s to cover the B-25 Mitchell bombers, and he was also involved in such missions as fighting, monitoring, ambushing, dive-bombing and machine-gunning the Japanese planes. He had even taken his Warhawk to attack Japanese troops and trains that carried weaponry and ammunition, flying as far as Guangzhou (Guangdong Province) in the south, Wuhan (Hubei

Province) in the north and Burma in the west. He had experienced countless injuries, some light, others more critical. Among the several forced landings he had made, one involved crash-landing his battered and burning plane in enemy territory. He was lucky to make it back under the cover of our army.

My husband was a proud recipient of the Three Star Medal awarded by the Nationalist Government's Military Committee; it was specifically designed for pilots in the Air Force who had destroyed enemy aircrafts, with each star representing the downing of one Japanese warplane. Back then the airplanes had no filming equipment on board. According to the memoir of one of his fellow pilots, my husband had shot down more Japanese planes than any medal was able to represent. He often worked with his American counterparts, either as comrades side-by-side or simply to cover their bombers, and had received the Air Force Cross from the United States Air Force. All my life I have been looking after the medals that the Chinese and American governments awarded him.

One day, due to bad weather, my husband's warplane didn't come back. He was still very young when he died. I was heart-broken.

Mills College

After my husband died, I went back to live with my father. That was the lowest point of my life. I was confused, unsure of where my future might be. There was no hope left, and I wasn't even 20 years old. Somehow I knew I couldn't rely on my father forever and managed to get a job. Every day after work finished at four o'clock in the afternoon, I would go to a foreign friend's place to practice typing. I soon became a typist for the United States Army, where I met a fellow Chinese employee who was rather knowledgeable about the West. He gave me a book introducing universities in the United States for me to start making applications. I was paid by the hour. That little money I earned was spent on application fees and stamps on letters to America. I applied for anything and everything that was available from more than 90 academic institutions.

Back then most people studying overseas were either from rich and prestigious families or subsidized by churches; I was neither. I had to apply for a scholarship because my father was famous as a newsman but poor. Some of the universities were willing to offer two or three hundred dollars which was far from enough. I waited, slowly losing hope, until the academic year was about to start. Then out of the blue a letter arrived from Mills College. Thanks to a presidential grant offered by the United States Federal Government after the end of the Second World War, the college was willing to waive my tuition fees *and* offered free room and board. I could even find a job on campus to earn some pocket money. My second sister, who worked for the United Nations by then, sent money to cover my travel expenses. As soon as I was issued a visa, I left Shanghai for America. It took me 18 days by sea to arrive in San Francisco.

Based in Oakland, California, Mills College is a medium-sized, privately-owned liberal arts college. It was well managed, forming a close relationship among the professors, administrative staff and students. Initially I majored in English Literature in the hopes that after graduation I could return to teach and eventually become a professor at Nanjing's Jinling Women's College. However, within a year of my starting school, China fell into communist hands so that for three whole months there was no news about the situation there. Later, officials from the United States Immigration Office notified me with this warning: "If you want to go back to China, do it now. Should you intend to stay, then you can never return. We will not spend money on your education and let you go back to work for the communists." As my father had by then arrived in Taiwan, returning to China wasn't an option. Where could I go? With my Pidgin English, who in America would hire me to teach English Literature? I realized I should major in education instead, as it suited me better and would lead to more job opportunities in this country. So I changed my major.

Patsy Peng (standing) with friends at the female dormitory, Mills College, circa 1948

Two years of living in Hanzhong and working in Chongqing had helped to boost my fluency in English. Having passed the English test for all new students at Mills College, I thought my English was pretty good. However, I soon discovered that people couldn't understand anything I said. Whenever I opened my mouth, others would ask: "Excuse me, what did you say?" Back then all university students in America were required to study a second language with one's native tongue excluded, which in my case was Chinese. Consequently, I studied both English and French. As I had no idea what the instructor was saying in the daily French classes, I could only ask my classmates for help and borrow their notes to copy at night which forced me to stay up until one o'clock in the morning or quite often even later. Worse, in order to keep my scholarship going, I had to complete four subjects per semester for the equivalent of 12 credits. I had to study hard, often working relentlessly at night while the others slept and on weekends while they went out for fun. With piles of books to read each week, I was so exhausted that it felt like dying. Indeed after only one semester my eyesight became very bad. The situation would have further deteriorated if I hadn't met the dean of academic affairs at the library one day and promptly accepted her advice to stay away from subjects that demanded a large amount of reading. At that time five out of the six international students receiving the Presidential Grants came from South America. I was the only one from China and the only one who completed a degree as the other five dropped out before graduation. I never wondered whether I could do it. I only focused on moving forward.

Upon arrival I discovered other Chinese students at Mills College. One of them was the daughter of Long Yun (Lung Yun), former governor of Yunnan Province, and another was the daughter of a Chinese banker. I was the only one among them who was poor. Long Yun's daughter stayed in the same dormitory as I. Our American classmates often asked me if the gold and diamond rings on her hands were real, and I would always say "yes." On one occasion Long Yun's daughter was absent during the first two weeks of the semester. When our dorm mother asked me to find out what happened, Long Yun's daughter simply said she didn't come to school because she hadn't finished ironing her clothes. Back then we could freely leave the dormitory on weekends but had to return before its doors were shut at eleven o'clock at night. On another occasion our dorm mother asked me to find out why there were so many men outside the building, but Long Yun's daughter only said they were her cousins. She was quite a mature person. However, as a result of her family circumstances, she rarely came into contact with ordinary people and their lives. She often stayed up late wanting someone to chat with her at night. When I insisted I had to study, she said it would only be a short while. She would invite me to her room and turned the clock's face away so that I couldn't see the time.

Then she would go on and on about how she missed her family and how she had to obey such and such rules enforced by her parents at home – things I couldn't understand because I had lost my mother at a very young age. It was nice to hear her talking, but I was really short on time. Initially, out of politeness I stayed with her, but she would talk non-stop until two o'clock in the morning. While her class started at eleven, I had to get up early and start working in the cafeteria at eight o'clock. How could I accommodate her needs every night? This had to stop. Later she transferred to New York to study art while I remained a country bumpkin at Mills College.

I had to work through the summer breaks which was tough, but I always had hope in my heart. My sister, who was working for Chinese representatives at the United Nations, asked me to go to New York. She knew how miserable my life as a poor student had become, but I refused. Being stubborn and proud, I refused to depend on her. Still, she would send some money to me every month. Eventually, after graduating with a bachelor's degree in education, I received another fellowship to pursue a master's degree in child development at Mills College.

Difficulty in Finding the First Job

Having received my master's degree, I was ready to find a job. It was only then that I discovered foreigners cannot teach in the United States as only American citizens and permanent residents can take the test for a teaching certificate. Furthermore, to teach in California would require a California certificate, and to teach in New York, a separate certificate for that city. At that time an American friend invited me to rent a house with her in San Francisco and proposed teaching me how to cook meals and clean walls. In China nobody cleaned their dirty walls, but here in America all the walls were painted and required constant cleaning. I followed her to San Francisco, but we couldn't find a place. The real estate agents refused to recommend potential residences to my friend because her house mate would be an Oriental. Eventually we found a place, and the next step was to find a job. Without a certificate, I could only teach kindergarten, but I eventually secured a position as an assistant teacher at a primary school in San Francisco.

All American schools finished early in the afternoon, and I had to stay on campus to look after those kids until they were picked up by their parents. They weren't all of the same age. Instead, there were kids of seven, eight, nine and ten years of age with considerably different personalities and family backgrounds. Having arrived from China, I was quiet and polite, unable to handle kids who threw rocks and other things at me and were even beyond the control of the principal. Later I found another position at a day care center that didn't require a certificate. I bought a jalopy, a car that was old and wrecked but still drivable, and dashed between the two jobs. The vehicle often broke down at intersections and caused me much grief. But I was too young back then to feel miserable.

Eventually it became too hard to survive, so I relocated to New York, staying with my sister while trying to work in special education and teach children with disabilities. However, my plan failed again as I didn't have a license in this field. I ended up working in a place that was more like a day care center than a kindergarten. After a while I found a newspaper ad in a restroom for a teaching position on Long Island. I promptly sent an application and was accepted. Every day I had to drive 36 miles from New York to work, but the salary was good. It was then that I met Benjamin B.K. Peng, a medical intern. We soon married.

Family Life and Public Welfare

My husband came from Guangdong Province. Born in 1920, he was five years older than I. We married in 1955 and experienced a tough beginning. Since he was only an intern, we lived on my meager salary as a teacher on Long Island, eating our simple meals on a cardboard box that served as a table. My husband studied medicine at Shanghai's Dongnan Medical College (today's Anhui Medical University in Anhui Province) and served as a major and surgeon at a military hospital in that city during the War of Resistance against Japan. Still, upon his arrival in the United States in 1949, he had to start as an intern in a residency program. Like me, his English wasn't good, especially for medical terminologies. From our wedding day onward, he studied all sorts of books and research materials, sitting on the same Chinese-style cane chair every day and eventually wearing through its seat. He was different from me. While I expressed my thoughts and feelings, he tended to internalize all his sadness and bitterness. Initially with neither citizenship nor permanent residence in the United States, he couldn't treat patients. Instead he conducted research on urological oncology at his medical school for many years earning many awards for his achievements. Eventually he received a license to work as a medical doctor, but had to be tutored for his English in order to master various specialized fields. I remember one evening when he came home he asked me to accompany him to visit a French doctor who worked in France before coming to America to pursue higher studies. That doctor studied so hard that he later died of a heart attack. It was truly tragic. Finally after many difficulties my husband became a specialist, working both as an instructor for the State University of New York's Medical School and as an urological surgeon in the hospital. He got up at six o'clock in the morning to prepare his own breakfast before driving more than an hour to New York City. He had to arrive at the hospital before eight o'clock to perform surgery often skipping lunch and relying on a bit of juice for nutrition. He was often starving by the time he came home.

Three years after our wedding, we finally had a child. Of my two sons the first one was born five weeks premature. Having arrived home after a one-week stay at the hospital, he needed nutritious food. I did not know much about baby formula, I had to cook any food I needed myself and wait for it to cool down. Every time I needed to sleep, my son would wake up and cry from hunger. I had never learned how to cook as my younger years were spent studying and fleeing from the turmoil of war. God knows how I did it, making meatballs and fishcakes and filling the refrigerator with various dishes, but I managed. After another three years our second child was born. His nose bled a lot, and I had to pick him up for feeding as soon as he cried at night to prevent him from waking my husband who needed to perform surgery at eight o'clock the next morning. Back then I wasn't aware of such hardship. I only knew I had to do what was required of me. There was no time for self-pity.

My husband once treated Cardinal Francis Spellman, the renowned archbishop of the Roman Catholic Church in New York. After Cardinal Spellman's death in 1968, the Vatican assigned Archbishop Terence Cooke whom we knew well to succeed him. In 1969 Archbishop Cooke invited my husband and me to witness his elevation to the cardinalate at a ceremony in Rome. As my husband was too busy to go, I made the trip alone, sitting in one of three specially chartered airplanes that were mainly filled with men wearing Catholic-style black cassocks. At the ceremony the first of the archbishops to be elevated as cardinals by the Pope happened to be Yu Pin, one of the few Chinese cardinals to be elevated. During those nine days of glory, I accompanied Cardinal Cooke as he attended all kinds of celebrations and functions including a visit to the church in Rome that had been assigned to him. Although my husband wasn't there, this was a unique and unforgettable personal experience that no amount of money could buy. Nor could I ever forget the Special Blessing I received during this trip. A year later on Palm Sunday my husband and I were invited for lunch at Cardinal Cooke's private residence. I presented him with a copy of the video recording I made of that trip which delighted him as he had been too busy participating in all kinds of activities to pay specific attention to anything else. As such you see there have been times of joy in my life to counter those of hardship. Some of my experiences are so unique that no one else could ever fully appreciate them.

B.K. and Patsy Peng (first and second from the left) and Cardinal Yu Pin (sitting).

As my first son was very naughty, Cardinal Cooke recommended that I should send him to a Catholic school. He spent his first year running around while others studied. When the nuns got upset and pretended to look for a rope to tie him up, he tried to volunteer one. I only heard about this many years later when mentioned in jest by a friend. I asked my son whether it was true – his response was affirmative. I said: "Weren't you embarrassed by this?" He responded: "There's nothing wrong with it." Indeed, our son was particularly naughty during the first few years of primary school. My husband was too busy to discipline him but would complain to me about his bad behavior, so I had to do something. I did try, but he was smart enough to numb his palm with ginger juice when I tried to hit it with a ruler. On those occasions when I wanted to smack his bottom, he would ask me to wait, then he tighten his bottom in order to feel less pain. I didn't know whether to laugh or cry, but that's the way we lived our life. When our second son was three or four years old, he announced one day that he and his brother had agreed for me to have another child. I said I couldn't – I wouldn't be able to handle another child should he/she turn out to be as naughty as our first son. So that's it – we had only two boys. Later, I sent the two of them to a nearby primary school that was operated by the United Nations. As the principal was too busy to teach full-time, I worked part-time there teaching in her place.

It was tough to be a doctor in the United States. My husband had his first heart attack in 1964 when our second son was just two years old. It happened in the middle of the night, and I had no idea what to do. Who should I call for help at such a time? I rang a friend whose husband was also a doctor and asked him to come and give my husband a cardiotonic shot. It sounds easy now that we're chatting about it but was truly horrifying as a personal, real-life experience. I had no idea how long he might live. At six o'clock the next morning, I took my husband to a clinic across the street from our place. They transferred him to a major hospital where the diagnosis indicated that coronary artery bypass surgery was needed. They would have to cut open his rib cage and use the great saphenous vein harvested from his leg to replace the clogged artery. Back in the 1960s, there were only a few hospitals and surgeons that were capable of performing this sort of dangerous operation. We had to wait up to six months for a specialist to become available at our hospital in New York. Meanwhile, although my husband had a weak heart, he was stubborn and tough and refused to stay home while waiting for the surgery. He still worked every day though for fewer hours. He had to work to sustain the family as I had to stay home and look after the children. He wouldn't let me discuss his condition with others – I could talk to no one about it at all.

When the specialist finally became available, I took him to the hospital. The doctor told me that the surgery would take six hours.

What should I do in the meantime? I refused to sit there grinding my teeth for six hours, so I found a coach who was willing to teach me tennis. After four hours of tennis, I returned to the hospital in the city. I hardly recognized my husband because his face was swollen all over like a pig. Soon after that, he started working and treating patients again. Yet he still refused to reveal his own condition, despite the fact that he would often become too exhausted or too sick to do anything. Whenever he had to take sick leave, he would pretend to be on vacation. When patients called and asked why my husband was having so many holidays, I wasn't allowed to tell them the truth. One day, an American friend who was also a psychiatrist asked me on the phone, "Patsy, tell me, exactly what's going on with your husband?" I burst into tears and told him everything because he was a very nice and straightforward person. When my husband heard this, he complained that it was I who should see a psychiatrist. You can imagine how these words saddened me.

After my husband's heart attack, the doctors suggested that he should eat vegetarian dishes containing less oil and salt. The whole family turned vegetarian, but after a while I decided to provide the children with at least one beef and one chicken dish each week to supplement the nutrition required for their growth. In the end, our second child didn't get to be tall and strong like his brother, something I always regretted later. During that period, when my husband was sick and kids were little, all I could do was to endure the hardships and hang in there.

Later, people described me as an excellent wife and mother, but I didn't know what it meant. Why? Because I had nothing to compare myself with. I never socialized, played mahjong or dined out with other people's wives. When people invited us over for a meal, I had to say, "Thank you for your kindness, but we cannot accept your invitation as we only have vegetarian dishes to return the favor." I would have loved to attend events such as Christmas celebrations, but all the invitations went straight to the trash can as my husband would throw them away without even asking me. He did not have the time and energy for social occasions.

In 1973 my husband launched a medical center in the Confucius Plaza in New York to provide a wide range of medical and pharmaceutical services to local Chinese communities. He set up a clinic there and worked two hours each day, while still maintaining his position at the State University of New York's Medical School and Hospital. On weekends, when other people went out for fun, I would help out at his clinic. All kinds of patients would come in including owners of restaurants and chefs who would present him with special dishes as gifts. As we never had time to eat out, he would ask for a fish for me to cook at home with our own vegetables. People often fantasized about how comfortable the life of a doctor's wife would be. However, back then I never had much chance to enjoy life. Before we married, I occasionally would go out for lunch with my sister at the United Nations Delegation Lounge. In contrast, throughout my life as a married woman, time had always been in short supply. There was no comfort in my life with him, but such is life. Not many people understood the bitterness I harbored.

Following my husband's operation, the doctors suggested we travel overseas for two weeks each year to give him a rest, as he couldn't continue to work as hard as he used to. I loved going overseas and traveling and had accompanied him on various occasions. However, when people started asking why he always fell asleep on the tour bus, I could only say he was exhausted. Consequently, I would travel by myself and record everything for his enjoyment later at home. Still, instead of watching the video tapes, he would dedicate all his time and energy to his patients. That's the way he was.

When our children were little, I had to look after the family while my husband worked. But later when the kids were in high school, I would go to New York's Upper Manhattan region in the afternoon to study painting. My instructor Ling-jia Li from Fujian Province was a relatively famous Chinese artist. Compared to his six other students who had already been painting for several years, I knew nothing about art and was only accepted as a favor. Unfamiliar with the names of the many types of paper and colors, I had to ask others, such as Theresa Chow and Florence Lin for help. They now live at Rossmoor (see chapters on Horace Chow and Florence Lin). Initially, according to Instructor Li, the bamboo in my painting looked shivery and weak as if the painter was too old to show any strength. However, I gradually caught up with the others. It is interesting that whenever we copied the same portrait of a lady, each of us would come up with a different style, especially the way the subject expresses emotions through her eyes.

Patsy Peng's paintings, Holding the Candle and Harvest 1977
(originally in color)

I have a scroll of Chinese calligraphy created by Liang Qichao, the famous Chinese scholar, who gifted it to my father in 1928 when he was working for Zhang Xueliang, Wengan Luo and Wellington Koo (a Chinese diplomat from the Nationalist Government) in Northeast China. *The Morning Post* ceased publication in Beijing that year, which led to my father's relocation to that region to be chief editorial writer for *The People's Herald* and a consultant to the commander of the Northeast Border Guards. Many years later when I invited Instructor Li for a meal at home, he saw Liang's scroll of calligraphy and loved it very much. I asked him to create an accompanying painting which took him three days. He even got up in the middle of the night to ponder it.

Apart from painting and playing tennis, I also helped to promote public welfare. For example, the China Institute in New York is a non-profit organization promoting cultural exchange between China and the United States. It was founded by renowned philosopher and educator John Dewey, publisher Henry Luce and then Chinese Ambassador Shih Hu with Boxer Rebellion indemnity money (paid by China to the United States) and Luce's donation. In 1944 the China Institute became part of the State University of New York as a continuing education organization and continued to remain active. I not only worked as a volunteer there, but at one stage also served as chairperson of the Women's Association. Every year we held a bazaar to raise funds for the China Institute. It was something I wanted to do, *had* to do, no matter how busy I was. On those occasions when my husband was sick and I couldn't leave home, I would ask my nephew to help. Despite my busy home schedule, I wanted to give something back to society.

My husband worked at the New York Downtown Hospital close to Chinatown and Wall Street. I served as the Auxiliary President there, helping the hospital to liaise with various departments of the city government, to promote its services and raise funds, etc. My co-workers included the wives of other doctors and many volunteers. Compared to my initial status as merely a member of the auxiliary, this position carried much more responsibility. I only agreed to take it because they insisted they desperately needed me. Many of our Jewish members were very kind to me. We often held meetings in the hospital's spectacular boardroom. It had a huge, long table, and as the president I would be sitting at one end, with the other members lined up on both sides. I bought some jewelry of considerable size and wore it at the meetings in order to be visible.

Patsy Peng as New York Downtown Hospital's Auxiliary President at a press conference

As soon as I became president of the auxiliary, I proposed the hospital should try to treat more patients from Chinatown. Most American patients owned cars or relied on public transport from Wall Street, but patients from Chinatown had no way of getting to the hospital. Therefore, improving this situation would be beneficial to both the hospital and the local Chinese communities. I held a press conference at the hospital, where I conveyed to the reporters that many patients from Chinatown were too ill or frail to walk to the hospital for help. One way to solve this problem was to schedule buses between the hospital and the Confucius Plaza in Chinatown to ferry patients back and forth at specific times and dates. This reasonable proposal was featured by both American and Chinese newspapers, which eventually led to launching a series of buses to serve the public. It was just one of many difficult tasks I resolved. Another achievement was to set up a staff lounge at the hospital where the staff could rest. When this was officially opened, I was invited me cut the ribbon.

Patsy Peng cutting the ribbon at the official opening of the hospital's staff room

On top of that I helped to raise funds for the hospital. The auxiliary would hold parties on the top floor of one of the fanciest hotels in New York where the doctors were invited to purchase a single ticket (which cost more than U.S. $100) or two for a couple. All the money received reverted to the hospital, a considerable amount back then. If any doctor refused to go, they would find us campaigning at the staff room or other public areas in the hospital, saying, "How can you refuse to support the hospital by not attending such a meaningful event?" That's how you raised funds, by making people feel obligated.

I used to take the subway to the hospital. One day someone pick-pocketed my money. I knew the thief was right next to me, but I was too afraid to move a finger. Luckily, some passengers realized what happened and offered me money to go home. After that I chose to go by car, but it was very arduous and time-consuming to drive to Manhattan often taking up to two hours. Still, it was a very well managed hospital, with a friendly director who offered me a valued parking spot. Indeed, to be a volunteer in New York required both a sense of giving back to society and much courage.

Having worked, taught and researched as a doctor in New York for more than 30 years, my husband became famous and received many awards. As his health continued to deteriorate, he finally retired in 1988 but not before refusing many requests for him to stay. More than 40 of his former students arrived from all corners of the country to see him at his farewell party; our families were invited as well. Even after retiring from the medical school, my husband continued to work at his own clinic until 1990 when he reached the age of 70 and passed it on to our first son. I donated US $40,000 to the medical school after my husband died and set up a seminar in his name which my son has attended every year. That was more than 20 years ago.

Our son managed the clinic well. He is a famous doctor now, a prestigious urological surgeon; his wife is a pediatrician, and they have a son and a daughter. Meanwhile, our other son is a pediatric dentist, his wife is a primary care doctor. They and their two sons live quite close to Rossmoor. We are a family of doctors except for me. Our first son was listed as one of the Top Doctors in America after ten years of work. In his 11th year he was chosen as a Super Doctor in New York as a result of his good service and friendly manner. A lack of medical incidents and a short stay for his patients in hospital were also contributing factors to his popularity. Considering he was such a naughty boy in the past, who could have foreseen his success today? Such is life – there's nothing you can do about it.

Retirement as a New Start

While in New York, we had a friend Shing-yi Huang who worked for the United Nations (see the chapter on Shing-yi Huang). After retirement he relocated to Rossmoor, in San Francisco's East Bay in 1987. After seeing deer wandering around the golf course outside his window in the photographs printed on his hand-crafted Christmas cards, we paid a visit to this place and liked it a lot. In 1990 after my husband retired, we decided to move here. One important contributing factor to this decision was my days as a student in California, a place that felt like home. Most importantly, I thought the gentle climate in California would enable my husband to exercise more and improve his health as his heart condition had become quite severe. Unfortunately, one and half years after we moved here, he passed away.

Back in New York there were 12 couples whose ages and life experiences were similar to ours. We would get together each month to play tennis, dance and play mahjong. As my husband was too busy being a doctor to learn mahjong, he wanted to go dancing which we all did. However, he disappeared even before the dance started and went downstairs to find a public telephone to contact his patients. It was the same the second time we tried. With patients on his mind all the time, he could hardly relax. Upon retirement some of the 12 couples chose to remain with their parents or children on the East Coast while others decided to move to Florida. The rest moved to Rossmoor, so I have many good friends here.

In 2001 *Time* magazine covered life in retirement here at Rossmoor. When asked why we moved here, we suggested it's good to be with friends in retirement because our children have their own lives and are busy. A photograph of us was thus published in the magazine (see the chapter on Peter Sih). After that some of our friends from the past expressed interests in moving here, so many Chinese friends at Rossmoor have known each other for a long time. I have lived here since the age of 65 when I was already an old lady. Now 25 years later I am practically ancient. Earlier this year I had my 90th birthday party with 200 family members and friends attending; more would have come if we had a bigger venue. Among the guests were some of my classmates from Mills College.

After graduation I often returned to Mills College and gave back what I could. As it is relatively close to Rossmoor, helping out is easy. I am grateful for all the opportunities my alma mater has given me which helped to change my life. Consequently, whenever I had some spare money, I would donate it to Mills College, initially to set up a scholarship for talented high school graduates whose parents never had a chance to go to university. Later, as China and the United States increased their cultural exchanges, I hoped that Mills College would set up a Chinese department. It would be valuable not only in language learning but also in boosting scholarly and cultural exchange and mutual understanding between the two countries. In fact, Mills College *did* have a Chinese department, but it was closed when the Communists came to power in China. Whenever I proposed to the president that the college should establish further contact with China, she simply ignored me as all she wanted was to have more buildings. From her point of view, I was simply a former student who kept nagging, demanding and writing letters. Eventually, 50 years after I graduated, a new president was appointed, who was willing to encourage and help with my request.

Certificate presented by President of Mills College in recognition of Patsy's Peng's donation that helped to set up a Visiting Professorship in Chinese Language and Literature

At that time the money I made from the stock market

considerably improved my financial situation. Consequently, I made a donation for Mills College to set up a Three-Year Visiting Professorship in Chinese Language and Literature starting in 2012. Upon receiving my donation, the college's fundraising officer reminded me that more money would be necessary in the future to sustain the professorship. Would I be able to afford it? Well, I didn't have any answer back then. I only knew it had to be done, so we'd go one step at a time. Even if I ran out of money, the college wouldn't be able to send me to jail, right? In short, when I made the commitment, I had no idea whether I could do it, but you never know if you don't give it a go. I sincerely wanted to set up a Chinese Department – that's why I did it. Such was life. Now those three years have come to an end. The visiting scholar has been promoted to receive a full-tenured professorship with a salary I no longer had to subsidize. Still, whatever is left of my money can be used to meet the Chinese department's other needs. It's something I'm truly happy to have achieved.

After moving to Rossmoor, I showed some of my travel recordings to my neighbor who was too frail to go out. She loved it and suggested I should share them with other residents via the community's television station. I agreed to do it because I thought it was important to share my experiences. For example, everybody here would have seen the Silk Road footage I made during a trip in 1999. Apart from my travels, I also recorded some of our activities here in Rossmoor which I edited myself on the computer after studying video editing at an adult education school. They even showed my photograph in an advertisement for the editing class. I did this for 15 years mainly to help physically disabled friends to maintain contact with the outside world.

In 1990 the year we moved here, the Chinese residents in our community established the Chinese-American Association of Rossmoor (CAAR, see the chapter on Peter Sih). From the initial 40, the number of members gradually increased. I served on the CAAR board for a total of six years, as its secretary in 1992, as the deputy chairperson in 1994, and as the chairperson from 1996 to 1998. At that time, those of us who played mahjong had to squeeze into a tiny room for our games. In order for the Mahjong Club to have a bigger room, whenever we had a pot luck lunch, we invited the person in charge of room management for a lion's share. Such "bribes" worked – they moved us to our current club room where we have dozens of tables for games. My fellow mahjong players have praised my resourcefulness. In 2010 CAAR presented two "achievement awards". One was for Shing-yi Huang, the other, for me.

As a large community, Rossmoor has more than 9,600 residents, the equivalent of a small city. Managed by the Board of the Golden Rain Foundation (GRF), the community has an annual budget of 1.6 million dollars with over 200 employees and a myriad of management issues. Members of the board, elected from the residents in various districts, take turns to be the chairperson. They meet once a month to discuss and decide major community issues. Several friends nominated me to run for the board to represent the voices of all Chinese residents. By the time I was elected as a member of the GRF Board, I was interviewed by *Diablo* magazine in San Francisco's East Bay as one of their ten outstanding women. They were amazed by the fact that I still played tennis at the age of 76 and spent more than three hours taking photographs as proof. These were published in the winter issue of the magazine in 2001.

76-year-old Patsy Peng on tennis court 2001

Whatever title I had is not important. What matters is to get things done. To be on the board, one has to be knowledgeable from building, piping and gardening to accounting and budget management. For every meeting we had to read a pile of documents. As the meetings were open to all community residents and had many items to be discussed, the decision making process was highly complex and often involved fierce debates. I often felt exhausted afterwards.

Patsy Peng at a board meeting 2001

During my time on the board, my most notable achievement was to have a movie theater built for our community. Previously our so-called movie theater was an ordinary room that was big enough to seat 80 people. There was no extra seating for latecomers and lacked quality audio and visual equipment. I proposed to the board that the present facility was inadequate for so many residents in our community who enjoyed watching movies. We definitely needed to build an appropriately sized movie theater. At subsequent meetings people fought over issues such as where the theater could be built and how big it should be. When others decided on a location and budget that would allow a maximum of 150 seats, I insisted it wasn't large enough, but the choice was made. Fortunately, one solution to this problem was to schedule more screenings, including daytime sessions which many of our residents might prefer. Another issue was the addition of a plaque next to the theater that listed the names of the donors. As a result of some objections, the plaque now remains black. Today what our movie theater lacks in size is compensated by its excellent audio and visual equipment and highly comfortable seating. The floor grades slowly from the front to the back, allowing easy access by the disabled and elderly. We have movies every day. A popular film may be screened up to four times each day for several consecutive days.

Many residents in our community enjoy playing ping-pong or table tennis. In 2006 when the GRF Board decided to rebuild the table tennis hall, a temporary portable building was erected after the old hall was demolished. However, after six years the new hall had yet to be built. Even though the board and members of the Table Tennis Club did a lot of work to plan, prepare and urge the progress of this project, at every meeting the GRF Board would set other items on its agenda, treating such issues as the expensive refurbishing of a meeting hall and a five-court tennis club as priorities. As members of the Table Tennis Club confronted the slow progress of this project and having no proper hall to play in, a club board member came to me for help. At that time I had already retired from the GRF board. Nonetheless, in such circumstances I made a commitment and decided I would do my utmost to help them achieve their goal. I asked a current GRF board member to find me an opportunity to speak at the forthcoming meeting. Apart from the three people already scheduled to express their views, I demanded a chance to present my argument. In order to make a strong stand and be perfectly persuasive, I did my investigation on the cost of renting the portable building and the potential expenses involved in building an Event Center and the tennis courts or maintaining the golf course. For days I didn't sleep well, as I had yet to think of a good argument.

Eventually I had my speech prepared. I suggested there were three reasons why our community needed a ping-pong hall. First, ping-pong is a sport enjoyed by people of all ages. When tennis fans become too old to participate in such a physically exhausting sport, they can switch to ping-pong. More importantly, a Table Tennis Hall would allow players to enjoy the sport in all sorts of weather conditions, which would be highly beneficial to both the community's public image and our quality of life. Finally, you don't need a team of players to enjoy ping-pong. All you need is a partner, which is good for our physical and mental lives. The incoming president of Table Tennis Club Bill Dabney submitted my remarks about table tennis to the Rossmoor News, our community newspaper. He said that he liked what I wrote. What I wrote was "As a retired tennis player and a retreating golf player, I judiciously beg to share the following. Table tennis is an extension of physical fitness! When the days of tennis and golf are beyond one's physical capability, one can still play table tennis. It accommodates age and minor infirmities. It requires no previous experience. It defies cold or rainy weather. It knows no difference between evening and daytime. One can never be too old to join. The novice is especially welcome. It is a challenging game with eye-hand coordination and swift skilful responses, yet it is also a congenial game. It is an everlasting sport for everyone who will give it a try for the benefit of one's own mobility and health. I fervently wish that the honourable members of the current GRF board will be long remembered for having made the permanent table tennis facility a reality." On the day the meeting took place, the Table Tennis Club also asked all supporters of the new hall to dress in red, to give the board a visual sign of the number of people favoring the plan. The copies of my remarks were placing in front of all who attended the Board meeting.

At the meeting after the three scheduled speakers had expressed their views and when the item about the Table Tennis Hall once again appeared to have vanished from the board's agenda, my friendly board member called my name. So I gave my speech. I started by describing how the board demolished our ping-pong hall and promised to build a new one but rented a portable building instead at a considerable yearly cost. To build a new hall would be a valuable investment, a one-off payment that would be much cheaper than the cost of annually maintaining the golf course. I concluded my speech with this: "Building a Table Tennis Hall is neither a matter of money nor one of priority. What is at stake is the credibility of this board. I hope the board can think over this issue carefully." Some considered this to be the most influential speech I had ever given to the board. At the second meeting all members of the Table Tennis Club dressed in red again. Finally, the board decided at this meeting that a professional quality ping-pong hall would be built and the standard five tables would be provided instead of the initially promised four. Now we have many people who enjoy playing ping-pong at the hall. I am so glad to have contributed to this success.

  People say I have talent as a leader. What talents do I have? It's just to meet the demand of circumstances as they arise. All I knew in the past as a student was to study hard and move forward, never to be bothered with other things. It was only later after my children had grown up that I started to work for public welfare. Considering the fact that so many innocent people had lost their lives in the turmoil of war and that I personally had suffered so much and could have died on several occasions but survived, it all feels like a dream. Those of us who survive should work hard to give back to society.

Ruby Chow 陳麗焜
At home in Rossmoor 2014

    Throughout her life, Ruby Chow has been pursuing her dreams in science, music and visual arts. Her house is graced by a large piano near the entrance and more than a dozen of her own paintings on the walls, most of which are abstracts. While some of them appear to have obvious backgrounds and meanings, I have to rely on her to explain the others. It is hard to imagine how such a petite figure is able to create paintings so magnificent in size. As a friend she has often provided me with advice and constructive criticism based on her more than 90 years of life experience. With this book her suggestion is also excellent – to enable each of our senior Chinese Americans to tell their unique stories instead of presenting a simple chronological documentation of what happened in their lives. During our interviews her words are often philosophical and wise, making it a great pleasure to converse with her. It remains her hope that her positive attitude towards life and its numerous twists and turns can be an inspiration for others.

Biography

Ruby Chow, whose Chinese name is Li-kun Chow (nee Chen), was born in Shanghai in 1923. After graduating from Shanghai's McTyeire School in 1942, she fled from the turmoil of war to Chongqing, Sichuan Province, followed by two years of study in nutrition at Yenching University in Chengdu. Later in the midst of the War of Resistance against Japan, she entered Bryn Mawr College in Pennsylvania where she received a Bachelor of Science in Chemistry in 1947. After getting married, she relocated to Long Island, New York, with her husband. A total of 36 years after that, having raised four children, she received a Bachelor at Music degree from the State University of New York at Stony Brook in 1973. A decade later she received a Bachelor of Fine Arts in Studio Art and has since focused all her energy in this field. She relocated to Rossmoor, Walnut Creek, in the San Francisco's East Bay in 1984 to continue pursuing her dreams in science, music and visual arts.

A Dreamer in Science, Music and Art

My father Tie-shan Chen was born in Hawaii around 1890. As the Chinese people had yet to succeed in their attempt to overthrow the Qing Dynasty, when my father graduated from university, he returned to China to assist his uncle Sun Yat-sen the revolution of the overthrowing the regime and establishing the Republic of China. I am not sure what my father studied at university in Hawaii, nor do I know what he did in China except that he devoted himself to helping the people there. When I was young, I enjoyed too many things to pay specific attention to events like that. By the time I was old enough to want to understand people like my father, they had already passed away as well as those who knew them intimately. Now I have a lot of regrets as I never thought about asking my father about such things. What he did back then must have been very interesting, but I will never get to know.

My mother Guo-fen Xiao was born in Guangdong Province but later moved to Shanghai. Her family owned a ship building and maintenance business and was rather affluent. My mother was the fourth among the family's twelve children, although six of her siblings died at a young age. With her big sister having bound feet and the next sister's failing halfway through the foot-binding process, my mother was determined not to have her feet bound. Also in contrast to her older sisters, she absolutely refused to have an arranged marriage. Having lived among the revolutionaries at a young age, my mother was a rebel herself. As a teenager, as soon as she met my father, she announced to my grandfather that she would marry only him and no one else. She was very young when they married.

Happy Childhood

Born in 1923 I was the oldest child in our family with a younger sister and brother. Although we lived in Shanghai, my Hawaiian-born father enjoyed outdoor activities and would often take the three of us and my cousins to play on the outskirts of the city. Up to ten of us had a lot of fun running around. Together we rested on a large bed sheet spread out on the grass. If it was too hot to sleep indoors during the summer due to a lack of air conditioning then in Shanghai, our servants would put up camp beds made of canvas around the garden for us to sleep where it was so exciting seeing twinkling stars at night. Without knowing there was such a thing called astronomy, I was interested in observing the stars and I always will be. It was only after retirement that I started reading books and magazines in this field.

Ruby Chow and her parents 1924

Several years ago my oldest cousin and our childhood playmate organized a family gathering. It was a grand event attended by more than 80 people. In our family's genealogical charts, Sun Yat-sen belonged to the 18th generation and I am in the 20th. With that said, I have no idea who our ancestors were. I grew up in a loving family and was always well treated. Now, in my own big family, my four children, nine grandchildren and I are all good friends. Although our family members live in various corners of the United States, we often meet and travel together. At our gatherings we all share the workload. Every Christmas we have a "Secret Santa" who collects presents from everyone and re-distributes them based on computer-generated random selections. I received an excellent book last year as a gift from the "Secret Santa". I truly feel that everything is and will be fine if you know your family loves you. I have always enjoyed the love of my relatives, my children and grandchildren, so I never become upset or depressed by the hardships and obstacles in my life.

Studying in China's Hinterlands

I graduated from Shanghai's McTyeire School in 1942. By then my brother's godmother had a daughter engaged to the son of a certain Chief Commander Yang, but the young couple lived in two separate locations due to the turmoil of war. Consequently, Yang sent a so-called special agent and a soldier to escort the young bride-to-be from Shanghai to Yunnan to get married. As my father recognized the importance of studying, he sent me along with the bride-to-be to the hinterlands. Also traveling with us were my brother, my cousin and another girl. The five of us wore long, dark blue gowns for warmth throughout the freezing winter trip. I also wore a long mink coat under my gown, which was hard to see from the outside. Each of us had various valuables hidden because it was too dangerous to carry money.

Even with escorts it took us a total of 55 days to travel from Shanghai to Chongqing. Wherever we went, we had to remain cautious and wait for the two escorts to arrange, check and ensure that everything would be safe. We walked every day, often without a place to sleep or bathe. It was too dangerous to carry luggage so we had no change of clothing. Worse, we dresssed as shabbily as possible and ate only simple meals, such as a glass of water and a piece of bread or a bun for breakfast before commencing a whole day of walking. Still, being only a teenager I had a lot of fun with no idea what hardship was. I recall memories of a place with dry and cracked ground with occasional rooftops and tree trunkss sticking out of the ground but not a single soul around. The roads were made of mud, and a so-called house had only half a wall standing. We were so exhausted that we simply used a wooden plank and slept on it as a bed. Once upon our arrival in an unknown location, we overheard noise on the other side of a wall that sounded like people interrogating a spy. We knew they were doing horrible things to that man, but we were too tired to do anything about it.

At the end of that 55-day journey, the four of us parted from that girl who would be married in Yunnan. After that a truck full of military supplies took us to Chongqing with us standing on the sideboards and hanging onto the carriage's steel poles for dear life. That's how we entered Sichuan Province where the dirt by the roadside was red. The mountain path was so winding and dangerous that our truck had to blast its horn at every turn as a warning so that vehicles coming the other way would be aware of our existence and stop to let us pass. Indeed we often saw wretched cars lying stuck in ditches after taking a tumble from the road.

Upon my arrival in Chongqing, I stayed with my uncle's family. Knowing that I would be coming, they purchased new clothing and arranged a school for me. My uncle had a huge study where he kept all sorts of books, the subjects of which ranged from geography and history to literature and philosophy. In my mind he was a well-read scholar. Then having been told that I could read any book I liked, I walked into that study and saw one titled "British Society of Extra Sensory Perception", something I truly wanted to understand. However, as I reached for that book, my uncle saw it and said, "Ruby, you're too young to read that book." I was so mad. Back then I really wanted to read that book, but even today I still don't know what it's about. Why am I interested in this subject you may ask? Well, when I was in high school, among my good friends were two daughters from a family surnamed Shi, who were two years older than I. Being twins, each sister knew exactly what the other needed at any moment, and that is why I developed much interest in things related to "extra sensory perception".

Perhaps it is something I still need to figure out.

After staying at my uncle's house for about a week, I went to study in Chengdu. At Yenching University, which by then had relocated from Beijing to the hinterlands, I spent nearly two years studying nutrition. Soon after my arrival there, we experienced a series of Japanese bombings. I dashed outside as soon as the sirens sounded and followed the locals to hide in the rice fields. I would come back and find my roommate studying as if nothing had happened, and the same situation repeated the second time. When I asked why she didn't leave, she replied, "You'll die if you're destined to die; otherwise, you'll live no matter what happens. We have to face examinations tomorrow." I then asked what we should do, and she told me to follow her. "How much money do you have? Let's go to a tea house and have our favorite buns for a meal," she further said. "Then let's come back here to sleep. Empty your mind of everything and tell yourself to sleep, sleep and sleep. Everything'll be fine once you're asleep."

At that time many students met, studied and ate together at local tea houses, so I did as my roommate said the next time the siren sounded and discovered a kind of crabmeat bun at our local tea house that was super delicious. How did I have money to buy buns? Well, when I left Shanghai, my mother sewed a number of lipsticks into the seams of my clothes. The lipsticks were highly valued in the hinterlands, so I sold them for money.

Our electricity supply was cut off every Friday, so we used small oil lamps instead. We put the lamps together to make it brighter and then studied as a group which helped to turn strangers into friends. At that time not every university in Chengdu was able to offer all the subjects required for a particular degree. Hence students like me were allowed to go to other university campuses to sit in their classes.

While at Yenching University a couple of senior students were really nice, treating me like a little sister. Once we organized a trip to Mountain Emei. A total of 100 participants were divided into groups of ten with the leader of each group carrying a pile of blankets for everyone's bedding. I was so happy because I could play the organ for those who wanted to sing hymns. Eight male students took turns transporting the tiny organ, which had only one and a half octaves but required one person on each side to carry it. It was a long way to the mountain peak through the narrow paths used by Taoist priests. People repeatedly kept saying we're nearly there, and it was wonderful when we finally reached our destination.

Outside the Taoist temple was a huge pavilion supported by five thick pillars. It was there that our group leaders organized a place for us to spread blankets on the ground to sleep on. Although we weren't allowed entry into the temple, there was a drum at the entrance. As soon as we beat the drum to announce our arrival, priests hurried out with all sorts of delicious vegetarian dishes for us to share. After that they scheduled us to see the "holy lamps" at two o'clock the next morning before witnessing the sunrise and then returning to pray at the temple.

At night it was pitch black on the mountain. We had one guide carrying a lamp, who told us to stay on the left side while walking. We soon discovered the so-called "holy lamps" were actually what is known as "will-o'-the-wisp" or *ignis fatuus* today, atmospheric ghost lights that resemble flickering lamps here and there at night. Later at the break of dawn, the sun appeared to be leaping out from behind the mountain instead of rising slowly into the sky. As soon as it was daylight, we realized why we had to stay to the left on our way here – we were standing on a cliff that was only accessible via a steep, narrow path. While we had so much fun coming up in the dark, we were now scared of going down along this path. I was frightened of heights, especially when we came upon an ancient suspension bridge that had lost most of its boards. I had to cross the bridge in order to go home, but I was so scared that it took me more than 20 minutes to do it. Talking about it now, I still feel unnerved. Anyway throughout that trip I played the organ on many occasions.

No one was concerned that we were singing Christian hymns near a Taoist temple on a mountain considered to be a Buddhist sacred place. Some of my high school friends had traveled through every mountain in that region, studying and sharing meals with Taoist priests and nuns who lived there like hermits. Decades later I wanted to go back to Mountain Emei for a visit, but all the Taoist priests had been driven away from that region.

As a new comer, I was allowed to share accommodations with a senior student who was two years older than I. On New Year's Eve she and her boyfriend invited me to come along to a dance party at someone else's house. There were so many people jumping up and down there that the floor collapsed and we all fell to the ground. As I stood there dazed and unsure what to do, the other students yelled, "Ruby, come on, let's go!" and hurried me away. I wonder what the owner of that house thought about the whole incident?

Back when I was young, I did a lot of silly things like that. While I can't remember a single book I studied in school, those unique memories have always remained with me.

Studying in America

I came to America in 1944 at the end of my second year at Yenching University in Chengdu. Remember that mink coat I mentioned earlier? I sold it in order to raise money for this trip. I flew from China to the United States in an army transporter, which had no seats but metal benches on both sides of military supplies in the center of the cabin. I sat on one of these benches as the aircraft flew over the "Hump" of the Himalayan Mountains and reached India as a stopover. All I experienced in India was a sense of inequality with the British people dressed in fancy suits surrounded by the locals who were either beggars or suffering extreme poverty. It was much worse than China, and I never wanted to go there again. From India, we flew to Washington, D.C., and finally to New York. No meals were offered on the aircraft and we couldn't even drink water because no toilet was available.

During China's War of Resistance against Japan, my uncle sent all his children to study in the United States. Hence my relatives had everything ready and organized for my stay at their place upon my arrival in New York. My cousin even prepared books and arranged a university entrance examination for me. He was a nice person who really looked after his family. I was never good with numbers, but the mathematics test in that examination was really easy. After that at a party organized by my relatives, I sat next to a professor who suggested that I had two choices as a newly arrived student from China. "You could go to the Columbia University in New York, or choose a smaller college." he said. "For example, Bryn Mawr College near Philadelphia is a private, girls-only school. They have excellent subjects in both liberal arts and science."

Assuming that Columbia University didn't have much campus in a big city such as New York, I decided to go for the open environment at Bryn Mawr College in Philadelphia. I was young and naïve back then, unafraid of anything and everything even though my relatives had organized everything there for me. Upon my arrival I immediately made three friends with whom I still maintain frequent contact today. Later one became a professor in mathematics, the other stock analyst, and the third a scientist. One of them used to invite me to stay with her family on holidays. Her father was a high-ranking manager at IBM.

Now that I was in Bryn Mawr, all the credits I earned during my two years at Chengdu should be able to be transferred here. My parents had a friend who was a retired diplomat and whose daughter was also attended this school. She offered me a lot of help. For example, how to transfer the credits. With a major in chemistry, I needed to study subjects in my own department and those in liberal arts. She told me about a professor in philosophy who was friendly with Chinese students and urged me to approach him. I took her advice and briefly read such famous philosophers as Aristotle at the library before meeting that professor. He spent two or three minutes interviewing me before agreeing that I could take his class.

At another time when I mentioned that I was not good in English, she told me the most important part of taking a particular professor's English class was to face him from the front row and to understand his opening statements as much as possible. She further explained that, no matter how hard I worked, there would be no way for me to finish all the required readings. Take our classmate Barbara Bunce, who later became a professor in chemistry and whom we referred to as "Bunsen Burner", as an example. She was so smart that as soon as she completed a chemical experiment, our professor would add another title to the reading list. There would be no way for me to catch up to people like her. Hence my friend told me to find a seat near the entrance of the lecture hall. "As soon as your professor issues a reading list and leaves the room, you should hurry to the library to grab the most important titles on that list," she said. "Just read those titles and you'll be fine. There's no need to read all the titles on the list." Throughout my days at the college, such suggestions from her were of tremendous value to me.

I entered the country with a student visa. In 1947 when I found a job after graduating from college, immigration officials announced that as an international student, I was not allowed to work in the United States. It didn't matter much then as I was about to get married. Still I immediately applied for and gained my citizenship because my father was born in Hawaii and was already a citizen of the United States.

My Husband and Children

My husband Joe Chow specialized in material science. He was a very smart scientist but extremely non-talkative. Back when we were dating, I wanted to cook a meal for us before going out to see an opera. However, because I knew so little about cooking and ended up burning the chicken, we had to go out for dinner. When I took my friend's advice and wore high heels and make-up, he told me to just be myself. After we married in 1948, I gave birth to four kids – bang, bang, bang and bang. Having previously received a bachelor's degree in chemistry, I was too busy looking after my children to do anything with it. I didn't even consider finding a job. Most of my friends had only one or two kids. When they asked me whether I was Catholic and I simply answered no, they said, "Ruby, you're silly." I was indeed young and naïve back then.

After we married, my husband worked for the Brookhaven National Lab in Long Island, New York. By the time our first child was born in 1955, my husband was teaching at the State University of New York at Stony Brook, where I occasionally attended seminars on various topics. At that time Chen-ning Yang was also there. As his son and mine went to the same kindergarten, we became acquainted via the parents' association. After Yang and Tsung-dao Lee received the 1957 Nobel Prize in Physics, I went to hear his speech at Stony Brook but was unable to understand anything he said. Being kept outside of a professional discipline was a rather upsetting experience, but the atmosphere on that occasion was very good.

Anyway my husband had a good friend at the Brookhaven National Lab, Dr Raymond Davis, who was conducting research at a deep, abandoned gold mine in South Dakota. In 2002 as a result of his detection of solar neutrinos and his subsequent discovery that their number is much less than previously and theoretically predicted, he shared a Nobel Prize in Physics at the age of 88. Dr. Davis loved sailing and introduced my husband to the sport which in turn led to our whole family becoming enthusiastic sailors. At one stage we were the proud owners of four vessels, including three sail boats and one motorboat, the last of which we used for water skiing and fishing. That was a really happy period in our lives.

Two years ago to celebrate my 90th birthday, my children and grandchildren rented a big house at Cape Cod near Boston on the Atlantic Coast. More than 20 family members stayed under one roof with the youngest being only 11 and the oldest 90. Everyday all of us would put on a T-shirt printed with the image of one of my paintings and participate in a particular water sport. As I was no longer able to sail, I chose to do kayaking with my son. We had a lot of fun together as a family.

Pursuing My Dream in Music

While teaching at the State University of New York at Stony Brook, my husband befriended many professors in various fields. Among them was a professor of music, Isaac Nemiroff, who introduced us to many pianists and musicians in our neighborhood. I enjoyed music so much that I formed a music club with several friends to meet once a month. I maintain frequent contacts with one member even today, a dancer. Among other members were a singer and a self-proclaimed dramatist, whose performances we often attended. They only performed for themselves without trying to sell tickets and attracting an audience; I helped back stage.

This was a rather nice little theatre club with the most active member being Dr. Nemiroff. Later a group of musicians created a new style called "chance music", which involved random and spontaneous addition of all sorts of sounds to their existing music so that each piece would sound completely different every time it was performed. My husband, another couple and I often tagged along when some of the professors conducted experimental recordings in the countryside on Sundays. We observed how they recorded sounds such as birds chirping and wind whistling. It was interesting watching them take turns composing different sections of a melody. Once in a performance at the renowned Radio City Music Hall in New York also used chance music. From time to time the audience would suddenly hear a bang here or a ding there or something that sounded like someone going down a slide on his bare buttocks. It was tremendously funny.

Both of my parents' families loved music. On my father's side, it was mainly Western music. He often had friends from Hawaii visiting and playing all sorts of musical instruments. They would also teach me, so I learned how to play the ukulele, Hawaiian guitar and various other instruments from childhood. My mother's family loved Chinese music and instruments such as *yangqin*, *yueqin* and *qinqin* that are commonly used in Peking Opera. While the *yueqin* (a four-stringed plucked instrument with a full moon-shaped sound box) produces high-pitch notes, the *qinqin* (a three-stringed plucked instrument mainly used in folk music) makes sounds lower in pitch and is rather like a banjo. Whenever I watched an older cousin and his friends playing these musical instruments, they would pick one and teach me how to play it.

At one stage when we lived in Beijing for a short while, whoever was aware of my passion for Peking Opera would take me along whenever they went to the local theater. That's when I was a kid. Much later as my own children grew up, I asked my husband whether I could study music as a student. He was always fine with what I did and wanted to do, so I was back to school and busy studying all day. I would tell the kids in the morning to put this or that dish in the oven after they came home from school. By the time I finished my classes and returned home at three o'clock in the afternoon, whatever was in the oven would often be burned to a crisp. The kids were little then, but they never got to have baked sweets for dessert because I wasn't a home-based mother. Still having studied for two years and transferred some of my old credits from Bryn Mawr College, I finally received a Bachelor of Music degree the State University of New York at Stony Brook in 1973.

While studying music I had to learn many things including musical theories, composition and even chance music. Students were required to hold something in their hands that made sounds, which could be a piece of wood or a bell. They were also given a timer and were told to make some noise whenever it was their turn. Once they wanted us to turn on a radio at the mark of 25 minutes, but there was no sound coming out of it. Was it chance music? Who knew? This musical trend lasted only a short while between the 1950s and 1970s. However, not so long ago, I heard some professors performing a new form of music that was similar to chance music. It sounded very nice as a modern style.

Apart from teaching children to play piano and enjoying life, I didn't do anything special after graduating from the Department of Music at the State University of New York at Stony Brook. I had started learning piano at the age of 9 and enjoyed it very much. The McTyeire School in Shanghai regarded music highly and required all students to take piano lessons with our instructor, a graduate of the renowned Oberlin Conservatory of Music in the United States.

I once mentioned the possibility of going to America and studying piano there in the future. She immediately responded, "Ruby, to become a professional pianist, you need to start learning at a very young age. You're not good enough to be a pianist because you only started learning at 9. It's impossible for you to have music 'naturally flowing out of your fingertips' the same way as those who started young. And, if you can't become a professional pianist, you'll only end up being a piano teacher like me." She further explained that piano teachers never earned enough money. Worse, in order to study piano at an academy, one needed to practice eight hours each day. As a result, they would have no time to go out with boys and end up getting married in their 40s or even 50s.

Because of her advice I never tried to learn piano in the United States. It was only after I gained my degree in music that I realized the reason why I played piano poorly was because I never had an opportunity to properly learn it. Hence I decided to find a good piano teacher in Manhattan. In 1977, I found an excellent teacher with very high standards. Apart from the homework he gave me each day, I had to borrow a pile of books from the Juilliard School's library to practice reading sheet music. I would start playing piano every morning and spend every available minute on it throughout the day.

However, because I was already 55 years old and had not played piano for many years, my hands became severely swollen as a result of such an intensive practice routine. Even my wedding ring had to be cut and removed from my finger. Eventually I couldn't move or control any of my fingers. I couldn't pick up or hold anything. I couldn't even sleep. My second son, then a medical student at the State University of New York, told me to stop practicing for a week. If my hands still didn't improve after that, he would take me to his medical professor for a check-up. That professor later announced that my hands were so severely injured that an operation was required to fix them. So, in 1980, I had an operation to have artificial joints inserted in my fingers. It was extremely painful, but I finally had my hands fixed. I could no longer play piano after that. I consider that starting intensive training on piano at a late age was the worst decision of my life.

Switching to Painting

In 1981 my husband and I had a dinner with a group of professors from the State University of New York at Stony Brook. When I mentioned how depressed I felt after my operation because I could neither play piano nor teach it to my children, a professor in visual arts told me to cheer up. "Ruby, don't worry," he said. "Times are different now, with the latest trend being large-sized painting. You could use your whole arm to create abstracts. Come and have a try in my class if you'd like. You could even become a formal student."

Of course I tried and later enrolled to become a student in Studio Art. It was quite a nice decision as I loved to work side by side with young students whom I referred to as little kids. The school would provide large-sized paper and all sorts of paints. We would have our paintings done and lined up against the wall before our professor walked in. He never knew in advance who did which painting, but his critique in general benefited me tremendously. We had a huge amount of homework and so many paintings to do that I often had to stay up late into the night. I also had ample opportunities to practice a wide range of styles by copying famous paintings. For example, I copied the style of the 17th-century portrait *Girl with a Pearl Earring* and then worked on a portrait of my husband in the same style. Specifically, I painted him wearing a jacket made of silk and focused on how to present the textures of light and silk.

We spent our second year working on abstracts. We needed to submit seven paintings at graduation, with the largest being 50x60 inches. Instead of purchasing existing canvases from a shop, we had to make our own wooden frames and stretch and glue canvases over them. Obviously we also had to create our own original paintings. I missed a lot of sleep over those seven pieces of work.

Later, that professor picked three of my paintings for an exhibition, one of which immediately sold. I didn't keep a photograph of it unfortunately, nor did I record the buyer's name or how much he paid for it. At our graduation seminar our professor explained that in order to become professional artists, we needed four things. First, you needed to know how to promote yourself. Second, the prices of your paintings needed to be high so that people would consider you to be already successful. Third, you needed a good agent. Finally and most importantly, you needed to maintain a unique style, something of your own, in the same way that people would take a look at Jackson Pollock's paintings and immediately recognize them to be his. When I mentioned this to my daughter at home, I commented on how boring it would be if I had to maintain the same painting style all the time. She responded that I studied painting for a completely different purpose than to become a professional artist and make money. I was doing it for fun, so I should simply enjoy painting whatever I liked and in whatever style I chose.

None of my family members painted in the past. I have some artistic friends working in ceramics and lapidary, but none of them painted. I had never felt the need to paint. I only continued doing it once I was into it. With some of my old credits from my studies in music, I managed to gain a bachelor's degree in Studio Art in two years. From then on I simply painted whatever happened in my life. This is why I often say my paintings are a record of my life. Never knowing where I get my inspiration from, I paint whenever I feel like it. I never do drafts either. Instead I would think about it, do it, and stop when it felt right. Drafts only limit my abilities.

Many of my paintings contain elements of music or dance. In fact all forms of art, visual arts, music or dance, share something in common. I am interested in the arts because they help me to express myself. While painting I can almost forget about my own existence. Indeed, I learned a little bit of ballet when my daughter was little, having taken her place in class for a while when she was unable to attend. I learned that while dancing you think not about oneself but about your movements and all the emotions you are supposed to convey.

The same applies to painting; facing a piece of blank canvas or paper, I simply focus on entering that empty space, which to me is almost like meditation. Whenever you visit a temple, you hear the monks chanting in a rather flat tone, a kind of "universal rhythm" as referred to by some people. You spin the prayer wheel along with this tone to calm your heart and mind. Indeed, my children once took me to a fundraising event where Tibetan monks conducted prayers for heavenly blessings. The sound of the Tibetan long horns could be heard from far, far away, which helped people to meditate. Instead of listening to sounds like this, I can immerse myself in the world of paper and colors and completely forget about my own existence.

After the Second World War ended in 1945, Chinese cuisine became popular in the United States. By the early 1960s there were so many Americans learning Chinese cooking that many Chinese, including my friend Florence Lin in New York, became instructors in this field (see the chapter on Florence Lin).

American scholars also discovered the *I Ching* or Book of Changes, which was translated to English. If people in the West knew about this ancient Chinese text, then I as a Chinese definitely needed to understand it. A friend of mine recommended a huge English book on this topic, so I bought a copy and read it; I understood the words but not their meaning. In order to further explore this field, I purchased another book from Chinatown in New York. Written by a scholar from the Qing Dynasty, it provides page after page of interpretation for each of the numerous sentences in the *I Ching*. It took me six months to finish reading a section of that book. However, that single section alone enabled me to understand the nature and significance of *yin* and *yang*. The image of *Tai Chi* contains two halves, one black and the other white, which are always together. Some describe them as opposites, but the truth is that they alternate and transform into each other when the whole *Tai Chi* revolves. Sometimes you'd see lots of black, at other times lots of white, and still at other times it would be half black and half white.

My understanding of this is that everything has two sides in our world with both constantly changing and evolving across time continuously in search for a balance within. As human beings, we need to insert ourselves into that balance between heaven and earth which is of utmost importance. Old events and important matters fade and disappear leading to the birth of something new, so that death means the production of a new life and our souls will never be truly gone. Here's another example of balance: Whatever we love or enjoy, having too much of it will only cause us trouble. It is never good to pursue the extremes. One of my paintings is a perfect expression of this view. It contains white and black colors as symbols of heaven and earth. While earth is constantly revolving and evolving, a simple dot of red color represents people and all the lives in this universe. In the eyes of an artist, black is not just a color. Instead, you can see many elements of it in the forms of such different colors as blue, green and brown.

I Ching: Tao as Yin and Yang (oil painting, originally in color) 36x48 inches.

I did two other paintings after our trip to the Silk Road with warm colors in one and cold ones in the other. To convey a sense of being in a dessert, I covered the canvas with two layers of cotton cheese cloth and brushed color all over them before removing the cloth. Against this large background, I cut and pasted a tiny human figure and a tent. Does this person want to enter the tent? Is there someone already in it? You can assume whatever you like. Meanwhile, all of this is being watched by a desert rat in the distance. I don't know where the sun is, so all the shadows in this painting are disconnected. I do not know from which direction the wind blows nor where the smoke will go. The whole painting offers plenty of space for the imagination.

Another series of paintings is worth mentioning. Back in early June, 1989, I was traveling with a high school friend in Luoyang in China's Henan Province. One morning on our way to the market to buy some stuff for cooking, we saw a large group of students demonstrating on the street. Holding banners that marked them as students from chemistry and biology departments, they appeared to be young scholars of science. Soon we heard about military tanks targeting students in Tiananmen Square in Beijing and immediately decided to join the demonstration right in front of us.

After I returned to the United States, there was so much agony in my heart that I was sleepless at night. I couldn't rid myself of the images of those young people being gunned down and crushed by tanks. So one day I got out of bed in the morning with a fierce desire to paint. I knew I had to express my emotions on paper, so I went to the local hardware store to purchase quarts of black glossy house paint which I felt at that moment was the only color I could use to convey my feelings. Blood does not have to be red. In this painting you can see thick, oil-like stuff spilling. You can also see abstract shapes of military tanks and bayonets. There are no human figures because I simply wanted to express a feeling of mine. Military stuff is used to launch wars, and I included tanks in this painting because they had been used in Beijing. While tanks are only tanks, I also wanted them to resemble human figures. This series has three paintings that I created using pieces of cardboard dipped in paint. Compared to the one below, the other two paintings are even more abstract.

Ruby Chow's painting in memory of June 4, 1989

Perhaps because of something in our genes, my children and grandchildren have always been interested in public welfare. Many of my paintings have no titles and are never intended for sale. However, in recent years my son has done well selling some of my paintings to raise funds for charities. He wanted me to create some Chinese-style paintings which I did using black ink over plain rice paper. They are not genuine Chinese paintings but have a Chinese feeling of it.

After my husband and I retired, when we were looking for a potential residence in Rossmoor, California, one of my conditions was to have my own studio. We ended up picking a condominium that was still being built. By the time we moved here in fall 1984, the garage became my studio. Once here, I attended many creative workshops in nearby towns such as Napa, Calistoga and Santa Rosa. I also joined a series of organizations for abstract artists and was very active in the Association of San Francisco Woman Artists.

Ruby Chow working in her studio
(photograph published on Rossmoor News in 2000)

Back then we had two cars with my husband driving the smaller one. I drove the bigger station wagon to bring my paintings to San Francisco, where unlike today, many parking spots were still available on the streets. Our association's gallery was situated right behind the renowned Davies Symphony Hall. As members of this collaborative operation, each and every one of us was expected to contribute something. I asked to do the registration at the front desk, so I was always the first person to admire everyone's new paintings. Because I am a tiny person who works on large-sized paintings, every time I entered the gallery carrying one of my works, people could only see my feet. Still everyone who saw my paintings would know it was me. That was a very busy but happy period of my life, leaving home with a sandwich in the morning and coming home very late at night. I kept my paintings on display in that gallery until my husband became ill.

Some of Ruby Chow's paintings (originally in color)

Caring for My Husband for 14 Years

In 1990 due to blood clots that formed as a result of his heart problems, my husband suddenly had a stroke and was in a coma for eight days. After that he was partially paralysed. My youngest son, a physician, decided to stay with us in order to visit his father at the hospital every morning. Several months later when my husband came home from hospital, he understood nothing. His brilliant mind had lost its ability to comprehend and respond. If I asked him to gather various items on a desk, he would sit there and stare at them for half an hour without knowing what to do. My children wanted me to find a caregiver so that I could still have my own life, but I couldn't do it.

That was a very strange period of my life. One day I tried my hardest to pray, "Whoever is in the heavens, please, please help me."

That evening I saw a program on the television channel Nova Science about a famous experiment using mice. A mouse, whose circumstances were the equivalent to those of a 79-year-old man, was placed in a cage full of toys. Initially it just sat there. Then as time went by, it became more and more physically and intellectually active. Eventually it was dissected and brand new neurological pathways were found to have formed in its brain. I immediately called my children and asked them to take turns visiting us on weekends. Their children, who were still little then, would run around my husband and create a lot of noise. The whole house was a mess and my children apologized, but I insisted such stimulation would be beneficial to their father.

As my husband suffered from diabetes caused by his physical trauma, I had to test his blood sugar level every night. My instructions were to contact our doctor whenever there was any problem with my husband's blood sugar level even in the middle of the night. I further went to the hospital to study how various nutritious dishes were prepared in their kitchen. Their recipes had a lot of fruit for breakfast and many vegetables for lunch and dinner. As my husband couldn't eat that much, I would boil more than ten different types of vegetables for five minutes then blended them into two bowls of "soup". Though the soup could hardly be called "tasty", my husband obeyed my orders and swallowed two bowls of this stuff every day.

Six months later our doctor was amazed by the improvement my husband had made. He even wanted me to publish my discovery, but I said it was only a mixture of ten different vegetables. Meanwhile I recalled that, when I was a child, one of our servants was a man from Shandong Province who always had garlic in his food. I had learned from him how valuable garlic is in terms of killing germs. Yet, concerned that garlic might be too potent for my husband, I used leek instead. Another article I read at that time mentioned the discovery of the complete remains of a man under layers of ice and snow in the Alps who was estimated to be 5,000 years old. Since mushrooms were found next to the Iceman, I thought they must be very good stuff. Finally, because of my husband's illness, my cousin often sent me news articles related to nutrition. One of these clippings discussed the benefits of kale. I ended up having three things – leek, mushrooms and kale – in our daily meals while adding seven other vegetables to make that "soup".

In those days whenever I had a bit of spare time to paint, there was always leek, onion, mushroom and carrot in my paintings. Other elements such as music and dancing would present themselves as well. For example, some of my paintings would have African Americans in bright and colorful dresses dancing with leeks.

Ruby and her husband Joe Chow at her *In Retrospect* art exhibition after his recovery 1993

On top of all this, I tried my best to make my husband laugh by dressing, speaking and acting funny. I drew this from another television program I had watched that mentioned the fact that when we laugh, the movement of our diaphragm would help to generate a particular hormone that is beneficial to our health. Having taken care of my husband like this for a total of 14 years, he finally recovered all of his brain's functions. Whenever I asked him to count from 0 and add 3 each time to form the sequence of 3, 6, 9, etc. or to count from 100 backwards and take off 7 each time, he could do them all.

Back to Music

When my husband was ill at home, I tried playing piano for him. I had brought my piano along when we moved to Rossmoor but I never touched it until 1992, when I asked myself exactly why I still kept it. I started slowly playing for only five minutes each day before increasing it to ten minutes. Then I proceeded to play with both hands for up to one hour. Later, as I was unable to handle many of the complicated movements, I started learning improvisation with my left hand. As a result whenever I played piano, people hardly knew that I didn't stick to sheet music. This is a lesson I learned: Some things happen in order for you to learn other things. If I hadn't damaged my hands back then, I would never have had the chance to learn new things such as improvisation.

My children once gave me a record by Bruce Springsteen as a Christmas present. It was my youngest son's advice that as a musician I needed to know both classical and modern music. Back then my children introduced me to rock and roll, folk songs and other types of music. Now my grandchildren insist that I know about rap. For example, my grandson recently participated in a Thanksgiving performance. One part of the program involved a section from the song *Bohemian Rhapsody* by the British rock band Queen. It sounded so interesting that I searched and eventually found the original melody and lyrics. This is how I keep in touch with new things. I may not like some of them at the start, but the more I understand them the more I realize that there's a reason for them to exist. I get to understand why young people like them which is very, very interesting. To me all types of music are good whether they are classical or modern.

Being Positive about Life

Decades ago, someone from the De Anza Optimist Club of Cupertino in Silicon Valley gave me a copy of the "Optimist Creed", written by Christian D. Larson, an American New Thought leader and teacher. He says: "Promise yourself to be so strong that nothing can disturb your peace of mind. To talk health, happiness and prosperity to every person you meet... To look at the sunny side of everything and make your optimism come true. To think only the best, to work only for the best, and to expect only the best... To forget the mistakes of the past and press on to the greater achievements of the future... To give so much time to the improvement of yourself that you have no time to criticize others." Reminders like this want us to remain positive when we face this world. Such an attitude has long-term benefits. It is obvious that all of us have encountered tragedies and bad things often take place in our lives. However, if you choose to remember these things all the time, then they will surely have a negative impact on your life even without you becoming conscious of it. It is my view that we should throw away these tragedies and bad things and stop thinking about them. We should strive not to worry about the "downs" of our lives, especially those that are likely to have little further consequence. Instead, we should concentrate on the "ups" of our lives, things that are positive and constructive. Concepts like this have a cumulative effect upon us, but I didn't feel it in the past. However, decades later, I have witnessed its profound impact on my life. Because I am always positive without being conscious of it, I have lived a happy life. It is such an important lesson that you don't even need to study it. All you need to know is that it's there as a reminder for you.

I also hold the view that we should be happy to accept new things. We should never stop learning. Some people would consider themselves to be incapable of doing this or that even before they actually give it a try. If they are afraid to try, then they will never find out whether they are capable of doing it. Indeed, if we are interested in something, then we should try our hand at it. Being capable of doing it is fine, but what harm would come if it turns out that we are unable to do it? Some experiences are so beneficial that they are definitely worth going through. For example, when my husband suddenly fell ill, I became completely lost. I knew nothing about our finances because he had always been the one who managed them. Eventually I approached Julia Ng, a Rossmoorian who understood stock investment. Thanks to her help, little by little I managed to take over the management of our finances.

Another example took place last May when I was invited to give a speech at the Rossmoor Arts Club. On the day I was scheduled to speak, my son, an experienced public speaker, arrived from New York to help me practice. When he asked me to give my speech to him, I could only make sounds like "mhhh" and "ahhh". Then he said, "Your friends will be there to listen to your speech, so you have to make it interesting and full of fun. Instead of saying this or that is my painting, you should try to explain what your painting is about." As a result I had to start all over again, and I had to do this three more times before my son considered it satisfactory. Thanks to such preparation, I was able to relax while giving that speech. Afterwards, some in the audience thought I was very funny, almost like a comedian. This is why I say we should keep learning whatever the subject or timing.

I think I have lived a rich life. I have worked hard in three fields: science, music and painting. As a matter of fact, they are all related to each other. Having studied chemistry and nutrition while hardly ever working in these areas, I still like science. I am interested in astronomy, solar neutrinos, and as earlier mentioned extra-sensory perception. Now that I have plenty of time, I read through every issue of *Scientific American* magazine.

I am currently reading other scientific books including *On Intelligence: How a New Understanding of the Brain will Lead to the Creation of Truly Intelligence Machines* whose author Jeff Hawkins is the son of one of our friends. As the inventor of the Palm Pilot, he is rather famous in Silicon Valley. Having sold his company Palm Inc. for a huge amount of money, he started studying neuroscience. When he published *On Intelligence* about ten years ago, he gave me a copy as a gift. In his book he described our brains as super-computers whose function is to cumulate knowledge. He also says human beings do not have souls with which I disagree. I have had plenty of arguments with him over issues like that. He thinks that way because he works with computers, but other researchers of artificial intelligence may come up with completely different conclusions in the future. Who knows? I don't know. Meanwhile, music and painting remain important aspects of my life. I also practice *Tai Chi* Qi Gong every day.

Ruby Chow, a dreamer in music and painting
(photograph published on Roosmoor News in 2000)

I hold the view that everyone in this world has an interesting life because there are always things in our lives that we cannot foresee. You know some things will surely happen, but you never get to know what exactly will happen or when. Some of these things will definitely make you happy, but there will always be others that will make you sad. You will surely have regrets, but you will always have hope. As I live my days happily, today will always belong to me. But I don't know to whom my tomorrow will belong.

Annie L. Toy 梁美瓊
At Rossmoor Fireside lobby January 2015

Among the 14 senior Chinese Americans whose life stories are collected in this book, Annie L. Toy, with "Toy" being her husband's surname and "L" as the initial of her own surname Leong, is the only one born in the United States as a second-generation immigrant. Our conversations were conducted in English. When I started planning this book, many people urged me to approach Annie as a potential interviewee. She was delighted when my friend Changlin Hua (another Rossmoor resident) and I visited her and treated us to many of her homemade sweets. She proofread the first chapter before asking a neighbor and former school teacher to edit it. She then invited us to her house to clarify various issues discussed in our conversations which demonstrated how serious she was about this project. To further my research, she lent me a book of personal essays that marked the 100th anniversary of the migration and settlement of her husband's family in the United States. According to Annie, she retired three times, the last being two years ago. Instead of staying at home, she is often busy driving everywhere which makes it hard for others to comprehend that she is already 95 years old. The story of Annie and her family is an illustration of how early generations of Chinese migrants achieved their American Dreams through their diligence and wisdom.

Biography

Annie L. Toy is a second-generation Chinese American, who was born in 1920 at home in Oakland, California. Her Chinese name is Mi King Leong. Her ancestral home is Xinhui in China's Guangdong Province. After the outbreak of the Pacific War, having graduated from a private girls' high school in San Francisco, she worked at a navy base. After working as an aircraft instrument panel maintenance technician for 28 years, she decided to retire but instead started to work for a medical clinic and later served as a volunteer to raise funds for the Children's Hospital Oakland. She continued to volunteer her services for public welfare organizations in Oakland until the age of 93.

Bitter-Sweet Life of Early Chinese Immigrants

As a second-generation Chinese American, I know very little about my father's hometown. I only know it to be Xinhui, in China's Guangdong Province and that Qi-chao Liang, the renowned Chinese scholar and reformist, was one of the distinguished people born and raised there. Many people left Xinhui to search for a better life overseas. Among them was my father Ping Leong who was born in 1871. He arrived in America at the age of 11 in 1882, but returned to China on the SS Mongolia in 1908. My parents married in 1910 when my mother was only 19 years old. In January 1911 my father returned to the United States alone on the SS Korea leaving behind my mother and their newborn daughter.

My father worked as a salesman in a Chinese company in Vallejo, California. He had to both support his family in China and save enough money to bring them to America. It was not until September 1919 that my mother, their nine-year-old daughter and other relatives were able to make it to America on the SS China. After a 28-day sea journey, they were detained on Angel Island in the San Francisco Bay. Unable to speak any English, my mother was so nervous during her interrogation by immigration officials that she failed to provide proper answers to three of their questions. Hence her detention was lengthened.

Today as we examine the archived documentation of the hearings conducted by the Immigration Bureau on November 3, 1919, it is clear that they asked my mother hundreds of questions on a diverse range of topics. These included the orientation of her home village; whether it was enclosed by walls and contained fish ponds; where her house was situated in the village; how many rooms were inside the house and the number of trees outside; where her family's drinking water came from and the number of wells in the village; the distance between her house and the nearby market; when she first met her parents-in-law; the names, ages and even wedding venues of her husband's numerous relatives – questions to which no one could possibly provide full and correct answers. Not only was my mother placed in a strange environment and faced with an unknown future, but she could hardly appreciate the foreign food or communicate with those around her. My mother was so frightened that she cried all the timewhich in turn caused her daughter to be constantly in tears. In the end it was my father who managed to convince the immigration officials to allow their entry; that's how my family was finally re-united.

I was born 95 years ago in 1920, at home in Oakland, California. My father named me Mi King in Chinese and Annie in English. Several years later my sister Mi Yee was born. Neither of us was delivered in a hospital. Back then there was already a Chinatown in Oakland. We lived on nearby Ninth Street close to Harrison Street. Whenever I go to Oakland these days, I still recognize the place where I was born although the building is gone.

At that time my father owned a laundry near the Carquinez Bridge in a town called Crocket about 30 miles to the north of Oakland. When I was several months old, my parents brought me there via the South Pacific Coast Railroad. I recall my mother making her weekly two-hour train journey to purchase food from Oakland's Chinatown. As a housewife she cooked for our family and many Chinese workers at the California and Hawaiian Sugar Factory in Crocket on Saturdays. It was on Saturdays that the various ethnic groups in that town conducted their own gatherings.

Annie L. Toy (second from left) and her parents and sisters 1928

While my mother still couldn't speak English, she was able to take the train back and forth between Crocket and Oakland. She often mentioned an incident in which she missed the train when it had been rescheduled to run at a different time. After she gestured for help and explained the trouble she encountered, people at the train station drew a clock on a piece of paper to indicate when the next train would arrive. On occasions where my mother needed to go to San Francisco, she would take the ferry and then a taxi. She would tell the driver to go to "Chi-na fout", which is how "Chinatown" is pronounced in Cantonese, and keep staring at him, so that she could tap his shoulder and point in the correct direction whenever he got it wrong. My mother was indeed a very brave and smart woman.

After we moved back to Oakland in the mid-1920s, my father opened a laundry there. Apart from doing housework, my mother also set up a small take-out Chinese restaurant behind the shop. After living in Oakland for several years, my father purchased another laundry in Benicia, a town on the opposite side of the Carquinez Strait from Crocket. We moved there where I started primary school. Several years later we moved to Oakland again because my father bought another laundry there. This is how I spent my childhood, moving here and there with my family. But we were not alone since many Chinese workers at the California and Hawaiian Sugar Factory were also constantly relocating.

Back then all laundrys operated on manpower instead of machines. My father got up at three o'clock each morning to boil water. To do the laundry, one had to rub, knead, beat and thump the clothing against a wash board before wringing and then hanging it up to dry. Then it had to be ironed and folded. I recall the fee for washing and ironing a man's shirt was only 15 American cents. We often had so much to do that all family members were required to share the workload. The iron was heavy and needed to be heated red-hot on a stove burning wood or coal. While I still have two of my father's irons as well as his sprinkler and mister for keepsakes, I have promised to leave these items of great historical value to my granddaughter.

The irons, sprinkler and mister in Annie L. Toy's collection

Having finished primary and junior high schools in Oakland, I went to a girl's high school in San Francisco. I clearly remember our school was situated at the corner of Scott and Geary Streets and I had to walk to the campus whenever the tram drivers went on strike. That school was small but boasted a long history with most of its students being white. When I graduated, we had only four or five Asians among the 42 students in our class. A couple of these Asians were from Japan, who were excellent students. I had never experienced any racial discrimination at that school. After the outbreak of the Pacific War, however, the local Chinese people would wear a small tag saying "I am Chinese" whenever they were outdoors. Even so I still worried that people would mistaken me for a Japanese. All the Japanese people had been detained by then. With their businesses shut down and carrying only a few personal belongings, they were sent to camps in various regions. I once visited my friends at these camps. One such camp was built on a race car circuit in San Mateo and had only temporary sheds for housing. It saddened me to see them being treated that way.

Because I wanted to be a school teacher, I planned to go to San Francisco State University near my high school. However, after the Japanese bombing of Pearl Harbor and the U.S. Government's declaration of war against Japan, my mother asked me to return to Oakland out of concerns of my safety. Unable to go to university, I tried to find a local job. I was lucky that the nearby Alameda Naval Base was looking for workers. After passing the entrance tests, I was hired to work on aircraft maintenance and repair and started with the most basic skill level at a huge aircraft hangar. Because of the war all available men were conscripted as soldiers, leaving ample opportunities for women to do the kind of physically and technically demanding work that was previously done by their male counterparts. A fast learner in all aspects of my work, I gradually was promoted to the level of aircraft instrument panel maintenance technician. My task was to disassemble the instrument panels and fix all the broken parts.

I spent 28 years working at the naval base. It was a very interesting job and my salary was good. However, the work had a negative impact on my eyesight because like fixing watches and clocks it demanded a high degree of accuracy and precision. Nonetheless, in spite of the degeneration of my eyesight, my request for transfer to other departments was denied. My work as an instrument panel maintenance technician continued until I retired in 1971.

Our Wedding January 1970

Annie L. Toy's wedding, January 1970
with her husband's son and daughter as best man and bridesmaid, respectively

While working at the naval base, I met my husband Carl Chun Toy, a maintenance technician on aircraft cabin windows. I knew of him, but we formally met at a social gathering a year after the death of his former wife. Having dated each other for six months, we married in 1970 with Carl's 19-year-old son as his best man and his 15-year-old daughter as my bridesmaid. I became a mother of two children as soon as the wedding ceremony finished.

My husband's family settled in the United States over 100 years earlier. A descendent of Chinese gold-rushers in America, he was born in Grass Valley, the famous "Gold Country" in eastern California. My father-in-law, a very nice man, owned a small grocery store there. My mother-in-law was only 17 years old when she arrived in the United States to be his bride. Initially she didn't even know how to boil water as she had always had servants at home back in China. She learned everything from scratch including housework and preparing food items to be sold at the store. Among those items was a type of watermelon jelly sold to their American customers. Both of my parents-in-law were hard-working people and started from the bottom level of society. By the time my husband and I married, they had already sold their business and relocated to Oakland.

Soon after our wedding, I retired from the naval base and started working at a medical clinic. I happened to visit our family doctor George Lee who asked me what I wanted to do in retirement. When I expressed my interest in the medical field, he asked me to work for him. Because of his reputation as a surgeon, I agreed to give it a try. Dr Lee wanted to pay me at least the minimum wage. However, unconcerned about income, I was willing to work there for free. His clinic was situated on the 30th Street on the opposite side of the street from Peralta Hospital which had since closed down.

We lived in Oakland but decided to relocate to Fremont before my husband retired. Tired of life in the city, we wanted somewhere quiet. Only a short distance to the south of Oakland, Fremont had a small population and reasonably priced houses back then. We moved there in 1979 with me driving to work at Dr. Lee's medical clinic every day for the following ten years until I retired for the second time. I was sad to leave that clinic because everyone there was like family to me.

Both my husband and I loved fishing. We also enjoyed traveling and had long agreed to travel around the world in our retirement. Throughout our 23 years of happy life together, we had indeed visited many places in America and around the world. But the thing we loved the most was to see our children and grandchildren growing up. My husband passed away in 1992. He is gone but left behind a wonderful, warm family full of mutual love and respect.

Annie L. Toy and her husband Carl

After my husband's death, I had to take care of everything and make my own decisions. I visited Rossmoor and, having fallen in love with that community, decided to purchase a unit there. However, I had trouble selling my property in Fremont because of a housing glut and potential buyers could afford to be picky. In order to sell the house, I did a lot of renovation by replacing the roof, garage door and the water and electrical systems. Meanwhile, the owner of the unit I desired in Rossmoor had kindly kept it for me in exchange for a deposit. Finally in 1994 I sold my house in Fremont and packed everything to move to Rossmoor, Walnut Creek.

While living in Fremont, I joined a quilting club and mastered the process of sewing numerous pieces of colorful fabric together to create patterned and padded quilts which I enjoyed tremendously. Our members not only made their own quilts but also helped to complete other people's half-finished products. All the money we raised which amounted to several hundred dollars at most was donated to our church. After relocating to Rossmoor, I continued to participate in our quilting club's activities in Fremont on Thursdays. While I didn't join the Rossmoor Quilting Club here, I was recommended by Mr. Song-sen Mo to become a member of the Chinese American Association of Rossmoor (CAAR) soon after I moved to this community. Our association was then headed by Patsy Peng (see the chapter on Patsy P.H. Peng). Since then I have made considerable contributions to this association and was once the secretary.

Since my retirement I have done a lot of volunteer work, mainly to raise funds for the Children's Hospital in Oakland. The hospital has a sizeable thrift shop between 55th and 56th Streets in Oakland to raise funds. From time to time many people across America donate clothing and household items that they no longer need to charity shops like this. I used to take the BART (Bay Area Rapid Transit) from Rossmoor to work in that shop as a volunteer, but finally stopped two years ago when I reached the age of 93. That was the third time I retired. Apart from that I have always been an active member of the Presbyterian Church in Walnut Creek.

My older sister was married at the age of 20. A matchmaker informed my parents that a man from Boston was available, so she married him. They had six children, three boys and three girls. My younger sister found her own husband who worked as a ship builder. They had only one child. As for myself I married too late to have children of my own. However, my husband's two children and their partners have been really good to me. At this point in time I have four grandchildren and seven great-grandchildren. I am lucky to have such a lovely family.

Back in our day and era, Chinese people married only their Chinese counterparts. These days are different and it is common for young people to marry those from other cultural and ethnic backgrounds. Three of my grandchildren are married to white people and have beautiful children who are interested in learning about their Chinese heritage. My grandchildren call me "*Po-Po*" (grandmother in Chinese), while their children refer to me as "*Tai-Po*" (great-grandmother in Chinese). Throughout my life I have witnessed how much times have changed, but it is my dear family and our church activities that have served as a spiritual guidance and source of strength.

I remember many things most clearly about my childhood. Back then we didn't have luxuries nor did we ever desire them. In the 1920s the rent of our single-room apartment was only US $7 per month. We didn't have electricity, only natural gas; my sisters and I studied under an oil lamp every night. We didn't even have a toilet in our apartment. There was a public toilet nearby, but it was hard to get there on cold days. We had a galvanized iron tub hanging on our wallk which my mother would take down and fill with hot water whenever we needed a bath. Those tough living conditions didn't last long, but once I lived through them, I never, ever forgot them. I am grateful that my parents worked so hard to raise us. They gave my sisters and me a tremendously valuable life.

I miss the times when I was growing up in Oakland. It was a peaceful and safe city back then, very beautiful, with many big shopping centers and small, ordinary stores. We never locked our doors when we went out unlike these days where iron bars are installed outside the windows. That was back in the 1920s and 1930s. Even during the Great Depression, when we had to line up to receive rationed soap and food items, no one would have thought of breaking into other people's houses to steal things. In comparison, everything is so different now.

My father enjoyed gardening and watching television at home after his retirement. He died peacefully in his sleep in 1956 at the age of 85. After his death my mother kept herself busy by visiting friends and relatives. She always wore a broad-brimmed hat and carried a shopping bag full of sweets and snacks which she would share with children of her relatives and friends and children on the streets. She insisted on maintaining various Chinese traditions and rituals. She was also famous for being superstitious, and she was always checking the almanac to prepare herself for things good and bad. Still, everyone around my mother loved her. She became so ill near the end of her life that I had to send her to a nursing home. She died in 1972, two years after I married.

Looking back, I feel lucky to have had a perfect life. Even though I didn't get to fulfil my dream of receiving a higher education, I did have ample opportunities to work on some very challenging and meaningful jobs. Now at the age of 95 I am still healthy. I attribute my health to the "*Luk Tung Kuen*" exercise that I have been doing every morning since 1996.

Shing-yi Huang 黃聖儀
Traveling in Europe, 2015

Shing-yi Huang is one of the earliest Chinese-Americans to relocate to Rossmoor. We call him S.Y. He is such an influential person that at least six Chinese-American couples decided to follow him from the New York area. As one of the founders of the Chinese-American Association of Rossmoor (CAAR), S.Y. is active among local Chinese groups as well as the Rossmoor community at large. Now over 90 he continues to act like a true diplomat, speaking clearly and logically and upholding his principles while taking all issues into consideration. While planning this book of conversations a year ago, I asked S.Y. for his suggestions. He said he too would have wanted to do something like this if he were ten years younger, especially since he had spent all his "youthful" days having fun. His words demonstrated his support and encouragement for this project but also gave me a sense of urgency.

From the very start he fully involved himself in this book, helping me unconditionally and providing everything he could think of that would be useful to me including the names of CAAR members from past years and old photographs of Chinese-American activities in our community. Whenever I had questions I would ask him first, treating him like a walking encyclopedia. S.Y. is a senior Chinese-American I will always respect.

Biography

Shing-yi Huang whose ancestral home is Ningbo, Zhejiang Province, was born in Shanghai in 1923 but fled to Chongqing at the start of the War of Resistance against Japan. In 1945 he graduated from the Central Chengchi (Political Science) University (today's National Chengchi University) before working for the Ministry of Foreign Affairs. Soon after that he was transferred to the Republic of China's embassy in America and studied part-time for a Master's degree in Political Science at George Washington University. In 1952 he began working at the United Nations headquarters in New York. His service at the U.N. Secretariat covered a wide range of personnel administrative duties. He retired in 1983 and relocated to Rossmoor, Walnut Creek, in San Francisco's East Bay in 1987. He remains active in community and public affairs.

From Diplomacy to International Civil Service

My independent life began at the age of 15 when I left home alone to study. With much hard work I established a home and career in a foreign land. This is the story of how I transformed from a young man in exile amid China's turmoil of war, to a civil servant in the international arena, and finally to an elder Chinese in mainstream

American society.

Leaving Home at a Young Age

I was born in Shanghai, the second oldest of six siblings in our family, but became the oldest after my elder brother died of tuberculosis. I studied at Chengzhong Primary School in Hongkou, Shanghai, before entering Chengzhong High School, a famous institution established by a ship builder from Ningbo called Chengzhong Ye. I left home in 1937 at the age of 15 during my third year of high school. As my parents felt that Shanghai was under threat by the invading Japanese troops, they decided I should take my brother, two years my junior, to Ningbo our ancestral home. At that time Ningbo was relatively safe.

Instead of living with my grandmother in the countryside, I boarded at Ningbo High School, an excellent and tuition-free provincial institution. However, not long after that even our ancestral home came under threat as Japanese troops took over Shanghai and expanded further south to capture the coastal cities in Zhejiang Province forcing us to flee. I followed my school as it moved to the mountainous areas further inland far away from the Japanese. We carried our own bedding and set up temporary dormitories in local temples. After relocating several more times, we finally settled in Sheng County, Zhejiang Province. We were students in exile.

It was tough fleeing from the turmoil of war with the threat of Japanese troops constantly behind us. To go to the hinterlands, we needed to pass Xikou which was the hometown of Chiang Kai-shek and was a major target of Japanese bombardment. We risked our lives escaping from the Japanese warplanes and machine guns. It was a truly chaotic time but we persisted with our studies.

During that time I learned English in high school. I also had an opportunity to learn Esperanto from a teacher in Chinese literature. Our studies went unabated throughout the war. Back then we did not have textbooks or study notes. Everything remained simple and crude as we were constantly ready to flee from the Japanese. While the students stayed in temples, our teachers faced even worse conditions. These brilliant men and women left their families and children behind during these difficult times and continued teaching and looking after us along the way. That was how I finished high school in Sheng County.

(Left) S.Y. Huang and other boy scouts from Ningbo High School entertaining the troops 1940
(Right) S.Y. Huang as a high school student in Shanghai

After graduating from high school in 1941, I wanted to go to university. When we were allowed to return to Shanghai, a city occupied by the Japanese, my brother went to Shanghai and later entered Nankai University in Tianjin in 1949. I did not go because I did not want to go to territory occupied by the Japanese. Instead more than a dozen classmates and I decided to continue our exile and spent about a month walking from Sheng County to Taihe, then the temporary capital of Jiangxi Province. Full of youthful passion we simply desired to continue our studies in the hinterlands. At that time underground branches of the Communists Party existed even among the exiled students. While these and other underground groups such as reading clubs that had been active since my youth back in Ningbo existed, I was rather naïve and did not get involved in their activities. As none of us had relatives in Taiho, we had nowhere to live but local temples. We also managed to cook our own meals.

Although China was at war, we still had unified university entrance examinations and could register for them. In an attempt to cultivate talent for the future of our nation and to look after students in exile, the Nationalist Government continued to promote education among young people. We had our university entrance examination in Taiho with the usual subjects such as Chinese, foreign languages and mathematics. At that time many universities accepted students including the National Central University in Chongqing, Sichuan Province; the National Southwestern Associated University in Kunming, Yunnan Province; Zhejiang University that had relocated to Fujian Province; and the newly established Chung Cheng University, named after one of Chiang Kai-shek's first names. Another option was the Central Chengchi (Political Science) University in Chongqing, Sichuan Province at that time, which had relocated from Nanjing and merged with the Central School of Cadre in 1946. It is now a prestigious institution, National Chengchi University, in Taiwan.

I received a rather good examination score making me eligible to enrol in three schools: Chung Cheng University's Department of Economics, Zhejiang University's Department of Chemistry, and the Central Chengchi University's Department of Diplomacy. I chose the last because it was the only school in the whole nation that offered a major in diplomacy to cultivate talent in this field. The Central Chengchi University admitted students by a national examination. In an attempt to attract young cadres nationwide, it imposed a quota on the number of students taken from each province. I clearly remember the quota for Jiangxi Province was 17, nine of which were taken by our group of students exiled from Zhejiang Province. We attended the examination in the capital city and took those spots.

These young people and I shared the ideal of going to the vast hinterland under the Nationalist Government's control to study in

Chongqing. After enrollment it was a tough journey from Jiangxi Province to Chongqing. All normal traffic routes had been disrupted by war, so several friends and I managed to make use of all kinds of transportation including boats, and hitchhiking to travel from Jiangxi Province to Guilin, Guangxi Province, then to Guizhou Province, and finally to Chongqing. Along the way were steep mountainous slopes and deep gorges where many cars had slipped off the roads. We were truly lucky to arrive safely in Chongqing after such a difficult trip. The city was then under Japanese bombardment, and many air-raid shelters had collapsed killing those hiding inside. It was truly tragic.

Situated in a mountainous area south of Chongqing, the Central Chengchi University boasted fantastic natural scenery. As a training ground for the Kuomintang's party cadres, the institution offered three majors, namely law and politics, diplomacy, and economics, to cultivate administrative talent for the nation; also included in its curriculum was military training. Most of the graduates became county heads, but we also had older classmates with previous administrative experiences who wanted to pursue further studies as a way to seek promotion. Our school had very high standards. All of us, even those of a younger age (including me), were well educated, qualified men and women. All three aforementioned majors, including our Department of Diplomacy, required four years of study. However, we also had specialty subjects such as statistics, land administration, journalism and oriental languages, which required only two years of study because of high demand for people with these skills. In the Department of Diplomacy we could study a foreign language of our choice with the majority of people choosing English. As I had already learned English from excellent teachers at both Chengzhong High School and Ninbo High School, I chose to study French for four years.

There was not much difference between my life as a student in the Central Chengchi University and at other institutions, as all the students here were also well qualified. As a matter of fact, our education under the Kuomintang's management was rather flexible. Apart from subjects such as the Three Principles of the People, we had courses that were similar to those taught in regular schools. In English we had Professor Dayu Sun, a renowned Shakespearean scholar, as well as teachers from the United States. French was taught in the same way as the department of foreign language in regular universities.

Other advantages were that our schooling was tuition-free and included a student allowance as part of the plan to cultivate talent for our nation. I remember the allowance being three to five Chinese dollars per month which was initially good money. However, as commodity prices went up with inflation, the amount became the mere equivalent of a pair of straw shoes. Still from the time I left Shanghai at the age of 15 to my arrival at the Central Chengchi University as a student, I supported myself with very little subsidy from home.

My family was then in Shanghai, a coastal city with neither communications nor banking service connections with Chongqing in the hinterlands. With one side occupied by the Japanese and the other under the Nationalist Government's control, my father sent money to me through private arrangements. At the university my schoolmates included the father of former Taiwanese president Ying-jeou Ma who majored in law and politics. The father of Gloria Kern, who also lived in our community, was my classmate in the Department of Diplomacy. After graduation he worked for the Ministry of Foreign Affairs before becoming China's Consulate General in Honolulu, Hawaii. I too found a position in the Ministry after graduation but was assigned to work here in America in 1947.

At that time our university was situated in Huaxi (Flower Creek), a district of Chongqing. It was there that I met my wife Carrie whose Chinese name was Xiaoxia Fang. Originally from Hubei Province, Carrie wanted to go to the same university. Coincidentally, and life is full of coincidences, she missed the deadline to register for the entrance examination but was ultimately able to do so after the registration period was extended due to the Japanese bombing. She took the examination, passed it and enrolled in my school. I often wonder what would have happened to our lives had she not been able to complete her registration and pass the examination. While Carrie only studied statistics for two years, we happened to be in the same literary study group as an extracurricular activity. With her beautiful handwriting, she often copied manuscripts for our group's periodic journals and posters. That was how we met and fell in love. We started university at the same time, but she graduated two years before me. She found a job and a place to live. A year after that, while I was still in my third year of studies, we married and lived together for the 68 years. Our wedding took place in Chongqing without my family as they were in Shanghai and unable to attend.

I clearly remember how I sang Franz Schubert's *Serenade* as part of my proposal to Carrie. That was more than 70 years ago. Back then my best man transcribed our wedding vows onto a piece of silk using traditional Chinese brush and ink with decorative patterns on the edges. It reads like this: "We believe marriage is a sacred institution, a union of the souls and bodies of the two parties involved. On the basis of such a belief, we wish to become husband and wife, to abide by the spirit of mutual love, care and respect, and to merge our two lives into one. We entrust our two destinies to the same master of the stars and are convinced that our constellation will cast an eternal light over the permanent night that is the universe." (Note: Punctuation marks added by the author.) I left this piece of silk behind when I departed for America. Magically, after 50 years of tumultuous transition in time and circumstances, this precious piece of silk returned to our hands in 1994 when my younger brother brought it from China to celebrate our golden wedding anniversary.

(Left) Celebrating Shing-yi and Carrie Huang's Golden Wedding Ceremony, 1994 (Right) Hand-written wedding certificate on a piece of silk 1944

Life as a Diplomat

I graduated from university in 1945 right after the victory in the War of Resistance against Japan. As my knowledge and skills in diplomacy were cultivated by the government via the Central Chengchi University, I was soon assigned to work for the Ministry of Foreign Affairs. Trouble occurred, though, as some party factions within the Kuomintang considered this school and its students to be untrustworthy because it was established by brothers Guo-fu Chen and Li-fu Chen. They were two prominent politicians whom the Communist Party referred to as the "CC Faction". Fortunately, Shi-jie Wang, the new Minister of Foreign Affairs, was able to negotiate with these factions to let us work in his ministry. After that we had unified examinations to select students from institutions across the nation for high-ranking positions such as administrators and diplomats. I also passed that examination and was thus better qualified than most of the university graduates of the time. I was very lucky.

Whole family portrait of Shing-yi and Carrie Huang (second and first from the right at back row) before the couple and their daughter left for America 1947

I was assigned to work as a junior officer for the Department of East Asian Affairs in the Ministry of Foreign Affairs. The department was responsible for handling China's relations with Japan, Korea and Thailand; in Japan's case, it was mainly to deal with war criminals and compensation issues. Within two years after I started working, an opportunity arose when our department's director, Yun-zhu Yang, was assigned to work in the United States. He wanted me to accompany him on the mission. At that time my wife and I had a two-year old daughter and were expecting another child. I wanted to settle in America first before taking them overseas, but my wife insisted on the whole family traveling together so that we would not became separated. Indeed soon after our arrival in the United States in 1947, China fell into ommunist hands. As a result our decision to relocate the whole family considerably impacted our lives in the years that followed. Had I stayed in China, I would have surely been targeted as one of Chiang Kai-shek's students and a Kuomintang agent by the Chinese Communist Party.

Shing-yi and Carrie Huang with two daughters in Washington, D.C, circa 1949

This opportunity that enabled me to come to America was a crucial turning point in my life, as most of the people I knew had retreated to Taiwan. I often wonder aloud to my children, what would have happened to them had I decided not to come to the United States? As a matter of fact, I could have stayed in China as my father had wished. Instead I took my wife and daughter on a ship that sailed from Shanghai to San Francisco and then on a train to Washington, D.C., where I worked at the Republic of China's embassy. Specifically, I worked for the Chinese Delegation to the Far Eastern Commission which controlled Japan on behalf of the Allied Powers. A total of 11 nations including China, discussed and decided at the Commission on the directions and policies in controlling Japan after it lost the Second World War. These policies were to be enforced by Douglas MacArthur, Supreme Commander of the Allied Powers who also had to obey their orders. As a recent university graduate, I was indeed very lucky to have such a valuable experience of working at international gatherings at the highest level. I also took advantage of my free time to study at George Washington University and received my Master's degree in Political Science in two years. My thesis was on the trial and judgement of Japanese war criminals.

Within three years after our arrival in America, the Nationalist Government retreated to Taiwan. After the establishment of the Communist Government, relations between China and the United States became highly sensitive. Many of the students and personnel related to the Nationalist Government were constantly in fear, unsure how their future would unfold. Many of the Chinese students were cut off from their families as well as sources of finance from China and had to find work to support themselves. They often secured jobs in three places: restaurants, laundries (washing and ironing), and libraries. It should be noted here that this generation of Chinese students came to study in America with plans of returning and working in China. They had no intentions of immigrating, but circumstances forced them to remain in the United States. They were cut off from their families and could no longer go home. Though they were the elites in China, here they had to struggle to survive.

At that time the Republic of China's embassy in the United States continued to be operated by the Ministry of Foreign Affairs in Taiwan with the Far Eastern Commission struggling to maintain its functions. However, under such tumultuous circumstances and facing an unknown future, many embassy staff decided to find jobs elsewhere. I too contemplated a way out. One of my options was to stay at work until it became absolutely necessary to find another job in America. Alternatively, I could follow my colleagues at the Ministry of Foreign

Affairs and return to Taiwan, a move I did not want to because my family was still in Shanghai. A third option was to return to China to help my father run his business in Shanghai.

My father, Rong-fang Huang, was a manufacturer of medicine and the founder of the patriotic Huaxingchang Pharmaceutical Factory. Back in the early 1950s the Communist Party had yet to forbid the operations of privately-owned industries and businesses. Life in general was rather tolerable at times before the large-scale upheavals caused by the "Three-anti" (which attacked corruption, waste and bureaucracy, 1951) and "Five-anti" (1952) political campaigns. Thus my father was of the view that I should return with my family to contribute to his business in China.

Entry to the United Nations

However, a once-in-a-lifetime opportunity happened to come my way in 1951 when the United Nations (UN) Secretariat conducted an examination for Chinese translators. The international organization was constantly in need of expertise in translation and simultaneous interpretation. Taking into consideration the People's Republic of China's intention to become a member of the UN, the Secretariat decided to hold an examination to select translators from Chinese scholars, postgraduates and students remaining in the United States. On top of that, such positions came with excellent salaries, a major reason why the UN was referred to as a "golden bowl" by the Chinese. In the end nine candidates were chosen from approximately 300 participants at the examination. Four among the nine enjoyed the benefit of their existing positions as Chinese transcribers at the UN, but the remaining five including me passed the tough examination fair and square. This was another crucial turning point in my life. From then on I abandoned my dream of becoming a diplomat and worked instead as an international civil servant.

The examination mainly consisted of translation from English to Chinese. Apart from common English, we had to choose one of three specialty areas: international politics, economics and law. I remember one of the questions required the Chinese translation of a famous English essay which contained a sentence written in an awkward grammatical structure. Luckily, I had studied such an English grammatical structure in high school and was able to provide a perfect Chinese translation for it. Happenstance like this can often have a huge impact on one's life. With that said, in my opinion, I passed the examination not only as a result of my familiarity with the UN and the formats of documents used in its international conferences but also because of my capacity to answer some of the extra questions requiring translation from French to Chinese. Among the six official languages used in the UN – Arab, Chinese, English, French, Russian and Spanish – I had the benefit of being able to use three, which were English, French and Mandarin. After that I informed my father of my decision to stay in the United States as I had entered the UN. It was lucky that I decided to stay put. Had I returned to China, I would have suffered greatly during all the "Three-anti" and "Five-anti" political campaigns and the Cultural Revolution. This is why I often tell my children how our family has been so fortunate.

An International Civil Servant

I started to work as an international civil servant in the Chinese Translation Service of the UN Secretariat in April 1952. My office was located on the 21st floor of the newly built UN headquarters on New York City's East Side. Our job was mainly to translate all UN documents from English to Chinese which involved a lot of writing. During those early days the UN's European branch in Geneva would borrow the Chinese translators whenever they held international gatherings, thus giving us frequent opportunities of traveling to Switzerland.

Since we translated the records of international meetings and agreements, extraordinary caution and constant reconsideration were required in our choice of wording. One of my most memorable work experiences took place at the "International Conference on the Settlement of the Laotian Question" in Geneva in 1962 where Chinese translation was crucial because China was one of the major participants in the meeting. It was the first time that our Chinese translators from the UN Secretariat provided service to a group of diplomatic representatives from the People's Republic of China. Their group leader, then Minister of Foreign Affairs Yi Chen, held a banquet to express their gratitude for our assistance.

I worked as a translator for 12 years at the Chinese Translation Service within the Documentation Division under the UN Secretariat's Department for General Assembly and Conference Management. In February 1964 I was temporarily transferred to the Secretariat's Department of Management to work as the Acting Secretary replacement of both the Joint Appeals Board and Joint Disciplinary Committees. As staff relations among the UN's numerous divisions and departments were extremely complicated, both committees had many cases waiting to be processed. I was assigned this task although for what reason I did not know. Upon my arrival in that position, I analysed all the cases and scheduled a series of dates for both Committees to assess them. However, because I worked on a temporary basis and was not assigned a permanent office, I could only work as a "nomad", that is, borrowing the offices of vacationing colleagues while carrying a huge cardboard box of documents with me wherever I went. Nonetheless, within a year all the cases were cleared. Some suggested that I worked so hard that I worked myself out of my job, but the truth was that I was permanently transferred to the Department of Human Resources as a result of my excellent work. In another five years I was promoted to the position of Section Chief in charge of Staff Rules and personnel administration manuals. During this period I went to Africa on three occasions to arbitrate various staff-relation issues.

Later I was nominated by the Department of Management to serve on the Joint Advisory Committee that consisted of representatives of the Secretary-General and all UN employees. In early 1979, for example, I handled a strike that took place at the UN headquarters in New York. It sounds incredible now when the use of computers is nearly universal. The strike took place because the typists at the Documentation Division under the Secretariat's Department refused to use computers for fear that they might emit health-threatening radiation. In spite of reassuring explanations and safeguard measures provided by the medical personnel, things came to a dead as the typists continued their strike forcing the aforementioned Joint Advisory Committee to conduct constant negotiations with representatives of all UN employees. On the weekend before negotiations successfully concluded, the Committee's chairperson, a lady from Belgium, asked me to accompany her when she reported the good news to the Secretary-General. This was the first time I met Mr. Kurt Waldhelm in his office on the 38th floor. While he was known for his exquisite taste in clothing, I used to dress casually at work on weekends. When the chairperson introduced me in jeans as the Secretary-General's representative who helped resolve the strike, he seemed rather surprised, an embarrassing moment for both of us.

Not long after that when a new Assistant Secretary General took over the Office of Personnel Services, I was assigned to work as a "special assistant director". My colleagues at the UN came from such countries as Jordan, the United Kingdom, Israel, the Republic of Tunisia, sthe Soviet Union, Belgium, Italy, Egypt and the Republic of Sierra Leone. We had friendly relation with one another.

I retired from the UN as soon as I reached the stipulated age of 60. In a speech given at my farewell party, I said: "I had promised to put the UN's interests ahead of everything else and to devote myself to the international civil service. It was we who served the UN, not the other way around. I believe I had truly achieved this goal, having worked for the UN for more than 31 years, including 19 years at the Secretariat's Department of Management." These words came from the bottom of my heart. Not long after my retirement in September 1983, I was called back to work for the UN for approximately two months each year as an advisor on human resources for the organization's various international organs. Between 1983 and 1993 until I reached the age of 70, I spent nearly every summer in Europe, mostly in Vienna. That city became my third home.

Returning Home After 25 Years

I had been in exile since 1937 when I left my family in Shanghai at the age of 15. I managed to keep in contact with my parents via letters, but delivery was often difficult due to my constant change of address. It was only after 1945 when I graduated from university and started working for the Ministry of Foreign Affairs that I left Chongqing for Nanjing, then our nation's capital. From there I returned to Shanghai but departed again in 1947 for the United States. My mother had passed away by then. I soon lost direct contact with my father as all our letters had to go through Hong Kong.

At the UN all international employees took home leave to their home countries every two years. Consequently after I started working for the UN in 1952, I returned to either Taiwan or Hong Kong every two years but never to China proper. The first time I returned to China was in 1973, 26 years after I left there in 1947. This was after former U.S. President Richard Nixon's visit to China, though the two nations had yet to establish formal diplomatic relations. While ordinary Americans could not go there, I was able to do so under the name of the UN and with a UN-issued passport. My return journey in 1973 was through Hong Kong and the Luohu Port near Shenzhen in China's Guangdong Province. I remember feeling this was a strange new world as it was still during the Cultural Revolution. In fact people in China already had a different view about us, the Chinese in America.

When the Cultural Revolution first started, people in Shanghai put up posters denouncing my brother's "crime" of having a brother working as a "running dog" for U Thant, the then UN Secretary-General. This was truly ridiculous. Because China opposed the UN back then, my brother was punished due to my work at the international organization. In sharp contrast, when we returned to China for the first time in 1973, it was a journey in glory. I remember traveling to Hangzhou, Zhejiang Province, and drinking the renowned Dragon Well tea with my children at a local teahouse. As the Chinese characters for Dragon Well (Longjing) were glazed on the tea cups, my children wanted to purchase one as a souvenir. When we asked a waiter whether we could buy the cup, he referred us to his superiors. A high-ranking party cadre then decided we could indeed have the cup because we came from the United States and therefore should be treated as Chairman Mao's guests. As a result we were the recipients of two free tea cups which I still have today. We were Chairman Mao's guests!

In the past there had been cases where some of the UN's Chinese staff's friendly gestures on their return to China were rejected by the Communist Party. It was only after President Nixon's visit to China in 1972 that the nation started to welcome people from the UN. In fact, because both the UN Secretariat and staff were politically neutral, China's gaining a UN seat in 1971 had no impact on the Chinese UN employees. I was even invited to give a speech at the Foreign Affairs College (today's China Foreign Affairs University) during one of my vacations in China.

When I returned to China for the first time in 1973, both parents had already passed away. I visited the families of my younger brothers and sisters in Shanghai and Beijing. My father's pharmaceutical factory had been passed on to my aforementioned brother who was in exile with me but later returned to Shanghai. Initially a private business, it was now partly owned by the state. The *Liberation Daily* in Shanghai once reported my brother as a model worker and a contributor to the nation's medical industry, though he suffered greatly during the Cultural Revolution. Another brother, ten years my junior, worked as a deputy party secretary in Beijing's Tsinghua University. After my retirement he invited me to teach English at the university for a semester.

Shing-yi and Carrie Huang (third and fifth from the left, front row) with relatives in China 1973

After 1973 I travelled to China every two years. Once, I think it was 1978 we went to Xinjiang Province in remote Northwest China because one of my wife's sisters had sent her daughter there many years before in response to the Chinese Government's call to support regional development. The daughter married a man in Xinjiang who worked in Hetian in the province's south, as deputy county chief. As a Han Chinese, he was actually the person in charge. Hence our trip to Xinjiang covered the southern part of the province, from which we went all the way to Kashgar in the far west in a car driven by the locals.

Hardly any Americans had been there as no foreigners were allowed entry. I only made it as a specially honoured guest from the UN since China had already entered the international organization by then.

Active and Fulfilling Life in Retirement

I retired in September 1983. Four years later, at the age of 65, I relocated with my wife from New York to Rossmoor in San Francisco's East Bay Area. I have spent 28 years here, nearly a third of my life. Why did we come here? As retirees we wanted to be closer to our children. Our younger daughter lives in Berkeley. Also as our older daughter received her Ph.D. from the University of California at Berkeley, we used to come here quite often. We chose Rossmoor because one of my friends knew Dolly, wife of architect Yen Liang who was already living here, and her sister (see the chapter on Yen Liang). Like me Dolly used to work for the UN. The couple moved to Rosemoor from New York after Yen's retirement in 1973, the earliest among all the Chinese American residents here. Dolly's sister married Mr. Shen in Taiwan. In order to play golf during retirement in the United States, he bought a house next to the golf course at Rossmoor. Back then the house was still in the planning stage, so he made the purchase purely on the basis of how nearby existing properties looked. Eventually the house was built but he still had several years to go before retirement. He inspected it several times while on vacations in America. However, tragically, he died of a heart attack before having a chance to move in. As the house had been empty since then, my friend showed it to us. We liked it so much that I asked my friend to inquire whether we could purchase it if Mrs. Shen decided not to live there of course. We ended up with a direct agreement between the two parties without the use of a real estate agent.

Living in New York for 35 years, we had many Chinese friends with whom we would often play cards and tennis, go dancing, and join in parties and holiday trips. After our relocation to Rossmoor, many came for a visit since they were also near retirement age and in need of a proper place to live. Our friends stayed with us as they holidayed and looked for houses in California. These included Peter and Helen Sih, C.D. and Doreen Tung, and Robert and Ellie Mao Mok. They all loved Rossmoor and moved here. Other friends, including Horace and Theresa Chow, Tian-Yi and Anna Yang, and Benjamin and Patsy Peng (see relevant chapters) among others, also visited and decided to relocate from New York. All of them followed our footsteps. That was 25 years ago.

Situated on land approximately ten square kilometres or 2,000 acres, Rossmoor is a retirement community built on a ranch formerly owned by Stanley Dollar who was also the owner of the Dollar Steanship Line. When we first moved here, the minimum age of residents was 45. Now it is 55. All Rossmoor residents live independently although about a third of them have yet to officially retire. The average age of residents here is mid-70. Some move out when they are no longer able to enjoy an independent life.

Rossmoor is the "land that favors poetry" in Chinese. How did this transliteration come about? After our friends moved here from New York, we formed an association in 1990 and were in need of a Chinese name. After much discussion, we agreed upon this poetic transliteration proposed by poet Hugh C. Chang (See the chapter on Hugh Chang), and named our group the Chinese American Association of Rossmoor (CAAR). Initially it had only 40 members. We gathered for dinners and celebrated the Chinese New Year at the Stanley Dollar Clubhouse, a private residence and historical building specially preserved as a tribute to the owner of the aforementioned Dollar Steanship Line. Coincidentally more than 20 of the Chinese residents including me had taken one of the company's four passenger ships across the Pacific Ocean to this country. Back then in our twenties or thirties, we arrived only to scatter to all corners of the United States and spend decades establishing our families and careers. Now in retirement we gathered in this beautiful land left behind by Stanley Dollar. It is fate that brought us together.

In January 2002 *Time* magazine published an article on retirement life. Using our Rossmoor group as an example, it reported that the latest retirement trend in America was not to build a house for yourself or to move in with the children but to be together with old mates who support one another in friendship. A group photograph was also published by the magazine.

The Chinese residents at Rossmoor are well educated and enjoyd prominent social status before retirement and raised children to be achievers as well. As a whole they were pioneers of a new Chinese settlement in America, a unique group throughout the history of Chinese migration. They all came to the United States from good families in China. Most of them came to seek higher education, arriving at the time when America opened its door to China. Early laws that discriminated against the Chinese were abolished in 1943. In 1945, with China being victorious in the War of Resistance against Japan, America welcomed the Chinese as allies.

At Rossmoor the Chinese residents are not concerned with personal fortunes or political controversies. We are different from traditional Chinatowns like the ones in San Francisco and elsewhere which are full of ancestral shrines or guilds that engage in commercial or political activities. The latter are based on clan or regional influences including those sharing the same surnames such as Huang, Li, Liu, Guan or Zhang, and those coming from the same provinces such as Guangdong, Jiangsu, Zhejiang or Fujian. CAAR as a group is dedicated to social activities beyond these worldly divisions. We are a new Gold Mountain full of hidden dragons and crouching tigers.

We travelled with many of our Chinese friends to such places as Canada, Alaska, Europe, Australia and New Zealand, and certainly China. Our last journey was to Egypt in 2003. Apart from traveling we also have many other activities including our monthly CAAR meetings and celebrations of traditional Chinese festivals. The first president of CAAR was Peter Sih (see chapter on Peter Sih). Our second president was Victor Young, an American-born Chinese whose wife's name is Tuck, and who enjoys playing golf and learning the Chinese language. Back then Sih had been very active. With donations he organized the building of a bus stop near the intersection of Terra Granada Drive and Horseman's Canyon Drive. Decorated with such Chinese words as "Sharing Life's Journeys", it was completed during the term of Horace Chow, our third president (see the chapter on Horace Chow). As our group continues to expand, CAAR had nearly 400 members at the time of this writing.

Soon after arriving at Rossmoor, I joined the local Lions Club and participated in its charity events dedicated to helping the general public, particularly those with vision and hearing disabilities. I was elected its president in 2001, which marked the 35th anniversary of the club's establishment. More than 120 members celebrated the grand event at the Rossmoor Fireside clubhouse with the mayor of Walnut Creek presenting her personal congratulations. Indeed, working as a volunteer in my spare time at Rossmoor and giving back to our society is a great way to complete my retirement.

As the number of our Chinese residents continued to increase, I have been working as a writer and photographer for the local weekly newspaper, the *Rossmoor News*, to enable the whole community to hear our collective voice. Throughout the past 20 years or so, I have published many articles on the activities of local Chinese communities and the Lions Club. In 2004 I published a collection of these articles in a book titled *Twilights in Rossmoor* and dedicated it to Rossmoor's 40th anniversary. An expanded edition of the book was printed in 2012 with proceeds derived from sales donated to the Rossmoor Fund, a local charity.

In September 2014 I became a member of a preparatory committee to coordinate celebrations for Rossmoor's 50th birthday as a community. In order to showcase the quality and contribution of our Chinese residents, I organized a concert featuring instrumental Chinese folk music and Peking Opera. I also arranged and hosted a pancake breakfast provided by the Lions Club, and participated in the design and planning of a parade float sponsored by CAAR. I feel much younger than my current age of 93 since I am constantly working on events like these.

People of my generation came to study in the United States as young men and women. They intended to return home and contribute to China's development but were forced to stay here because of circumstances of the time. We have lived successful lives and take pride in the success of our children. Having received traditional Chinese education at home, our sons and daughters understand hardship and self-improvement. They are brilliant people, but our next generation are surely different from us.

I will briefly mention my daughter Belle here. Before graduating from Wellesley College, she served as president of its Student Association. She was succeeded by Hillary Clinton, who is one year her junior. When Belle completed her studies, my wife and I were invited to attend her graduation ceremony and sit next to the president of the college. However, my daughter was absent. She was leading a group of fellow students in Boston to support a minister who was on trial for campaigning against the Vietnam War. Back then Hillary Clinton belonged to the conservative Republicans. Later she became the Secretary of State of a Democratic administration. After graduating from Harvard University's Medical School, Belle worked as a psychiatrist. She is now retired, enjoying family life and traveling. She taught her son to appreciate his Chinese cultural heritage. As he continued to study Chinese, he was able to use Chinese calligraphy to copy the text of a couplet from the family code of ethics that my father had written for me. The two panels of Chinese Calligraphy written four generation apart are hung side by side on the wall of my home.

Shing-yi Huang and children at his 90th birthday party 2013
From left to right: Belle, Bessie and Sidney

Rossmoor is like a garden full of trees, flowers and singing birds. We have deer, geese and wild turkeys walking in our front yard and the nearby golf course. We participate in all kinds of activities. I used to play tennis; then I switched to golf. In recent years I have been practicing Qi-gong four times a week while taking advantage of other community facilities to learn dancing and play bridge. Every time I returned from a trip overseas and drive through our community's gate, I feel this is the best place to enjoy retirement.

My wife Carrie and I have lived here 26 years, and celebrated the 50th and 65th wedding anniversaries in this community. Our Golden Anniversary celebration was held in the newly built Del Valle Clubhouse that was well attended by many old friends from all corners of the world. Among them were nine guests who had been present at our wedding near Chongqing. Though another friend was unable to attend he sent his wife and daughter from Canberra, Australia, as his representatives.

Shing-yi and Carrie Huang at the 65th anniversary of their wedding 2008

We are lucky to have overcome all the obstacles on our way from Huaxi in Chongqing to Walnut Creek in California and to spend the last years of our quiet, fulfilling and happy lives at Rossmoor, the community that we refer to as our Shangri-La. Unfortunately, after sharing much of life's joy and hardship throughout the past 68 years, my wife Carrie passed away in 2012. I buried her in Ningbo, my hometown at a lakeside cemetery. Then in 2013, my children and friends held a grand party to celebrate my 90th birthday. More than 100 guests gathered at the Rossmoor Fireside Clubhouse where I sang Franz Schubert's *Serenade*, the same song I sang as part of my proposal to Carrie some 70 years before to her now who is in heaven.

At that party my dear friend Ruby Chow, who was also celebrating her 90th birthday (see the chapter on Ruby Chow), played the piano to accompany my singing. In order to prepare for this truly important performance, I even practiced along with another dear friend, vocal instructor Ellie Mao Mok (see the chapter on Ellie Mao Mok) for weeks. At the Ching Ming Tomb-Sweeping Festival in 2015, my children and I went back to Ningbo to pay tribute in front of my wife's grave. It rained that day. As all fallen leaves shall return to their roots, that place will be where I belong.

Shing-yi Huang sang Schubert's *Serenade* at his 90th birthday Party 2013

Linna Wu 蔣婉青
At Home in Rossmoor, November 2014

I admire Linna Wu's calm and peaceful attitude. She said her life has been so uneventful that there is nothing worth mentioning. However, savoring a cup of tea and listening to her life story while contemplating how people spend their lifetime pursuing fame and wealth, I realized how extraordinary it is to be content with an ordinary life in this world. Now in her 90s, Linna communicates with her grandchildren on her Apple computer, reads books on her Amazon Kindle, and sends hand-written Chinese e-mail messages from her mobile phone. Both of her parents came from distinguished "Navy Families". Her father, Zhi-zhuang Jiang, came from Yutou in Fuzhou, Fujian Province, and her mother, Ya-zhen Yang, also from Fuzhou. Their various ancestors had served as commanders-in-chief and secretaries of the navy for the Qing Dynasty, the Beiyang Government and the Nationalist Government. She suggested that I check the stories of her grandfathers and great-grandfathers on the Internet as she herself has done. To me, it is this desire to keep advancing with the times that enables Linna to remain young at heart. As penned by Xi Zhu, a renowned poet of the Southern Song Dynasty: "Thanks to the flow of running water, the stream is always clear and fair."

Biography

Linna Wu, whose Chinese name is Wan-qing Jiang, was born in Fuzhou, the capital of Fujian Province in 1923. Having fled from the turmoil of war to Nanping on the northern border of the province, she studied in the mountains before graduating with a degree in education from the Hwa Nan College. After the victory in the War of Resistance against Japan, she relocated from Fuzhou to the United States to marry Hsia Wu. Apart from raising her daughter and working, she spent her spare time studying and learning new skills and changed jobs several times in order to find one that best suited her interests. In retirement she and her husband moved to Rossmoor in Walnut Creek, California, in 1990.

It is Never about Fame and Wealth

My ancestral home is Fuzhou in China's Fujian Province. My father Zhi-zhuang Jiang graduated from the Yantai Naval School in Shandong Province in 1920 and was stationed in Mawei, a district of Fuzhou at the mouth of the Min River during the War of Resistance against Japan. His command included four naval vessels although they were not fully-armed military ships. I was born into a big family with my grandmother and four of my father's brothers and their dependants all living with us. My 11 cousins were like siblings to me. We had a large traditional compound where dozens of family members would gather at meal times. When the communists arrived, they demanded that we sell them the compound at such a cheap price that they practically got it free. The whole family split into smaller groups and lived separately in accommodations elsewhere. Eventually all the children grew up and left leaving only my mother and one of my uncles in Fuzhou.

Being my parents' only child, everybody in our extended family loved and looked after me. We were a family of Buddhists and had dharma masters come to pray for heavenly blessings whenever any of the children celebrated their birthdays. The masters in their yellow robes would set up a door frame of paper maché. While they blew their ceremonial horns, chanted and performed their song and dance, all the children were told to go through that door frame as if to march to eternal happiness and leave all bad things behind. But we were very naughty as kids. While the masters sang and danced, each of us would go and hit them on their buttocks. Normally they would complain, but on occasions like this they were too busy singing and chanting to fend off our attacks. However, once while we were having so much fun, we were caught by one of my aunts. Two of my cousins were smacked as punishment.

My husband Hsia Wu, also from Fuzhou, was five years older than me. He was one of my distant cousins, but Fuzhou was such a small place that all of us were related to each other to some degree. With that said Wu and I were not related biologically. Our two families were close friends and so I had known and liked him since childhood. He was the second of four boys in his family, so I referred to him as Second Brother. We often bumped into each other on the street but never conversed. Whenever my parents and I visited his family, I would hope to meet him, but he was never there. Later, it was said that after graduating from high school, he went to study at the Chiao Tung University in Shanghai. "Second Brother has left," I thought then. "I will never see him again."

Fleeing from War to Study in the Mountains

A couple of years later, because Fuzhou was in danger of being bombarded by Japanese warplanes, my father decided to send my mother and me to live in the Shanghai International Settlement. At that time Fuzhou and Shanghai were still connected by boat. As Wu's parents had taken his siblings to Shanghai as well, our two families as relatives rented a house and lived together. "I can see Second Brother again," I thought. Indeed, his younger sister and I were classmates at school and would often hang out together. Being a junior high school student at the age of 15 or 16, I had sensed that things were changing. As Wu lived on campus, I would find it funny in a silly way whenever his sister talked about his interests in girls at school. One day I tried on my mother's lipstick and bumped into Wu on the street. "Ai-ya, you have lipstick on your lips!" he teased. It upset me a great deal but it encouraged his younger sisters to start using lipstick. Later, for some reason, Wu gradually started paying attention to me and we ended up being rather close. In 1940 after he graduated from university, our families returned to Fuzhou together. By the time I started senior high school, he had gone to Chongqing, Sichuan Province, in China's hinterlands.

I went to the affiliated senior high school of the Hwa Nan College, a private girls-only school operated by the Methodist Episcopal Church (part of what is known today as the United Methodist Church). It was said to be an institution for rich people, but my not-so-affluent parents only wanted to give me, their only child, the best education they could. By then, all the academic institutions in Fuzhou had already relocated inland to Nanping more than 100 kilometers upstream along the Min River to the north where the Japanese could not reach. Still, the river was dangerous there with mountain cliffs on both banks and rocks of all sizes and shapes below the water surface. Only boatmen highly skilled and very familiar with the surroundings could sail upstream. By the time I returned to Fuzhou from Shanghai, the affiliated senior high school of the Hwa Nan College had already moved to Nanping and taken over the old dormitories owned by the Jianjin Middle School on Mount Huangjin. As the college itself was situated on top of another hill, it was rather inconvenient traveling back and forth everyday. I was all alone in Nanping but felt OK because it wasn't particularly far from Fuzhou. Though a high school student in Nanping, I still returned to Fuzhou for summer and winter holidays.

In 1941 while in school I suffered from a severe toothache. As there were no good dentists in Nanping, my father told me to return to Fuzhou during the Chinese New Year holiday to have the problem fixed. I ended up having my last wisdom tooth removed. Within a week suddenly the Japanese arrived and captured Fuzhou. Since there was neither a battle nor any sound of gun or canon fire, it was said that they parachuted down, formed groups of troops and marched into the city. One of our servants reported that the Nationalist army had already evacuated which was bad news for civilians trapped in Fuzhou. The circumstances were so dangerous that we stayed indoors and did our best to keep quiet.

Later since my teeth were fixed and there were no books at home, I wanted to go back to Nanping to resume my studies. While it generally took an overnight trip to travel upstream from Fuzhou to Nanping by steamship, one of my cousins and several other relatives and me had to squeeze into five or six tiny boats due to a lack of larger vessels. Powered by men who pushed against the river bed with long bamboo poles, our boats had no cabins or seats, so we had to sit on the deck which was dangerous. We also had to smear our faces and hands with dirty ashes.

After a day or so into our journey, we were told to turn around to avoid being attacked by local bandits who were active in areas where neither Japanese nor Chinese troops existed. All of the boats then returned to Fuzhou, but our next attempt to escape was successful when our boats met Chinese troops who took us onto their steamship. Still by the time I arrived in school, the semester and even the end-of-year examinations had finished. The principal told me to join a lower grade class which was fine with me as I was too young then to be concerned with matters like that. Better yet I made friends with students in both grades. That's my story of fleeing from the turmoil of war. I don't remember many of these events very well because they took place more than 70 years ago.

One day in 1942 we had a fair on campus. To our surprese our principal brought three Americans onto the stage and introduced them as pilots from the United States. They looked strange wearing Chinese-style robes with sleeves too short to cover their long arms. Being so young then, we knew them as foreigners and nothing else. It was not until much later that I learned they were three survivors out of 80 American crew members who crash-landed in China and Soviet Union after bombing military targets in Japan on April 18, 1942. Today it is known as the Doolittle Raid or Tokyo Raid.

Further upstream from Nanping was a bigger town called Yangkou. One of my classmates had family there and invited me to spend a couple of days with them. On our journey back, while happily eating biscuits and sitting on the deck of one of those tiny man-powered boats that I mentioned earlier, our boat bumped into a rock and turned violently, and we lost all our biscuits overboard. As our boatman worked hard to push against the rocks scattered across the river bed with his long bamboo pole, we were too young and naive to sense the danger we were in. Luckily, in the midst of our innocent cries of "Biscuits! Biscuits!" our boatman managed to turn the vessel around and scoop out most of the water it had taken on.

Due to the delay it was already getting dark by the time we were near Nanping. Our boatman decided to stop there because it was too dangerous and the river bed too full of rocks for us to keep going. However, we could see the lights of Nanping in the distance and insisted on giving it a try. So instead of spending the night safely on the boat, we left it behind and started walking along a narrow mountain path that we supposed would lead to Nanping. The path was steep and might be a site for wandering snakes, but we began to feel nervous only after night had fallen. It was ghosts, not wild animals, that we were afraid of. We linked our arms together and encouraged each other to be brave, but all of a sudden we heard a noise behind us that sounded like an old man heaving a loud sigh. We looked hard, but there was nothing we could see. As we moved forward that noise kept coming up periodically behind us until we finally reached Nanping. What a journey it was with our destination seemingly so close yet so far away. They said there were tigers in the mountains around Nanping, but that noise definitely did not come from a tiger.

Years later after my relocation to America, I once took my children to see a Disney movie about a boy's friendship with a mountain lion. The sound made by the lion in that movie was exactly the same as what I heard so many years ago on that mountain path near Nanping. It could have been a mountain lion following us back then, but why didn't it attack us? Two years ago our community newspaper *Rossmoor News* reported that we also have mountain lions here in California. They will not attack you if you leave them alone. But, if they approach you, you should make yourself look as big as possible by holding up your jacket and spreading it out, etc. I immediately recalled how my classmate and I linked arms together while walking, which surely would have made us look twice as big on that eventful night so many years ago. When I called my classmate and told her about this new realization, we both laughed so hard that our stomachs hurt as it had taken us more than 70 years to figure out what that strange noise was. I remembered all the details of that incident more than ten years ago but have forgotten some of them since then.

When I went to Hwa Nan College as a university student, it was still in Nanping. Initially I majored in Home Economics but soon changed to Education. Some of my friends later became teachers while others worked as librarians after moving to the United States. As for all the education-related knowledge and skills I learned, I only used them on my own children.

Getting Married in America

Upon his arrival in Chongqing, Hsia Wu joined the Bank of China and was later transferred to the United States to work at its bank in New York. As a result we were apart for several years, but we kept writing letters to each other saying things like, "I'll wait for you, so please wait for me as well." We kept saying we were engaged although we never went through the formal process. After the victory in the War of Resistance against Japan and my university graduation, Hsia asked me to go to America, but I refused. I said, "Come back here if you want to get married. I'm the only child and my father died when I was a high school student in Nanping. I have to stay with my mother." Later, as he had to stay and continue working in the United States for another year, he asked me to go there to get married while taking the opportunity to do some sightseeing. With my mother's permission, I went to Shanghai to get my passport and organize the sea transport and arrived in America in 1947.

After our wedding Hsia and I had a lot of fun traveling everywhere. The only problem was that I soon became pregnant, but Hsia promised we could return to China even with a newborn baby. At that time, Hsia's older brother lived in the United States but was planning to return to China for his wife and son. We asked him to inform us about the situation in China, and we would then return too if the circumstances were good. The two brothers agreed on a set of secret words that would be used if the situation in China turned out to be less than ideal. Later when we discovered those very words in a letter he sent us, we realized we should remain in the United States.

Back in 1947 when I came to America, I paid for a first-class ticket but ended up staying in steerage. Why? Well, my initial travel plan was to sail from Shanghai to San Francisco on the SS General Meigs (owned by Dollar Steanship Line). However, someone from the Bank of China kept saying how bad the ship was and urged me to purchase a ticket for the next sea passage available on the SS General Gordon which he too would take in order to keep me company. Despite the fact that both ships were used for troop transport and had been converted to ferry passengers, I was too young and naive to doubt that man's words. So I canceled my ticket for the SS General Meigs. Then, before I was able to secure a ticket to the SS General Gordon, I bumped into one of Hsia's friends from Chiao Tung University in Shanghai, who scolded me, "How can you be so silly as to give up your chance to take the SS General Meigs? Some of our friends will be on that ship to look after you!" Still, what could I then do? In order to get me onto the SS General Meigs together with his friends, he was determined to get me a ticket. Having gone through his connections and spent money on buying gifts in exchange for personal favors, he told me to buy a ticket for first class but that the only real spot available would be in steerage.

That is what happens when you are too young and innocent to understand anything and everything. So, I paid for a first-class ticket but stayed in steerage and met many nice people there including Florence Lin who later became my good friend (see the chapter on Florence Lin). With that said, the so-called first class back then with six people in a cabin, was no big deal when compared to the beautiful cruise ships today. In contrast, the SS General Meigs steerage was bigger than my current apartment with more than 100 passengers sleeping on triple deck bunk beds. I met Florence because her bed was nearby, and we ended up living in the same city (New York) and attending each other's weddings. We lost contact with each other after that for a long time.

It took 17 days for our ship to sail from Shanghai to San

Francisco where I was received by the manager of the Bank of Canton in that city, as requested by Hsia, who was at the Bank of China in New York. The manager's daughter was about my age. She drove me around for sightseeing. She seemed to know everybody everywhere and would even say hello to the elevator operator at our hotel. I thought, "What a strange girl!" It was only later that I realized how common it is in America to express a polite word or sign of recognition to strangers. What a country bumpkin I was!

After staying one night in San Francisco, I took a train to New York with the girlfriend of one of Hsia's colleagues. That train was called Pullman Rail and the journey was so long that we spent two nights sleeping in our carriage. In the dining car we met five or six young American military officers. They were interested in girls and asked us a lot of questions which we managed to answer. By the time they left the train, they stood outside our cabin to say goodbye and blow kisses. One of them even yelled out, "I love you!" which gave me a big shock as I couldn't believe how rude and frivolous these Americans were! No one in China would openly express such personal feelings after only a few words with each other in public! Luckily they left as I never wanted to see people like that again! It was only much later, having lived in America for a long time that I realized the phrase "I love you" can be a common expression often with no special meaning at all.

Upon my arrival in Grand Central Station in New York, I stepped onto the platform from the train and looked up to see Hsia waiting for me above the escalator. It was almost like a dream as I had never walked on an escalator before. After all those years of being apart, we were finally together again. I was so happy that I could almost hear the wedding music playing in my ears! From that moment on we lived together through all sorts of triumph and hardship for 65 years. Those 65 years were absolutely marvellous.

Linna and Hsia Wu at their wedding in New York 1947

Full-Time Wife and Mother

We worked together to create a good life. However, upon my arrival in America, I didn't know anything at all. As a kid I was never allowed in our family kitchen. As a result after I left home, I had to write a letter to ask my mother how to cook noodles. Knowing how spoiled I had been, Hsia's mother urged us to hire a servant after we married. When our first child was born, she again told us to employ a nanny. What she didn't know was that due to our lack of money, I had to do everything myself. I didn't get a chance to study in a university or pursue a Ph.D. like many other people. Instead, I only lived an ordinary life and looked after our two daughters at home.

At that time Hsia had a friend who sent his son to a day care center. Because the child cried constantly and was relatively neglected there, our friend asked me to help look after him. "Why not? A bit of income would be nice." I thought. I now recall he paid me about US $10 a week. For the following one or two years, his son was very happy to come and play with my two children every day. At home I would speak to my kids in Mandarin instead of Fukienese; otherwise, they would have a problem communicating with other Chinese people in the United States. Still, as soon as my girls started school, they switched to speaking English all the time. What a disaster! Back then it was difficult for the younger generation to study Chinese unlike today where we have Chinese language schools everywhere. There were Chinese language teachers in Chinatown in New York, but they only taught Cantonese. It was too far for us to travel there anyway.

Linna Wu and her daughter, granddaughter and great-granddaughter, circa 2010

Working and Taking Care of Mother

By the time my children reached five or six years in age, I started looking for work. We hired a nanny to look after the kids in the morning; she left as soon as I returned home in the afternoon. I started out as a filing clerk at an insurance company which sounded easy but still required training. Having studied English since my junior high school days, I was able to do an adequate job. I remember my salary back then was US $37 per week. Even though it wasn't much, I was happy to send it to China to help my family and other relatives there.

Later I saw someone using the comptometer, the first commercially successful key-driven mechanical calculator that is no longer used today. While many people used only two fingers to add or subtract numbers, a skilled operator could enter all the digits of a number almost simultaneously, using as many fingers as required. Having spent one month learning how to use the calculator from my boss, my salary was raised to more than $40 each week which made me very happy.

This is how I slowly enhanced my work skills. For example, I saw people typing and concentrated on leaning that skill at night school. Many of the night schools no longer exist along 40th Street in New York City. After studying typing for several months, I passed another insurance company's entrance examination and worked as a typist for the following five or six years with an even better salary. I then enrolled in an accounting course at night school, and worked another six years at Hertz after quitting the typing job. At Hertz my job was to respond to queries from various branches regarding the current locations of their trucks. Whenever a branch manager from a certain city called to ask where a particular truck was, I needed to search through our files for details such as the truck's location, whether it was ready for use or still getting ready, etc. Whether the truck *per se* was in transit, or was borrowed from one branch but had since been driven to and returned at another, I was still required to know exactly where it was. That was my job. Back then, there were no computers but many trucks of various sizes and shapes. As a tiny person, I had to climb a ladder to reach the big heavy files kept in a particular order on top of the company's numerous shelves. Even today I consider that job title "associate accounting clerk" to be rather interesting. While there was no accounting involved at all, I only found this job after I had studied accounting.

And that is the way I am, constantly wanting to experience something new: from Home Economics to education, then to various night school courses and new jobs. As my salary slowly increased through the years, so did my savings. In the midst of all this, I had my mother com to the United States to live with us for a while. Since my father's death many years ago, there remained only my mother and me. Unable to return to China, Hsia and I decided to bring her to America. By the time we were successful in our application for a visa for my mother on the grounds of family reunion, it had been three years since she had paid smugglers to hide her in a boat that sailed from Fuzhou to Hong Kong where some of her relatives lived. I still recall that upon her arrival in the United States, we celebrated her 60th birthday with an acute sense of how old she was. Well, now that I am in my 90s, people in their 60s look like kids to me. Still, by then my children were old enough to travel between home and school by themselves, so my mother only helped to look after their meals.

When my mother was young, my uncle as an important government official often had parties. She always enjoyed having guests plus with the hustle and bustle around her. My uncle Shu-zhuang Yang was much older than my mother. He was the first Secretary of the Navy of the Republic of China and later served as the Governor of Fujian Province. By the time he passed away, I was already a teenager, but I always remembered how he spoiled me like a little baby.

After my mother came to the United States, both Hsia and I worked during the day and had to leave her alone at home. On occasions where I had night shifts, we were too tired after work to spend quality time with her. Later, knowing how unhappy she had become after living with us for six years, I decided to send her to live with our relatives in Taiwan. My family, all the older generation Jiangs, had relocated from Fujian Province to Taiwan when the Chinese mainland fell into the hands of the communists. I was still young at that time. Then as time went by, the number of the Jiang family members increased to nearly 200. There were so many birthdays and weddings to celebrate that my mother had a great time living in Taiwan.

As I was determined to visit my mother as often as possible, finding a job at an airline company seemed to be a good idea. I eventually secured a position as a senior accountant for Pan American Airways. While it sounded like a high-ranking job, my task was merely to liaison with other airline companies in order to specify their shares of the profits and losses derived from codeshare agreements. The term "codeshare" means Pan American Airways might have published, marketed and sold seats of a flight under its own airline designator and flight number, but the flight was actually operated by a cooperating airline company, and vice versa. So, my job was to calculate the profits and losses of each flight and to ensure each of the airline companies involved in the codeshare agreement would get its fair share. It was really no big deal.

There was a huge room in the Pan American Airways headquarters building that was full of shelves with dozens of people managing all the documents stored there. Back then before the advent of computers, the company hired many employees for this work. They were so well trained and doing such a good job that they knew every one of the numerous air routes across all the nations of the world. Whenever I needed information regarding the origin and destination of a particular flight, I called with the flight number and the results would be delivered to me. It was such an interesting job. Later after my retirement in 1985, the company slowly started using computers. The number of employees was reduced considerably after that.

While working for Pan American, I had three weeks of vacation every year. I would spend two weeks visiting my mother in Taiwan while using the remaining week to travel with my husband and children. I had a great time working there because it was cheap for us to travel. Instead of purchasing tickets in advance, all we needed to do was to wait until the last minute to find out whether there were seats available. Indeed, throughout the years that I worked for the company, our annual travel expanses to Taiwan were very reasonable. Initially, we only paid US $10 per person. Then, as time went by, we didn't even have to pay for the tickets at all, just the service fees, i.e. our in-flight meals. Both Hsia and I loved traveling. We went to Paris, his favorite place, many times especially during the long weekends. I worked for Pan American for a total of 24 years until I finally retired.

That is the way I am, step by step, with new things happening every year. Every job was brand new and full of fun, and I enjoyed all of them. Although I was the only child in our family, I was good-natured and easy-going and always maintained excellent working relations with my colleagues. No one ever discriminated against me on the basis of my ethnic and cultural background probably because I was only an ordinary employee. In contrast, my husband worked for the Bank of China from the moment he arrived in America until his retirement. Unlike me, he preferred stability to change.

Too Young at Heart to Feel Old

My husband retired in 1985 and was keen to move to Oakland, California, where our older daughter lived. Hence I decided to retire early at the age of 62 to enable us to move from New Jersey. Our daughter lived in a mountainous area overlooking the tunnel that connects Rossmoor and Oakland. She arranged a nearby townhouse for us with a staircase leading up to the second story from the garage below. We had quite a good time there. As my husband and I enjoyed traveling but never had enough time to do it while working, we traveled extensively after retirement visited nearly every country in the world and all the places we could and wanted to see.

We also had frequent trips to China where many people to me looked older than their stated 50 years. My relatives and friends all had different life stories to tell including those of various family members and former classmates who had committed suicide. I recall that in 1979 when we returned to China for the first time, I met my cousin Zhi-hong Yang, the son of my aforementioned uncle Shu-zhuang Yang, in Shanghai. Yang was only several months older than my husband Hsia Wu, yet he looked so old, almost like Hsia's father. Yang went to study Economics in Oxford England in 1939 and returned to Shanghai after concluding his studies. In 1958 he was accused of being a "rightist" and sent to Ningxia Province in remote Northwest China for re-education through hard labor. His whole family was also forced to move there; they must have suffered a lot along the way. Yang was told to mind the pigs in Sanying Village (today's Guyuan City in the Ningxia Autonomous Region for the Hui people, one of China's minority ethnic groups). For the following 16 years, all he saw were the pigs but none of his family. By the time I met him in Shanghai, he had been "rehabilitated" and all his "crimes" "redressed" by the Communist Party. They gave him a small amount of money as compensation but he managed to survive with both of his daughters growing up there, and then studying medicine in Ningxia. Now that my cousin has passed away, his daughters live in Hong Kong and keep in constant telephone contact with me. I visited Shanghai, Taiwan and Hong Kong two years ago, mainly to visit relatives including them. Most of them were living quite a good life.

While living in the Oakland Hills, we often attended social dances held at Rossmoor on Saturday nights. Our good friend Sheng-yi Huang, whom we met in New York, was already a resident in Rossmoor then (see the chapter on Sheng-yi Huang). He urged us to move to Rossmoor to save the trouble of driving 20 minutes each way. In fact he insisted that we move there because many of our good friends from the past had already done so. However, in spite of his gentle but consistent advocacy, we didn't think we were old enough to move to Rossmoor. Although my husband and I were already in our 70s, we still felt quite young. Nevertheless, we eventually decided to find a place in Rossmoor because my husband found it increasingly difficult to negotiate the stairs in our Oakland Hills home.

In 1990 after several months of browsing, we finally purchased and moved into a condominium at Rossmoor. It made my husband very happy. There were so many activities here that he vowed never to move away. I, too, attended a wide range of social events such as singing and dancing. We used to do quite a bit of ballroom dancing. I also learned line dancing, belly dancing and the Hawaiian-styled hula dancing, which was a lot of fun, but I have since forgotten how to do it. I also went swimming every morning back then, a very good sport. I am too old for that now and only go on rare occasions.

When we first moved here, the Chinese American Association of Rossmoor (CAAR) had only 42 members. By the time I took charge of the association's finances in 1992, I had made friends with all of them (see the chapter on Peter Sih). Unlike today, our relatively small group of people would often have meetings, play mahjong and dine out together. It was all very spontaneous. If someone proposed something, we would simply get up and go. Later, the number of Chinese residents increased. Many people decided to move here after visiting families and/or friends at Rossmoor in the same way that we came because of Sheng-yi Huang's recommendation. As of today, CAAR has more than 400 members.

Soon after our relocation to Rossmoor, Florence Lin also came which made both of us very happy. One day in 1997 Florence proposed a celebration to mark the 50th anniversary of our arrival in the United States on the same ship. I suggested a trip to San Francisco, which my husband Hsia Wu wanted to participate in and pay for it despite the fact that he wasn't a passenger on the SS General Meigs back then. In the process of organizing the trip, we discovered three more people at Rossmoor who were also on that ship including Ellie Mao Mok and her sister Frances Sheng, formerly Hao Mao (see the chapter on Ellie Mao

Mok). I can't remember the third person's name; she passed away recently. Still, what a coincidence. The five of us were in the same steerage room, on the same ship, and arrived in America on the same day. Later, instead of traveling to San Francisco, we decided to have a banquet at Florence's place. All the dishes were delicious because she is such a great chef. The five of us also brought our husbands. Then, because of the coverage of this event by *The Rossmoor News*, we discovered three more people who had come to America on the SS General Meigs. The eight of us came from various regions across China, arrived in the United States on the same ship, established our families and careers in different corners of this country, then gathered together in the same retirement community 50 years later. Isn't that fantastic!

Five ladies celebrating the 65th anniversary of their arrival in the United States on the same ship sailing from Shanghai in 1947 –(from left) Ellie Mao Mok, Florence Lin, Frances Sheng (Hao Mao), Linna Wu and Luciana Yang 2012

In 2012 the five of us met again to celebrate the 65th anniversary of our arrival in America on the same ship. Today, 68 years after that event, with three of the original eight having passed away and another two having moved to the East Coast, only Ellie Mao Mok, Luciana Yang and I remain at Rossmoor. We are so old now that it is difficult for us to get together at anyone's place. As a result, I often contact Ellie by telephone. A great woman who never gives up, she still travels frequently by plane. While I am also a firm believer in the "Never Give Up" principle, I am too old to walk far.

As my husband grew older, it became increasingly difficult for him to walk. In 2008 we moved into a unit at the Waterford, the building with elevaters. It is an independent living arrangement providing aged care for those in need. We received a special meal each day. Initially, my husband strongly opposed the idea because he disliked western food. However, after much persuasion by our daughters and me, my husband finally agreed to face the fact that our original place had steps at the front that could potentially endanger his life and cause trouble for me in the unfortunate event he fell. Luckily, once we moved into the service apartment, he enjoyed living in our unit and dressing up to attend dinner in the public dining room. No more complaints about the western food, either. He had three good years of life here before passing away.

Linna and Hsia Wu and their two daughters in Rossmoor 2008

I have now lived in this building at the Waterford for six years. Apart from walking along the corridors that lead in every possible direction, I also do sports from nine to ten o'clock in the morning Monday to Friday. The classes on Monday, Wednesday and Friday are very good as we can participate in all sorts of sports; those in wheelchairs and walkers also have their own exercise courses. As for the yoga classes on Tuesday and Thursday I don't like them because I always think of food whenever I am told to close my eyes and meditate. So on those two days, I go to the Tai Chi Qi Gong classes organized by CAAR, which take place from ten to eleven o'clock in the morning. Our instructor, Gus Kao, already in his 90s, is a good friend of mine (see the chapter on Gus Kao). In the beginning it was just a few of us casually practicing Tai Chi Qi Gong on the grass outside. Later, as the number of participants increased to more than 40, we became sort of a club with plenty of members my age.

To practice Tai Chi Qi Gong, I have to walk from my building on the south side through the one on the north side to the fitness center, and then walk all the way back afterwards. A round trip like this together with the Tai Chi Qi Gong class usually takes up to one and a half hours. Having committed to such hard work twice a week, I think I have been doing pretty well. To play mah jong I also have to walk to the activity center. My husband used to drive me. Even after I took over the driving as a result of his deteriorating health, he would always sit next to me for moral support. After he died, I felt very depressed and would panic whenever I had to drive alone. When I mentioned this to my daughters, they insisted that I stop driving. They even told me to sell the car to prevent me from driving. That was three years ago.

With that said, it is really convenient here with community buses running frequently and stopping everywhere including the supermarket, post office, bank and medical clinic. There is even a bus stop right at our front door. For places beyond our community, my daughter takes me, such as shopping at Chinese grocery stores and going to movie theaters. I still enjoy doing fun things, but I am too old to do mosy of them now. That is the problem with getting old, but we should never give up the things we want to do.

I have two excellent daughters. My older daughter who lives nearby visits me two or three times each week. Her work is flexible, so she can spend a whole day with me on a relaxing day or only a couple of hours when she is busy. I ask her for help if things can be done by telephone, as I have been wearing a hearing aid in recent years. Otherwise, I am able to manage my own bank statements and all the bills.

These days I spend a lot of time watching television and using computers. I have a lot of fun with new inventions like these. For example, I often use Skype to chat with my younger daughter who lives in Alaska. A while ago when she participated in a ten-day cycling tour in Colorado, I got to know her schedule and all the things she did everyday. A great cyclist, she once spent a whole month riding along the Silk Road. Now although I am old, I still enjoy traveling and would often envy those who travel everywhere and even by cruise ship. Knowing this, whenever my daughters travel, they share all the details with me. I also use the Internet to check the places they visit, just to get a feeling of the things they have seen and done. Sometimes I am even able to point out to them things that they haven't experienced yet.

I want to learn about all the new inventions. Apart from browsing the Internet and doing online shopping, I also use Amazon Kindle to read ebooks at night. I also have an Apple iPhone, which is so small and convenient that I carry it with me all the time. My daughters often send me all sorts of things. I usually remember the useful items and forget the rest, but I can always re-learn the things I have forgotten whenever the need arises. However, although I worked as a typist for five years, I can no longer type very well and often make mistakes when writing emails to my daughters. I guess this is why people say they tend to remember things from the distant past while forgetting recent events.

As the only child in my family, I didn't have to remember everything because my parents would do it for me. With such great support from my parents, I often forgot the things they wanted me to do. Later after Hsia Wu and I married, he had a great memory and would always remember everything for me with or without my request. I had always thought my memory was bad. Then ten years ago as my husband's memory increasingly deteriorated, he started teaching me everything including the management of all our finances and bills. Although I didn't like them and would rather spend my days doing fun things and all the details he told me would "go into one ear and out the other", I managed to keep some of them in my head. Indeed, I had been too lazy to remember things until the day I had to do them. Then I was surprised to discover that my memory was not so bad after all. I can remember anything, and I can do anything. Even when my husband failed to recall something, I was there to remind him of it. Also, I still maintain a sense of curiosity and want to learn new things. I ignore some people's advice that I should stop learning simply because I am old. Like today, I learned how to write Chinese by hand on my Apple iPhone. It made me really, really happy.

I have lived an ordinary and uneventful life. I used to think I had suffered. However, compared to the hardship and bitterness that some of my fellow Rossmoor residents such as Anna Yang encountered (see the chapter on Anna Yang), and the pain and misery that some of my friends and relatives experienced back in China, I have nothing to complain about at all. Now, as I sit in the quiet and tidy restaurant of this retirement community while admiring the evergreen grass, beautiful flowers and chirping birds outside the window, I should say that I have never, ever suffered much at all. I have lived a smooth and joyful life. It is good.

Peter Sih 薛君仁
At Home in Rossmoor, February 2015

Peter Sih always attends concerts at Rossmoor. Whenever we get together to enjoy music, he always sings in high spirits. He is one of the founders and the first president of the Chinese American Association of Rossmoor (CAAR). Now that he is in his 90s, it is difficult to trace the fascinating details of his work as an engineer on major construction projects around the world. However, from his recollection of the past, we can gain a glimpse of the daring and energetic young man he was back then.

Biography

Peter Sih, whose Chinese name is Jun-ren Sih, was born in Shanghai in 1920. After graduating from the Henry Lester Institute of Technical Education in that city, he received the top score on the Nationalist Government's examination for overseas studies and then enrolled at Cornell University in 1947. After receiving his Master's degree in engineering, he joined TAMS Consulting Engineers in New York City. Throughout the following years, he was involved in the design and implementation of a series of major hydraulic engineering and airport construction projects in the United States and other parts of the world. In addition he studied computer engineering at Columbia University in the 1960s and was one of the pioneers in the use of computers in engineering design and application. He relocated to Rossmoor, Walnut Creek, California in 1989.

An Engineer Facing a Brand New World

Though my ancestral home was Beijing, my father arrived in Shanghai at the age of 6. The oldest of six children, I was born in Shanghai in 1920. The character "ren" in my Chinese name, Jun-ren, means "benevolence". The first of the "Five Constant Virtues" in traditional Chinese culture, it is followed by the characters "yi" (righteousness), "li" (propriety), "zhi" (wisdom) and "xin" (fidelity), each of which were included in the names of my younger siblings. One of my brothers and I now live in the United States. My sister Jun-zhi, an expert in Russian Literature, lives in China and was once a visiting scholar in America and the president of the Harvard Alumni Association in Beijing. My other siblings are also successful professionals in science, technology and medicine.

Top Graduate of a Distinguished Institution in Shanghai

My father was a successful businessman in Shanghai and our family was rather affluent. After graduating from high school, I enrolled in the Henry Lester Institute of Technical Education in Shanghai once I passed its entrance examination. A private all-male university with an engineering focus, the institute was established in 1934 and funded by the estate of Henry Lester, a prominent British architect and real estate merchant in the Shanghai International Settlement. Academically, it was considered as distinguished in China as the Massachusetts Institute of Technology (MIT) is in the United States. While a group of British scholars served as core instructors, most of the teaching staff were former graduates of academic institutions in England and the United States. All subjects were taught in English which laid a good foundation for my growing fluency in the English language.

Back in Shanghai in the 1930s and 1940s, graduates from the Henry Lester Institute of Technical Education were among the most admired and sought after. In that era the subtext of our prominence consisted of academic excellence, diligence, professionalism and elegance which implied true talent and refinement in taste and manners. Unfortunately, the Institute lasted only eight years. The Japanese shut it down after the outbreak of the Pacific War and sent all the British and American teachers and other staff to concentration camps. It was only later that I learned that the Shanghai Seaman's Hospital was constructed on the former site of the Institute. The war did not affect our family too much because we stayed in the Shanghai International Settlement.

Studies and Marriage in the United States

In 1947 I received the top score at the Nationalist Government's examination for overseas studies in Shanghai. I was one of two engineering students allowed to study abroad on government expense that year. While my family has always taken pride in my achievement, I think it was my fluency in English that helped a great deal. Indeed, thanks to my frequent higher-than-average English test scores, I had a better chance of getting scholarships. I left Shanghai in 1947 to study

Engineering at Cornell University on a full scholarship which meant I did not have to work. After two years I received my Master's degree in 1949.

Peter Sih receiving his Master's degree in Engineering at Cornell University, 1949 with dedication to his wife Helen in writing

At Cornell University I referred to two good friends and myself the "Three Musketeers". One day, at one of their homes, I met Helenwho later became my wife and whose father was also a good friend of my father's. Helen, whose Chinese name is Xun Qiu, specialized in singing and was already a famous singer during her days as a student at Beijing Normal University. After graduating from the renowned Juilliard School in New York, she was selected as a B-list actress for the Broadway musical *Flower Drum Song* but later gave up the role as a result of her pregnancy. My favorite hobby has always been singing. Unable to read sheet music, I often committed the melodies and lyrics to memory. I really enjoyed singing with my wife.

I was the one who was always looked out for opportunities to perform, while she didn't care to sing that much. My wife was indeed a much better singer than me.

Peter and Helen Sih at Cornell University

There was an amazing coincidence in our family involving my sister and future wife. After my sister Jun-zhi passed the Nationalist Government's examination for overseas studies, she gave up the opportunity to study abroad at the last minute in order to marry. Her husband-to-be was a high-ranking military officer who had accompanied Mao Ze-dong on the Long March and who later became the Deputy Commander of the Chinese Navy. The precious opportunity that my sister gave up coincidentally went to Helen, who enrolled in a small institution in Georgia before transferring to New York. My sister and I still did not know Helen back then. We only discovered this coincidence much later.

Successful Career and Life

As a government-sponsored student, I was supposed to return to China to work at least two years after finishing my studies in America in 1949. However, considering the current change of political circumstances in China, the American Congress passed the Displaced Persons Act to allow all Chinese students in the United States to apply for permanent residency. Hence, I was able to quickly gain a Green Card and later American citizenship. After that, perhaps also thanks to my strength in English, I found a job at TAMS Consulting Engineers in New York.

The word "TAMS" was an acronym from the initials of four American military generals' names: Tippetts, Abbett, McCarthy and Stratton, who jointly founded the company. Based in New York City and with branch offices all over the world, the company was renowned for its expertise in consultancy and management of major construction and civil engineering projects including the design and building of a series of mega-sized dams and airports in America and other regions. Thanks to my Master of Engineering degree, I started my career as a proper engineer.

However, in order to advance my knowledge and skills, I worked for the company by day and studied Computer Engineering at Columbia University at night. Computers were still a relatively new invention then. While I planned to get a Ph.D. in this field, the company preferred that I supervise construction projects in South America and other places; in other words, lead and teach less-experienced engineers. On top of that, I was soon to marry. Even though I was a graduate student learning a lot about Computer Engineering, I was still one step short of receiving a Ph.D. in this field. I was really busy during those years in New York. For a year or two in order to improve my income, I also taught mathematics at the City University of New York's Queens

College.

While working for the company, I was involved in diverse mega-sized construction projects around the world such as the Tarbela Dam on the Indus River in Pakistan. Completed in 1976, it is still the largest earth-filled dam in the world to date. In addition, I worked on the Dallas/Fort Worth International Airport that was completed in the early 1970s. The company managed a series of constructions in Iran and South Africa as well as design reports on many major projects in other regions.

I wrote a computer program for the company in 1970 on algorithms to measure airport runway traffic, such as the number of runways required for landing, the selection of specific runways for particular flights, the direction of landing traffic, just to name a few of its options. Doing this through computers was quite a complicated task then, but the project eventually won an award in Washington, D.C., and received a fair bit of limelight. I worked for the company from 1950 until my retirement in 1989. After decades of service, I eventually took charge of our company's computer department as Chief Engineer.

My many friends in New York were mostly Chinese as I did not have many close American friends. Many of them are members of the Alpha Lambda (AL), an association of Chinese graduate students from academic institutions across America. While the association's functions are similar to fraternities formed by American students, it also continues the traditional Chinese custom of close friends pledging brotherhood and sisterhood. Chinese associations like AL appeared in various American states in the 1950s assisting but also competing against similar organizations. At AL our members looked after each other like a big family. We organized all sorts of activities together including dancing on Christmas Eve, sightseeing trips for summer holidays, sporting events such as golf and tennis, and of course singing and playing mahjong. People often pointed out how similar my son and I are as we both enjoy sports, singing and dancing. It is probably because he frequently accompanied me to AL events. Indeed, while living in New York, we visited Chinatown almost every weekend, eating, shopping and watching Chinese movies. Life was wonderful there.

Peter Sih and family in New York 1960

Friends Together in Retirement

Shing-yi Huang (S.Y. Huang) and I have been good friends since our days in New York (see the chapter on Shing-yi Huang). We both lived on 168th Street in Flushing in the northeastern part of Queens, a borough of New York City. While our children grew up together and were also close friends, my office at TAMS Consulting Engineers was close to his at the United Nations. He often gave me a ride to work. After retirement we even followed him by moving to Rossmoor in Walnut Creek, California.

We called S.Y. Huang the Pied Piper of Rossmoor as it was due to his high praise of this community that we followed him here. Indeed, one of our friends initially decided to move to Florida after retirement. By the time he met Huang, who insisted the climate there was too humid for proper living, he and even a group of other people immediately cancelled their Florida plans and relocated to California instead. Many of our AL members in New York also moved to the San Francisco Bay Area after retirement. Apart from myself at Rossmoor, there's also Joe Chow, Shing-yi Huang, C.D. Tung, Daval Chang, Ronald Sun and Hsia Wu, although some of them have since passed away. Throughout the 1990s we often got together with AL members already in the Bay Area. Once, we even organized a dance at a luxury hotel for all the AL members across the United States. However as time went by, old members faded away with no new generation to take their place. Student fraternities like AL slowly became a mere monument in the history of Chinese immigration and settlement in America.

When we moved to Rossmoor in 1989, we shared a huge moving truck with Tian-yi and Anna Yang's family (see the chapter on Anna Yang). A small earthquake happened soon after our arrival causing our New York friends to immediately joke that we were the cause. Still, having lived here for 25 years, I prefer Rossmoor to Florida. We were not even in our 70s when we moved here. We golfed and played tennis, in which I taught my friends many tricks. I am a better player at mahjong than bridge, but now I am too slow for my friends to take pleasure in these games. I still enjoy music and attend every concert at Rossmoor.

In 1990 we felt the need to establish an association for all Chinese residents at Rossmoor. Together with Yen Liang, who had lived here the longest, Shing-yi Huang and Victor Young, a second-generation Chinese American and a great golf player, we established the Chinese American Association of Rossmoor (CAAR). I served as the first president. Irving Hsi was our secretary while Huang's wife Carrie managed our finances. After much discussion, we decided on a two-year term for board members to be elected during the Chinese New

Year festivities.

Handover of duties from inaugural CAAR board members to the incoming board, Chinese New Year 1992 (From left): Shing-yi Huang, Irving Hsi, Carrie Huang, Victor Young, Peter Sih, Patsy P.H. Peng, Doreen Tung, Horace Chow and Linna Wu

CAAR was inaugurated at the Rossmoor community activity center, followed by a banquet consisting of numerous dishes offered by the families involved. At the launch, we decided the Association's mission and charter. Liang, an architect, even designed an emblem for us (see the chapter on Yen Liang). We further decided that members should meet each month and conduct annual celebrations for the three important traditional Chinese festivals, namely Chinese New Year, Dragon Boat Festival and Mid-Autumn Festival.

We have been organizing these activities for 25 years now. Back then, with a limited number of members, we only needed to drive around the neighborhood to inform everybody. Later, we developed a "telephone tree", a communication system involving each person contacting several other members by telephone to pass on the decisions made by the Association. That system was enough to quickly reach 40 members. However, with the member census bordering 400 today, we have long since switched to electronic mail.

Helen and I loved to travel. Back then we were too busy to

travel far, not to mention the lack of desire to explore other places while living in New York. After retirement, we often traveled with old friends who had moved from New York to California. Apart from traveling, singing, dancing and playing sports, I also participated in a project that raised funds to provide scholarships for young students in need. Another activity was to teach computers to people around my age in nursing homes.

Photograph of Chinese American residents in Rossmoor published by *Time* magazine, January 2002.
(Back row from left): David Hsu and wife Jin-Yun Zhang, Ellie Mao Mok, Anna Yang, Peter Sih, Patsy P.H. Peng, Doreen Tung and husband C. Dong, David Chang and wife Pauline Chang (Bao-qiong Pan).
(Front row from left) Horace Chow and wife Theresa (Ren-lin Wang), Helen Sih (Xun Qiu), Carrie (Xiao-xia Fang) and husband Shing-yi Huang.

In 2002 *Time* magazine published an article about us. Citing an interview with Rossmoor Chinese residents as an example, the article suggested the latest social trend in America is to retire with friends. It quoted Helen's recommendation that retirees like us should not move in with our children. Besides, our children would be too busy to spend quality time with us, and they might change jobs and move elsewhere. Instead, we should live in the same area with friends to entertain and care for each other. A photograph of us with our names was also published by the magazine.

Both our son and daughter were born and raised in New York and are now living in California. They used to live near Washington, D.C. However, since our relocation to Rossmoor, they have both found jobs in California in order to be close to us. My son Andrew is a professor in biology at the University of California, Davis. He often recalls how I taught him mathematical puzzles when he was little, such as algebra. For example, a rabbit has four legs while a man has two. Given a certain number of legs, how many rabbits and men are involved? I also taught him about computer, which serves him well today. My daughter Barbara, a graduate of Yale University's School of Law, once served as a member of the Board of Education in the Stanford University District. That was a difficult task, as every parent with children studying at Stanford University thought their kids to be the smartest. Now she heads a small company that organizes Stanford University students to tutor children in the inner city. Although I have been living alone since my wife Helen passed away, my son and daughter take turns to visit me on weekends which makes me very, very happy.

(This chapter was written with the assistance of Andrew Sih, Peter's son, and Shing-yi Huang.)

Anna Yang 錢重慈
At courtyard of Waterford in Rossmoor October 2014

When I contacted Anna Yang by telephone to request an interview, her first reaction was to inquire who I was. Having submitted my personal details and one of my books, a biography of my parents, I was lucky to include her life story in this book. During our conversation she often mentioned how fortunate her life had been as if everything that ever happened throughout her life should be attributed to fate which is a view I would dispute. Indeed, apart from the fact that she was born into a rather affluent family, every other success in her life was a result of her own intelligence, diligence and perseverance through much hardship. It was I who was fortunate to have a chance to learn from such a unique person and her rich, extensive life experiences. I truly admire her logical thinking and crystal clear memoryin in addition to her beautiful, tidy calligraphy. She was born in the Year of Dragon. She is the most senior among all the senior Chinese Americans whose stories are collected in this book.

Biography

Anna Yang, whose Chinese name is Chong-ci Yang, was born in Wuhan, Hubei Province. After graduating from the National Southwestern Associated University in 1942, she worked for the Women's Advisory Council in Chongqing under the guidance of Mei-ling Soong, wife of President Chiang Kai-shek. This was part of the New Life Movement launched by the Nationalist Government in 1934. Having passed the national examination for overseas study in 1944, she pursued further studies in the United States before becoming one of the first Chinese professionals employed by the United Nations. She worked for the Chinese Translation Service of the U.N. Secretariat before gaining a Master's degree in statistics; she then transferred to the Statistics Division of the U.N. Department of Economic and Social Affairs. After her retirement in 1989, she relocated to Rossmoor in Walnut Creek, in San Francisco's East Bay.

Such a Fortunate Life

My ancestral home was Ningxiang, Hunan Province, but I was born in Wuhan, Hubei Province. In accordance with the custom of preventing government officials from favoring relatives and friends in their own regions, my father, a judge, was frequently assigned to work far from home. Apart from Wuhan, he had spent decades working in such cities as Zhenjiang, Huaiyin and Nanjing in Zhejiang Province before finally becoming one of the Supreme Court's nine public prosecutors. I had an older sister, an older brother and three younger brothers. Supporting a family of six children was one of my father's burdens, forcing him to work hard throughout his life. As a kid, I spent a lot of time living with my grandparents. I went to a primary school in Ningxiang where one of my uncles was the principal. Then I transferred to Changsha, the capital of Hunan Province, about 25 kilometers away from Ningxiang.

We were reunited with my father when he worked in Huaiyin and Nanjing. However, after the Shanghai Incident on January 28, 1932, in which Japanese troops attacked the city under the pretext of protecting citizens from local rioters, circumstances in nearby Nanjing became increasingly dire. My parents considered it too difficult for our whole family to flee from the turmoil of war. Hence, between my older sister and brother who were relatively independent and the two youngest siblings who still required constant care, the two kids in the middle, my younger brother and me, were sent to live with our grandparents in Hunan Province. Later while boarding at school in Changsha, I missed home so much that I cried every day. Fortunately, by the time I entered the affiliated experimental senior high school of the National Central University, I was reunited with my parents in Nanjing.

By the end of 1937, my father was supposed to follow the Nationalist Government as it moved from Nanjing to Chongqing, Sichuan Province. However, considering his own parents' advanced age, he decided to retire and return to Hunan Province. My siblings and I had already entered universities by then which eased some of his burdens. With my older sister studying law and politics, my older brother in Guangxi Province, my younger brother in Guangdong Province and me in Kunming, Yunnan Province, we were scattered across the nation, a family torn apart without peace and stability. Back in Hunan Province, my parents took it upon themselves to look after my grandparents as well as their household and land. As a result, they were accused as "landlords" and suffered greatly in the following years. I think my father made the wrong decision by returning to Hunan Province. He should have gone to Chongqing with the Nationalist

Government. My father suffered greatly, but he was only trying to be a good son back then.

My University Days

After graduating from high school, I traveled with a friend from Nanjing to Shanghai to attend the entrance examinations for Ping University and National Tsing Hua University. Upon our arrival on July 7, 1937, the Marco Polo Incident happened in Beijing causing the cancellation of all examinations. Besides being a complete waste of my time, my father scolded me for going to Shanghai during such a tumultuous period. I guess I was just too young and full of energy to feel scared. After the War of Resistance against Japan started, many government agencies relocated from Nanjing to Changsha. Also moving to China's vast hinterlands were Beijing University, National Tsing Hua University and Nankai University which later jointly established the Changsha Temporary University. Originally from Hunan I was able to return to that province and enter the Changsha Temporary University with my high scores from the University of Nanking's entrance examination. A follow-up examination in Changsha formalized my enrollment there, and I thought everything would be fine from then on. However, Japanese troops advanced so fast that they had captured both Shanghai and Nanjing by the end of 1937. As the situation in Wuhan deteriorated, Changsha appeared to be increasingly in danger. This forced various government agencies to move further inland including the Changsha Temporary University, which was ordered by the Ministry of Education to go to Kunming, Yuannan Province. All of its students also relocated from Changsha to Kunming. The institution was officially renamed the National Southwestern Associated University in April 1938.

How then did we get there? Male students spent more than a month walking there, while continuing their classes along the way. As for the female students, we took the train from Changsha to Guangzhou, Guangdong Province, before taking a ferry to Hong Kong and then a ship to Haiphong, Vietnam. After that, the Yunnan-Vietnam Railroad would lead us from Haiphong to Kunming, a round-about way you may say. Upon our arrival in Guangzhou, however, there was no ferry to Hong Kong. We stayed at the Lingnan University dormitories for a month waiting for the ferry to start operating again, but we were too young to worry about anything like that. Besides, the food and accommodations at Lingnan University were excellent. All of us had quite a bit of fun there.

After reaching Kunming we stayed at a local agricultural institute while the university set up classrooms and dormitories. Still, the weather in Yunnan Province was so good that it was like spring year round. The living standard in Kunming was very low at that time. Everything was cheap. Many students traveled from other cities and regions with much money, like me as an example. I had relocated from Nanjing to Changsha and then to Kunming with plenty of clothes and shoes. Even a small allowance, such as 200 dollars in Flat Money (a currency issued by the Nationalist Government since 1935), would last a long time. With that said, as inflation continued to rise, life eventually became increasingly harsh. Eventually, we could not even afford second-hand products and goods.

As university students we were just a group of big kids with very little awareness of the real turmoil of war. The Japanese bombing had not started when we arrived in Kunming, so we often had picnics in the countryside. When the Air Force Academy moved to Kunming from Hangzhou, Zhejiang Province, its students often came to the National Southwestern Associated University to find potential dates. These young men looked so handsome and were always in such good spirits that some of our female classmates married them. With that said, the students at the Air Force Academy experienced much hardship. Many of them were killed or missing in action during the war. It was truly sad.

I majored in History at the National Southwestern Associated University. We had many senior professors, including philosopher You-lan Feng, physicist Ta-you Wu, and another physicist You-xun Wu. There was also the mathematician Wu-zhi Yang who taught me calculus; his son was Chen-ning Franklin Yang, co-recipient of the 1957 Nobel Prize in Physics. At that time young students like me were highly enthusiastic about serving our nation, a common sentiment during the war. We were so passionate about social welfare that we were willing to sacrifice our personal interests for the public good. For example, when we first arrived in Kunming, some friends and I founded a public school to teach reading and writing to illiterate laborers. I was even given the title "Dean of Academic Affairs". Furthermore, as a member of our university's drama club, I participated in a series of theatrical performances to help "save our nation from extinction". I was the leading actress in *The Night Before the Storm*, a stage play written by Han-sheng Yang that exposed various traitors to China by patriotic Chinese youths.

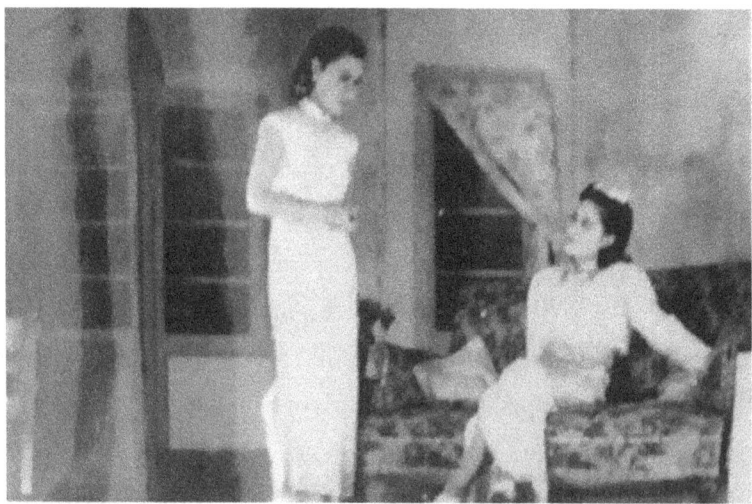

Anna Yang (standing) as leading actress in stage play *The Night Before the Storm*, February 1942

As students of a national university in exile, the National Southwestern Associated University took care of our tuition fees as well as food and accommodations on behalf of the government. We were fortunate to be studying at a government-sponsored institution unlike students at many other schools. All my life I have been very fortunate. Indeed, I consider myself to be luckier than most people of my generation. Anyway, at that time, we tutored children of military personnel in Yunnan Province whenever we needed money. This often happened during the summer holidays.

Upon our arrival in Kunming, Yunnan Province was still a rather isolated and backward place. The locals had a hard time getting used to us coming from the middle and lower reaches of the Yangtze River. If we happened to walk down the street without buttoning our jackets, the local police hasslled us. Still, as the number of arrivals from the outside world increased, there was nothing the locals could do. I recall we caused quite a stir by simply riding horses on the road. The locals could not tolerate women riding horses.

Hence, our being there helped turn Yunnan Province into a civilized place. With the National Southwestern Associated University from Beijing and the Air Force Academy from Hangzhou, Zhejiang Province, we were like pioneers that completely transformed Kunming from an ancient and isolated country town into a modern city. The more people arrived from the outside world, the less traditional customs and habits existed. Later, after arriving in the United States, I happened to live next door to the daughter of Yun Long, former governor of Yunnan Province. I used to jokingly refer to her as a "princess" without realizing it was a real title the locals had once presented to her due to her father's powerful presence as the "King of Yunnan".

Finding Employment in Chongqing

While I was studying at the National Southwestern Associated

University in Kunming, all of my relatives were living in Chongqing. After my graduation in 1942, they asked me to explore employment opportunities at a number of government agencies that had recently relocated there. It was a difficult time to be in Chongqing because of a food shortage and the constant threat from Japanese bombing. The air raid siren often sounded at meal times forcing us to abandon our food and escape to the countryside. By the time we finally returned, we would be too exhausted to eat anything. Worse, due to a lack of chairs, we had to stand around the table for the meals. Very often the big rice bucket contained porridge that was so watery we had to scrape the bottom to search for the grains of rice. Some short people sometimes tried so hard that they fell into the big bucket.

People today may find it difficult to imagine such a tough life. With not enough rice to eat, we had to rely on peanuts every day. We counted ourselves lucky to have such a nutritious food, a luxury item in spite of its relatively cheap price. Anyway, as one of the three renowned "furnace cities" in China, Chongqing was incredibly hot during the summer. While our bamboo beds were nice and cool at night, we often had to share them with relatives or friends arriving from other cities and regions. With two people on a single narrow bed, one of us often had to squeeze hard against the wall.

I worked as a government employee for the Women's Advisory Council in Chongqing. Led by Mei-ling Soong, wife of President Chiang Kai-shek, the council was in charge of teaching reading and other basic skills to women whose husbands were sent to war and who therefore had no alternative way to survive. A series of vocational training courses was established including sewing. We also provided consolation to soldiers injured in battle, as well as to children who lost their parents in the war.

We all lived a hard life during the war. Without any financial assistance from my family, I supported my two younger brothers, their studies and myself. I worked for money and would take any job as long as there was payment. On occasion when more than one decent job became available, I would pick the one with better salary. I always wore the same threadbare clothes and patched shoes, and my eyeglasses were so broken that the lenses and frame were held together by layers of tape. Constantly starving, I looked and felt haggard. The only joy in my life was a rare meal paid for by my sister-in-law at a small restaurant. Somehow we survived as we soldiered on in high spirits with faith in the future. We held on to the hope that one day we would recover our homeland from the Japanese and reunite with family at home. We were so young and innocent back then that we remained happy despite the harsh and chaotic circumstances around us. Everything was and would be fine.

Attempt to Study Overseas

I never thought I would be able to study overseas. In October 1943 the Nationalist Government announced a series of regulations regarding self-sponsored overseas study. Although we would be spending our own money, those of us interested in studying overseas were required to attend a national examination and have two years of work experience after graduating from university. The application needed to be approved by the Ministry of Education. By the time the first examination was held in Chongqing in December 1943, I was lucky to have been working in that city for a while as no such opportunity became available in Kunming.

I also happened to have a friend who encouraged me to attend the examination even though I had neither money nor intention of studying overseas at that time. Not only did my friend promise to lend me money, he also taught me a trick. By exchanging the US $100 he lent me in the black market, where US $1 was worth several hundred dollars in the government-issued Flat Money, I would have enough Chinese money to exchange for the US $4,400 required by the government. The official exchange rate between American and Chinese dollars was a mere 1:20. In other words, the difference between the official exchange rate and the black market was a wonderful gift. It enabled government-approved Chinese students to have enough money to study in the United States. This was the only way for people like me to make it abroad. As the majority of us were low-ranking, low-paid government employees with families in Japanese-occupied regions, it was almost like the government paid us to study overseas.

By the time I heard about the national examination for self-sponsored overseas study, I had only two months to prepare. With friends' encouragement, I did it purely for fun as I had neither the money nor confirmation that my friend's trick would work. With my history major at the National Southwestern Associated University, I chose International Politics as my test subject with the intention of eventually finding a job at the Ministry of Foreign Affairs. With so many people attending the national examination, and with tests ranging from English, Chinese and essay writing to the usual subjects required for a university degree, only those who were already advanced in their studies could possibly pass. Of about 40 female students across the whole nation who made it that year, I was one of them. Among the people I knew, a medical student called Yi-ling Yu (nee Tang) also passed the first national examination; she is now in San Francisco. Anyway, there was one more examination in 1946 with test venues held in nine cities across the nation. The event ceased to exist after the Nationalist Government relocated to Taiwan.

After passing the national examination, we had to attend a party cadre training class organized by the Nationalist Government's Central Training Corps, with a separate unit especially established for female students like me. The class was held at Fotu Pass in Chongqing where all high-ranking government officials were trained. While President Chiang Kai-shek often gave admonitory talks there, all sorts of government ministers were also keen to meet us because we were considered the future party cadres after returning from the United States. I remember one of them was the warlord Yu-xiang Feng who mumbled a lot of nonsense such as why government employees like us had to work so hard. Meanwhile, we had many photographs taken with Chiang Kai-shek. Sometimes it would be just one or two of us; other times it was the whole class.

Anna Yang (second from right, back row) at the conclusion of her cadre training class in the Central Training Corps May 1944

As it is today, we had to personally apply from China for our own American universities. Also like today, we were able to learn from students who had already studied in the United States which institutions were better, had higher Chinese student enrollment, required less tuition fees and were an area of lower living expenses, etc. Thanks to these older students, we gained a good understanding of academic institutions in America. Among the best choices was the University of Michigan. It was not in big city and was friendly to Chinese students. With more than 100 Chinese students enrolled there each year, it was considered a good match for us.

My family never knew of my plan to study in the United States. It would have been a very novel concept to them. Among the six of us, my older sister and brother had long ago married and established their own families. As for my three younger brothers, they were too lazy about their studies to even notice opportunities like this. Our parents never paid attention to our academic careers; none of the older generation was able to help anyway. My father had been to Japan (many Chinese students around his age had gone there to study law) but he was now too old to give me any advice on studying and living in America. Hence I had to be self-reliant.

Fortunately, at the National Southwestern Associated University, there were many former students from academic institutions in Britain and the United States to provide assistance in this matter. I was lucky to have opportunities like this which are so important to a person's future prospects. I still remember how I sold off my personal belongings in Chongqing in preparation to go to the United States. For as little five Chinese cents, every item was sold. As my travel expenses were already paid for by the government, all proceeds from the sales were donated to students who could not make it to America.

Last Visit to My Parents

Considering the fact that I would soon be on the other side of the world, I knew I had to visit my parents in Hunan Province. It was extremely difficult to travel from Chongqing to Hunan during the war. As I did not have money for public transport, I hitched rides with the "yellow fish" instead, i.e. trucks that ferried goods and products from one place to another. Various people told me about a truck going in this direction or a postman's vehicle going to that town, enabling me to hitch rides along the way. With generous assistance from both friends and strangers, I visited my parents in Hunan Province and later returned to

Chongqing. There was still such a thing called *friendship* at that time where people were willing to help one another in tough times. This helped people like me to overcome obstacles. It was fortunate that I visited my parents then as that was the last time I even saw them.

That trip was risky. Once, at a hotel, a patron overheard two people discussing what they would do to a single female traveler such as me. The amazing coincidence was that this man was one of my former students back in Kunming, Yunnan Province, when friends and I taught reading and writing to illiterate laborers. In his attempt to disrupt the plans to harm me, he spent the whole night coughing and spluttering to show that he was awake. It was only the next morning that he informed me of this matter and warned me how dangerous it was to travel alone. Happenstance like this is why I always consider myself to be fortunate as one rarely gets to know the consequences of what almost happened because of something one decides to do or has done. Had I not participated in the teaching activities at that public school in Kunming, I would never have known this person who ended up probably saving my life many years later. Back when I was young, I only volunteered my service out of compassion. I never expected any pay back for helping at that school. Having my life saved is probably the best unexpected reward I can ever receive.

Studying in America

My journey to American began with an airplane from Chongqing over the "Hump" of the Himalayan Mountains to Calcutta, India. We were like country bumpkins in poor health going overseas for the first time. Having endured the severe lack of food in Chongqing for so long, we were shocked to discover how healthy looking the other Chinese students who had arrived ahead of us were. They had enjoyed a whole week of milk, eggs and toasted bread.

We spent more than a month waiting for our ship to arrive in

India. As there was nothing else to do, we visited many scenic spots such as Mumbai, New Delhi and the famous Taj Mahal. Being young and inexperienced students, we were so happy to be able to go to America. We felt rich with money in our pockets, especially after we had exchanged some US dollars into Indian rupees. We used this money to eat at cheap Chinese restaurants as we had no way of cooking for ourselves. In sharp contrast, I felt so sad about the poverty in that country where so many people were homeless and slept in the streets. Even worse were the snakes that looked absolutely terrifying when the locals played with them.

Finally, we boarded the ship which took another month to arrive in the United States. Though horribly seasick, I was able to remain cheerful in the company of so many students from universities across China, especially those from the National Southwestern Associated University. Being around the same age, we had ample topics to chat about. No one felt lonely on that ship.

Upon our arrival at the University of Michigan without scholarships, we paid our own tuition fees and applied for subsidies from the Nationalist Government in Chongqing. The money was then sent to us through international bank transfers. Again, the difference between the official exchange rate and the black market helped pay our tuition and living expenses in America. It was almost like the Chinese government was directly sponsoring our studies in the United States. All of us were ordinary men and women. None of us were particularly rich. Having arrived in America, we had to find our own accommodations due to a lack of dormitories on campus. The rent was low because many local men had been conscripted for war. American universities needed money and we were there as paying students. Fortunately, Japan surrendered in August 1945, several months after my arrival in the United States.

Initially, my English was not good enough for me to understand everything in the classes. In particular I had trouble listening and speaking the language and often sat through a whole class without comprehending anything the instructor said. Although I had studied English in high school in Nanjing, our teachers may not have used the correct English pronunciation. Worse, we rarely had a chance to listen to real-life conversations in English not to mention the academic terminology we encountered every day on an American campus. So, what else could we do apart from extending ourselves beyond the limits of our capabilities? Whatever we wanted to do, we had to struggle extremely hard. Hence we suffered. Still being so young, we endured the struggle without bitterness and kept working until everything was done.

An even bigger problem was the lack of Chinese food. It was impossible to find the proper ingredients to cook our own meals. Nor could we afford to dine at the local Chinese restaurant. Life was tough back then, being away from China while having difficulty acclimating to America. We could cry when we felt homesick, but as long as we kept soldiering on, we believed everything would turn out to be all right. One has to seize his or her own opportunities. Whatever you want to do, whatever goal you need to achieve, you have to be relentless to get it yourself. Nothing is easy.

I was fortunate to come to America. It was pure luck because such an opportunity came only to the few. Worse, if you didn't seize the opportunity when it appeared, it would soon be gone forever. Take one of my relatives as an example, he was a graduate of the National Central University in Chongqing. When I urged him to take the national examination for self-sponsored overseas study, he refused, saying he did not have any money. Being far more capable than me, he could have done it the way I did: pass the examination and then sort out the money issue, but he did not. Why? Because he was already married by then and instead of pursuing his own dreams, he spent money looking after his family and kids. He could have easily found employment in America if he had made it here. Everybody is indeed different. I found a job soon after my arrival in United Stetes, writing Chinese subtitles for a movie produced in Hollywood. It is easy to find work in the United States if you are willing to work hard. You can be a tutor or do this or that. There is always a way.

While studying in Michigan, I met Tian-yi Yang (T.Y.) who later became my husband. Though we both worked in Chongqing, we had never met. In 1945 after he graduated from Chiao Tung University as an engineer, he was in charge of a maintenance and repair factory under that city's Public Bus Management Office that was situated in Xiaolongkan, a suburb of Chongqing. With two older sisters he was the only son in his family. While fleeing from the ravages of war, he rode a bicycle from Jiangsu Province to Chongqing with his older sister sitting behind him. It was a truly amazing feat. I have a photograph of him sitting in the midst of his colleagues at the factory. He was a good, capable man, with a sense of responsibility and willingness to endure hardship. Everybody loved him.

Anna and Tian-yi Yang, July 1948.

T.Y. passed the national examination for self-sponsored overseas study the year after I did. His goal was to pursue studies overseas and then return to develop China's automobile industry, to become China's Henry Ford, but the aforementioned factory in Chongqing insisted that he stay another year. Hence, T.Y. came to America two years after me. We met at a social gathering of Chinese students at the University of Michigan at a time when only a limited number of Chinese students were in America. Very few were females. He received his Master's degree on June 12, 1948. We married on July 3 and spent our honeymoon at Niagara Falls.

While he was in Chongqing, an older couple with several daughters appreciated T.Y.'s talents and treated him like their own son. Though they failed to turn him into a son-in-law, I believe he and I were destined to become husband and wife. On our wedding photograph he wrote: "With a partner like you, I'm no longer afraid of the hardships ahead. Instead, we'll face our bright future with a smile." Somehow these words foreshadowed the many obstacles we would face together in the years to come.

Working for the United Nations

Halfway through our studies in America, the government in China dramatically changed hands. That was the summer of 1948 when many Chinese government agencies disintegrated in the midst of the tumultuous and chaotic civil war. Among them was the Ministry of Finance whose Foreign Exchange Control Board ceased processing all transactions between American and Chinese currencies. As a result, overseas Chinese students suddenly lost their main source of income. Nor could their families and friends in China provide any financial assistance. Many Chinese students in America faced the same problem including us. While I washed dishes at a local restaurant to make US $0.5/hour, my husband was earning the minimum wage by working night shifts at a factory.

As we wondered how to survive, a friend of mine working at the United Nations sent a letter to inform me that the United Nations Secretariat was looking for Chinese translators and interpreters. With no other options available, I abandoned my studies and went to New York to give it a try. I did not attend any examinations the way Shing-yi Huang later did (see the chapter on Shing-yi Huang). Instead, I entered the international organization by recommendation. All I did to get the job was to appear for an interview and write a brief autobiography using Chinese calligraphy. My grandparents and parents used to tell me to practice calligraphy after school every day, but I never expected such a skill would be of tremendous advantage to me so many years later.

At that time before the U.N. Headquarters buildings in Manhattan were completed, the Secretariat was temporarily situated at the Sperry Gyroscope Plant at Lake Success, Long Island. My task at the Chinese Translation Service within the U.N. Secretariat's Documentation Division was to proofread and copy the Chinese translation of transcripts of U.N. meetings and conferences. As there were no Chinese typewriters available then, everything had to be handwritten, neat and tidy before the course of printing began. Again I was fortunate to have been in the right place at the right time. Desperately needing a job, I happened to be the kind of employee the U.N. was looking for.

Upon our arrival in New York, it was still difficult to find employment due to the economic depression. One day while visiting the U.N. Headquarters buildings still under construction in Manhattan, my husband and I saw the name of one of the contracted builders at the front entrance. That was Almirall, a company specialized in fitting modern buildings with air conditioning modules. T.Y. wrote them a letter and received a request from them a week later asking him to come for an interview at the UN construction site. He started out at Almirall as a mechanical draftsman before eventually taking charge of installing air conditioners for the company's numerous clients. To some degree, his job was also related to the U.N. After that he worked for Almirall during the day while studying analog computers at the Brooklyn Polytechnic Institute at night. That was before the digital computer was invented.

By then, our first child was born. Upon my arrival at home in the evening, I had to immediately switch to the role of mother and housewife after our babysitter left. T.Y. often returned home at 11:00 p.m. when we were finally able to sit down for dinner together. That was the most difficult period of our married life. It was lucky that the U.N. was able to help process an American visa for our babysitter from Hong Kong.

Anna Yang in her office at the U.N. Secretariat in Long Island, New York, circa 1950

One thing I like about America is that as long as you are willing to learn, anybody and everybody can go to school. You can study at night, during the day, with or without children; it does not matter, and no one will laugh at you. It is different in China where studying as an older student can sometimes be embarrassing. My husband and I took turns pursuing our studies. By the 1960s after T.Y. had completed his course and secured a steady job, I started outlining my own career and future. I wanted to pursue something practical, so I tried calculus and statistics at New York University by taking the subway to class after work. During the weekends I studied on a park's picnic table in the early mornings while my family slept. That was another difficult period of my life.

As a practical person I soon decided to focus on statistics because it would help me to find a good job. One semester later I applied for leave-without-pay in order to study full-time at NYU's Department of Business Administration. After receiving my master's degree, I returned to the U.N. and transferred from the Chinese Translation Service under the Documentation Division to the Statistics Division under the Department of Economic and Social Affairs. From then on we finally had stability in our lives. I worked for the U.N. for the following 30 years until retirement.

Although this was a really tough period for us, my husband and I were willing to soldier on, to fight and endure any hardship. It is hard to imagine now how busy we were and how we managed back then. We did not have to study any more, especially since we both had good jobs. But we kept urging ourselves to think ahead: with three children to raise but with neither contact nor any support from our families in China, what if we lost our jobs in America? What should we do? This sense of urgency, the anticipation of unexpected developments, prompted us to pursue further studies because we believed that an academic degree would make it easier for us to find jobs in the United States. On top of that, we also had a desire to learn, to constantly improve ourselves. Many of the goals that we deemed impossible then, somehow we managed to achieve them all.

In 1971 the Republic of China on Taiwan lost its seat in the U.N. to the People's Republic of China. Prior to that Chinese employees like me at the U.N. were concerned about our jobs due to rumors that we would all be sacked. However, once the new Chinese representatives arrived in New York, they went out of their way to be really nice to us.

Indeed, having isolated themselves from the world for so many years with absolutely no understanding about the inner workings of either the United States or the U.N., they had to depend on us for all sorts of information gathering and networking. With a particularly friendly attitude towards the long-term employees at the U.N., they often invited us to visit as their special guests. As a result all the Chinese employees decided to remain at the U.N. including me. None of us left simply because the China seat had changed hands. That was certainly a very unusual transition period in the history of this international organization.

Chinese Pioneers in America

Back then there were not many Chinese students in the United States. Before World War II the majority of them returned to China after completing their studies overseas, so later those of us staying on were akin to Chinese pioneers in America. In our attempt to establish new lives and careers here, we paved the way for future generations of Chinese students to come. Take my husband T.Y. as an example. Initially, no one would employ a Chinese person like him. Even when he asked to wash dishes for various restaurants, they simply looked at him and assumed he lacked the capacity. And we were the fortunate ones when compared to others. At least I already had a stable job at the U.N. by then. Still, upon our arrival in New York, we were often discriminated against on the basis of our ethnicity. Even where vacancies were advertised for apartments, the owners would change their minds as soon as they saw our faces. They simply refused to let in any Chinese people, and that was that. Later, as the number of Chinese immigrants gradually increased, we started seeing apartments and houses built by Chinese owners. We witnessed this noticeable change throughout our years in America.

With that said, the majority of Americans are very open-minded. Take Almirall for example. Before my husband approached them in New York, they had never hired a Chinese. Although they had no idea whether or not Chinese people were good workers, they were willing to give T.Y. a chance to prove himself. Fortunately, my husband was a practical person with a fierce sense of responsibility. Undaunted by any hardship and willing to confront all sorts of obstacles, he often did far more than what was required of him while trying his best to assist others. Hence everybody liked him as a colleague. He proved to them that the Chinese were diligent and serious employees. From then on, Americans in general slowly recognized the intelligence and skill of Chinese workers. This is how we were raised; this is our trademark as a capable and hard-working people. Once such recognition was achieved, American companies started competing to employ Chinese professionals. And that is how they changed their stereotype. Still, Chinese people in general endured much bitterness and difficulty here in America. In order to succeed in any field, they relied only on themselves. We were fortunate to be among these pioneers. We helped to pave the way for others.

Almirall was the name of the company's owner. A specialist in the installation of air conditioning facilities, the company had contracted to work on numerous famous buildings in New York such as the U.N. Headquarters buildings, the Lincoln Center, the Empire State Building and the Time-Life Building just to name a few. It was quite an achievement for a middle-sized company such as Almirall. The timing helped, too, as the Second World War had just ended. America experienced a construction boom which helped launch air conditioning and other industries.

My husband spent the rest of his working life with this company despite the fact that it had nothing to do with automobiles, his original ambition. He was an unusual employee. Even his boss respected his professional opinion and gradually promoted him to more senior roles.

Eventually when the boss retired, my husband bought the company and started employing American workers. While it was only a middle-sized company with 80-to-100 workers, it had taken my husband a total of 18 years to rise from the lowest level to the most senior position as the owner. Back in the 1950s, who would have expected a Chinese person to achieve this in the United States? It was indeed quite a success. It was also fortunate that he had purchased the company since it considerably improved our living standards. He was such a nice and capable person that some of his friends in New York jokingly referred to him as "Millionaire Yang". They said he would have been able to establish an automobile factory in China had circumstances there remained unchanged.

After leaving China we had planned to return following our studies in the United States. We always wanted to go home. No one initially thought of remaining in America, to take roots here, because it was not our country. After all, China was our homeland. We came here to study. However, when China suddenly changed hands, we felt confused, unsure whether or not we should return home. We felt the need to give back to our nation because it was our government that helped cultivate our careers, but where could we go? Should we go to Taiwan or the Mainland China? It was hard to decide where we could go.

Indeed for a while, facing an unknown future in America, we wanted to return to China. Some of our friends made the trip against the strong advice from their families and friends there. Among them was my friend, an engineer who felt that his talents were wasted while working as a translator for the U.N. He promised to contact us if the circumstances in China were ideal; otherwise, he would simply keep quiet. We never heard from him again. It was only years later that we learned how unhappy my friend became. His wife, a music teacher, managed to bring a German-made Steinway grand piano back to China. Even though she gifted it to a local music academy, she was soon refused entry there. It was certainly depressing, but the Chinese are such a practical people that we get used to it. More importantly, our life in America was relatively stable. Without knowing our fate were we to return to China, we simply decided to stay put in the United States.

A Bitter-Sweet Trip Home

We eventually made a trip back to China nearly 30 years after we left. For many years after our arrival in America, we did not even dare write letters to our families in China not to mention sending any money which I had once tried to do while my mother was alive. Since my mother passed away, however, I stopped contacting my siblings for fear of causing them trouble. It was only after U.S. President Richard Nixon visited China in 1972 and forged formal communications and transport channels between the two countries the following year that I made the trip. Perhaps as a result of my ability to easily tap into these channels as a U.N. employee, I was among the first group of Chinese Americans to make it back to China.

Unfortunately, my mother passed away in 1962 and my father even before her. Fortunately, I had visited my parents just prior to coming to America as I never had another chance to see them. After learning about my parents' deaths from my brother when I called him from Hong Kong, we both burst into tears.

At that time to return to China, one had to go through Hong Kong. I bought a lot of things for my family in China, as they had nothing. Nothing was available to them even if they had coupones. Anyway, I bought many things in Hong Kong without thinking of the logistics to transport these items, such as television sets, bicycles, sewing machines, numerous items of clothing made of velvet, wool and nylon; you name it. As there was no way to hire anyone to carry these things, I managed to have them dropped on the other side of a bridge that served as the Chinese-Hong Kong border. That was in 1973.

When I arrived at the Wuhan Iron & Steel Corporation where my older sister worked, it was such big news that everyone came out to see us. Even the general manager of the company offered a personal meeting and was highly polite towards both my sister and me. Initially, I did not dare to get too close to them for fear that any connection with the West would cause them trouble. However, as the general manager insisted on treating me to a grand banquet, it was obvious that circumstances in China had already started to change.

From then on I started bringing my family to China every two or three years. Thanks to my work at the U.N., we were able to make free family trips to our home countries every two years. Such employment benefits were mostly wasted on me prior to the establishment of official relations between China and the United States although I did travel to Taiwan twice. With that said, without any direct family members in Taiwan, it was rather tiresome visiting remote relatives there.

Since I was the only one in my family to leave China, I decided to bring out the next generation, especially those who genuinely wanted to study overseas. Since that first trip to China in 1973, I have sponsored most of my siblings' children to study in the United States. This is counter to the fact that the majority of Chinese students in America have come from either Taiwan or Hong Kong. Worse, it was quite a difficult process to get my nieces and nephews out of China. Still, those who have made it to the United States have all achieved success including my older brother's son, my older sister's daughter and my younger brother's son and daughter. The children of my two youngest brothers did not come to America because they lacked a university education from China.

Golden Years in Retirement

By the time my husband and I retired, our children had

already settled in California. As some of our friends from New York were already living in Rossmoor in Walnut Creek, California, we paid a visit to this community and found it a very nice residential area. In 1989 we relocated to Rossmoor, sharing a moving truck with our friends Peter and Helen Sih. That was 26 years ago. Initially, with a limited number of Chinese residents here, we were able to travel, play cards and enjoy sports together as close friends. We had a wonderful life here until my husband passed away in 1998. We shared 50 years together, experiencing not only hardship but also much joy. I truly think I lived a fortunate life. Thanks to all the luck that came my way, I feel I have hardly suffered at all.

Yen and Dolly Liang 梁衍, 薩本蓮
1997

Mr. Yen Liang passed away many years before our relocation to Rossmoor. As a result, we have no way to personally converse with him regarding his legendary life story. His friends remember him as a renowned architect once involved in designing the United Nations headquarters and other famous buildings in New York. By the time the other senior Chinese men and women represented in this book arrived in America to pursue their studies, Mr. Liang had already returned to China before being invited back to the United States a second time. Later, when medical professionals in New York failed to find a cure for his life-threatening illness, he decided to relocate to Rossmoor. Somehow, he continued to live another 27 years in health and happiness.

This article, written on the basis of my research and a series of commemorative articles composed by his friends, can only help to outline Mr. Liang's extraordinary achievements as an architect. As the first Chinese American to become a resident at Rossmoor, his move had a profound impact on his friends in New York. It is thanks to Mr. Liang and friends who followed him here that the Chinese community was established at Rossmoor as a unique cultural group.

Biography

Yen Liang was born in 1908. He was a graduate of Tsinghua College (today's Tsinghua University) which was established in 1911. using the excess Boxer Rebellion indemnity payment reimbursed by the American Government, as a preparatory school for Chinese students who would later study in the United States. Liang left China in 1928 in the midst of armed conflicts between the warlords in the country's north and the Nationalist Government in the south. After graduating from the Yale School of Architecture in 1931, he studied under the famous American architect Frank Lloyd Wright until his return to China in 1935. Through the following years, he traveled between Beijing, Chongqing (Sichuan Province) and Kunming (Yunnan Province) while building a career in architectural design. After the War of Resistance against Japan, Liang was invited to return to America and work in Wright's Taliesin Studio in 1947. He later joined Harrison & Abramovitz as Chief Designer and was involved in a series of major construction projects in New York. In 1973, he retired and relocated to Rossmoor in Walnut Creek, in San Francisco's East Bay Area, and played second violin in the Diablo Symphony Orchestra for many years. He passed away in 2000.

An Architectural Master's Swan Song

Yen Liang's ancestral home was Xinhui, Guangdong Province, He was born in Japan in 1908 while his father was studying there. His academic name was Yen-zhang. After returned to China in 1910, his father worked as a high-ranking officer of the Beiyang Government. Liang and his siblings, older brother Zhi-zhang and younger brother Juzhang, later went to study at Tsinghua College. Among the students were another three brothers sharing the same surname and hometown as well: the three sons of renowned Chinese scholar Qi-chao Liang, whose study names were Si-cheng, Si-yong and Si-zhong. Another student in Liang's class was Ben-yuan Sa, the grandson of Admiral Zhen-bing Sa of the Qing Dynasty's Imperial Navy, whose younger sister Ben-lian later became Liang's wife.

As Tsinghua College was a preparatory school for Chinese students to study in the United States, graduates like Liang qualified to commence their academic career as second-year students at American universities. In Liang's own words (citation source provided below):

"After graduating from Tsinghua Collage in Beijing, China, I decided to go to the United States and take up architecture. All I knew was that an architect designed buildings. Interviews with a few practicing Chinese architects who were graduates of the University of Pennsylvania influenced my decision to register there in the fall of 1928 for the five-year architecture course."

"That school year found me studying French and calculus, doing meticulous drawings of the Roman orders and charcoal sketches of plaster casts, solving design problems by using Renaissance motifs and, of all things for a Chinese student, learning the intricacies of grinding Chinese ink sticks into ink for use in renderings. So, at the end of my first school year, feeling that I was not getting architecture, I decided to change to a better school. To pick a new school, I looked at old copies of *Beaux Arts* bulletins to determine which school had won medals most frequently. Yale, MIT, Cornell and Harvard were all very close. Thinking that pure engineering was perhaps the direction I should follow in order to become an architect, I registered for summer school at Cornell."

"There, I soon had my fill of empirical formulas while getting nowhere nearer to an understanding of building principles. I began to see that learning to choose the appropriate eclectic veneer, be it Roman,

Gothic, or whatever, was the prevailing architectural objective in America and Europe."

"After more summer work at MIT, I transferred to Yale and was able to finish the five-year course in three. Then I enrolled in the Harvard graduate school for advanced study, but still felt no closer to understanding architecture. Moonlighting in a Boston architect's office offered no help. I did not see how I could force Roman orders and the like on buildings when I returned to China to practice, and still call myself an architect." (p.127-128)

And here came the turning point:

"...During that year in Boston, pure luck brought me a copy of *Frank Lloyd Wright: An Autobiography*. Of course, I had heard about Mr. Wright and his work, but nothing was taught about him in the architectural schools or in the schools' libraries. Looking back, I realize there was a silent boycott, a kind of taboo."

"My awakening from reading *An Autobiography* was ecstatic. 'This is architecture,' I excitedly told myself. Therefore, with a sense of urgency (for I had already spent too much time studying the wrong things) during the middle of the spring term at Harvard, I dashed off a short note to Mr. Wright, asking to work [for him]. He answered with a similarly succinct note for me to 'come along', together with the first draft of his Taliesin Fellowship application form typed by his then-secretary Karl Jensen." (p.128)

Liang's words above are collected in *Frank Lloyd Wright: Recollections by Those Who Knew Him* edited by Edgar Tafel and published by Dover Publications in April 2001. Taliesin was Wright's self-designed home and estate in Wisconsin; it is now a National Historic Landmark. Wright established the Taliesin Fellowship in 1932 to enable up to 60 apprentices to study under him. Later, many of them also became famous architects in the history of American architecture. One of Wright's cutting-edge architectural concepts back then was to place a building's occupants close to the natural surroundings. Years later, he was recognized by the American Institute of Architects as "the greatest American architect of all time".

In the copy of Wright's *An Autobiography* that he autographed and gave to Liang as a personal gift, he wrote that Liang was the "first to accomplish the Taliesin Fellowship" among the first group of 32 apprentices. In Liang's own words: "I was twenty-three in 1932 when I drove up to Taliesin in a two-seater gray and black Stutz with a rumble seat. I approached Taliesin the wrong way, up a steep back road and stopped behind Mr. Wright's Cord convertible... [Mr. Wright] was concerned about my having spent money on such a fancy car, funds I could have spent at the Fellowship [which was US $670 per year back then]." (p.128) In fact, Liang had first taken a train to Chicago, where a former Chinese classmate informed him that he needed a car to get to Wisconsin. Liang then bought the Stutz from a second-hand car dealer at a reasonable price. Prior to that, Liang had never driven a car. The short driving lesson from his classmate sustained him all the way from Chicago to Wisconsin. More importantly, Liang did not have to worry about funds. It would be another year of studying in the United States before his Chinese government sponsorship ended, based on the aforementioned excessive Boxer Rebellion indemnity payment returned by the American Government.

In Liang's words: "Taliesin was designed by Mr. Wright to hug the hills with the hilltop exposed, affording the stroller a panoramic view of the valley over the low sandstone parapets. And through the seasons of the year, Taliesin wore the mantles of the changes well. The snow of winters piled on the serene Buddha, adding to his passive countenance on top of the grand stairway at the entrance. The sight of a pine branch through the clerestory window, with a couple of birds chirping away on it, was subject enough to inspire a painter in the spring. When I ploughed (trying hard to get a straight row) the corn field in the spring, I often became distracted by looking up at Taliesin to admire its loveliness from down below. Fall came with a blaze of colors.

Husking corn was better than a party! When I was told about the legendary rite of a kiss from the girls when you husk a red ear of corn, I worked like a demon to reap the corn." (p.129)

"It was the introduction to living so closely to the earth that gave me an understanding of the cycle of living as nothing else did. A stable, a pigsty, a garage, and a woodshed, all usually ugly places in the average establishment, were at Taliesin, beautiful because of their design. Aside from the revelations, which opened new vistas on architecture for me from close contact with the fertile mind of Mr. Wright from living at Taliesin, rich in architectural ideas and heartbreakingly beautiful, from working in the drafting room, and from actual hands-on constructions in masonry, carpentry, plumbing, furniture building, and even lumber milling, I learned without realizing it at the time a way of life. His free and natural mingling among us imbued all daily activities with beauty, richness, and meaning."

"For instance, he decreed that the decoration of the theater for the weekly theater-dinner event was one of the duties of the apprentices. This was Mr. Wright's idea to train the youngsters in a sense of design. Each of us would take turns as the chief decorator of the week. The usual would be some foliage of the season spotted around the place in pots. I remember once, when it was my turn at captaincy, I went out with my gang and gathered pine branches by sawing off a substantial number of handsome limbs from a pine tree, trucked them home and hung them off the theater balcony with spotlights to highlight them as if the pine grew there naturally." (p.130) That unique design ended up being highly regarded by Wright. Also, having enjoyed playing violin since childhood, Liang often performed violin sonatas at the Sunday musicals in the Taliesin living room with Edgar Tafel, his close friend and fellow apprentice and later editor of the aforementioned *Frank Lloyd Wright: Recollections by Those Who Knew Him*, at the piano.

In 1934 on his journey back to China, Liang stopped by Europe to study the architecture there. Historical archives reveal that he arrived back in China in 1935 to join Beijing's Kwan, Chu and Yang Architects, the earliest and the biggest private architecture firm in Northern China. It is with this important firm in the history of modern Chinese architecture that Liang designed the International Club in Nanjing. He relocated to Kunming, Yunnan Province, during the War of Resistance against Japan, and designed the Yunnan Trust Building, the Bank of Yunnan Mining Industries, as well as a residence in Chongqing for then President Chiang Kai-shek and his wife. During his last years in Kunming, Liang worked for the U.S. Army.

After the war Frank Lloyd Wright wrote a letter to Liang inviting him and his wife for a visit. In 1947 Liang and Dolly sailed from Shanghai to San Francisco on SS General Meigs (owned by the Dollar Steamship Line) and then arrived at Wright's new studio in Arizona that was also named Taliesin (which is known today as Taliesin West). In Liang's words: "When we arrived, Mr. Wright said, 'Yen! You look like your own grandfather.' And to my wife he said, 'Why do all Chinese women look like Mme. Chiang Kai-shek?'" (p.131) During his six-month stay in Taliesin, Liang worked at the drawing board in the Hillside drafting room on drawings for the renowned Obler House in Southern California.

After leaving Taliesin Liang joined Harrison & Abramovitz architectural firm based in New York, and worked for the United Nations Planning Office in Manhattan as an expert on loan from Harrison & Abramovitz. Meanwhile, Dolly worked as a secretary for the Chinese Translation Service of the U.N. Secretariat before transferring to a similar position at the General Services Division. In 1953 after the United Nations headquarters buildings were completed, he became Chief Designer at Harrison & Abramovitz and was involved in a series of major construction projects in New York including the John F. Kennedy Center for the Performing Arts, Battery Park, and the expansion of LaGuardia Airport. Among them was the Battery Park City project in Lower Manhattan, which was launched by the New York

City Government in 1966. It was later praised by the Urban Land Institute as "a model for successful large-scale planning efforts and marking a positive shift away from the urban renewal mindset of the time".

In 1973 due to a life-threatening illness, Liang was diagnosed to have only six months to live. He immediately retired as ordered by the doctors, and relocated to Rossmoor in Walnut Creek in the San Francisco's East Bay Area. Once there, he started to play golf, and he went on to enjoy another 27 years of healthy living. The goal for his everlasting love for that sport was to maintain his health rather than competition. Everyday he walked alone or with friends around the nine-hole golf course in Rossmoor, carrying only three clubs in his bag and swinging away wherever he found his balls until the year before his death at the age of 92. As the first Chinese American to relocate to Rossmoor, Liang's move had a profound impact on his friends, many of whom also moved from New York to this community. Throughout his 27 years of life here, he was a passionate supporter of local community activities. He was a founding member of the Chinese American Association of Rossmoor (CAAR) and was the designer of the organization's emblem when it was officially established in 1990 (see the chapter on Peter Sih).

Emblem of the Chinese American Association of Rossmoor (CAAR) designed by Yen Liang (right) inspired by the Rossmoor logo (left)

While living at Rossmoor, Liang also produced illustrations for the 12 Chinese zodiac animals, one for each year, until 1999. These were the major decoration for CAAR's annual party celebrating, the Chinese New Year Festival (see the chapter on Peter Sih).

Yen Liang and his last Chinese zodiac animal illustration 1999

A talented artist-cum-genius, Liang enjoyed drawing (part of his training as an architect) as well as music. Not only was he a professional violinist, but he also played the Erhu, a traditional Chinese musical instrument, and was an ardent supporter of community concerts. For more than 20 years, he played second violin in the Diablo Symphony Orchestra, worked there as a volunteer, and attended every one of the orchestra's numerous rehearsals and performances. His gentle manner, his wit and humor, his musicianship and his devotion to the orchestra endeared him to all.

Liang and Dolly moved into a nursing home in 1999. Shortly after Dolly's death, Liang passed away on December 27, 2000, at the age of 92. To support musical education, Liang's assets were used to set up funds for the Yen Liang Young Artist Competition, which is dedicated to showcasing the talent of local musicians less than 23 years of age. On top of a cash honorarium, first prize winners are offered an opportunity to perform in two concerts with the Diablo Symphony Orchestra.

To pay tribute to Liang as a noted architect and artist, renowned composer James Bethel was engaged by the Diablo Symphony Orchestra to compose the symphony *Overture of the New Age*, which premiered at the Lesher Center for the Arts in Walnut Creek in 2011. It may be seen as a coda to Liang's colorful life.

(Author's note: This chapter was based on a commemorative article written by Yen Liang's close friend Shing-yi Huang, as well as Liang's own writing about his early life in the book "Frank Lloyd Wright: Recollections by those who knew him")

Yen Liang's illustrations of the 12 Chinese zodiac animals

Hugh C. and Elsie L.C. Chang 張厚群, 陳嵐君
Celebrating the 65th Anniversary of Their Wedding,
April 24, 2007

Hugh C. and Elsie L.C. Chang married in Chongqing, Sichuan Province, in 1942 during the War of Resistance against Japan. After arriving in the United States to pursue further studies, both achieved successful careers and were talented citizens. On Thanksgiving Day 2008 they perished in a boating accident at Angel Falls, the world's highest uninterrupted waterfall, in Venezuela, a testimony to the ancient Chinese romantic statement that true lovers, though not lucky enough to be born on the same day, may wish to end their lives at the same time. This chapter was written on the basis of the couple's own written records, a series of commemorative articles composed by their friends, and information gathered from media reports and the Internet.

Biography

Hugh C. Chang, whose Chinese name was Hou-qun Chang, was born in Chongqing in 1916. His ancestral home was Fuling, Sichuan Province. Having spent his childhood in that city, he studied at Sichuan University's Department of Physics in Chengdu, the capital city of Sichuan. During the War of Resistance against Japan, he joined the army and later reached the rank of colonel in the Armored Regiment of the 200th Division of the National Revolutionary Army. In 1942 he was assigned to Washington, D.C. In 1949 he entered the University of California at Berkeley to study Nuclear Engineering. Having gained his Ph.D. in this field, he proceeded to work as a researcher at the Lawrence Berkeley National Laboratory operated by the United States Department of Energy. Outside of work, he enjoyed calligraphy, painting, composing classical Chinese poetry and playing the Erhu, a traditional Chinese musical instrument. In 1990 he retired and relocated to Rossmoor in Walnut Creek, in the Fan Francisco's East Bay Area. He died on November 27, 2008.

Elsie L.C. Chang, whose Chinese name was Lan-jun Chen, was born in 1918. Her ancestral home was Jintian Village in Guiping, Guangxi Province. She spent her junior high school years in Guangzhou, Guangdong Province, before entering Nanjing Huiwen Girls' Middle School in 1931. During the war she followed Fudan University in its relocation from Shanghai to Guangxi and later graduated from National Guangxi University's Department of Economics. After the war she went to America to pursue further studies at San Francisco State University. She later worked at the East Asian Library of the University of California at Berkeley before resigning to study Chinese painting. A highly successful artist at porcelain painting, she also enjoyed playing the piano. In 1990 she retired and relocated to Rossmoor in Walnut Creek, in the San Francisco's East Bay Area. She died on November 27, 2008.

A Loving Couple to the Very End

Hugh C. Chang, whose ancestral home was Fuling, Sichuan Province, was born in Chongqing in 1916. Having spent his childhood and teenage years in that city, he went to the university in Nanjing and promptly fell in love with Lan-jun Chen, a student at Nanjing Huiwen Girls' Middle School. After he graduated with a university degree in physics, he joined the army and was involved in various battles across China before retreating to Guilin, Guangxi Province. In 1940 during the famous Battle of South Guangxi, Chang was a colonel in charge of a maintenance and repair factory operated by the Armored Regiment of the 200th Division of the National Revolutionary Army. Commanded by General Yu-ming Du, the 200th Division was created in 1938 as the first mechanized division in the National Revolutionary Army. The Armored Regiment was established in Xiangtan, Hunan Province, and led by Major-General Xian-qun Hu.

Lan-jun Chen, or Elsie, was born in Jintian Village in Guiping, Guangxi Province, in 1918. As the first daughter in her family with five older brothers, she was particularly well looked after by her father. Having spent her primary school years in Guiping and junior high school years in Guangzhou, Guangdong Province, she entered Nanjing Huiwen Girls' Middle School in 1931. In 1937 she followed Fudan University in its relocation from Shanghai to Guilin, Guangxi Province. It was there in the midst of the turmoil of war and constant bombing by Japanese warplanes that Elsie, then a student of the National Guangxi University, again met up with Chang.

In 1941 the United States Government enacted An Act to Promote the Defense of the United States, or the Lend-Lease policy, to provide other Allied nations with weaponry, supplies and capital in exchange for leases on army and naval bases in Allied territory during the war. In 1942 the Chinese Government set up a liaison office in

Washington, D.C., to both facilitate the supply and transport of defense-related materials and to select outstanding officers from all branches of the armed services to study in America. Chang was among the first group of military officers who passed the written examination for overseas study. However, during the interview, his superiors assigned him to work at the aforementioned liaison office in Washington, D.C. Later that year Chang and Elsie married in order to travel to America together. Soon after Elsie received a telegram that confirmed her acceptance by Columbia University as a student, the then U.S. president Franklin D. Roosevelt announced a temporary ban or limit on private communications between America and foreign countries. Elsie had to remain in Chongqing while her husband travelled to the United States. She suffered greatly from the turmoil of war, with life becoming particularly tough after her father passed away.

After the war, Chang entered Harvard University in September 1945 with the intention of pursuing a research degree. Having been separated from each other for five years, he and Elsie were finally reunited in Boston in January 1947 as a result her acceptance of a scholarship from Wellesley College in Massachusetts. Soon after that the circumstances in China suddenly deteriorated as communist troops advanced southward to pose a considerable military threat to the Nationalist Government. Chang received orders to return home. He, Elsie and their baby daughter left Boston for San Francisco where their second daughter was born. The communist troops eventually swept through China's vast hinterlands and established the People's Republic of China in October 1949. As the Nationalist Government retreated to Taiwan, all communications between China and the United States were cut off. Chang and his family were forced to remain in San Francisco.

Chang joined the University of California at Berkeley to study Nuclear Engineering. Having gained his Ph.D. in this field and commenced research work at the Lawrence Berkeley National Laboratory operated by the United States Department of Energy, he was able to financially support Elsie's studies. By then Elsie had received a scholarship from the San Francisco State University. However, in order to secure a financial future for her family, she chose to study economics instead of painting, her favorite subject as well as her speciality. In 1963 Elsie became an assistant to Professor Elizabeth Huff, the founding librarian of the East Asian Library of the University of California at Berkeley. Throughout the following years, her task was to procure books for the library. This provided her with ample opportunities to explore Chinese art and history while studying Chinese painting under a number of renowned artists. In 1968 she resigned from the library in order to focus on painting. She also served as a broadcaster for the Voice of Free China and as a teacher for Chinese language schools in Oakland. She and Chang also started traveling around the world.

  Elsie often accompanied Chang when he travelled to Taiwan and Southeast Asia to give lectures. In the 1970s and 1980s, the couple visited numerous museums and galleries around the world. Back in the United States, Elsie joined a series of Chinese painting and porcelain painting clubs including the Oriental Art Association in San Francisco where she actively served in various positions. She also composed articles for arts magazines, organized arts exhibitions, and gave lectures at schools, universities and on television. She pioneered a technique of assembling colorful porcelain tiles into large-scale porcelain paintings, with her largest work measuring 18 feet wide and 4.5 feet tall, created for a private collector. Many of her other works were also purchased for collections. In 1976 Elsie launched an art studio and gallery to teach porcelain painting. In 1983 when her best pieces and those of her students went on display at a museum in Los Gatos, the exhibition period was extended from one to three months so that local students could have ample viewing opportunities to be informed and inspired by these fascinating works of art.

Elsie L.C. Chang's large-scale porcelain painting "Phoenix with Bells" (originally in color) with inscription by Hugh C. Chang: "For the Exhibition Marking the 10th Anniversary of the Establishment of the Peninsula Porcelain Painting Association Autumn 1983"

From the Lawrence Berkeley National Laboratory, Chang transferred to Sandia National Laboratories in Livermore at the edge of in the San Francisco Bay Area. He later held positions at Aerojet General Corporation, the renowned engineering firm Brown and Root, and General Electric until his retirement in 1983. Outside of work, Chang enjoyed calligraphy, Chinese painting and composing classical Chinese poetry. Indeed, most of Elsie's porcelain paintings were accompanied with Chang's Chinese poems as inscriptions. They also had electric kilns at their home studio where he fired porcelain vases, tiles and any newly created porcelain paintings.

In 1984 Chang and Elsie visited China as part of a Chinese American arts group. They were invited by the China International Cultural Exchange Center to hold a porcelain painting exhibition on the Chinese mainland with all associated expenses paid for by the Chinese authorities. However, the project was canceled out of safety concerns over the transportation of fragile porcelain tiles. In 1980, after a trip to Kauai, oldest of the main Hawaiian island, Chang and Elsie were so impressed by the beautiful environment there that they purchased an apartment and lived there for the following four years. Kauai, a small but irresistibly attractive island, witnessed the earliest wave of Chinese migration and settlement in the Hawaiian archipelago. Both Chang and Elsie were active participants in local Chinese art circles with Elsie's porcelain paintings displayed at Kauai Community College, a branch of the University of Hawaii. In 1989 more than 100 of her porcelain paintings were exhibited at the Kauai Museum as part of local celebrations for the 200th anniversary of Chinese arrival in Hawaii.

In 1990 Chang and Elsie relocated to Rossmoor in the San Francisco's East Bay Area. As multi-talented artists, they never retired from life. Instead, apart from regular travel, they continued writing, playing music and dancing and were active participants in the community's arts association. Chang twice served as president of the club while giving lessons in calligraphy. Elsie held a number of art exhibitions and taught Chinese painting both within and outside of the community. Chang's "Wai Tan Kung" exercise group was highly beneficial to other senior residents in Rossmoor.

Since China opened its door to the outside world in the 1980s, Chang and Elsie frequently visited their relatives and friends there. Like most of their fellow Chinese migrants, the farther away they drifted from their homeland, the more they felt connected to it emotionally. After much hard work Elsie helped a younger brother and two younger sisters to migrate to the United States. Her siblings have since established families and careers here. Because both Chang and Elsie had studied in Nanjing and because Chang also studied at Sichuan University, they gifted an album of their works of calligraphy and paintings to the Nanjing Museum and the university's library. According to media coverage of this event, Chang and Elsie were close friends to Si-yuan Cheng, the former deputy leader of the Chinese People's Congress who, like Elsie, was from Guangxi Province. They further played a major role in the decision of Zong-ren Li, formerly a prominent warlord and military commander for the Nationalist Government who was also from Guangxi, to return to China from the United States in his old age.

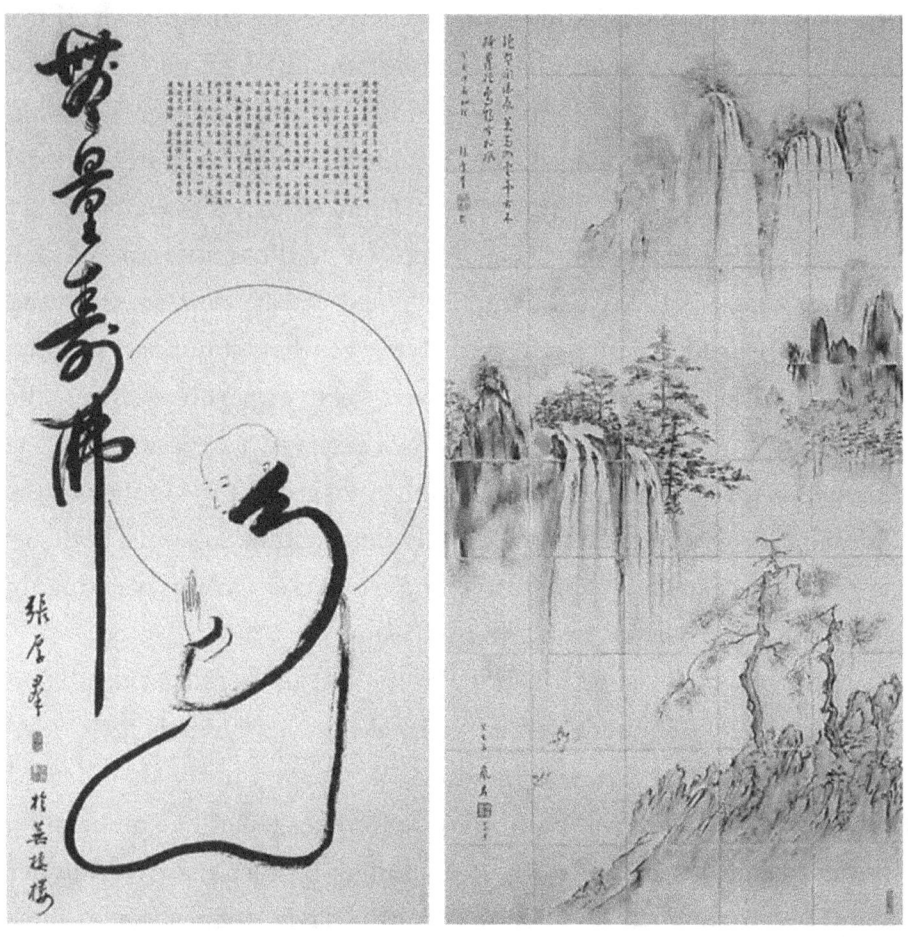

Left: Hugh C. Chang's painting and calligraphy "The Heart of Prajna Paramita Sutra" Right: Elsie L.C. Chang's porcelain painting "Visiting a Friend in the Mountains" with inscriptions by Chang, 30" x 60", (originally in color)

Left: Hugh C. and Elsie L.C. Chang celebrating their diamond wedding anniversary 2007 Right: The couple at their wedding ceremony 1942

In 2007 Chang and Elsie held a grand party in Fireside room at Rossmoor Gateway Clubhouse to celebrate their 65th wedding anniversary. At 91 and 89 respectively, Chang and his beloved wife danced a waltz to a commemorative song that he had composed specifically for this occasion. After the party the couple embarked on a journey to the North Pole in the same way that any newlyweds would spend their honeymoon in a special location. Starting from the port city of Murmansk in the extreme northwest point of Russia on July 8, 2007, it took six days for their nuclear-powered icebreaker NS Yamal to sail across 2,000 miles before reaching the North Pole. The whole trip took 15 days and cost tens of thousands of U.S.dollars. On board the icebreaker, Chang and Elsie met a lady named Mary who had also travelled around the world. Originally from Kunming, Yunnan Province, and now based in Australia, Mary later reported her admiration for the senior couple and their extraordinary journey on the "Tianya Club", one of the most popular Internet forums in China. According to Mary, there were five passengers on that icebreaker who were then in their 90s with the oldest being 97. On a photograph that

Chang and Elsie took with Mary, Chang inscribed the following poem:

"One's talents are only revealed to someone who truly knows him.
With good friends, one advances by leaps and bounds like a magnificent horse.
His footprints are everywhere between the North Pole and Antarctica.
The world being his backyard, a traveler takes delight in every journey."

Hence it was obvious that Chang and Elsie already had Antarctica in mind.

Hugh C. and Elsie L.C. Chang with Mary on board the North Pole-bound icebreaker NS Yamal 2007

As soon as Chang and Elsie announced their plan to travel to Antarctica, families and friends tried to stop them but to no avail. It is uncertain why they were so determined to go on this adventure. We only know that on December 22, 2007, Mary flew from Chile to Antarctica and that in July 2008 she published an illustrated book in which her travels around the world, including Antarctica, were documented in detail. It is therefore reasonable to assume that Chang and Elsie learned about Mary's forthcoming trip to Antarctica at some point during their trip to the North Pole.

As a part of their trip to Antarctica, Chang and Elsie also included in their grand plans a side trip to Angel Falls in Venezuela, the world's highest uninterrupted waterfall with a height of 979 meters. Formed by the water from the Churun River flowing over the edge of the Auyantepui mountain within the Canaima National Park, the waterfall mostly consists of the 807-meter main plunge, then about 400 meters of sloped cascades and rapids, and a further 30-meter plunge to the bottom. A 150-meter-wide pool is formed at the base in the midst of dense tropical jungle deep in the mountains. It is only accessible in summer, the rainy season in South America, when rivers run deep and rapid and boating upstream becomes possible but still risky. Unfortunately, the boat carrying Chang and Elsie capsized, drowning them both. That was November 27, 2008, Thanksgiving Day in America.

More than 200 people attended Chang and Elsie's memorial service in Rossmoor on December 14, 2008. As Elsie was a Christian and Chang a Buddhist, the service was held in accordance with formal rituals of both religions, an unusual decision that was covered by the *Sing Tao Daily* in America. The event was further reported by Chinese media worldwide causing numerous Chinese readers to lament the deaths of a couple in their 90s in their attempt to visit the world's highest waterfall on their way to Antarctica. This loving couple, who met in the midst of the tumultuous war in China and then spent 71 years together in the United States, lived a rich and colorful life before dying on the same day. This is a perfect testimony to the ancient Chinese romantic statement that true lovers, though not lucky enough to be born on the same day, may wish to end their lives at the same time. One almost feels sure that they will remain a loving couple even beyond this world.

Afterword

I once posed a question to singer Ellie Mao Mok whose story is among those collected in this book: While at the time when she was growing up in the early 20th century, China was full of intelligent and brilliant masters in all walks of life, one wonders why that golden age of talents is there no more. Her brother Yua, answered casually: Because back then, at the end of the Qing Dynasty and the beginning of the Republic of China, the government's control over public thinking was much more lenient than it was later. As all the senior Chinese Americans depicted in this book lived through that period, their life stories may be seen as perfect examples of the saying, "Heroes emerge in troubled times."

Compared to the sixteen couples depicted in this book, the first half of our own parents' lives were very much like theirs. However, throughout the second half of our parents' lives in China, they went through one political upheaval after another. They tried their best but were prevented from achieving the kind of lives that they would have loved to have, because of the spiritual oppression and shackles enforced upon them.

The first half of our own lives was very different from those of these senior Chinese Americans although there are some similarities between the second half of our lives and theirs. As members of a younger generation, Zong-Yi and I did not have the direct experience of war. However, we happened to grow up in an era where the government enforced the fiercest control over public thinking. In spite of our enthusiasm as young men and women to study hard and give back to our nation, during the Cultural Revolution we were sent to the remote countryside in the Loess Plateau in Northern China for eight years. It was only after the Cultural Revolution that we were allowed to take and pass the national examination, return to our hometown Beijing, and enter graduate school to pick up the books that we had abandoned 12 years earlier. More importantly, it was only after China opened its door to the outside world that we were able to come to the United States via the generous assistance of senior Chinese Americans like those depicted in this book. For example, thanks to my mentor Tsung-dao Lee (T.D. Lee), co-recipient of the 1957 Nobel Prize in Physics, I was able to pursue further studies at Columbia University beginning in 1981. Thanks to an invitation from renowned ophthalmic pathologist Mark O.M. Tso at the University of Illinois at Chicago, Zong-Yi was able to commence her research in ophthalmology there in 1983. We were among the fortunate ones who came to study, work and live in America in the early 1980s. That was more than 30 years ago.

Left: Zong-Yi Li consulting with Professor Mark O.M. Tso, 1983
Right: Tianchi Zhao during a Christmas gathering at Professor Tsung-dao Lee's residence 1981

Zong-Yi spent more than a year planning, interviewing, transcribing and writing this book. As for me, even in retirement, I still travel between Beijing and the United States to assist in various neutrino-related research projects at the Institute of High Energy Physics of the Chinese Academy of Sciences. Among the 14 stories collected in this book, I only authored the chapter on Annie Toy, based on transcripts of her English interviews and research results from other historical materials. I also wrote the two short chapters at the end of the book to commemorate the two couples who had passed away. As editor, I collated, revised and polished various passages in this book. I also did the formatting and cover design.

Although the writing, editing and publishing of this book was an exhausting task, it was also highly rewarding. After it was finished, I heaved a big sigh:

> "Leaving my homeland, I felt torn apart, forced into exile.
> Looking back from afar, I wondered to whom I could lean on.
> Only now, in my old age, do I give vent to all my deep feelings:
> How many have succeeded and how many died in silence?"

It remains my hope that this book can help to preserve the footprints of these senior Chinese Americans in the pages of our history.

– Tianchi Zhao, September 2015

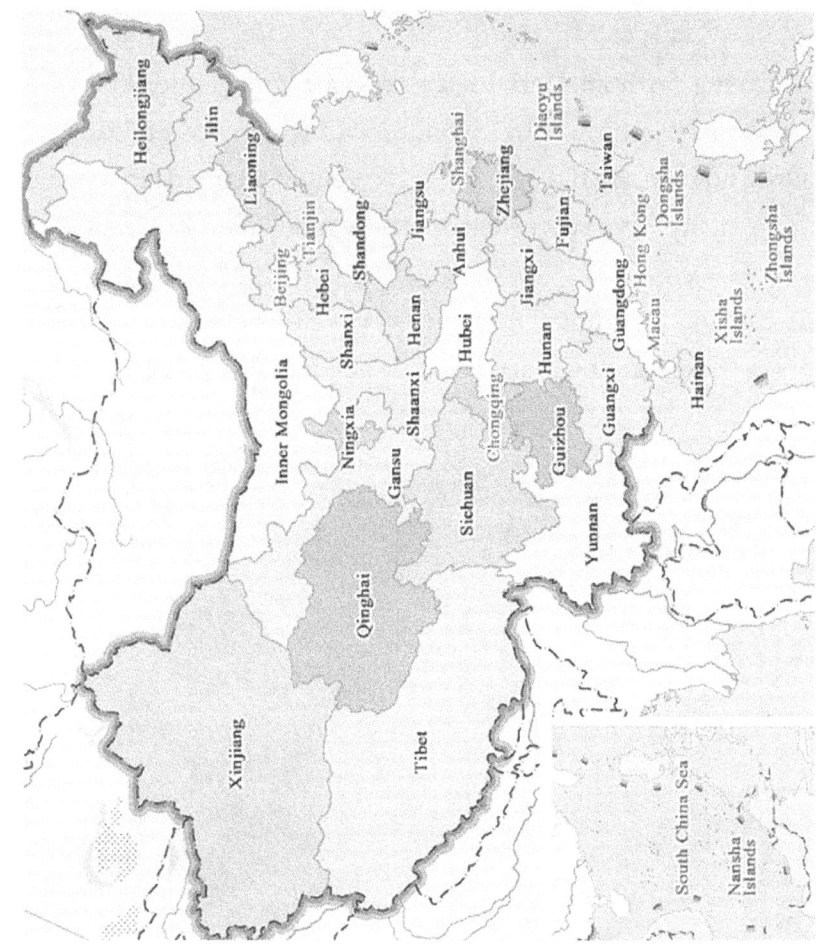

China's provinces

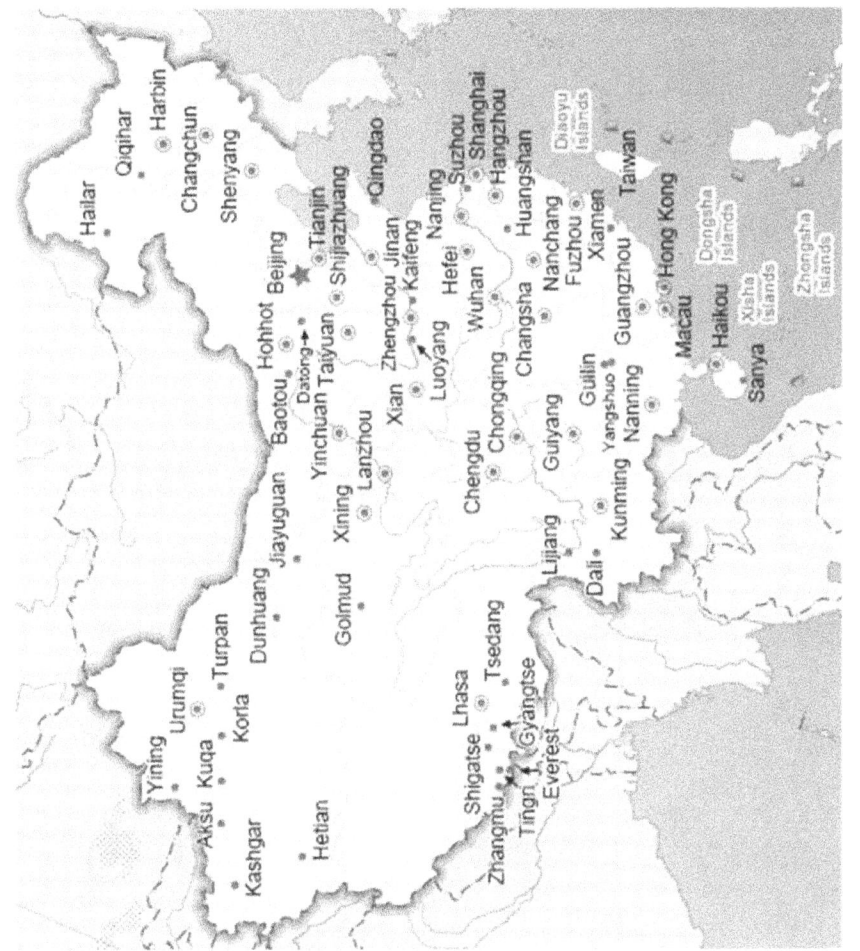

China's major cities

www.ingramcontent.com/pod-product-compliance
Lightning Source LLC
Chambersburg PA
CBHW080437170426
43195CB00017B/2801